CN00971073

HANDPLANE
ESSENTIALS

WOODWORKING
MAGAZINE

HANDPLANE ESSENTIALS

Christopher Schwarz

Cincinnati, Ohio

Handplane Essentials. Copyright © 2009 by F+W Media. Printed and bound in China. All rights reserved. No part of this book may be reproduced in any form or by any electronic or mechanical means including information storage and retrieval systems without permission in writing from the publisher, except by a reviewer, who may quote brief passages in a review. Published by *Woodworking Magazine*, an imprint of F+W Media, Inc., 10150 Carver Rd., Blue Ash, Ohio 45242. (800) 289-0963. First paperback edition, 2013.

Distributed in Canada by Fraser Direct
100 Armstrong Avenue
Georgetown, Ontario L7G 5S4
Canada

Distributed in the U.K. and Europe by F&W Media International LTD
Brunel House, Ford Close
Newton Abbot
TQ12 4PU, UK
Tel: (+44) 1626 323200
Fax: (+44) 1626 323319
E-mail: enquiries@fwmedia.com

Distributed in Australia by Capricorn Link
P.O. Box 704, S. Windsor NSW 2756 Australia
Tel: (02) 4560 1600; Fax: (02) 4577 5288
Email: books@capricornlink.com.au

Visit our web site at www.woodworking-magazine.com.

Other fine F+W Media Books are available from your local bookstore or direct from the publisher at woodworkersbookshop.com

17   16   15   14   13   5   4   3   2   1

Library of Congress has catalogued hard cover edition as follows:

Schwarz, Christopher, 1968-
  Handplane essentials / by Christopher Schwarz. -- 1st ed.
     p. cm.
  ISBN 978-1-4403-0298-5
  1. Planes (Hand tools) 2. Woodwork. I. Title.
  TT186.S345 2009
  684'.08--dc22
                                              2009022825

ISBN: 978-1-4403-3298-2 (pbk : alk paper)

media

PUBLISHER: *Steve Shanesy*
COPY EDITOR: *Megan Fitzpatrick*
DESIGN AND LAYOUT: *Linda Watts*
PHOTOS BY THE AUTHOR, EXCEPT WHERE NOTED.
PRICES ARE CORRECT AS OF MAY 2009, EXCEPT WHERE NOTED.

PHOTO BY AL PARRISH

About the Author

Christopher Schwarz is the editor of *Popular Woodworking* and *Woodworking Magazine*, a contributing editor to *The Fine Tool Journal* – a quarterly that covers hand tools – and a woodworking instructor at several schools.

Born in St. Louis, Mo., and raised in Northwest Arkansas, Chris began woodworking as a boy in his dad's home shop. His father prohibited him from using the powered machinery, so he built his projects – including his first workbench – with a small set of hand tools. Chris became further enmeshed in the world of hand work when his family bought an 84-acre farm in Hackett, Ark., and began building two houses without the benefit of electricity.

Chris trained as a newspaper journalist and graduated from Northwestern University's Medill School of Journalism in 1990 and earned a master's degree in journalism from The Ohio State University.

After covering mill fires, plane crashes, murders and train wrecks for the *Greenville* (S.C.) *News*, Chris went on to cover politics for *State Government News* magazine. Then he founded the political newspaper *The Kentucky Gazette* in Frankfort, Ky., with a partner. At nights, he took classes in furniture making at the University of Kentucky and built projects on his back-porch shop in Lexington, Ky.

As *The Kentucky Gazette* faltered, Chris joined the staff of *Popular Woodworking* magazine in 1996 as managing editor, worked his way up to editor and helped establish *Woodworking Magazine* in 2004.

Since joining the staff of *Popular Woodworking*, Chris has expanded its coverage of hand work – though he uses both hand and power tools in his work. He's also hosted five DVDs on hand tools that were produced by Lie-Nielsen Toolworks and has taught hand tool skills at the Marc Adams School of Woodworking, Kelly Mehler's School of Woodworking and the Northwest Woodworking Studio.

After writing his first book, "Workbenches: From Design & Theory to Construction & Use"

(Popular Woodworking Books), Chris and a partner established Lost Art Press LLC, a side business that publishes historical woodworking texts; their first project was to revive Joseph Moxon's "The Art of Joinery" in 2008.

Chris remains an avid woodworker, building projects for the magazines, his family and occasionally for sale. When he's not woodworking, he's cooking or working on his 1969 Volkswagen Karmann Ghia. He lives in Fort Mitchell, Ky., with his wife, Lucy, who is also a journalist, and his two children, Maddy and Katy.

"Basically, I no longer work for anything but the sensation I have while working."

— John Gay (1685 - 1732)
English poet & dramatist

Table of Contents

*"In 20 years on this mountain,
I've never been cheated by a hoe."*

— Stonehouse (Shan shi)

poet

Introduction

I can't imagine building furniture without handplanes any more than I can imagine building furniture without wood.

Planes touch almost every surface of my projects. They flatten panels and prepare them for finish. They define and refine my joinery so it's tight. They add the mouldings, beads and chamfers that differentiate my work from a shipping crate.

Most power-tool woodworkers assume that I do all this because of some political choice. That I have an affection for the pre-Industrial age. That I live off the grid with goats, granola and two grimy children.

Nothing could be further from reality. I own a full suite of machinery in my shop for the brutal processing of rough timber. Instead, the reason I use handplanes is that I believe they are the most highly evolved wood-cutting system ever developed. And that basic handplane technology has yet to be eclipsed by anything with an electric cord.

And in many cases, handplanes are faster than the equivalent power-tool. I know this sounds absurd. Bear with me.

Sure, a router can cut 200 feet of moulding in a couple minutes. But consider this: How often does a garage furniture-maker need to cut 200 feet of anything? And how does a router-cut surface compare to one cut with a moulding plane? It doesn't. Router-cut surfaces require sanding. And the more complex the profile, the more grueling the sanding. Hand-cut mouldings are ready to finish right from the tool.

What about dealing with flat surfaces? In my years of sanding and planing, I have found that dressing my stock with sandpaper is slower than doing it with a plane. Good sanding requires careful attention to detail as you progress through the grits. With a plane you can make two swipes and be done.

To be certain, industrial machines like wide-belt sanders can leave planes in the dust, but these are out of reach for most home woodworkers.

THE COST OF DOING BUSINESS

Because you're holding this book, I suspect some of these ideas have crossed your mind. And by now you're probably wondering: What's the catch?

The catch is that you have to learn some skills to become good with handplanes. It won't take you years or even months. But it will take time, effort and risk. You see, the difference between handplanes and power tools isn't the electricity. It's the engineering.

Power tools have brilliantly eliminated the need for the first-time user to be highly skilled to do basic operations. Even beginning woodworkers can turn out stunning feats of woodworking thanks to the cleverness of the tools themselves.

I'm not saying that power-tool users are unskilled. In experienced hands, power tools can do amazing things. The difference is among the beginners. It takes a lot longer to learn to make mouldings with a plane than it does with a router.

So where do you begin? To use handplanes, you need to learn to sharpen. It's the gateway skill to everything else. This book includes the essentials for getting you started, but nothing beats hands-on teaching. Find a weekend sharpening class in your town if you can.

After you learn to sharpen, the puzzle pieces will fall into place. Mastering one tool (such as a block plane) will get you halfway to taming the bench planes. Understanding the bench plane system will prepare you for the joinery planes. And mastering the odd cutters and grips of the joinery planes will pave the road to mastering the moulding planes.

And here's the final note: The learning process with these tools never ends. I picked up my first block plane when I was about 11 or 12 and raised a panel in my dad's garage shop. I've used handplanes to build almost every project I've completed since graduating college. And I am still learning.

This book is a compilation of a lot of the things I've written about handplanes during the last 10 years, but it is incomplete. Though I cover the bench planes and joinery planes fairly well, the section on moulding planes is inadequate – I'm still not good enough with these tools to teach others to use them.

This is supposed to be heartening – not discouraging. Even the best plane users are still learning something new with every stroke. And the universe of these tools is rich and deep – enough for a lifetime. So before I waste any more of yours, let's get started.

Christopher Schwarz
April 2009
Ft. Mitchell, Ky.

BASICS

THE MINDSET

ABOUT THE TOOLS

IMPORTANT DETAILS

PLANES PLUS WOOD EQUALS …

Why Use Hand Tools?

Hand work is remarkably straightforward —
once you overcome one barrier.

L earning to use hand tools is far easier than acquiring the hand skills to type on a keyboard. I should know – I cannot type worth a dang (despite being a trained journalist) and yet I've picked up the skills to use chisels, planes, rasps, hammers and braces with little effort.

That's because I've found that using hand tools successfully is not really about manual dexterity. It's not about having natural gifts. It's not about years of frustrating training. And it's not about being an apprentice and having an old-world master to guide the way.

Instead, it's about overcoming a barrier that stymies many home woodworkers: the fear of taking a gamble and messing up the project you're working on by trying a new process. I see this all the time with woodworkers. After we experience success with a certain operation, we then resist trying a new way to do that operation because it seems risky. And because most of us (though not all) learned the craft with power tools (through shop class, television or magazines), that's what we're comfortable with.

I, however, was lucky. When I was 8 years old or so, my parents embarked on a crackpot adventure. We bought an 84-acre farm in rural Arkansas and decided to build two houses there. There was no electricity on the farm, so the first house was built using mostly hand tools – a handsaw, brace and hammer. This kindled my interest in woodworking, and I lusted after my father's table saw and radial arm saw, which he kept at our house in town.

For obvious reasons, I was banned from the machinery. But I was allowed to use any of the hand tools, and I had my own small kit in the garage. I built a workbench with the help of my grandfather. I built an embarrassingly wretched tool tote. But it was all with hand tools, so I knew that these tools could actually work in the hands of a kid.

As a result, when I started to get back into woodworking after college I had little fear as I picked up my first dovetail saw, plow plane and outcannel gouge. That fearlessness has taken me a long way and it continues to pay dividends as I've begun experimenting with turning and carving.

I can't give you the same experience I had growing up, but I can give you this truth: If an awkward 8-year-old can build a workbench with hand tools, then you can do it, too. Overcoming your fear of failure is the first step. The second step is to

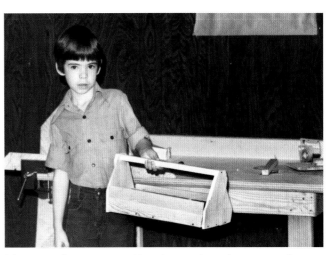

ME AT AGE 8 WITH *my workbench (note the enthusiastic nailing on the legs) and my first tool tote. Being limited to only hand tools as a child removed my fear of them in later years.*

understand what the tools are used for – there's not as much information about hand tools out there as there is about power tools. And the third step is to learn basic sharpening. Acquiring this skill is absolutely the Rosetta Stone to all the other hand skills, and that's why we've devoted significant space to these topics in this book.

THE MYTHS OF HAND TOOLS

There are some woodworkers who see little reason to even mess with hand tools. After all, we have all these amazingly fast and precise power tools at our disposal. Why should we "devolve" to an earlier technological state? That's quite against our progressive nature. Well the reason you should incorporate hand tools into your work is because just about everything you hear about hand tools is likely wrong. Let's look at some of the myths.

Myth 1: Hand tools are slow. The truth is that some people are slow. Hand tools have always been built to work as quickly as possible. They just have to be set up and wielded correctly. And you have to pick the right tool for the job. You wouldn't try to reduce a board in thickness with a sanding block, so why would you try to do that operation with a smoothing plane?

All tools are slow when used incorrectly. About seven years ago, one of our editors for our woodworking book line decided to build a cradle for his newborn child. It was a small project, yet he spent three full days planing down all the wood for the project on our Delta 13" cast-iron industrial planer. Why? Because he refused to remove more than $\frac{1}{64}$" in a pass. He was afraid he'd mess up.

The truth is that both hand tools and power

FORE PLANES ARE ROUGH TOOLS *that can hog off ¹/₁₆" in a pass. The jointer plane's long sole then trues the surface and takes a thinner shaving (about .006" thick). The smoothing plane is then used to remove a thin shaving (about .001" to .002" thick) to prepare the surface for finishing. You need all three planes to surface lumber and you need to use them in the correct order.*

THIS SHAVING IS .001" THICK *and you can easily set a hand plane to remove this amount (or more, depending on your needs). Setting power tools to remove such small increments is almost impossible.*

tools can be remarkably fast when set up properly and used appropriately. You have to know that a fore plane is used for hogging off ¹/₁₆" of material in a stroke. You have to know that a 7-point hand saw will fly through a board in half the number of strokes you'd make with a 12-point saw. You have to know that a cabinet rasp will shape wood faster than a pattermaker's rasp. Once you know these things, you'll pick up speed.

Myth 2: Hand tools are less precise than power tools. Whenever I hear this one I laugh and ask the person if they can set their table saw to remove .001" from a board's edge. This is virtually impossible to do with a table saw, router, jointer or planer. Yet it is child's play for a handplane. After an afternoon of practicing with a handplane, you will be able to set any handplane to remove a .001"-thick shaving. Imagine the sort of power that gives you. Fitting and trimming your joints can be effortless when you have that skill. And it's an easy skill to get.

The real truth is that hand tools free you from a lot of these arbitrary measurements anyway. Your door panels don't care if they are .0625" thick or .061". All they care about is if they fit in the rails and stiles. If you cut a panel too thick to fit into its groove on a table saw, you end up engaging in the endless cycle of: Cut, go to the bench, check the fit, tweak the setup; cut, go to the bench, check the fit. Then you have to sand the panel for finishing. When you fit a panel with a handplane you do it all at the bench. Take a few passes, check the fit, take a few passes, check the fit. And here's the real kicker, once it fits you don't have to sand it – the handplane

produces a ready-to-finish surface. So now you're both faster and you're more precise.

Myth 3: Hand tools require great skill. A lot of people are under the assumption that to use hand tools you need years of practice to develop a feel for the tool. While true mastery of any tool (hand or power) is probably unobtainable, most hand tools can be learned after a couple hours (not years) of practice. Go down to the shop and decide to practice on some scrap. Drill it, cut it, plane it, shape it, carve it. When you have some success, then apply those skills to a project.

There's another bit of missing information that helps propagate this myth about hand tools: people think they are used entirely freehand. This is wrong.

THE BENCH HOOK GUIDES YOUR *backsaw and keeps it in place on your bench as you cut. It's a remarkable workshop appliance. Having the right jigs and fixtures is absolutely key to making your planes, saws and chisels work well.*

GOOD HAND TOOLS NEVER WEAR *out (unlike even the best routers or cordless drills). So spending a bit more money on them is a good idea because you'll never have to buy a replacement and you'll never outgrow it.*

There are a number of simple "appliances" or jigs that will help you guide your hand tools. Shooting boards assist you in planing perfect square edges and ends on boards. Bench hooks hold and guide your work while using a backsaw. Sawbenches help make your handsaw fly through the work. Planing stops eliminate complicated workholding apparatuses.

Building a few of these appliances (I'd start with a bench hook or shooting board) will immediately unlock the hidden abilities of your hand tools.

Myth 4: Simple hand tools aren't cut out for complex work: We have an amazing array of commercial and shop-made jigs for power tools these days. There are dovetail jigs that cost more than my first pickup truck. Believe me, these modern jigs work. I've used a lot of them. And I think that these jigs sell so well because some woodworkers really like gizmos (nothing wrong with that) and some woodworkers think they need a complex jig to per-

form a complex operation, such as cutting a mortise-and-tenon joint.

Hand tools largely free you from complex jiggery. Think for a moment how difficult it is to cut a compound miter on a table saw, particularly on a panel. There is an immense amount of setup and test-cutting involved. Lots of wasted sample pieces. And if you really want to do it well, you should buy an aftermarket miter gauge that is accurate to half a degree.

When I want to cut an unusual angle, I mark it out on my workpiece and simply saw to the line. Then a couple strokes with a plane clean up the cut and get it precisely fit. No test cuts. No wasted material. No jigs. Mark the line; cut the line. It is one of the most liberating feelings you will ever experience. And it's not hard to do. An 8-year-old can handle it.

Or how about fitting a door in a face frame? If your door or face frame is crooked (let's say it's off by $\frac{1}{32}$"), how are you going to correct that error when using power tools? A tapering sled on the table saw? A few stopped cuts on the jointer? A tapered straightedge guide for your router with a bearing-guided pattern bit? I've used all these methods. Here's what I do now: I mark the taper I need on the door's rail or stile. I plane to that line by using a quick series of stopped passes. When I get to the line, I'm done. As a bonus, the edge of that door is ready for finishing, too.

Myth 5: Hand tools are cheaper than power tools: I bet you weren't expecting me to say that.

FITTING A DOOR WITH A *handplane is fast and accurate. First mark out how much material you need to remove and draw a line on the door showing what you want to remove (right). Then plane to that line and the door will fit perfectly (far right).*

Good tools cost. Period. End of story. It's true you can buy vintage hand tools or vintage machinery for a lower up-front cost. But getting these tools to work correctly can cost you time and effort. If you have a lot free time and enjoy tinkering with metal things, then this is the route for you.

For those of us for whom time is scarce: Buy the best tool you can. You will end up sharpening it less, fooling with it less and using it more. This has always been the case, even hundreds of years ago. In Joseph Moxon's "Mechanick Exercises" of 1678, he exhorts craftsmen to buy superior steel saws over the less expensive iron ones and even tells them exactly where in London on Foster Street to get them. And virtually every other old text on woodworking I own insists that you should always buy the best you can afford. "Audels Carpenters and Builders Guide" (Audel Co. 1947) puts it thus: "(I)t is important to buy only the best regardless of cost."

As a kid, my first coping saw was a Craftsman. Some tools from Craftsman are good; some are not. This one was decidedly a piece of junk. The blade clamp never worked right. The frame buckled under normal use. The riveted handle was loose. The mechanism that controlled the angle of the blade routinely came loose. Pretty much everything on that saw was a stinker. So it was no wonder I struggled with that tool. I now have a nice Olson Saw Co. coping saw. The day I started using that saw my sawing skills increased tenfold. Cheap tools are barriers to good work. Good tools make the work as easy as possible.

WHERE TO BEGIN

If this all sounds good to you, you're probably wondering where you should begin your journey. The first step is to educate yourself about the tools before you start buying them and using them. While there's indeed sound information about planes in this book, you need a few books to help you really get the critical mass of information you need. I have a number of favorite books about hand woodworking. You need at least two: One on sharpening and one about the tools. I'd buy the book on sharpening first.

There are two sharpening books I really like: "The Complete Guide to Sharpening" by Leonard Lee, and "The Complete Illustrated Guide to Sharpening" by Thomas Lie-Nielsen. Both books are from The Taunton Press and both will guide you in all the basic moves required to sharpen a wide variety of tools.

For an overview of hand tools and their uses, here are some good sources to look for at the bookstore and the library (some of these books are out of print but still available used and at libraries).

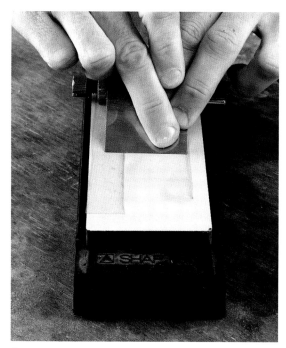

SHARPENING YOUR TOOLS IS THE *first skill to master. Once you get past this hurdle, you will find yourself able to master any edge tool.*

■ "Hand Tools" by Aldren A. Watson (Norton). Although Watson has a bit of a boatbuilder's perspective, the information and his beautiful hand illustrations are solid gold. This book is inexpensive, readily available and packed with excellent information you'll turn to regularly.

■ "Traditional Woodworking Handtools" by Graham Blackburn (Blackburn Books). The first woodworking book I ever owned was written by Blackburn. This book combines many of his columns for magazines during the years into a very nice reference book on hand work.

■ "Tools for Woodwork" by Charles H. Hayward (Drake). Sadly, this fine book is out of print. Hayward explores all the basic tools you need to do woodworking with clear explanations and perfect illustrations.

■ "Restoring, Tuning & Using Classic Woodworking Tools" by Michael Dunbar (Sterling). If you are going to go the route of fixing up vintage tools, you need this book. It can be difficult to find, but it is worth the effort.

■ "The Workbench Book" by Scott Landis (Taunton). You need a good workbench for hand work, and Landis's book is the classic. Avoid imitators; this is a great bench book.

And then you should get a catalog from Astragal Press, which specializes in publishing and selling books on traditional craft work. You will find many excellent books that will help take you down paths that interest you, such as handplanes or braces or saws. How to contact Astragal: Visit astragalpress. com, call 800-330-6232, or write to them at: 8075 215th Street West, Lakeville, MN 55044.

NOT A REJECTION OF ELECTRICITY

There's one final point I'd like to make about hand tools. Using them does not force you to reject power tools or machinery. Many people who visit my shop at home are puzzled by my big 8" Powermatic jointer, Delta Unisaw and Grizzly 15" planer. "I thought you were a hand tool guy," is the inevitable comment that falls from their lips.

Then I point out the obscene number of braces hanging on the wall behind my band saw and the collection of handplanes stored in a cherry cabinet above my grandfather's workbench.

"I like all tools," is my standard reply.

Hand tools and power tools co-exist very peace-fully in a modern workshop. The two perspectives complement one another in surprising ways and allow you to work faster, more accurately and with less waste and more joy.

You can blend the two perspectives to your heart's desire. I use my powered planer and jointer for prepping all my rough stock, but the hand tools handle all the final truing and make the work ready to finish. I use my table saw for ripping and cross-cutting (its true purpose in life) and use my hand tools for most of the fine joinery. The rough work is handled by the power tools in my shop and the fine work is done by the hand tools.

The result of knowing both hand and power tools is that I'm a more fearless woodworker. New tools, techniques and projects are much more do-able when you have a lot of different ways of going about any given task. And when I do hesitate or cringe at a task ahead of me, I simply remind myself to act more like an 8-year-old boy.

A GOOD WORKBENCH MAKES THE *work easier and faster. Buy a book on workbenches to learn everything you need to know before you build or buy one.*

Coarse, Medium & Fine

Using bench planes with your machinery will speed your work.
But first you must understand how the bench plane system works.

   PHOTO BY AL PARRISH

Too often we hear that hand tools are slow and power tools are fast. Even people who love hand tools talk about how they enjoy handwork because it forces them to slow their work on a project, to ponder the details, to enjoy the smell of the freshly cut lumber and to labor in quiet harmony with the wood.

That's all very bucolic – but it's also a bit ill-informed.

To my mind, people who think hand tools are slow are either using the wrong tool for a task, or they are people who will work slowly no matter what tool is in their hand. I have found that to become truly efficient at woodworking is to first ignore whether or not the tool in your hand has a power cord or a finely honed blade. Instead, you should make sure that you know whether that tool is a coarse tool for hogging off material, a medium tool for refining and truing the work, or a fine tool that's the last to touch your work.

This classification system – coarse, medium and fine – works for many of the tools of the craft, from sandpaper to handplanes. And putting each tool into its place is the first step toward knowing its true use at the bench.

Once you know what each tool is used for, you'll also be able to figure out which tools (if any) should be used before it and which tools (if any) should be used after it. Plus you'll know – in general terms – how long you should be using that tool before you switch to a finer one.

The net result of this is you will become much faster because you'll always have the right tool in your hand.

To show how this approach works, let's look at surfacing lumber. This coarse, medium and fine system will first help you understand what bench planes are for then show you how bench planes can be blended seamlessly with powered jointers and planers and other surfacing tools.

First Understand the Bench Plane System

Bench planes are the mainstay of a shop that uses hand tools or blends hand and power tools. Bench planes were designed to make lumber smooth and true before any joinery operations (and before applying a finish).

To surface wood with bench planes, you need three planes: a fore plane, a jointer plane and a smoothing plane. It sounds simple, but the problem is that over the years, handplane manufacturers have designed bench planes in many lengths and widths (too many, really), and they have given them misleading numbers. Stanley, for example, numbers its bench planes from the diminutive No. 1 up to the massive No. 8. And there are more than just eight planes in that numbering system (there are Nos. $4\frac{1}{2}$, $5\frac{1}{4}$, and $5\frac{1}{2}$, too). Do you need all 11 planes? No. Do you need to start working with the No. 1 then progress to a No. 8? Absolutely not. So which planes do you need? Good question. Let's hit the books.

"One machine can do the work of 50 ordinary men. No machine can do the work of one extraordinary man."
— Elbert Hubbard (1856 - 1915)
author and teacher

Ignore Some Numbers

What's more important than the model number that's cast into a plane's bed is the overall length of the tool – that's the key to unlocking its function.

And once you understand the plane's intended function, then you'll know how to incorporate it into your shop, no matter what set of tools or machines you own.

In a nutshell, the fore plane is the tool for coarse work, and it does a job similar to a powered jointer and power planer. The jointer plane is the medium tool, and it works like a random-orbit sander, drum sander or belt sander (in the right hands). And the smoothing plane is the fine tool; it does the detail work performed by powered pad sanders, hand scrapers and sanding blocks. So let's first take a close look at these three planes.

Fore Planes: Rough & Ready

Fore planes are between 14" and 20" long and are so named because they are the planes that are used "before" the other handplanes. They are the "coarse" tool – the roughest of the bunch. They require more strength and stamina to use than any other hand tool, and I use mine as little as possible now that I own a powered jointer and planer.

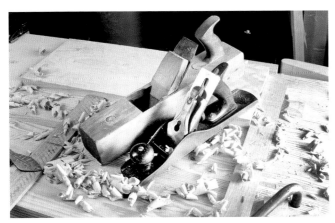

Like a powered planer, the *fore plane produces thick curls so it can rapidly reduce a board in thickness. Shown is my crusty-but-trusty Stanley No. 5 (some people call this a jack plane) and my sweet Scioto Works 16" wooden-stock fore plane.*

Working diagonally or across the *work is the key to using the fore plane. The diagonal motion reduces tear-out and assists in truing the face.*

In the Stanley numbering system, the No. 5 (14" long and commonly called a jack plane) and the No. 6 (18" long) planes qualify as fore planes.

The fore plane is used to rapidly take a bowed or cupped board to a state where it's reasonably flat. Fore planes don't take a fine shaving. They take coarse curls of lumber so the work gets done quickly. Their middling length is an advantage. They are long enough so that the sole touches a lot of the surface of the board. This helps you true the face of the board more easily and prevents you from over-shooting your mark – turning high spots into deep valleys by accident. (Why are scrub planes so short, then? I think these 10"-long tools were used more for hogging wood off edges or for localized, very rough work – but that's another story.)

If the length of the fore plane is an asset, why not make them really long? Working with fore planes is strenuous, so having them shorter and lighter makes them easier to handle than a longer plane. Whenever I use my fore plane, I marvel at its perfection of design. It's exactly long enough – but no more.

Once you know that the fore plane is for roughing, this also tells you how to set up the tool for use. The flatness of the sole isn't a concern for rough work. If the sole looks flat and the tool won't rock when the tool is flat on your bench, you're in good shape.

Fore planes need a wide-open *mouth to pass the thick shavings they produce. A tight mouth will clog and slow you down.*

A silhouette of the shape *of my fore plane's cambered iron. It's an 8" radius, which allows me to take an almost $1/16$"-thick shaving in softwood.*

Cambering the iron on a *fore plane is a task best handled on a bench grinder.*

I wouldn't recommend you spend hours flattening the sole of your fore plane so you can take .001" shavings. Save that drudgery for another plane (or avoid the drudgery – more on that later).

My metal fore plane is a sorry old Stanley No. 5 with a handmade tote that looks like it was fashioned by a blind beaver. The tool is rusty in spots. The sole's flatness is questionable – but it works like a dream.

Back to setup. Because you want to remove thick shavings, open up the mouth of the tool and make the tool easy to push by cambering the tool's cutting edge. A fore plane with a blade sharpened straight across (like you would with a chisel or block plane) can be quickly immobilized by a tough patch of wood. And the cambered iron (I like an 8" radius) helps reduce tear-out because there are no corners digging into the wood. If your plane has a chipbreaker, set it so it's back at least $^1/_{16}$" from the corners.

Fore planes are pushed diagonally or directly across a board's face. Work diagonally one way across the face, then diagonally the other. Check your progress with winding sticks. Working diagonally will generally get you where you need to be, but if there's a persistent high spot, work at it selectively with the fore plane. The goal is to get the board flat and almost to your finished thickness – as close as you dare.

JOINTER PLANES:
JOIN THE FLAT-WORLD SOCIETY

When the work is nearly flat and nearly to finished thickness, fetch your jointer plane – sometimes also called a try plane. Jointer planes are tools with soles 22" long or longer. Longer is better in the world of jointer planes. In the Stanley system, the No. 7 (22" long) and the No. 8 (24" long) are the jointers. Wooden-bodied jointer planes can be much longer.

The jointer plane is the "medium" tool. It brings the surface of the board to a state where joinery can be performed. Jointer planes take a finer

A JOINTER PLANE'S MAJOR ASSET *is the length of its sole. The longer the sole, the flatter your board will become. Shown is a Lie-Nielsen No. 7 plane (left) and the Veritas bevel-up jointer. The jointer I covet (not shown) is the Clark & Williams jointer, which can be as long as 30".*

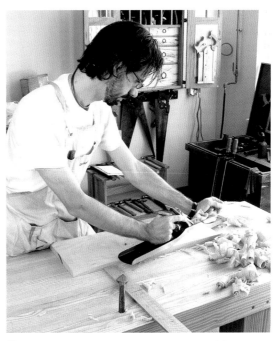

ON NARROWER CABINET COMPONENTS, THE *jointer plane works along the grain. Skewing the tool slightly during the cut makes it easier to push and does assist in flattening. One wider panels – say 14" and wider – I'll begin with a few diagonal passes before switching to long-grain ones.*

WINDING STICKS (I LIKE ALUMINUM *angle) exaggerate any warp or high spots on the board's face. View the winding sticks so they are in line with one another.*

THERE ARE LOTS OF WAYS *to get the proper camber on the iron for a jointer plane. Shown is the Odate crowning plate from Powell Manufacturing – essentially, it's a diamond sharpening stone that's concave in the middle.*

THE MOUTH OF THE JOINTER *plane is a fine balance. You want it open enough to pass a fairly thick shaving, yet tight enough to limit tear-out as much as possible.*

A SILHOUETTE OF THE SHAPE *of my jointer plane's cambered iron. I placed a feeler gauge on the end to see how far back the corners were swept: it's .008".*

shaving than the fore plane, but nothing that would be called gossamer. I generally go for a shaving that's about .006" thick. That's about the thickness of two or three sheets of typing paper. The length of the jointer plane is its greatest asset. When you can push a jointer plane across the entire surface of the board and remove a full-width, full-length shaving from every point, the board is quite flat (flatter than most machinery can get it, I've found). The plane's sole rides over the valleys of a board and flattens the hills. When the hills are the same level as the valleys, you're done.

If this tool is so accurate, why not begin work with a jointer plane and skip the fore plane? Though a .006"-thick shaving sounds like a lot, it's not. With rough-sawn wood, you could work one face all day with a jointer plane – a fore plane can remove much more wood in a hurry. And the jointer planes are more unwieldy. I'd much rather push my fore plane, which weighs less than 5 lbs., for a lot longer than my No. 8, which weighs 10 lbs.

Because the jointer plane is a precision instrument, it requires more attention than its coarser, shorter cousin. The sole should be reasonably flat. There's been a lot written about this topic, but the bottom line is that the tool must work – that's its true test. Can you flatten the sole of an old metal jointer plane yourself? Perhaps, but I can't. Though I've flattened the soles of many planes, I end up making jointer planes worse. There is too much cast iron to work with there.

And that's why I recommend you spend a little money when buying a jointer plane. In fact, if I had to buy only one precision plane, it would be a toss-up between the jointer plane and the smoothing plane. There's a good argument for buying a premium metal jointer plane and a vintage wooden-soled fore plane and smoothing plane. Then you could use the metal jointer to true the soles of the two wooden planes.

No matter which jointer plane you acquire, the setup is similar. Some historical texts recommend an iron sharpened straight across, but I prefer a slight camber to the cutting edge, which is also historically correct – it depends on who you read. The camber should be much slighter than the curve on your fore plane. I like a curve that allows a .006"-thick shaving that's almost the entire width of the iron. Practice will get you where you need to be.

The mouth needs to be fairly open to pass this shaving, but there's no need for a gaping maw. Keeping the mouth fairly tight can reduce tear-out. And though the jointer plane isn't generally a finishing plane (that's the job of the smoothing plane), reducing tear-out will make less work for the smoothing plane. The chipbreaker needs to be somewhere between $\frac{1}{16}$" and $\frac{1}{8}$" from the cutting edge in my experience.

When I work a board's face with a jointer plane, I tend to work in the direction of the grain – not diagonally like with the fore plane. However, when I'm flattening a big tabletop, a largish panel or my benchtop, I'll begin with diagonal strokes. This helps keep a larger surface in true.

As you start to work, the first pass or two should produce irregular shavings as you remove the high spots left by the fore plane. After a few passes, long and wide shavings should emerge from the mouth. When this happens all the way across a board's width, you are ready to work the other face of the board.

If you're surfacing the board entirely by hand,

use a marking gauge to scribe the finished thickness on all four edges of the boards and work that rough face with the fore plane almost to the scribe line. Then true the second face with your jointer plane.

This is the point at which I'll typically perform joinery on the piece (with some exceptions). If you proceed to the smoothing plane before you cut your joints, you can make more work for yourself in the end.

That's because joinery can be hard on a board. You'll mark it up with the typical shop bruises from cutting and clamping. When the joinery is complete, I'll generally assemble the project and then smooth the exterior – if possible. Sometimes you have to go to the smoothing plane before assembly. Experience will be your guide.

Smoothing Planes:
An Addiction for Some

The smoothing plane is the tool that usually hooks woodworkers into hand tools. They're the "fine" tool in the troika of handplanes and they pro-duce gossamer shavings and leave shimmering surfaces. I like my smoothing planes, but if I've done a good job with my other planes, the smoothing plane should see only a little use.

This is a good thing because it saves you on sharpening and setup. Fore planes are the easiest tool to set up and sharpen (they don't have to be surgically sharp), jointers take a little more work in both departments and smoothing planes are the trickiest tool.

Smoothing planes require a cutter with a gently curved super-sharp cutting edge, a fine mouth, perfect alignment of the cutter in the center of the mouth and a lot of other fine tweaks that demand fussing, fussing, fussing. So if you're using your smoothing plane as little as possible, then you're also spending less time tweaking and more time woodworking.

There are a lot of sizes of smoothing planes, but in general they are 7" to 10" in length. The Stanley No. 4 is the most common size at 9" long with a 2"-wide cutter. The bigger planes, such as the No. 4½, are suited for larger-scale work, such as dining tables. The smaller planes, such as the No. 3, are suited for smaller work, such as narrow door stiles and rails.

SMOOTHING PLANES ARE THE ELITE *(and most demanding) planes in your shop. Shown is a Lie-Nielsen No. 4, a Veritas bevel-up smoother, a wooden-bodied Clark & Williams smoother, and my most guilty pleasure: a custom-made plane by Wayne Anderson (bottom right). Yes, it's a smoothing plane, too.*

THE MOUTH OF A SMOOTHING *plane should be as tight as possible. This requires tweaking and experimenta-tion. Once you get the mouth set, however, you shouldn't have to change that setting.*

SMOOTHING PLANES REMOVE WISPY SHAVINGS *and pre-pare a surface for finishing.*

A SILHOUETTE OF A SMOOTHING *plane iron. The cam-ber is slight: .002" or maybe a little more.*

The smoothing plane needs to take a fine shaving, anywhere from .002" thick down to stuff that cannot be measured. So you need the sole to be as flat as possible to consistently take this shaving. You can try to tune the sole of your smoothing plane, or you can do what I do – let someone who knows what they are doing handle this job with a surface grinder. If you purchase a nice handplane from Veritas, Lie-Nielsen or Clifton and the sole is out of whack, then send it back. You shouldn't have to flatten the sole if you pay more than $175 for a plane.

Other considerations: The mouth needs to be as tight as you can get without it clogging with shavings. The chipbreaker needs to be set near the cutting edge. I like about $\frac{1}{16}$" – as close as I can get without clogging. And the iron needs to have the slightest camber, just a couple thousandths at the corners. I achieve this by applying selective finger pressure at the iron's corners while sharpening. I also find that smoothing planes are the place to lavish your sharpening skills. To get the edge as perfect as you can, polish it up to the highest grit you have available. In my experience, sharper edges reduce tear-out as much as a tight mouth or the pitch of the blade (higher pitches reduce tear-out but make the tool harder to push).

When working with a smoothing plane, make passes parallel to the grain of the board, making sure that your strokes overlap slightly. Work from the edge of the board near you across to the far edge. Your first strokes will remove the high spots left by the jointer plane and your shavings could look inconsistent. Once you make a couple passes across the face, you should be able to get full-length shavings that are as wide as your blade allows. When this occurs and the board looks good, put down the plane. Clean up any localized tear-out with a hand scraper.

HAND SCRAPERS AND SANDING BLOCKS *are an accepted and historically accurate way to prepare a piece of wood for finishing.*

If necessary, I'll make a few strokes with #220-grit sandpaper to blend the planed surfaces with the scraped ones. This should take only a few strokes.

WHAT THIS MEANS: BLENDING HAND AND POWER

Armed with this understanding of handplanes, you can now unlock an important secret. Almost all of our power tools can be classified as coarse, medium or fine tools – just like the handplanes used for surfacing wood.

Think about your powered jointer and planer as coarse tools, like the fore plane. Their job is to remove lots of stock in a hurry. But their surface needs to be refined before finishing (unless you build only chicken coops).

What are the medium tools? I classify large random-orbit sanders, belt sanders and drum sanders as medium tools. They remove the marks left by the coarse machining process and can indeed true a board when wielded by a skilled user. Some people are satisfied to stop at this phase – and truth be told, I'll sometimes stop after using my jointer plane for interior surfaces or when building something intended for the shop or for pure utility.

But most power-tool woodworkers go a step further. They scrape and hand sand to remove the scratches left by random-orbit sanders and pad sanders – the so-called pigtails you see on so many fur-

THE POWERED JOINTER (RIGHT) AND *planer (above) are faster than a fore plane (though they won't burn as many calories during use).*

THE CONCEPT OF COARSE, MEDIUM *and fine works with other operations as well. For cutting curves, think of your band saw as the coarse tool, your rasp as the medium tool and your spokeshave as the fine tool.*

A DRUM SANDER (ABOVE) CAN *level and true a panel much like a jointer plane. A random-orbit sander (right) is ideal for removing machining marks in a power-tool workshop.*

niture-store pieces. In the power-tool world, these hand tools are the "fine" tools.

Once you classify your power tools, you can use them in conjunction with your hand tools. Let's say that the only bench plane you own is a smoothing plane. When should you use it? First joint and plane your stock (a coarse operation). Get it as true and flat as possible with your drum sander or belt sander (that's medium). And then finish things up with the smoothing plane, scrapers and sandpaper (fine).

This information can also be used to guide your tool purchases. What plane should you buy at the flea market if you don't own a powered jointer or planer? (A fore plane.)

Here's how I personally blend power and hand tools in my shop. My coarse tools are my powered 8" jointer and 15" planer. Though I own two fore planes, I use them only when a board is too wide for my powered equipment.

Once the coarse stuff is over, I use my jointer plane to true my stock before cutting my joinery. This medium tool removes snipe and machine marks, and makes the boards flatter than my power equipment can. Finally, my smoothing plane is my primary fine tool, although I scrape and hand sand, too.

It's important to use the tools in the right order (start with coarse; end with fine) and that you don't skip any steps between. Skipping wastes time. It's

frustrating to use a fine tool right after a coarse tool. Try using a smoothing plane on a larger board that's fresh from your powered planer. Then use a smoothing plane on a board that you first dressed with your jointer plane. You'll notice a significant difference.

The other important idea is to work as long as you can with the coarse tool. You wouldn't remove $\frac{1}{16}$" of a board's thickness with a random-orbit sander. So don't use your jointer or smoothing planes to do that, either. This is a common error and is one way hand tools get a reputation as slow.

One last thing: I don't use hand tools because of a romantic obsession with the past. Once I adopted this system of coarse, medium and fine, I became faster, my joinery became tighter (because my boards were perfectly true) and my finished results looked better.

And once you understand how coarse, medium and fine works with surfacing lumber, you can apply the idea to other workshop processes. Here's a hint at the possibilities: When cutting curves, the coarse tool is the band saw, the medium tool is the rasp and the fine tool is the spokeshave. And there's more. A lot more.

FOR MORE INFORMATION

Anderson Planes
andersonplanes.com, 763-486-0834

Clark & Williams
planemaker.com, 479-253-7416

Lie-Nielsen Toolworks
lie-nielsen.com, 800-327-2520

Odate Crowning Plate
toolsforworkingwood.com or 800-426-4613

Veritas (Lee Valley Tools)
leevalley.com, 800-871-8158

Pretty, Stupid

When a vintage plane looks like it's brand new, something might be very wrong with it.

I have a shiny bronze edge plane perched on my bookshelf that's nestled in an attractive red velvet bag. Wait, let me clarify that. It's actually a plane-shaped object. The thing couldn't cut its way out of a wet paper bag.

The plane's adjuster is hopelessly coarse, the iron is warped like a potato chip, and the tool's integral fence isn't 90°. But it is a pretty thing and visitors often pick it up to admire it.

Me, I hate the plane, but I keep it around to remind me not to be such a crow – a hoarder of bright and shiny objects. It's a lesson that I apparently needed to learn.

When I first started buying vintage hand tools I went for the ones that looked new. And if the tool was still in its original box, even better.

I soon discovered that often there are reasons a tool has survived for 100 years with nary a blemish or chipped handle. Sure, sometimes you get lucky and you stumble on a perfectly preserved tool that was put away new and forgotten.

But more times than not, vintage tools in pristine condition are usually the victims of poor design or faulty manufacturing.

I have a gorgeous jointer plane with a rear tote that is designed to come loose after 15 minutes of use – no matter how tightly you screw the tote to the body of the plane. I have a pristine bird-cage awl that hurts your hand every time you use it. I have a marking knife that slips from your fingers like a watermelon seed no matter how tightly you squeeze it.

In the category of tools that were made by a drunk monkey, I have a jack plane with a sole shaped like a banana. I have a gorgeous hammer with its original handle rotated about 5° off from its head. And I have a brace (it was still in the original wrapper!) with a pad that wobbles like a newborn's oversized noggin.

On the other hand, there is my Stanley Type 11 No. 5 handplane. I bought the thing at a flea market for just $12 – the hippie selling it normally dealt in books and was tired of toting the thing from show to show.

The tool had been repainted (poorly). The rear tote had been replaced with a somewhat-crude shop-made handle. The metalwork was a dull battleship gray. But if I ever enter a handplaning contest someday, that's the tool I'm going to bring along. I swear the thing is haunted. Despite its dowager appearance, the tool is unerringly precise and stable. It will be the last tool I sell when I am penniless and hungry.

These principles of buying tools also apply to furniture. Too often I encounter products that are dresser-shaped objects or table-shaped objects. Just like the tools, these things (I hate to call them furniture) are the victims of poor manufacturing, poor design or both.

In fact, when I look at old furniture, I am now drawn to pieces that are well-worn but still sturdy. Case-in-point: My wife and I used to haunt an antiques store stuffed with European imports. We always walked past the pristine and imposing bureaus and highboys to wander among the French farmhouse tables with worn edges and scarred tops.

"People forget how fast you did a job – but they remember how well you did it."
— Howard Newton (1903 - 1951)
advertising executivee

The fact that these tables had survived so much use and abuse was more impressive than any finial or carved knee block.

So no matter how much my daughters scratch the dining table, I refuse to refinish its top, though it would take only an afternoon to restore. I allow my tools to patinate (though not to rust). On one of my brass-walled planes you can clearly see the whorls of my fingerprints.

These are the marks that these objects were useful in life, as telling as the lines in our faces that show up from smiling or frowning a lot.

And when I pick up that bronze edge plane, I do my share of both smiling and frowning. I frown because I spent $85 on something that's as useful as a rock for building nice furniture. And I smile because the company that made this object in the 1990s is now out of business.

So perhaps there is hope.

Lending a Hand to Power Tools

The four most useful handplanes for the modern power-tool woodshop.

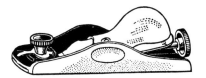

LOW-ANGLE BLOCK PLANE

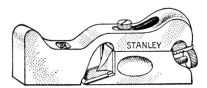

SHOULDER PLANE

SMOOTHING PLANE

JOINTER PLANE

It's easy to get labeled by your fellow wood-workers as a power-tool junkie (a Normite) or a hand-tool Luddite (a Neanderthal). The truth is that most woodworkers fall somewhere between those two extremes. And with good reason.

Using a combination of hand and power tools can be an effective one-two punch of quickness and accuracy. Power tools excel at converting rough stock to usable lumber, which is exhausting and tedious if done by hand. And hand tools provide the fine detailing and perfectly fit joints that can be a challenge to achieve with power tools.

So where do you start? Most of us begin woodworking with power tools, which allow us to accomplish great feats of furniture-building when our woodworking skills are in their infancy. As our skills develop it's natural to become interested in hand tools. But many early attempts with planes and chisels are usually stymied by one missing skill: sharpening.

A keen edge is the secret to success with hand tools. Sharpening takes a little study and practice, but everyone can learn it. Our best advice? Take a sharpening class. If that's not an option, get one of these books: Leonard Lee's "The Complete Guide to Sharpening" or Thomas Lie-Nielsen's "Complete Illustrated Guide to Sharpening" (both from The Taunton Press).

Once you commit to sharpening, you will want to purchase some planes. But which ones? Stanley alone made hundreds of styles. And while many of these tools look useful, you don't need many to get started. In fact, after much historical research and work at the bench, I've found that most woodworkers need only four handplanes to complement their power tools.

LOW-ANGLE BLOCK PLANE

The first plane you should buy is a low-angle block plane with an adjustable mouth. They are the simplest plane to sharpen and set up. They will open your eyes to what other planes can do. And they begin tuning your fine motor skills (such as where to apply pressure and sensing when you are cutting square) to handle other planes.

So what is it good for? You should first assign it to one of the most dreary jobs: dressing the edges of your work. Without a doubt, one of the worst tasks in woodworking is hand-sanding the edges of your boards to remove machine marks. With one or two light swipes, a block plane slices away the saw and jointer marks and leaves a bright and shimmering surface behind that's ready for finishing. It is a fast and effective way to prepare your edges; and this act is the first reward for those who learn to sharpen.

A BLOCK PLANE CAN SKIM *the machining marks from the edges of your boards, leaving a ready-to-finish surface behind.*

THE SMOOTHING PLANE IS THE *thoroughbred of the shop and is kept highly tuned. Make sure the shavings come out of the center of the mouth.*

Other tasks for the block plane: Whenever you have two parts of a joint that aren't flush, a lightly set block plane can trim the proud part of the joint flush with a few well-placed swipes. This is not a task to assign to a belt sander (too aggressive) or a sanding block (too tedious). Block planes also trim small doors and drawers to fit their openings (larger doors require longer tools). The low angle of the tool allows you to trim end grain. In general, I avoid planing end grain. But it's occasionally unavoidable, and the low-angle block plane is ideal for this job, especially after you wet the surface with denatured alcohol. I also use the block plane to round over sharp edges of workpieces and even plane chamfers. These take a little practice to master, but your skills will advance quickly with a block plane because it will never be far from your hand.

Sharpening tip: Sharpen it so the edge is square to the sides. It can be straight or slightly cambered.

SMOOTHING PLANE

The next plane to buy is a smoothing plane. This is the name for just about any plane that is about 9" long. Using Stanley's numbering system, these are typically a No. 3 or a No. 4 plane. These tools are designed to be the last tool that touches the surface of the wood before finishing. They are supposed to take a very fine cut and remove the top layer of wood cells that has been marred and compressed by our machines (or other handplanes) during construction.

In a traditional woodshop, the smoothing plane shares equal importance with the longer planes that make stock flat and true. But in the modern workshop, machines do most of the flattening and straightening tasks. In practice, I have found the smoothing plane to be an effective replacement for a random-orbit sander. I go from machine-flattened wood to the smoothing plane, then (if necessary) a card scraper and some quick hand sanding with #220-grit paper.

Why use these planes instead of sandpaper? Once you get some practice, a smoothing plane can be as fast as sanding. And it's definitely more enjoyable than power sanding. It takes some skill to sharpen and use a smoothing plane properly, but the rewards are substantial.

For many woodworkers, smoothing planes become as indispensable as block planes. In fact, as you become skilled with them you'll start to use them for almost any trimming task: truing edges, trimming joints flush and the like. I like to use the smoothing plane to fit a workpiece into a dado or rabbet with amazing accuracy. Here's an example: Say you have a ¾"-wide dado for a shelf but the shelf is just a shade too thick. Running it through the planer is risky and sanding it is tiresome. Get your dial caliper and measure the width of the dado and the thickness of the shelf. Let's say the shelf is .006" too thick. Set the smoothing plane for a fine cut (it's easy to dial the tool in to take a .001"-thick shaving). Make three passes with the plane across each face of the shelf. Chances are, the shelf will fit perfectly now. And you have the added benefit of the shelf being ready to finish.

Sharpening tip: The cutting edge of a smoothing plane needs to be slightly cambered across its edge, usually by just a few thousandths of an inch. Achieving this camber isn't tough; we show you how to do it in the section on sharpening. The camber prevents the corners of your cutting edge from digging into the work and cutting little tracks that you can see and feel.

Setup tip: The iron needs to be perfectly centered in the mouth of the plane. I set this close with the plane's lateral adjustment lever and then fine-tune its position with small hammer taps.

SHOULDER PLANE

The shoulder plane is the ultimate fitting tool. Because the tool's iron extends to the far left and right edge of the tool's sole, you can completely

THE SHOULDER PLANE IS A *joint-trimming maestro. This tool will fit tenons, rabbets, raised panels and shiplaps with ease.*

THE JOINTER PLANE EXCELS AT *truing stock, both the long edges and faces of boards. The pencil marks on the wood in the photo are low spots found by the plane after two passes over the board – which was fresh from the planer.*

trim one surface while pressing the tool against another adjacent surface. Most people use these tools to trim the cheeks and shoulders of tenons. I also use this tool to increase the depth and width of rabbets. And I use it to fit shiplap, tongue-and-groove and half-lap joints.

Some power-tool people deride the tool as a fix for poor machinery setups. I disagree. No matter how well you set up your router table or table saw, there will be variation in your joints. And a few thousandths of an inch can ruin a good fit. These inaccuracies can be due to the fact that the wood is slightly bowed. Or that you have released internal tension in the board as you have machined it. Or that you didn't hold the workpiece with the exact same downward pressure that you did with your test piece. No matter what the cause of these inaccuracies, the shoulder plane will make things fit.

Sharpening tip: The cutting edge must be sharpened square to the sides of the iron.

JOINTER PLANE

This long-bodied plane is one of my favorites. It's like having a steel straightedge that can fix any problems it finds with bowed stock. And when the jointer plane is working right, your other planes work faster and better. Here's why:

Sometimes the wood that comes from a powered jointer and planer can still have some problems, such as snipe on the ends. While boards with a little snipe might be acceptable in some cases, sometimes you need really flat stock. A few swipes with a jointer plane can fix the problem.

Perfectly flat stock is always a boon for accurate joinery, no matter if you are headed to the dovetail jig, the router table or the table saw. The jointer plane also has the added benefit of bringing all your surfaces to the point where they can be touched up quickly with a smoothing plane. With the snipe eliminated, the smoothing plane has a lot less work to do.

As you become adept at using your jointer plane, you'll also find it more accurate than your powered jointer at truing edges for panel glue-ups. I know that sounds like a stretch, but it's true.

Sharpening tip: Like a smoothing plane, the cutting edge of a jointer plane needs to be slightly cambered across its edge by just a few thousandths of an inch.

HOW TO BUY THESE TOOLS

I'm frequently asked which brand of plane is best. Even lousy hand tools are expensive. Here is my philosophy: If you enjoy fixing antique tools, breathing life back into a piece of history, vintage tools are for you. Rest assured that this route (though it seems cheaper) requires hours of research, hunting down the tools and fixing them up before you'll ever put them to wood.

As far as new planes go, I don't recommend the current Stanley, Anant, Kunz or low-end handplanes from the Far East. These tools can be tuned for rough work, but not for fine woodworking.

This brings me to my point: To buy a good tool that will go to work immediately, you need to spend a little money. But rest assured that this is an investment for several lifetimes.

While almost everything with a power cord on it ends up in the landfill, good hand tools last several lifetimes. Lie-Nielsen Toolworks, Veritas and Clifton (to name a few of my favorites) make tools that will exceed your expectations.

And when your tools work at a higher level than you do, you'll strive to keep up. And that's when you can dispose of the labels of Normite or Neanderthal for a new one: Craftsman.

Understanding Bench Planes

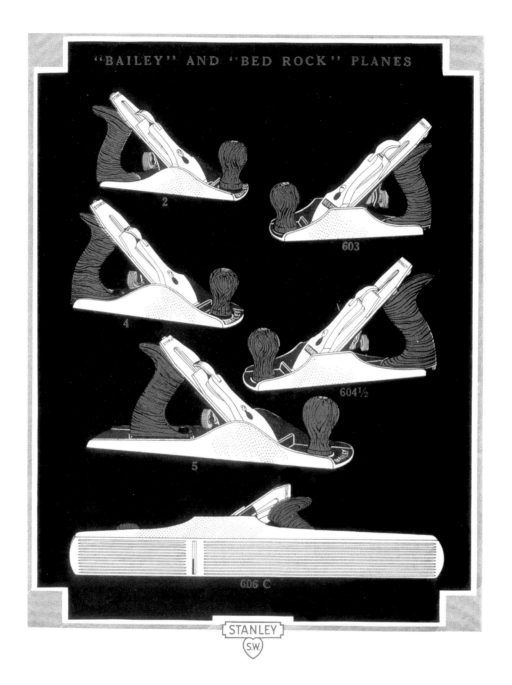

Many woodworkers are confused by the large number of bench planes. We explain what each plane is used for.

ILLUSTRATION: STANLEY TOOLS CATALOG NO. 120

The bench plane has three jobs in the woodshop: to straighten the wood, to smooth it and to remove it.

It sounds so simple when you put it that way, but many woodworkers are confused by all the different sizes of bench planes available, from the tiny 5½"-long No. 1 smooth plane up to the monstrous 24"-long No. 8 jointer plane.

Add into the mix all the new bevel-up bench planes that are available in the catalogs now, and it's bewildering enough to make you want to cuddle up close to your belt sander.

Believe it or not, there is a way to make sense of all the different sizes and configurations of bench planes out there and to select the few that you need in your shop. You don't need one bench plane of each size to do good work (though don't tell my wife that). In fact, it's quite possible to do all the typical bench plane chores with just one tool (more on that later).

In this article, I'm going to walk through the entire line of forms of the metallic-bodied bench planes and describe what each tool is good for. Because people can work wood in so many weird ways, I'll admit that what follows is equal doses of traditional workshop practice, personal preferences (formed by years of planing) and stubborn opinion that comes from growing up on a mountain.

But before we jump headfirst into describing each plane, let's first divide the tools into three broad categories: smoothing planes, fore planes and jointer planes.

THREE JOBS FOR THREE PLANES

You can tell a lot about what a plane is supposed to do by the length of its sole.

■ Smoothing planes have a sole that ranges from 5" to 10" long. The primary job of the smoothing plane is to prepare the wood for finishing. It is typically the last plane to touch the wood.

■ Fore planes have a sole that ranges from 14" to 20" long. The traditional (but by no means only) job of the fore plane is to remove material quickly. By virtue of its longish sole it also tends to straighten the wood to some degree. The fore plane is typically the first bench plane to touch the wood to get it to rough size.

■ Jointer planes have a sole that ranges from 22" up to 30" (in wooden-bodied planes). The primary job of jointer planes is to straighten the wood, a task it excels at by virtue of its long sole (the longer the sole, the straighter the resulting work). The jointer plane is used after the fore plane but before the smoothing plane.

SMOOTHING PLANES

Let's begin at the small end of the scale and look at the smoothing planes. People tend to end up with several of these (sometimes even in the same sizes). Why? Well there's a lot to choose from and different ways to configure them.

THE NO. 1 BENCH PLANE
■ Sole length: 5¹/₂" ■ Cutter width: 1¹/₄"

Prized by collectors, the No. 1 bench plane is like an exotic little dog. It is designed to make people pick it up and say, "It's so cute!" And it's designed to empty your wallet – it's easy to spend $1,000 on a vintage No. 1 plane. With a price like that, it's got to be one amazing and useful plane, right? Nope.

Some woodworkers like to use the No. 1 in place of a block plane – woodworkers with arthritis report that it's easier to cradle in their hands than a block plane. Some woodworkers buy a No. 1 for their children. Some woodworkers have special small-scale applications for the No. 1, such as working linenfold panels.

THE NO. 1 PLANE IS *cute, but is it useful? Some woodworkers think so. Other woodworkers regard it as workshop jewelry.*

But in reality the No. 1 is not a useful size for building most full-size furniture. You can't hold it like a regular bench plane because there's not enough space in front of the tote. You kind of have to pinch the tote to hold the tool. And adjusting the depth of cut is no fun either because of the cramped area behind the frog. Add to that fact that the cutter is so narrow and you can see why you'd be working way too hard to plane a typical carcase side.

Buy one because you want one. But don't fool yourself into thinking that you're going to use it all that much. Most woodworkers end up putting it on a shelf and admiring it.

THE NO. 2 BENCH PLANE
■ Sole length: 7", Cutter width: $1^5/8$"

Pity the poor No. 2 bench plane. It's not as rare as its smaller and cuter sibling, nor is it all that much more useful. Collectors love them, though the No. 2 doesn't fetch the same prices as the No. 1. Woodworkers are bewildered by them. It's almost impossible to grip the tote because things are so cramped in there. And holding the tool makes you feel like you're an awkward giant.

I do hear occasionally that the No. 2 is a good smoothing plane for children. It's usually big enough for their hands, and it isn't terribly heavy. The vintage ones were $2^1/4$ lbs. And I've heard from maybe one woodworker in all my years that they had abnormally small hands that were suited for a No. 2. But other than that, I think it's best to avoid the No. 2 bench plane unless you stumble on some unique application – or you just want a complete collection of bench planes.

THE NO. 3 BENCH PLANE
■ Sole length: 8", Cutter width: $1^3/4$"

The No. 3 is one of the most overlooked planes in the pantheon. Because of its small size, it gets lumped in with the No. 1 and No. 2 in the category of "cute but useless." Nothing could be further from the truth. If I were manufacturing a line of handplanes, the No. 3 would be the smallest plane I'd offer in my line. It truly is a useful tool.

You can actually get your hand comfortably around the tote and work the controls with great ease. The front knob is big enough to grasp like a traditional bench plane. And the cutter is just wide enough to be a useful size. So what is it good for? I use a No. 3 for two things: smoothing small-scale parts (such as narrow rails, stiles, muntins and mullions) and for removing tear-out in very localized areas in a larger panel.

The tool is ideal for small parts because you can easily balance it on stock that is only $3/4$" wide

without tipping or leaning problems.

As for removing tear-out, it's the sole's small length that makes this possible. The shorter the sole, the more that the tool is able to get into localized areas on a board and remove tear-out. The long sole of a No. 4 or larger plane will actually prevent the tool from removing more than a shaving (maybe two) in a small area. The No. 3 goes where my other tools simply won't.

THE NO. 4 BENCH PLANE
■ Sole length: 9", Cutter width: 2"

The No. 4 smoothing plane is historically the most common size of smoothing plane. It is an excellent balance of sole length and cutter width to be useful for typical furniture parts. And the last part of that sentence is what is important here: typical furniture parts. Typical furniture parts range from 2" wide to 24" wide and 12" long to 48" long. That's a gross generalization, but it works.

Here's another clue that the No. 4 is useful and popular: When you are searching out a vintage one, you'll find 10 No. 4s for every one No. 3.

I use a No. 4 for most of my typical cabinet work. And because I work with hardwoods, I have equipped my No. 4 with a 50° frog, which helps reduce tearing (a 55° frog also is available for reducing tearing in curly woods). This is not the tool I'll use for really tricky domestic woods or exotics – I use a bevel-up plane for that (see below).

A No. 4 SMOOTHING PLANE *is the most common smoothing plane. Why's that? I think it's the most useful all-around size.*

THE NO. 4¹/₂ SMOOTHING PLANE *has become quite popular in recent years. Perhaps as we have gotten larger, our taste in tools has done the same.*

Another important detail of the No. 4: It's not terribly heavy and won't wear you out as quickly as the bigger smoothing planes.

THE NO. 4¹/₂ BENCH PLANE
■ Sole length: 10" ■ Cutter width: 2³/₈"

What a difference an inch makes. The No. 4¹/₂ is a little bigger than the No. 4, but that additional metal is a game-changer. The No. 4¹/₂ smoothing plane is more popular now than it was when Stanley was the only game in town. Why is that? Good press. Lots of high-profile woodworkers have sung the praises of this size tool. And, as Americans, we also seem to like things that have been Super-Sized.

In truth, the No. 4¹/₂ is an excellent-size tool, though it's more apt to wear me out faster because it's heavier and has a wider cutter. So it requires more effort to push the tool forward.

Of course, the advantage of the wider cutter is that you'll get the work done in fewer strokes, so that might be a wash. And the advantage of the extra weight is that the tool will stay in the cut with less downward pressure on your part. So it's not the simplest of trade-offs to calculate.

I think the No. 4¹/₂ is ideal for woodworkers who like a big and heavy plane (a legitimate preference) and those woodworkers who work on larger-scale furniture. If you build jewelry boxes, the No. 4¹/₂ likely isn't for you. If you build armoires, you'll love it.

THE NO. 5¹/₂ BENCH PLANE
■ Sole length: 15" ■ Cutter width: 2¹/₄" or 2³/₈"

No, this isn't an error. I meant to put the No. 5¹/₂ in the smoothing plane section. Despite the fact that the No. 5¹/₂ is 6" longer than a typical smoothing plane, I think a legitimate case can be made today that it serves as a smoothing plane more often than not.

Why is this? English craftsman David Charlesworth. Charlesworth has been a passionate advocate of setting up this sized tool as a so-called "super smoother" that is used in a modern shop to both smooth and straighten the wood. The No. 5¹/₂ is midway between a jointer plane and a smoothing plane, which is why this arrangement works.

In a nutshell, the No. 5¹/₂ is the same size as a historic English panel plane, a form of tool that was uncommon in the United States. English craftsmen would use a panel plane for smoothing large surfaces.

The modern No. 5¹/₂ is a perfect companion to the woodworker with a powered jointer and planer and who doesn't want to set up a bunch of planes. Here's the drill: You dress all your lumber with your machines and then use your No. 5¹/₂ to refine the stock; the No. 5¹/₂ trues up the work more than the machines can and it smoothes the work simultaneously.

There are disadvantages to any "one plane" approach. The middling size of the sole makes it difficult for you to get into localized areas to remove tear-out (shorter tools do this with ease). Plus, the tool is difficult to use to shoot long edges for a panel glue-up – a real jointer plane makes this task simpler.

However, the No. 5¹/₂ does handle more than 90 percent of your work-a-day chores if you own machines. I've worked the Charlesworth way on several projects and have found his methods to be correct and reliable.

BEVEL-UP SMOOTHING PLANES
■ Sole length: 9¹/₂" to 10" ■ Cutter width: 2" to 2¹/₄"

The modern bevel-up smoothing planes have become quite popular recently. They are simpler tools (with no chipbreaker or movable frog), they're less expensive than their bevel-down counterparts, and they are easily configured to plane at high angles that reduce tear-out.

With all those advantages, why did I even write about all the bevel-down smoothing planes. It seems a no-brainer.

Well, it's not that simple. With the bevel-up tools you have to give up a few things. These are important to some woodworkers (myself included) and insignificant to others. You have to be the judge here.

HERE'S A VERITAS BEVEL-UP SMOOTHING *plane. These are easy for beginners to set up and excel at removing tear-out when sharpened with a high angle.*

First, there's the position of the controls. Traditional bevel-down planes have the blade adjuster right where you want it: in front of your fingers. You don't even have to remove your hand from the tote to adjust the depth. In fact, you can adjust the cutter while the plane is moving. I do this all the time.

With bevel-up planes, the controls are low on the tool – too low to reach without removing your hand from the tote.

Second trade-off: lateral-adjustment controls. With traditional bevel-down planes there are separate controls for depth adjustment and lateral adjustment (which centers the cutter in the mouth of the tool). With Veritas's bevel-down planes, both controls are integrated into one adjuster, called a Norris-style adjuster. Some people love this arrangement. Some struggle with it and find that they cannot separately control the two functions (depth and lateral adjustment). The Lie-Nielsen bevel-up plane, the No. 164, is adjusted laterally with hammer taps, so it has a different feature set.

Third trade-off: comfort. If you like a traditional bevel-down plane, working with the bevel-up planes can be disconcerting. There's no place to rest your index finger except on the tote itself. And if you were trained to extend your index finger, you feel naked, weird and alone (or maybe that's just me).

All that said, the bevel-up planes are extraordinary tools for eliminating tear-out. Because the bevel faces up, you only have to hone the cutter to a higher angle to raise the cutting pitch of the plane. This is a tremendous game-changing advantage and is the reason that I really like the bevel-up tools and keep one handy that's set with a high cut-

ting angle. (I like 62° because it seems to eliminate most tearing problems. Angles higher than that are difficult to push and make a surface that looks like it's scraped.)

If you work with exotics or curly woods, I wouldn't even bother with the traditional bevel-down tools. Sorry, but that's how I feel. I'd go straight to the bevel-up models. You'll be happy.

But if you work with mild domestics (I do), you should consider the trade-offs between the two forms before you make a purchase. In fact, the two formats are so different in the hand that I think it's worthwhile to take a test drive of each form to see which you like better.

THE FORE AND JACK PLANES

Welcome to the weird middle ground of plane sizes, where any tool can do any job and trade-offs abound. Historically, this size plane was used for roughing. You'd put a heavily cambered iron in the tool, open up the mouth all the way and take off huge ribbons of wood. In this day and age of inexpensive and accurate machinery, few people use this size tool in this historical manner. Let's take a look.

THE NO. 5 BENCH PLANE
■ Sole length: 14" ■ Cutter width: 2"

Commonly called a jack plane, the No. 5 is the most common plane out there. If a pre-war homeowner bought one plane, it was most likely a jack plane. Why? Well the jack plane can be set up to do almost any job on a job site or in a workshop.

A STANLEY NO. 5 JACK *plane. This tool was the most popular size sold. Why? Because it can be used for almost anything.*

A STANLEY NO. 6 FORE *plane with a scraping insert installed. This particular scraping insert is no longer available, though Veritas of Canada makes a similar insert.*

Camber the iron (I use an 8" radius) and it can be a fore plane for removing stock in a hurry. Set it up with a straight iron or a slightly cambered iron and it can be a shortish jointer plane. It won't work as well as a jointer plane for this, but you can get away with a lot, actually. I've found it to be accurate when working boards up to about 30" long or so. Set it up with a minutely cambered iron and take a light shaving and you can use the jack as a long-ish smoothing plane. Once again, it won't be the end-all smoothing plane because it won't get into the hollows of your boards, but you'll be surprised what you can do.

I know all this because this is how I worked when I had only one bench plane, a vintage No. 5. When people ask me what plane to buy if they only bought one, I usually recommend a No. 5 or its bevel-up equivalent.

Now that I own many more planes, I use the No. 5 as a fore plane. With a heavily cambered iron, I use it to dress stock that is too wide for my jointer or planer. With a sharp iron and mild material I can remove almost $1/16$" at a time. It's a powerful, effective and useful tool, even in a shop filled with machines.

THE NO. $5^1/4$ BENCH PLANE
■ Sole length: $11^1/2$" ■ Cutter width: $1^3/4$"

Sometimes called the junior jack plane, tool collectors tell me that this plane shows up in a lot of inventories of manual training programs at public schools. It was a little lighter and shorter than the traditional jack, which made it easier for the shop-class misfits to wield.

I have only limited experience with this tool and have never owned one. My short stint with the tool was enough to convince me that there's a reason that it's an uncommon size. It was really too short to joint an edge accurately. The cutter width was the same as a No. 3, but the longer sole prevented it from getting into hollows like a smoothing plane.

If you're a devotee of this tool, I want to hear from you.

NO. 6 BENCH PLANE
Sole length: 18" ■ Cutter width: $2^3/8$"

The No. 6 bench plane, which Stanley actually called a fore plane, gets a bad rap. Patrick Leach, who administers the excellent Blood & Gore plane-reference site at supertool.com, runs down the No. 6 as a fairly useless chunk of iron. Here's how he puts it: "You Satan worshipers out there might find them a useful prop during your goat slicing schtick by placing three of them alongside each other."

I've owned a few No 6s and actually like them. I've set them up as fore planes, and they work quite well at that task. I've set them up as jointer planes, and they work surprisingly well at that task. In fact, I've found that it's easier to teach someone to joint an edge with a No. 6 than one of the longer planes. There's just less iron swinging around I guess.

HERE'S A VERITAS BEVEL-UP JACK *plane on a shooting board. The tool is ideal for shooting edges and ends, though you can set it up to do almost any task.*

I also have one set up with a scraping insert. Did I hear you say that's nuts? Well, I thought so too, but it's a great set-up for glued-up tabletops. Here's why: When you glue up a tabletop from narrower boards, it's tough to get the grain in all the individual boards going the same direction and looking good.

So when you go to plane down the tabletop, you run into lots of grain reversals. One way around this problem is to change planing directions several times while working the top. That can be tough sometimes. Or you can scrape the top – and that's one of the best tasks for a scraper plane. And with a scraper plane that is long (like my No. 6) I can scrape the entire top without leaving any dished areas, which is more a problem with cabinet scrapers, card scrapers and short scraper planes.

The good news is that No. 6 planes are fairly plentiful on the secondary market and reasonably priced. Thanks Patrick!

BEVEL-UP JACK PLANES
Sole length: 14" to 15" ■ Cutter width: 2" to $2^1/4$"

One of the most common questions I get here at the magazine goes something like this: "I'm a beginner. I want to buy one premium handplane, and I want it to do as many tasks as possible because I cannot afford a whole set of tools. Which tool should I buy?"

The answer is to buy one of the bevel-up jack planes. Yes, there are trade-offs (see the previous section on the bevel-up smoothing planes), but these bevel-up tools are extraordinarily useful, versatile, adaptable and easy to use.

If you buy a couple extra irons, you can have a longish smoothing plane with a high cutting angle. You can have a shortish jointer plane that is good for jointing edges up to 30" long. And you can put a straight iron in the tool and use it for shooting the ends of boards. No other plane that I own can do all three things like the bevel-up jack planes.

The one thing the tool doesn't do very well is to work as a fore plane with a curved iron. I haven't had much luck putting a heavily cambered iron in the tool and taking a super-thick shaving. There's some geometry at work there.

You can use the tool as a fore plane if you purchase a toothed iron for the tool. Toothed irons have little steel fingers for edges. They were traditionally used for roughing up a surface before veneering it with hot hide glue, but they also can remove wood without leaving tear-out.

JOINTER PLANES
The longest tools in the bench plane family are designed to straighten and flatten the work. They are among the most important tools in my kit, though many woodworkers go their entire careers without picking one up.

NO. 7 BENCH PLANE
Sole length: 22" ■ Cutter width: $2^3/8$"

Some woodworkers use a No. 7 plane for all their planing needs. Woodworking legend Alan Peters is said to use a No. 7 for jointing, smoothing and shooting. And if you set the tool up precisely and are a careful craftsman, you'll find this is quite do-able. Like my experiments with a No. $5^1/2$, I tried using a No. 7 for everything as well. I was surprised how easy it was, once I got used to the weight of the tool and balancing it on small pieces of work.

In a traditional shop, the No. 7 is the most common size of jointer plane. It is used for shooting the long edges of boards to form them into a wider panel. And it is used for dressing the faces of boards to make accurate surfaces for joinery.

Here's how I use a jointer plane in my shop. I dress my stock using the machines, and then I further refine the faces and edges with a jointer plane. Sound fussy? Try it some time. Most machinery can get your boards only so flat. A jointer plane can take them one step further. And accurately prepped stock can help you when it's time to cut your joints.

I also use it to joint the edges of boards for glue-ups. The jointer plane allows me to add a spring joint to a panel glue-up. A spring joint is where you plane the middle section of the edge a wee bit hollow. When you close up the joint with a clamp at the center, it closes the ends tightly. This allows you to use fewer clamps and keeps the ends of the joint in tension. This can be helpful with some stock because the ends of your panel will lose and gain moisture more rapidly than the center. So the extra pressure keeps everything together when the dry season hits.

There's a lot of controversy about how the jointer plane's iron should be sharpened. Some like it straight. Some like it curved. I use a slightly curved iron because it makes it child's play to correct an out-of-square edge. And when I plane the faces of boards, the curved iron reduces the chance that the corners of the iron will dig into the work. But you can use a straight iron – with practice.

No. 8 Jointer Plane
Sole length: 24" ■ Cutter width: $2^5/8$"

The No. 8 seems only a little bigger than the No. 7. But in reality, the No. 8 is a big beast of a tool compared to the No. 7. There seem to be some tipping points when it comes to the sizes of planes, and the No. 8 definitely tips the scales into a whole different class of tool.

Some people really dislike the extra weight and width of the tool. Other woodworkers love it. I fall into the "love it" category. Though I use a No. 7 at work, I keep a No. 8 in my shop at home (perhaps so I don't have to share).

I've found that the No. 8 works like a freight train. Once you get it started, there's little that will stop it. This is useful when dealing with patches of tough grain. The No. 8 just snowplows through.

The extra weight does come at a price: Surfacing boards (particularly large panels) can be more tiring. And you have to keep the iron sharper than you do on the No. 7. All the extra mass and width makes the No. 8 harder to push around when the iron gets a little dull. Oh, and you'll want to keep some paraffin on hand to wax the sole. That's a good idea for any plane, but it's particularly true for the big boy of the planing world.

Bevel-up Jointer Planes
Sole length: 22" ■ Cutter width: $2^1/4$"

Because of my affection for the bevel-up jack plane, you'd think I'd have the same enthusiasm for the bevel-up jointer. Not so much.

The bevel-up jointer plane is easier to use than its bevel-down cousin. And it is less expensive. But it also has a lower center of gravity, and I think that's why I'm not as fond of it. The high center of gravity of the bevel-down jointer plane makes it easier for me to sense when the tool is tipping to the left or right. In other words, I can feel "plumb" better with a bevel-down jointer plane. The bevel-up jointer plane doesn't give me that same feedback.

Other than that detail, the trade-offs are the same when you consider a bevel-up vs. a bevel-down tool.

THE NO. 7 IS THE *most common size of jointer. However, some people like the additional mass and length of the No. 8 and are willing to pay for it.*

Important Differences Between Bevel-up & Bevel-down Planes

It's more than just which way the bevel faces.

At least once a week I'm asked if I prefer handplanes that have the iron's bevel facing up (like in a block plane) or facing down (like in a traditional Stanley/Bailey-style bench plane). It's a tough question that I've struggled with for years, as both Veritas and Lie-Nielsen have expanded their lines of bevel-up planes.

I first learned to plane with the old-school Bailey tools, but I've made a strong and serious effort to get comfortable with both styles of tools from both makers during the last seven years or so. Here, then, is what I see are the important differences between the two kinds of tools.

DIFFERENCE 1: ADJUSTING THE BLADE

This is the most important difference for me. In general, I've found the Bailey-style adjustment mechanism (shown above right) to be the superior one. It's a bold statement, but here's why: It allows you to adjust the setting of your iron on the fly as the tool is moving. As I plane, I make subtle adjustments to the iron, usually increasing the cut to remove material as fast as possible. The adjustment knob of the Bailey planes can be tweaked without moving your hand from the tote, and this allows a level of speed, sensitivity and feedback I can't get from any bevel-up plane.

All of the bevel-up planes have their adjuster knobs that are out of reach of my fingers as I'm planing. So I have to stop my stroke, remove my hand and adjust the cut. Then I resume planing. This slows me down, breaks my rhythm and requires more thought. This is the same reason I sometimes struggle with infill planes and other planes with Norris-style adjusters. Generally, those adjusters are above the tote or generally inaccessible to your fingertips during a stroke.

Also on the topic of adjusters is the difference in "lateral adjustment." This is where you tweak the position of the iron so it's cutting evenly on the left and right side of the mouth. Bevel-up planes can have a Norris-style lateral adjuster that is incorporated into the depth-adjustment mechanism. One knob handles it all, such as in the Veritas planes – I've found this adjustment to be a bit coarse. Or the plane has no formal lateral adjustment, as with the bevel-up Lie-Nielsen planes, and you have to adjust the iron laterally with your fingers or a small hammer.

THE BAILEY-STYLE ADJUSTMENT MECHANISM IS *(in my opinion) the best. It is robust and located right where you need it.*

YOU CAN USE A THREE-FINGER *grip with some Veritas bevel-up planes, such as this smoothing plane. But most tools encourage a four-finger grip.*

The Bailey-style planes have a separate lateral-adjustment lever above the tote. It's also a coarse adjuster, and so I generally use it very little and handle my lateral-adjustment chores with a small hammer – tap left, tap right.

What's important here is that ultimately, all the planes need fine tweaking laterally by some other method than the lateral-adjustment lever. So don't get hung up on it.

DIFFERENCE 2: GRIP

One subtle difference is that the bevel-up planes encourage a four-finger grip, while the Bailey-style planes encourage a three-finger grip. Some people really like the four-finger grip, and I believe them and think that bevel-up planes are ideal for this sort of hand preference. I like the three-finger grip and use it on my drills, saws and planes. I think having the index finger extended is a cue to your brain and helps guide your work straighter.

You can use a three-finger grip with bevel-up planes (I do) but it feels weird having your finger suspended above the tool in space with nothing much to support it.

HERE'S THE CLASSIC THREE-FINGERED GRIP *on a bevel-down tool. This is more comfortable to me than a four-fingered grip.*

THE BEVEL-DOWN PLANES ARE A *pain in the tuckus when it comes to adjusting the mouth aperture. Shown is the nicest system for adjusting the mouth, and it's still complex.*

DIFFERENCE 3: CHIPBREAKERS

I say this all the time: I dislike chipbreakers. I think they're the No. 1 source of clogging and frustration with handplanes. Chipbreakers are found on all Bailey-style planes, and this is one of their major demerits. There are aftermarket chipbreakers available from Lie-Nielsen and Hock Tools that helps things out, but they're not a panacea.

The bevel-up planes have no chipbreaker. And I marvel every time at how easy they are to set up because of that. If you hate chipbreakers, you'll like bevel-up planes. Period.

DIFFERENCE 4: THROAT ADJUSTMENT

If you want to adjust the throat on your Bailey-style plane, settle in. It's going to take a while. Even the best Bailey planes (with a Bed Rock mechanism) require some fussing and back and forth to get a tight throat opening. Older Bailey planes require you to disassemble the frog.

I don't change the throat much on my Bailey planes – I have one tool set up for each of the three jobs bench planes do. But when I do tweak the throat, it's a pain.

WITH BEVEL-UP PLANES, YOU TWIST *the front knob of the tool, move the throat plate and twist again to lock it. The small brass wheel is a stop for the mouth to prevent you from striking the blade with the mouth.*

In contrast, the throat on a bevel-up plane is a cakewalk to adjust. You loosen a knob and slide a shoe plate where you want it. Nothing could be simpler or more intuitive. This is another big advantage for bevel-up planes if you make any throat adjustments in your work – and many people with just a plane or two do this.

OTHER DIFFERENCES

The bevel-up planes have more of their mass low on the tool. The Bailey-style planes can be a bit top-heavy. The funny thing is, I like top-heavy. And I don't know why, it probably is just what I'm used to. Beginners report that the bevel-up planes' low center of gravity makes the tools easier to balance when working on narrow edges. I believe it, but I think it's easier to balance a top-heavy tool. I chalk this up to what you are used to. I have become comfortable with the balance of the bevel-up planes, but I still favor the top-heavy feel of the Bailey.

Also, the bevel-up configuration allows you to change the angle of attack of your tool by honing a different angle on your cutting edge. With the bevel-down planes, this is harder to control and involves back bevels, shims or other work-arounds. If you work with difficult material (exotics in particular), you'll like having a bevel-up plane around that cuts the wood at a high angle – 60° or even higher.

But if you work with mild material, you won't find this a striking advantage because the stock 45° angle of attack is fine.

BOTTOM LINE

Get a bevel-up plane if you're going to have only one or two planes in your shop, if you're a beginner or you deal with a lot of oddball planing situations that require you to quickly change the angle of attack and the throat. Get a bevel-down plane if you have a fair-sized arsenal of planes and like tools that are dedicated to one function alone.

Metal-bodied Jack Planes

A well-tuned jack plane can quickly trim doors,
fit drawers and eliminate edge-sanding forever.
If you've never successfully used a plane before,
here's how to set one up and use it.

et's be honest: Teaching yourself to use a handplane without guidance is a challenge. It's like trying to teach yourself to drive an 18-wheeler. Don't let anyone tell you different.

Back in the day – before the apprentice system was disbanded – journeymen cabinetmakers showed their apprentices how to properly sharpen the iron, how to adjust the tool and how to cut paper-thin shavings. Perhaps most important, the master was there to tell the apprentice what he was doing wrong when the plane stopped working well. "Your iron is dull; your frog is too far forward; your chipbreaker is set too far back. Here, this should fix things."

These days, unless you take a good class, you're on your own. So it should come as no surprise to you if you've had terrible luck using a handplane. Unlike many power tools, there are myriad adjustments that must be made to adapt the tool to different planing situations. A plane set up to cut perfect shavings on sugar pine might not do so well on ash, white oak or hard maple.

Now before you give yourself up to a life of power sanding, let me tell you this: Learning to use a plane is worth every minute of agony and puzzlement. In fact, I couldn't imagine woodworking without handplanes – or without my table saw and jointer, for that matter.

The jack plane was once reserved for rough work in a shop with a full array of job-specific planes. But if you have just a few planes (or even just one) you should probably get a jack plane. With some tweaking, it can be used like a short jointer plane, or even as a longish smoothing plane.

Equipped with a fence, my jack plane cleans saw-blade marks off the edge of boards. I never worry about rounding over edges with a random-orbit sander. This isn't about "hand-tool heritage." It's simply a better and faster way to do things.

The same goes for trimming doors and drawers. The inset doors I fit with my jack plane fit better than those I've fit with a power jointer or table saw. Why? I have more control over where the cut stops and starts, so things are less likely to spiral out of control.

Finally, my jack plane excels at cleaning up band-sawn edges. I'll taper table legs on my band saw and clean up the tapers with a jack plane. Again, I have more control, and the tapers need no sanding when I'm done.

First, Learn to Sharpen

Before you'll have any luck with a jack plane, you need to get familiar with sharpening. The iron's edge must be keen, or the plane won't work. All the sharpening systems work; you need to find one that's right for you. Also key is choosing the shape of the cutting edge of your jack plane. You can sharpen it straight across for general work, or with a slight curve (just .002" at the edges) for fine smoothing work, or a large curve (an 8" radius) for coarse stock removal.

Once you learn to sharpen, you need to purchase a decent plane. Some years ago, I reviewed all of the jack planes then available on the market. Bottom line: the ones from the Far East had a lot of problems. If you want to buy a new tool that

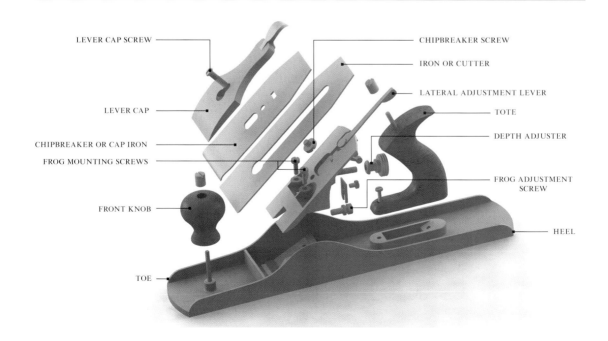

LEVER CAP SCREW

LEVER CAP

CHIPBREAKER OR CAP IRON

FROG MOUNTING SCREWS

FRONT KNOB

TOE

CHIPBREAKER SCREW

IRON OR CUTTER

LATERAL ADJUSTMENT LEVER

TOTE

DEPTH ADJUSTER

FROG ADJUSTMENT SCREW

HEEL

requires no tweaking, I recommend you buy a premium plane from Veritas, Lie-Nielsen or Clifton. If you're short on cash and have some free time, I recommend one of Stanley's classic 100-year-old planes, which you'll see at flea markets almost anywhere.

SET UP YOUR JACK PLANE

All planes require some degree of "fettling," also called tuning. In general, the more money you pay up front for your plane, the less fettling you're in for. On average, expect to spend anywhere from 10 minutes to six hours to fettle a plane.

If you've bought an old plane, you might need to work on the sole if you cannot get the tool to take a consistent shaving. But if you've bought a new premium plane and the sole isn't flat, send it back.

There are people out there who insist the sole must be lapped dead flat and be as shiny as a mirror. Others say that sole flatness is overrated and you need only to be worried about major warps.

It's been my experience that the truth is somewhere between. If you are going to use the tool for coarse work, the sole doesn't have to be even close to flat. If you're going to use this as a precision tool, sole flatness is a factor. In general I lap my soles so that the area in front of the mouth is flat. And I make sure that most of the sole (especially the edges) is flat behind the mouth. I don't worry much about the extreme front and rear of the sole. These are more likely to be out of kilter, especially if the plane has ever been dropped. And as to the required final sheen on the sole, I'm not much of a purist here, either. I've made a few soles look like a mirror, but it didn't seem to boost performance much. Lap until the tool works.

There are several ways to lap the sole, but the most important thing to remember is that the surface for lapping must be flat. Your choices include thick glass, a marble pastry slab or a metal casting – usually the wing on your table saw.

SANDPAPER OR SILICON CARBIDE?

Next you have to choose an abrasive. Most people use either sandpaper or silicon carbide grit. In sandpaper, the choice product these days is called Alumina-Zirconia (and sometimes it's called Zirconia Alumina). This light blue-colored sanding belt is used for thicknessing wood in belt sanders and abrading stainless steel and titanium; so it's fine for a plane's sole. You can purchase it in belts from a home center (about $6 for two belts; get some medium- and fine-grit belts to start), or order it from Klingspor (800-645-5555). Attach the belts to a flat surface using a spray adhesive.

LAP THE SOLE WITH THE *plane fully assembled (but with the iron retracted into the body). I start with #90-grit silicon carbide powder and kerosene. Rub the sole on your flat surface in a figure-8 pattern, being sure not to concentrate your efforts in one certain place on the sole or on the surface (above). It's like a big sharpening stone, and you don't want to dish the center.*

The other option is silicon carbide powder. You sprinkle a few pinches of powder along with a light-bodied oil or kerosene on your flat surface and rub the sole until it's flat (see the photo above). You can buy a 4-ounce jar of #90-grit powder for $6.50 from Lee Valley Tools (leevalley.com or 800-871-8158). Or you can buy a kit of five grits for $22.50. One thing worth mentioning is that if you use the powder on your table saw wing it will lower the sheen of the cast iron to a dull grey.

Usually, I prefer the sandpaper over the powder. It makes much less mess and leaves a shinier surface on the sole of your plane.

No matter which abrasive you choose, the method is essentially the same. Affix the sandpaper to or mix up a slurry on your flat surface using a few pinches of powder. Put your plane together as if you were going to plane wood, but retract the blade into the body. This is critical because the lever cap exerts pressure on the base casting and it can affect the shape of the sole slightly.

Now take a permanent magic marker and color the sole of the plane. I like red. Rub the plane for about 30 seconds on your abrasive surface and turn the plane over. The red spots are your low-lying areas. Continue rubbing the plane on the abrasive until you get as much red off as you can.

With the sandpaper, you will periodically have

RED MARKS

RED MARKS

TURN THE PLANE OVER AFTER *a few minutes and check your progress. Here I'm looking for red marks on the sole. When most of them have been removed I'm ready to move up to a finer-grit powder or call it done.*

I USE A DMT DIAMOND *stone to flatten the face of the frog, but any medium-grit stone will do. You'll have to work around the lateral adjustment lever, but you'll get most of the frog flattened this way.*

to use a brush to clean off the metal filings. With the silicon carbide, you will have to occasionally refresh the slurry with another pinch or two of the abrasive powder. When your sole looks good, move up a grit and continue your work. Keep doing this until you run out of finer grits or patience.

FIXING YOUR FROG

The frog is the soul of your handplane. It holds the iron steady so it won't chatter and hop across your work like, well, a frog. Essentially, you want your iron to seat firmly against the frog and the frog to screw firmly to the base casting.

First, fix up the face of the frog. On a medium-grit sharpening stone, rub the face of the frog to remove milling marks and high spots. As with your plane's sole, you can check your progress with a magic marker. Move up in grits as you did with the sole. Unlike the sole, this is quick work. I find that vintage planes usually benefit from this tweak – premium planes are always good to go.

Now screw the frog to the base casting. Notice the black rib between the two legs of the frog. Keep an eye on that rib. First position the frog about where you will keep it for general-purpose work. You want your mouth to be about 1/16" wide, perhaps smaller if you're going to use this occasionally as a smoothing plane.

Put the iron and cap iron in place and lock the lever cap. Check the mouth. If it's about the right

HERE YOU CAN SEE THE *difference a little stoning makes to your frog. Your iron is going to seat much more firmly against the frog once it's flat.*

size, remove the lever cap, cap iron and iron. Rub your finger over that rib. If it protrudes past the frog, you've got trouble. A protruding rib prevents your iron from seating against the frog. File the rib.

You also want to make sure that the base casting isn't interfering with the mating of the iron and frog. If your frog is set too far back, the blade will rest against the base casting and some point at the back of your frog. The result will be chatter. So move the frog forward a bit.

QUICK CAP IRON FIX

Another oft-neglected part of the plane is the cap iron, also called the chipbreaker. There are two common problems with this part. First, it doesn't mate tightly with the cutting face of the iron. And second, it doesn't have any "spring" to it. Luckily, both are simple fixes on new and vintage planes.

If you screw the cap iron to the iron and the cap iron doesn't have to bend even a little, that's usually a problem. If the cap iron bends so much that the

The Venerable and Affordable Stanley Type 11 Jack Plane

I'm sorry to say it, but Stanley just doesn't make handplanes like it used to. Though some Stanleys can be tuned to perform adequately, you can easily purchase a plane from the Stanley Works' glory days for less. The only catch is that you might have to do a lot more tuning and cleaning than you would on a premium plane. But the results are worth it.

Without a doubt, the best bench planes that Stanley ever produced were the Bed Rock line of professional planes, which began production in 1902 and were discontinued after World War II. These planes are different than other Stanley planes in the way the frog mates with the base casting. Simply put, there's a lot more contact between the frog and base, so there's less opportunity for blade chatter. It's such a good idea that Lie-Nielsen Toolworks and Clifton use that same 100-year-old technology on their premium planes. But trust me, it's tough to afford a Bed Rock plane (unless you're prone to dumb luck at yard sales). They can be as expensive as a new Clifton or Lie-Nielsen.

In my opinion, the next best thing is a Stanley "Type 11" plane ("Type" is sort of like the model year for a tool. The first version Stanley made is a Type 1, for example). These planes, produced between 1910 and 1918, are common sights at flea markets. I've fixed up four of these planes and find them excellent. Here's why: The face of the frog of the Type 11s (and earlier planes) is a flat casting. Properly prepared, this frog will give rock-solid support to your iron and chipbreaker. Modern-day frogs have small ribs on the face of the frog that support the iron, so blade chatter is more likely.

So how do you know if you have a Type 11? It's pretty easy. Type 11 planes have three patent dates cast into the base behind the frog: March 25, 1902; Aug. 19, 1902; and April 19, 1910. As far as I know, it's the only Stanley bench plane with three patent dates. Additionally, the front knob is a low mushroom-shaped thing. Later planes have the same "high" knob as on planes today. There are some other trademarks of planes of that era, including the fact that the lever cap does not have "Stanley" cast into it, a feature found on planes made from 1925 until today.

Sometimes you'll find a plane that has some Type 11 characteristics, but the plane might have a high knob or a lever cap with Stanley's logo cast into it. Likely you have a plane that has been assembled from parts from different eras. If the frog still has the solid cast face, it's worth considering. However, be sure to ask for a discount.

So how much should you pay for a Type 11? That depends on how pretty you like your tools. Nice examples fetch $30 to $40 on eBay. Planes with defects, such as a split in the handle or rust pitting on the iron, can be had for as little as $7.50. I've bought all mine for between $12 and $15, but each one needed a little work.

Many of these Type 11 planes have corrugated soles. The thought was that the corrugations would reduce friction while planing. The corrugations do make it easier to flatten the sole of the plane. You have to remove only about half the metal as you would on a sole without the corrugations.

Finally, I recommend you purchase a new iron for your tool. Most catalogers sell aftermarket irons that are thicker and better made than stock irons. You'll be glad you did.

THE LOW KNOB IS AN *immediate clue that the plane you're looking at may be a Type 11, a desirable and inexpensive option to many modern-day planes.*

iron bends, that's also a problem. Put the cap iron in a vise and bend it using your hands to increase or decrease the amount of spring in it. It's easy.

Now, screw the cap iron to the iron and hold the assembly up to a light. If you can see light between the cap iron and iron, you need to stone the edge of the cap iron. This is a quick fix, and I've found it necessary for all planes, regardless of the price tag. Put a scrap of wood next to your sharpening stone and stone the leading edge of the cap iron. It

shouldn't take a lot of time; cap irons are made from soft metal. The scrap of wood keeps your cap iron at a consistent angle.

Reassemble the iron and cap iron and check your work. When the fit is tight, you're done.

Finally, while you're working on the cap iron, polish the top of the curved edge, too. Anything that reduces friction between the plane and the shavings will make your tool work better.

TRICKS FOR A PERFECT SETUP

The hard part is over; now it's time for a test run. Attach the cap iron to the iron. Set the cap iron so it's a little less than $1/16$" back from the edge of the iron. This is a good, all-purpose setting. For rough work, set the cap iron back a little more. For fine work, move the cap iron forward slightly.

Put the iron assembly in place on the frog and put the lever cap in place. Now is a good time to check the setting of that screw in the middle that holds everything together. The screw should be tight against the lever cap but you should still be able to smoothly adjust the iron's cutting depth by turning the wheel behind the frog.

Turn that wheel until the iron protrudes from the mouth just a bit. Now hold the plane as shown in the photo at right and move the lateral adjustment lever until you can see that the cutting edge and sole are parallel. Now, without touching the lateral adjustment lever, retract the iron so it's almost protruding from the sole.

TAKE A FEW MINUTES TO *polish the top hump of the cap iron. Anytime you can reduce friction you'll improve planing performance.*

YOU CAN STONE THE EDGE *of your cap iron freehand, but a scrap piece of wood will make the operation foolproof and quick. Stone this edge until it seats tightly against the iron.*

HERE YOU CAN SEE THE *rib between the two legs of the frog. If this protrudes past the face of the frog, your iron isn't going to seat properly. File it down or adjust your frog forward.*

Get a piece of scrap. Try something easy at first, like poplar. Just like with your woodworking machines, you need to read the grain direction on a board when deciding which direction to plane. You want to plane with the grain. The wood fibers will likely tear out if you plane against the grain.

Turn the iron adjustment knob just a bit to advance the iron. It's important to note that you should always adjust the iron by increasing the depth of cut. This avoids what is called "backlash." If you retract the blade and then start cutting, the blade can back up during use because there is slack in the adjustment mechanism.

Push the plane over the board and see what happens. How you hold and push the plane is important. Skew the body of the plane about 5° left or right as you push it forward; this will make the tool easier to push. When you begin the cut, keep most of the downward pressure on the front knob. In the middle of the cut, keep the downward pressure even on both the front knob and rear handle. As you finish the cut, most of the downward pressure should

be on the rear handle. This takes a bit of practice, but it's worth it because your boards will remain true as a result.

After your first stroke, advance the iron in tiny increments until the plane starts to cut. If the plane seems to be cutting on one side only, tweak the lateral adjustment lever left or right. Just like with a ham radio, it's all about small adjustments. In a perfect world, shavings for a highly tuned smoothing plane should be the width of the blade (2"), about .001" to .002" thick and fluffy.

You'll also know if you're in the ballpark by the sound the plane makes. When things are going well, it sounds like "swish." When your cut is too heavy, the sound will have a grinding quality.

TROUBLESHOOTING

Lots of things can go wrong for the beginner, so here are some things to think about. If the plane chatters or skips across the work, look for something loose. Is the frog screwed tightly to the base? How about the iron? Is it seated correctly on the frog? Is the screw that comes up through the iron assembly tight enough to keep everything in place? Have you checked for backlash?

Another common problem is shavings choking the mouth. Check the location of the frog. If it's too far forward for the cut you're making, the shavings will bunch up in the mouth. Next, check the fit between the cap iron and the iron. If it's not airtight, chips will bunch up there.

If the plane seems to cut inconsistently – that is, it cuts in some places on a board but not in others,

HOLD THE PLANE UPSIDE DOWN *and look at it head on as you tweak the lateral adjustment lever. When the cutting edge and sole are parallel, back the iron out and go to work.*

THIS IS WHAT YOUR SHAVINGS *should look like when your plane is properly set up for smoothing. This is the perfect setting for removing saw marks from the edge of a board or smoothing a board before finishing. If you want to hog off more wood in a hurry, advance the blade just a little more.*

you need to check two things. First, the board might be twisted, so you're only able to plane the high spots. Second, your lateral adjustment might be out of wack. Try adjusting the lever this way and that a bit.

Finally, just keep at it. Start working with some pine 2x4s; it's a forgiving wood that begs to be planed. Then try some poplar, which gives up wispy shavings easily. Then move on to oak, maple and cherry. With practice, all your common cabinet woods will do as you please.

And when you're ready to be humbled again, move on to the exotic woods. That's a bit like teaching yourself to steer the QE II, and that's another story.

The Jack of all Planes?

Many handplanes have nicknames that describe what they're used for: smoothing planes for smoothing, jointer planes for jointing, shoulder planes for trimming shoulders etc. But what does "jack" have to do with a "jack plane?"

Ever since I got into woodworking, people have told me that the "jack" refers to the expression "jack of all trades." The jack plane, it was explained, was a good all-around plane , so that's its nickname.

So I asked Graham Blackburn, the author of "Traditional Woodworking Handtools" (The Lyons Press) and a longtime hero of mine, about jack planes. According to Blackburn, "jack" is an expression used since the Middle Ages to describe something that is common, such as jack boots or a jack knife. The jack plane is indeed one of the most common sizes you'll find on the shelves of hardware stores. However, it could be argued that the "jack" refers instead to the most common sort of carpentry and construction work performed with this plane.

Indeed, Blackburn explained how carpenters called the plane a "jack plane" while cabinetmakers called the same instrument a "fore plane." And to make things even more complex, the premier English plane manufacturers of the day tried to separate their products from the common ones by calling the same-size plane a "panel plane."

But in the end, the people spoke, and in this country we call it a jack plane – no matter if the tool is used for the coarse surfacing of a piece of rough lumber, for fine furniture work or for trimming an interior door to fit its jamb on the job site.

USING MACHINERY TO TRIM INSET *doors so you have a perfect $^1/_{16}$" gap all around is a real skill because it's easy to go too far. With a jack plane and the Veritas jointer fence, you can sneak up on the perfect fit. This method also removes any milling marks from your doors' edges, so you don't have to sand the edges once the door fits.*

THE VERITAS JOINTER FENCE IS *a great accessory. It really shines when it comes to removing machinery marks from the edges of your boards. With the fence attached to a well-tuned plane, you'll produce shimmering straight edges that are ready for finishing. No more edges rounded by your sander, and no more toiling over the edges with a sanding block.*

WITH YOUR JACK PLANE SET *up for smoothing, you can easily trim fitted drawers to a perfect flush fit. If you have to plane the end grain of the drawer front and the grain direction of the sides dictates that the drawer front is at the end of your cut, be sure to clamp a back-up block to the drawer front (not shown). This will help prevent you from blowing chunks out of your drawer front.*

Instead of Sandpaper, Use a Smoothing Plane

Tune up a smoothing plane and you will greatly reduce the amount of sanding you do. Here's how to select, fine-tune and use this oft-neglected traditional tool.

In the days before sandpaper was common, fine furniture was prepared for finishing using planes, scrapers and little else.

Smoothing wood surfaces with a handplane is a skill, and doing it well takes practice. But the rewards are substantial. With a well-tuned smoothing plane, you can quickly take a piece of flattened wood to a ready-to-finish state. In fact, I find that in many situations, using a smoothing plane can be faster than using a modern random-orbit sander.

Also, surfaces that have been smoothed are different than surfaces that have been sanded. The wood fibers have been sheared cleanly instead of abraded. So the wood looks – in my opinion – luminous after it has been smoothed.

And finally, smoothing is healthier. It's a mild upper-body workout, though nothing like running a 5K. But more important, smoothing is better for your lungs. You're not producing clouds of the unhealthy lung-clogging dust that power sanding kicks up.

But before you can start smoothing, there are three important hurdles: selecting the right plane, tuning your tool and learning the basic strokes.

PICKING A PLANE

For some, choosing a smoothing plane is like picking a computer operating system, spouse or religion. It's personal, and people tend to get worked up and argumentative about it.

So let me say this: All good-quality smoothing planes can be tuned to handle most workaday

HERE YOU CAN SEE THE *different angles that smoothing planes commonly come in: a low-angle, a Norris $47^{1}/_{2}°$ pitch, 50° and 55°. The higher the pitch, the better the performance on tough-to-plane woods (but the harder the tool is to push).*

smoothing tasks. Each kind of plane has its strengths and weaknesses – and in the end, you'll probably end up owning several smoothers. But before we talk about the different varieties of smoothing planes, let's look at the factors that make smoothing planes work well.

A WELL-BEDDED IRON

Without a doubt, the most important characteristic of any plane is that the iron be firmly fixed to the body of the plane and not rock or vibrate in use (even the tiniest bit). If the iron isn't seated well, it's going to chatter.

THE ANGLE OF THE IRON

Garden-variety Stanley smoothing planes have the iron bedded at a 45° angle to the work. This angle allows the plane to be pushed without too much effort and handles most straight-grained domestic woods without tearing out the grain. Some smoothing planes have irons bedded at $47^{1}/_{2}°$, 50°, 55° or 60°. The higher angle makes the plane harder to push, but it increases the plane's performance on some tricky woods such as curly maple and situations where the grain is interlocked or wild. You'll get less tear-out with a high angle.

Other smoothing planes have an angle of attack that's lower: usually 37°. These low-angle smoothing planes have their irons bedded with the bevel up. This feature allows you to use them with a low cutting angle of 37° for end grain, or to sharpen a high angle on the iron so that you can use them to smooth wild grains.

What is a Smoothing Plane?

All planes smooth wood to some degree, but not all planes are "smoothing planes." Smoothing planes – or smoothers as they are sometimes called – put the final finishing cuts on your work. Typically, they are $6^{1}/_{2}$" to 9" long and $2^{1}/_{4}$" to $3^{1}/_{4}$" wide, according to R. A. Salaman's "Dictionary of Woodworking Tools" (Astragal). In the common Stanley plane-numbering system the No. 2, No. 3 and No. 4 planes are considered smoothing planes. Wooden smoothing planes that have been made since 1700 are typically coffin shaped. Infill smoothing planes – which are based on Roman planes believe it or not – are usually the most expensive planes and are highly prized by collectors.

THE CLIFTON NO. 4 SMOOTHER *is an excellent modern-day handplane.*

THE THROAT SIZE

This is a matter of some debate in the world of handplanes, but many woodworkers contend that a tight throat (the opening between the cutting edge and the plane's sole) is another key to reducing tear-out. There are a lot of physics involved in the reason why. But the dime-store-novel explanation is that a tight throat keeps the wood fibers pressed down before they are sheared by the iron so tear-out is less likely to start and then progress ahead of the cutting edge. I've found that a tight throat seems to help sometimes; and other times it doesn't seem to make a difference at all. It depends on the wood.

For many of the planes on the market, the throat is adjustable so you can try it either way and decide for yourself.

There are basically four different kinds of smoothing planes available: wooden-bodied planes, Bailey-style planes, bevel-up planes and infill planes. See the story on page 56 "Choosing a Smoothing Plane" for a discussion of the strengths and weaknesses of each type of plane.

SHARPENING FOR SMOOTHING

Without a sharp iron, smoothing is impossible. You must learn to put a keen edge on your iron and shape the edge for smoothing.

For a basic lesson in sharpening, check out "Sharpening Plane Irons & Chisels" on page 94. For a complete education on the topic, read Leonard Lee's "The Complete Guide to Sharpening" (The Taunton Press).

FOR SMOOTHING WORK, POSITION YOUR *chipbreaker between 1/32" to 3/32" from the cutting edge.*

TAKE A LOOK AT THE *throat on this Clark & Williams coffin smoother. See it? Neither can we. This is a tight mouth.*

Unlike a chisel or the iron for a block plane, the cutting edge of the iron for smoothing planes needs to be shaped differently. With a chisel, you want a straight edge that's perfectly perpendicular to the sides. With a smoothing plane, you want the edge to have an ever-so-slight curve.

Here's why: If you smooth a piece of wood with a perfectly straight iron, the corners of the iron cut a small shelf in the wood. These are called "plane tracks," and they are undesirable. They feel like small ridges to your fingers and they can be noticeable after you finish your project.

To reduce or eliminate the plane tracks, I like to do two things to the plane's iron. First, I clip the corners of the cutting edge. I usually do this on a belt sander or with a file. You only want to take off

MOVE FILE IN THIS DIRECTION

TO AVOID "PLANE TRACKS," CLIP *the corners of your iron by filing a tight radius on the corners of your cutting edge.*

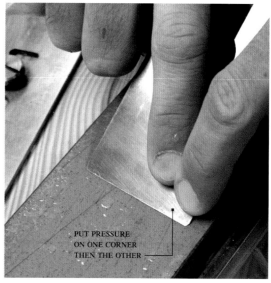

PUT PRESSURE ON ONE CORNER THEN THE OTHER

TO SHARPEN AN IRON FOR *smoothing, work the corners on your sharpening stones. This will give your cutting edge a bit of a camber – which is perfect for smoothing.*

about $\frac{1}{32}$" of the corner or so. And you want it to be a smooth curve – like the radius of the smallest roundover router bit you can imagine.

Then you need to sharpen the iron so it has a slightly cambered edge – so the iron actually scoops out the wood. The tooling marks left by an iron sharpened this way are far less noticeable.

Luckily, it's easier to sharpen an iron this way than it sounds, especially with a honing guide. As you sharpen your iron, most people start with a coarse grit, move up to a medium grit and finish on a fine grit.

At the coarse-grit stage, finish sharpening at that stone by moving your hands' downward pressure on the iron to one corner of the iron and then making about a dozen strokes. Then shift your pressure to the other corner for another dozen strokes. Sharpen at the medium and fine grits the same way. When you hold up the iron against a square, you should be able to see a curve or belly in the edge of just a few thousandths of an inch.

OTHER TUNE-UPS

With your iron in good shape, make sure your chipbreaker (if your plane has one) is seated firmly on the back of the iron. Place it so its leading edge is $\frac{1}{32}$" to $\frac{3}{32}$" from the cutting edge. Placing it farther back allows you to tighten up the throat more on planes that have adjustable frogs without the danger

of the tool's mouth clogging with shavings.

In general, the rest of the tuning is much like you would tune any plane. For smoothing, the sole of the plane should be as flat as you can make it. I flatten vintage plane soles on #120-grit sandpaper stuck to a flat piece of granite. Then I finish up on #220 grit.

The iron needs to fit perfectly on the plane and be secured as tightly as possible. For metal planes, this might involve tuning your frog: Flatten the face that contacts the iron, remove any burrs and make sure the frog attaches securely to the plane body.

With wooden planes and infills, this usually involves filing the wooden bed of the tool.

Then turn your attention to the device that holds the iron in place. On wooden planes, this is a wedge that might require a little sanding to seat just right. For infills and metal planes, the lever cap must be screwed down tight.

Now set your iron square to the sole. For planes with adjusters, set the iron so it projects a little from the sole. Turn the plane upside down and look down the sole from the front of the plane. Adjust the iron until it projects evenly from the sole, then retract the iron. Now advance the iron until it takes the lightest cut possible. Your wood should already be true – either from machining or earlier planing. Final smoothing removes just a few thousandths of an inch of wood.

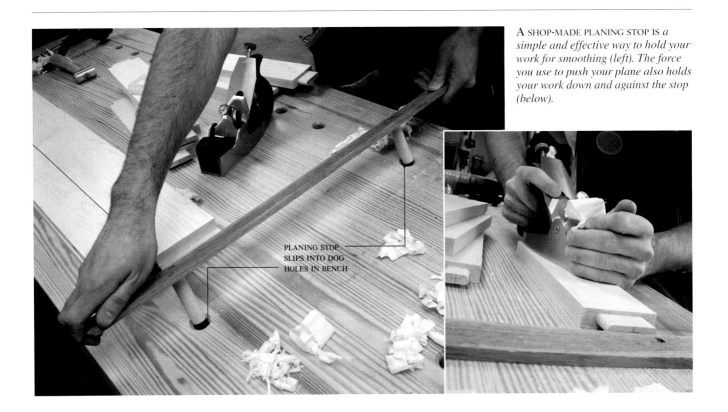

A SHOP-MADE PLANING STOP IS *a simple and effective way to hold your work for smoothing (left). The force you use to push your plane also holds your work down and against the stop (below).*

PLANING STOP SLIPS INTO DOG HOLES IN BENCH

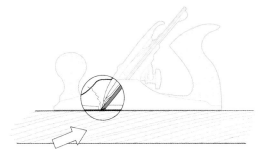

PLANING AGAINST THE GRAIN — TEAR-OUT

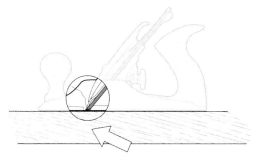

PLANING WITH GRAIN — NO TEAR-OUT

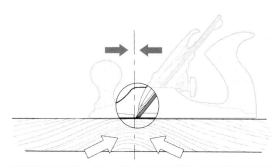

REVERSE GRAIN — PLANE BOTH DIRECTIONS
TO AVOID TEAR-OUT

THIS IS WHAT TEAR-OUT LOOKS *like. Avoid it. When a finish is applied, it looks terrible.*

A STOP BEFORE YOU START

The boards you plane need to be fixed on your bench so you can smooth them quickly. Some woodworkers use bench dogs and a tail vise equipped with a dog to secure the wood. This works, but it can be slower than more traditional methods.

In my opinion, the best way to keep your boards in one place during planing is to use a "planing stop." This simple jig is a piece of hardwood that's $7/16$" thick, about 2" wide and as long as your bench is deep. My planing stop has a couple dowels screwed to it that allow the whole thing to be slipped into two dog holes on my bench (see the photo at below left).

Place the far edge of the wood to be planed against the stop. The downward and forward pressure of your plane will keep most work pieces in place against the stop. Very narrow wood or irregular shapes require some thought to clamp. This little jig works for about 90 percent of my needs.

One more thing you should consider as you set up your area for planing: A lower benchtop height (34") is better for planing than a higher bench (36" or higher). With a lower bench you can use your weight to hold the plane against the work instead of relying mostly on your arms. Old-time benches were 28" off the floor. People were shorter then, but you get the idea.

READING THE GRAIN AND ACTUALLY PLANING

It's almost always best to plane with the grain. The illustrations above show you what I mean better than words ever could.

Now rub some wax on the sole of your plane. I use squares of canning wax that I buy from the supermarket. It's cheap and effective. The wax cuts

down on the effort required from your arms. Apply the wax again after a dozen or so planing strokes.

Grip the plane. Many smoothing planes require a three-finger grip on the rear handle. If your four fingers feel jammed in there, remove your index finger and wrap it on top of the iron.

The body mechanics you use when smoothing are the same as when you use a jack plane or other bench plane. Begin with the toe of the plane (the part below the front knob) on the wood with most of the downward force on that knob.

Start moving the plane forward. As you begin cutting, shift the downward pressure so it's evenly distributed between the front knob and rear handle (called the tote). At the end of the cut, shift your pressure to the rear handle or heel of the plane.

The shavings should emerge from the middle of the iron only. The edges shouldn't be cutting if you sharpened your iron correctly. To remedy this, you should tap the iron left or right to get it projecting squarely from the mouth.

Start planing at the edge of the board that's closest to you. After the first pass, make a second pass that slightly overlaps the first as you work your way to the other edge, and so on. Think of it like mowing a lawn. You want to avoid going over the same areas again and again.

I recommend that many beginning woodworkers start by planing Baltic birch plywood. I know that planing plywood sounds nuts, but it's good practice. The plywood has been sanded at the factory so it's easy to see where you are planing and where you aren't. Plus, the grain on this stuff is generally easy to plane.

When you have made it across your practice board, take a close look at the surface for tear-out and to make sure you're hitting everywhere on the face. A bright light at a raking angle helps this process. If the board looks good, run your fingers across its width to make sure you're not leaving plane tracks. If you are, it's probably one of three things:

■ Your iron doesn't have enough (or perhaps any) curve at the cutting edge.

■ You're taking too deep a cut.

■ One corner of your iron is cutting deeper than the other; tweak the lateral adjuster.

PROBLEM GRAIN

Of course, wood is cantankerous. Sometimes the grain in a board will switch directions. Or sometimes you'll plane with the grain and get tear-out. Or – even more frustrating – a small section of the

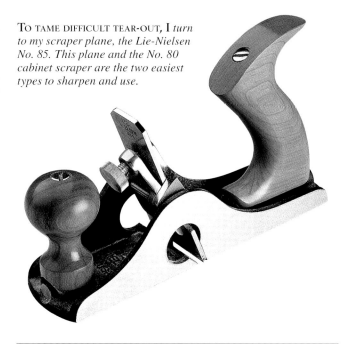

To tame difficult tear-out, I *turn to my scraper plane, the Lie-Nielsen No. 85. This plane and the No. 80 cabinet scraper are the two easiest types to sharpen and use.*

board will tear out but the rest of the board will be perfect.

Tear-out can happen with every wood: domestics, exotics, you name it. What do you do? The trick is to try different approaches until you find one that works. You might have to plane most of a board in one direction and reverse direction for a small part of the board. Here are the things I do to tame tear-out:

■ Try skewing the plane. Sometimes by angling the plane's body (which effectively lowers the cut-

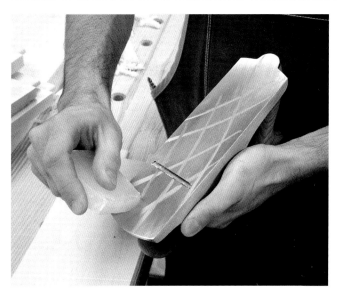

A little canning wax on *your sole makes the work easier and your cuts lighter. Some craftsmen prefer a little mineral oil.*

See how the shaving emerges *only in the middle of the mouth? That's how you know your iron is sharpened and set correctly.*

ting angle) magical things happen. But sometimes things get worse, too (black magic?).

■ Try a different plane or reconfigure yours. Depending on the length of the plane's body, the mouth, the angle of the iron and the wood, some planes work better on some woods than others. If you can tighten up the throat of the plane, try that. Or switch to a different tool with a higher angle of attack or a tighter throat.

■ Sharpen the iron. A sharp tool is always less likely to tear out the grain than a slightly dull one. If you are planing a board that refuses to be tamed, try touching up your iron on a sharpening stone and then attacking your problem area immediately.

■ Go against the grain of the board. Once in a great while I'll plane a problem board against the grain and it solves all or most of my problems. Wood, as I mentioned before, can be a vexing material.

■ Shellac. Wipe on a spit coat of thin shellac to the problem area and let it dry for 10 minutes. Then give the area a try. This tip, which I picked up on the Internet, has worked for me. The shellac stiffens the fibers and allows you to shear them more easily. You only get a couple passes, though, before the shellac is gone.

■ Scrape. My last resort is my scraper plane and my card scraper. The scraper plane handles the larger problem areas (half a board). The card scraper is for the small sections that refuse to behave.

Finally, just keep at it. Refuse to give up. Smoothing is one of those skills that seems to develop in fits and starts. Don't be ashamed if you have to resort to sandpaper or power sanding.

Another suggestion I give beginners is to begin developing their planing skills by smoothing the interior parts of their casework. If you botch things there, it generally won't show.

Then, when you think you've got that down, I encourage you to plane all the parts of a project and then power sand it with #220-grit paper. This will quickly point out where you planed too little or too much. Depending on how messed up things are you can continue with the sandpaper or go back to the plane.

Just remember: Sometimes a plane is the right tool for the job, and sometimes you need to resort to the random-orbit sander or the scraper. But as you get more experience with a smoother, I think you'll find your power-sanding equipment sitting dormant for longer periods of time.

Skewing the plane body during *the cut can help in tricky grain situations.*

A little shellac on a *problem tear-out will stiffen the wood fibers and allow them to be sheared cleanly – sometimes.*

Choosing a Smoothing Plane

There are lots of brands of smoothing planes available, especially if you start adding in all the vintage flea-market specimens available.

I do have some old smoothing planes, but for budding hand-tool users, I usually recommend they buy a new,

premium smoothing plane. Restoring a plane is a separate skill unto itself, and smoothers are tricky enough to tune anyway. Here are some of the smoothing planes I use in my shop, and their advantages and disadvantages.

VERITAS BEVEL-UP SMOOTHING PLANE

Bevel-up (sometimes called "low-angle") smoothing planes are odd birds. Sometimes they are the only plane that will get the job done. Their advantages are that they have no chipbreaker to adjust, they work well on all different kinds of grain and you can adjust the throat as tight as you please – these tools have an adjustable throat like a block plane. The Veritas version is simple, well-made and costs only $199, a bargain in the premium-plane market. Veritas also makes a wider version of this tool that sells for $219.

One bonus is you can adjust the angle of attack simply by grinding a steeper bevel on the iron. That's because the bevel faces up in these planes. Grind the iron's bevel at 35° and you have a 47° smoother. Grind the iron at 48° and you have a 60° smoothing plane.

Lee Valley Tools
leevalley.com
800-871-8158

LIE-NIELSEN NO. 4 WITH A HIGH-ANGLE FROG AND A LIE-NIELSEN NO. 3

These Bailey-style planes are heavy, expertly made and easy to tune to a high level for beginners. I used to use the No. 3 ($265-$325) for about 80 percent of my smoothing. But since Lie-Nielsen has come out with a No. 4 plane with a 50° blade angle ($300-$350), I now turn to that for problem-grain boards, too.

The nice thing about Bailey-style planes is you can adjust the size of the throat so the planes can be used for rough and fine work. I am partial to the way you adjust the irons in this style of plane. The Bailey-style adjuster and separate lateral-adjustment controls are precise and hearty systems. These are world-class tools that you'll be glad you own for the rest of your years.

Lie-Nielsen Toolworks
lie-nielsen.com
800-327-2520

RAY ILES A5 INFILL SMOOTHING PLANE

Several years ago I built an infill plane from Shepherd Tool Co. and produced an excellent tool. If you don't want to build your own infill, I recommend the Ray Iles A5 ($999.95). It's a reproduction of the legendary Norris A5. Iles has made many improvements to the Norris design, including the well machined blade-adjustment mechanism. He also makes a Norris A6, which has straight sides instead of the coffin shape of the A5.

The iron is bedded at 47^1/$_2$°, making it a bit better than the standard Stanley 45° angle for tricky grain. The Ray Iles plane looks and performs beautifully. I recommend you check it out.

Tools for Working Wood
toolsforworkingwood.com
800-426-4613

CLARK & WILLIAMS 2^1/$_4$" COFFIN SMOOTHER

Time for some honesty. I never liked wooden-bodied planes much until I tried those made by Clark & Williams. Vintage wooden planes can be more difficult to tune than metal ones, in my opinion. These plane makers have truly revived the art of wooden planes in this country. I'm partial to the Clark & Williams plane shown ($325, pictured) because of its particular ergonomics. The plane has no chipbreaker and a .005" throat. With the iron installed for a light cut, you can barely even see the throat. This is my plane of last resort. When I encounter grain that no other tool can tackle, the Clark & Williams with its 55° blade and tight throat has yet to let me down. Of course, because of the tight throat, it's good only for smoothing. These are beautifully made tools and finished to a high degree. Other sizes are available.

Clark & Williams Planes
planemaker.com
479-253-7416

The Curious Scrub Plane

Modern woodworkers use the scrub to thickness and texture
the faces of boards. But the tool might have been designed
for some other part of the board, too.

The scrub plane is a survivor in a world where even the die-hard hand-tool enthusiast will own a powered jointer and planer to transform rough lumber into cabinet parts. Dressing anything more than a few boards of rough stock by hand is tough work. I've done it, and I can say without shame that I prefer my powered jointer and planer.

But I own a scrub plane. I use it quite a bit. And I'm quite attached to it.

In fact, the first Lie-Nielsen plane I ever owned was the Maine company's adaptation of the Stanley No. $40^1/2$ scrub plane. And I must not be alone in my affection for the simple tool. Veritas, the manufacturing arm of Lee Valley Tools, started manufacturing its own version of the tool that has some notable differences (including a smaller price tag).

This new Veritas scrub plane prompted me to dive a bit into the history of this rough-and-ready tool form and compare it to the Lie-Nielsen version. In the end, what I found was that most woodworkers aren't using their scrub planes for the tasks they were likely manufactured for.

AN ODD BIRD, OR PERHAPS A COW

The scrub plane is unusual in that it doesn't fall neatly into the traditional English system of classifying bench planes. Rough stock was prepared first with a "fore plane," which is a metal or wooden plane that's anywhere from 16" to 20" long and has an iron that has a significant curve to its cutting edge. Then you refine the board's surface with a jointer plane followed by the smoothing plane.

The scrub plane doesn't jibe with this English system. The scrub is between $9^1/2$" and $10^1/2$" long and its iron is even more curved than what I've seen on fore planes. In fact, the scrub plane outwardly resembles the German Bismark plane – a wooden stock plane with a horn up front that's about the size of a smoothing plane and is used for removing stock quickly in European workshops.

R.A. Salaman's "Dictionary of Woodworking Tools" (Astragal) classifies the scrub plane as a "roughing plane" and says it also goes by the name of scud plane, scurfing plane, hunter plane or cow plane. (Apparently a "cow cut" is an old-country term for a radical haircut.)

"The difference between genius and stupidity is that genius has its limits."
Albert Einstein (1879 – 1955)
scientist, mathematician, inventor

WHEN WORKING THE FACE OF *a board with a scrub plane (or a traditional fore plane), work in a diagonal manner across the face. Then work diagonally the other way. This action will assist in bringing all four corners of the board into the same plane.*

Another part of the puzzle is when you consider that Stanley made the No. 40 scrub plane between 1896 and 1962. The scrub plane wasn't introduced until after the Industrial Revolution and the invention of powered jointers and planers. In 1896, fore planes were fast on their way to becoming relics – so why would Stanley introduce such a plane as the scrub?

One answer might be in Stanley's 1923 catalog. It states that the scrub is for "planing down to a rough dimension any board that is too wide to conveniently rip with a hand saw…." So the scrub plane was perhaps designed instead to work on the narrow edges of boards, to quickly reduce a framing member in width before the house carpenter had a portable circular saw (an invention of Skil after World War II).

If the plane was indeed a carpentry tool for ripping, this might explain why Stanley japanned the entire body of the plane, including the exterior sidewalls. Home sites are a lot less friendly to cast iron than workshops. It also might explain why so many of the vintage No. 40s I see look like they were dredged from the bottom of the sea.

This theory also makes sense from a workholding point of view. The fastest way to reduce a board in thickness by hand is with a hatchet or drawknife. But neither of these tools would be convenient to use with the workholding devices common in the long carpenter's workbenches shown in "Audel's Carpenters and Builders Guide" (Volume 1). However, working an edge on a long carpenter's bench with a plane is a natural and simple operation.

Curiously, Audel's excellent books on carpentry don't shed any light on this topic. The books show a scrub plane, they repeat Stanley's description of the tool and they don't mention a scrub in the list of tools a carpenter should own or discuss it in the chapter that deals with the coarse removal of wood.

The trail of tool catalogs had gone cold there. So it was time to head to the shop.

Much Fancier Cousins

Modern scrub planes are significantly refined compared to their ancestors. They have nicer knobs – the Lie-Nielsen uses cherry; the Veritas uses rosewood. Both tools have some brass or bronze fittings; and the level of machining, fit and finish far exceeds the vintage No. 40s I've laid my hands on. Of course, one might argue that these niceties are superfluous on such a coarse tool – like socks on a squirrel.

And though the two tools are quite similar, there are important differences that appear as you work with each. Most significant is the difference

ONE OF THE SIGNIFICANT DIFFERENCES *between the two premium scrub planes is in the totes. The Veritas's (left) is wider. Also worth noting is that the Veritas's tote is secured to the plane's body with two screws. The Lie-Nielsen's is secured with one.*

in weight of the tools. It's not much, the Veritas weighs 3 lbs. 1 oz. and the Lie-Nielsen is 2 lbs. 8 oz, but you can feel the weight difference in use. The reduced weight of the Lie-Nielsen makes it less tiring to use during long planing sessions. Little differences do add up.

But the extra weight is sometimes welcome. I found the Veritas easier to wield one-handed thanks to the extra mass. I frequently find myself holding my work against a stop with my left hand and hogging out a high corner with the scrub plane in the other.

Also, the extra mass offered a slight advantage when dealing with knots. The Lie-Nielsen would occasionally bounce off of nasty knots that the Veritas could plow through. Speaking of knots, the Veritas has small setscrews on either side of the iron that help keep the cutter centered in the mouth of the tool. The company states that this is to keep the iron in position when the cutter hits a tough knot. In truth, I've never had this iron shift around with my Lie-Nielsen (which doesn't have the setscrews). In other Veritas planes the setscrews are useful for centering the iron in the mouth of the tool when setting it up. But the scrub is so dead-nuts simple that even the rank amateur can position the iron perfectly without too much fuss. So don't get too excited about the setscrews; I don't think they offer much advantage.

Another significant difference is in the shape and size of the knob and tote. The Lie-Nielsen tote is skinny and more curved than the Veritas version. And though the Lie-Nielsen feels more comfortable when you first pick it up, Veritas officials contend

THE TWO MAJOR MANUFACTURERS OF *premium planes now make scrub planes. Both are more refined than the original Stanley versions and are useful for rough work.*

that their handle design is more ergonomic and will dissuade you from using a death grip on the tote when working. Ultimately, I found both totes satisfactory in use, though I give a slight advantage to the Lie-Nielsen – my hands have always favored their totes. However, I prefer the Veritas's larger front knob, which was simply more comfortable to grasp.

The Veritas is a little longer. It's a shade more than 11" long; the Lie-Nielsen is $10^1/4$". Both have the same size cutter – $^3/16$" thick, $1^1/2$" wide and ground with a 3"-radius curve at the edge. The Veritas is available with a high-carbon blade or with an A2 blade for a slight upcharge. The Lie-Nielsen comes standard with a cryogenically treated A2 blade.

Both tools were easy to set up initially and went a long time between sharpenings. When you do have to sharpen the tool, some people are intimidated by the curved edge, which makes it almost impossible to sharpen with most standard honing guides. But I've found an easier way.

SHARPENING A RADICALLY CURVED BLADE

Most sharpening maestros recommend you sharpen a scrub blade freehand and rock the curved edge on the sharpening stone. I did this for years, and then I got a bit wiser. The real trick is to make a concave sharpening surface that helps you sharpen the radius of the cutting edge.

This is easier than it sounds thanks to sandpaper sharpening technology. The fastest and most accurate way to sharpen a convex blade is to make a shaped piece of wood with sandpaper stuck to it. Then you clamp the blade upright in a vise and work the curved edge.

Making the "sharpening stick" is easy. With your scrub plane straight out of the box, set it to take a light cut. Clamp a fence to a piece of softwood scrap, much like you would create a fence for a dado plane to ride against. Press your scrub plane against the fence and make a few passes until it stops to cut the softwood. Extend the iron out a bit more and make a few more passes. Repeat this circular process using you have created a trench that is almost $1^1/2$" wide. Now rip the softwood scrap so it's about $^3/4$" wide. Crosscut a couple 5" lengths off your stick and adhere some PSA sandpaper to each curved face. I've had the most luck with the 15-micron paper and the 5-micron paper. (Both grits are available from Lee Valley Tools, 800-871-8158 or leevalley.com).

Clamp your iron straight up in your vise and work the edge with your sticks until you turn a wire

TO MAKE A SANDING STICK, *first cut a trench in some softwood with the plane guided by a temporary fence. Then rip a section of the curved shape from the board.*

edge on the unbeveled face of the blade. Remove this wire edge on your polishing stone and keep sharpening until you get a smooth and sharp edge without and snags on the edge, which can be detected by running a thumbnail lightly across the edge.

AND THEN TO BUSINESS

Once you start working with a scrub plane you realize why they are so popular. They are a blast to use. Using a smooth plane seems fussy and slow once you've reduced a board in thickness with a scrub. It can be done by working directly across the grain or diagonally. Then check your work with winding sticks and go after the high spots on the face. When the board won't rock when this scrubbed face is pressed to the benchtop, you're ready to move on to the jointer plane.

This is a useful skill – even today – when dealing with boards that are too wide for your jointer or

STICK ADHESIVE-BACKED SANDPAPER TO THE *curved portion of your stick and mark the grit on the wood – you should be able to get at least 10 sharpenings out of this stick before replacing the paper.*

SECURE THE IRON UPRIGHT IN *a vise and work the edge with your sanding stick. Start with the coarse grits and work up to the finer grits.*

planer. Instead of ripping them into narrower widths (a crime, really), you can true up your wide boards to make impressive tabletops or door panels.

And though I do regularly use my scrub for this sort of operation, I've found that my fore plane (a beat-up Stanley No. 5) is more reliable at truing a board's face. The longer sole of the fore plane is one of its assets.

I also use the scrub to simply texture surfaces before finishing. With a sharp iron and a steady hand, you can produce a regularly scalloped surface with a scrub plane. It can create a rustic look, and can even be successfully used in contemporary furniture.

Another fine use for the tool is in removing the backsides of baseboard moulding to fit it against a less-than-stellar drywalling job. I found out this excellent use for the tool when trimming out an addition to our house a few years ago.

But then there's the matter of the scrub plane's true mission in life. Could it be a good tool for reducing a board's width? Is it a ripping plane? Intrigued,

I fixed a long length of framing lumber to my bench and tried to remove $1/4$" from the edge. Removing that amount of wood from an 8'-long 2x12 would be a good deal of effort with a rip saw.

The scrub did the job remarkably well, especially when I didn't try to use the tool like a jointer plane. Instead of taking a long continuous pass on the edge, I started at the left end of the board and took short, choppy strokes to get down to my scribe line. It was indeed faster than any ripsaw I've used and was on par with the stock removal rate of a drawknife (but with more control). I'm not ready to call this mystery solved. But I am going to start collecting some more books on early 20th-century house carpentry. Maybe they will help reveal the true nature of this aggressive and durable plane.

FOR MORE INFORMATION

Lie-Nielsen Toolworks
lie-nielsen.com, 800-327-2520

Lee Valley Tools
leevalley.com, 800-871-8158

The Scrub Plane Litmus Test

Were metal scrub planes primarily a carpenter's tool? We ask a lifetime carpenter his opinion on the matter.

My boss at my last job had a test he gave to all job applicants. He simply asked them: "How many hours do you sleep at night?" If they answered "seven" or anything less, then you were hired. Here's another one: Among trim carpenters in Chicago, simply knowing what a scrub plane was could get you a job.

Recently Carl Bilderback called me to share some of his thoughts about the intended use for a scrub plane. Was it commonly used in cabinetshops to dress rough boards – as many woodworkers contend? Or was it used more for dressing the edges of boards? And what about the furring plane? (See the illustration below.)

Bilderback is a long-time trim carpenter and noted tool collector who specializes in saws. As a career trim carpenter in Chicago, Bilderback always kept a scrub plane handy for fitting mouldings against irregular plaster walls. The scrub plane could remove large amounts of material from the backside of moulding so it would sit tight against the plaster and the floor.

Bilderback also was a primary supplier for scrub planes among trim carpenters in the region. He'd pick them up at flea markets and resell them to his co-workers and buddies. During one job, Bilderback said he had to hire 75 carpenters for a huge job that involved seven miles of moulding. One of the problems of the job was finding enough good carpenters to work on the project; Bilderback

was going to have to hire people he didn't know personally.

So when the job applicant came down for an interview, Bilderback had a scrub plane sitting out. He'd ask them: "Do you know what that thing is?" If they answered "scrub plane" then he hired them. So now there is one more reason to make sure you know what all the planes are – it could help get you a job someday.

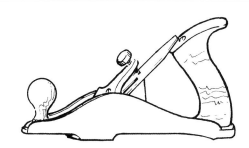

STANLEY SAID ITS FURRING PLANE *was "for preparing lumber as it comes roughly from the mill, to remove the fur and grit before using a Smooth Plane."*

ILLUSTRATION FROM VINTAGE STANLEY CATALOG IN THE AUTHOR'S COLLECTION

Geeky Scrub-plane Data

Vintage catalog descriptions of the scrub plane point to its utility on edges as well as faces of boards.

SCRUB PLANES

For planing down to a rough dimension any board that is too wide to conveniently rip with a hand saw, an operation that is sometimes called "hogging." This is made possible by reason of the peculiar shape of the extra heavy cutter the cutting edge of which is round instead of square. Handle and Knob of beech.

No.		Each
40	9½ in. long, 1⅛ in. Cutter, Japanned	
	Wgt. each 2⅛ lbs.	**$2.65**
40½	10½ in. long, 1½ in. Cutter, Japanned	
	Wgt. each 2½ lbs.	**3.55**

Let's talk about the historical and controversial scrub plane. First a little history, then the controversy.

Whenever I talk about the fore plane, the handplane used to get boards to rough dimension and flatness in the English system of bench planes, there's always someone handy who asks if the fore plane is the same as a scrub plane.

They're not the same. A scrub plane has a shorter sole and a cutter that has an edge that is far more rounded. Traditionally, scrub planes were a Continental tool, and fore planes were an English tool. Yet Stanley made two metal-bodied scrub planes between 1896 and 1962, and Lie-Nielsen and Veritas make them today. So confusion abounds as to which tool one should use for roughing lumber to build furniture.

You can use both. I think the longer sole of the fore plane makes it easier to get a board flat, but I've seen people who can do wonders with a scrub. I also know people who use the scrub plane for really rough work and then follow it up with a fore plane – there are many ways to work.

OK, that's the history. A few years ago I wrote an article that discussed a little theory of mine that the metal scrub plane was more useful for working down the edges of boards on a job site than for working down the faces. And I have taken a beating for that article from a few people. And hey, that's fine. I like a good airing of the grievances.

Recently a reader, Jeff Ross, passed me a few entries from old Stanley catalogs that helps shed further light on the scrub plane and its historical role. It turns out that it was used both to remove wood from edges and from faces. Here is the text from an 1898 Stanley catalog:

"It is particularly adapted for roughing down work before using a jack or other Plane."

OK, that sounds like it was used in a cabinet-shop for processing rough lumber: Point: Critics. Let's read an entry from a 1914 catalog:

"With these planes the user can quickly plane down to a rough dimension any board that is too wide to conveniently rip with a hand saw, an operation that is sometimes called 'hogging.' "

OK, that sounds like working on edges. Point: Me, mostly, I think. And then the 1958 catalog:

"A time and energy saver! When you have to remove quite a bit of wood from the edge or surface of a board – not enough to rip with a saw but a great deal to plane – use a Scrub Plane …. Use it to back out baseboards, true up sub flooring, size rough timber, clean gritty boards etc."

OK, that sounds like carpentry work, mostly, a view supported by Carl Bilderback, a retired union carpenter I interviewed a few years ago. So I'd say that the scrub plane was probably used for any operation that was rough. Use it on edges. Use it on faces. Use it anywhere you need to remove a bunch of material in a hurry.

No More Iron Bananas

*The so-called 'transitional' handplanes marry a metal frog
to a wooden body. They are inexpensive and work well
(for the most part).*

Memory is a funny thing, especially in my family. But I swear that during my last days as a college undergrad there was a car dealership in Chicago that offered a special deal to its customers.

Buy a car and get a Yugo for just $1.

If there is a Yugo of the woodworking world, it has to be the Stanley planes that are called "the transitionals." These poor suckers have a wooden body with a metal Bailey-style adjustment mechanism that works a bit like an Australian toilet (that is, they spin backwards compared to what we are accustomed to).

Most modern woodworkers first encounter these planes through Patrick Leach's venerable web site "Patrick Leach's Blood & Gore" (supertool.com). This site offers commentary on almost every plane made by Stanley. Tool collectors print out every page of this enormous site. They put the pages in a three-ring binder. They live by the advice, which is, for the most part, totally dead on the money.

For example, Leach contends that the Bed Rock series of planes are overrated (bingo). He laments the mere existence of fiberboard planes (fair enough, but so do small children, invalids and lunatics). And he mocks the No. 55 combination plane (which deserves it). But he also runs down the No. 6, a plane that I find quite useful. And he advocates the ritual burning of almost all the transitional planes. He even has photos!

Let me be the first person to say that the transitional planes aren't perfect. Many of the defects he points out are dead-on. But some of these tools have some distinct advantages that, when realized, are impressive. Here's my take.

ARE THEY WORTH MESSING WITH?

The transitional planes are excellent for some jobs, and are fairly worthless for others. You just have to think about it for a minute. Personally, I think the transitional planes that are jointer planes and fore planes are outstanding. I'm not so fond, however, of the many transitionals that are smoothing planes.

Let's take a look at the way these planes work and I think you'll see where I'm coming from.

In essence, these planes marry a Bailey-style blade adjuster with a wooden body. The advantages of this sort of tool are:

THE ADJUSTER TAKES SOME GETTING *used to. It's small, and it operates the reverse of how the adjuster on a metal Bailey-style plane works.*

1. The sole is tremendously easy to true compared to a metal plane. The sole is wood, and most of us should have some woodworking tools lying around.

2. The tool is lightweight, thanks to the wooden body. Some people really like lightweight planes for long planing sessions.

3. You can purchase enormously long and accurate jointer planes (up to 30") in this form because the wood is so inexpensive.

4. You can dial in your shaving thickness with great accuracy thanks to the patented Bailey adjuster.

5. You get the same sweet wood-on-wood feel as you would when working with a traditional wooden plane.

The disadvantages are:

1. Closing up the mouth of this tool is a stupid exercise in shimming under the blade with cardboard. I've never had good luck with this. I prefer using an all-metal Bailey-style plane or a bevel-up plane that makes this process simpler.

2. The tote and knob are poorly attached to the plane (most are wobbly). This is a major problem with these tools. Other woodworkers think so, too. I once saw a transitional where they removed the rear tote and replaced it with a broom handle that went all the way through to the plane's sole. Sure, that

fixed the problem but boy was it ugly – like a prom dress made from duct tape.

3. The blade-adjustment mechanism works opposite of the same adjuster on a Stanley metal plane – you spin the wheel counterclockwise to advance the blade.

4. The blade-adjustment wheel is too puny. This makes the plane almost impossible to adjust on the fly (at least with the transitionals I've picked up). You have to stop working to adjust the projection of the blade.

If you carefully sort through these advantages and disadvantages you'll see why these planes make excellent jointers and fore planes. First, the soles are easy to true – far easier than truing the sole of a metal plane. When I fixed up my first jack plane, I spent days (yes, days) lapping the sole to dead flat. I want those days back.

When I flatten the sole of a transitional plane, I set my power jointer to the lightest cut I can manage and make a pass on the plane's sole. Then it's dead-

flat and done. When readers ask me how to flatten the sole of a metal jointer plane, I'm at a total loss. I've never been able to manage it to my satisfaction. I just make the sole worse, turning it into an iron banana.

Forget the Mouth. Really

With a fore plane and a jointer plane, the mouth aperture is fairly unimportant. So the fact that it gets larger as you true the sole is immaterial. However, it's this problem that makes the transitionals troublesome as smoothing planes. You can stupidly adjust the plane's frog forward to close up the smoother's mouth, but that just makes the iron chatter because the wooden bed and the iron bed that hold the iron are then out of alignment. The best way to close up the mouth on a transitional is by patching the mouth with an extra piece of wood.

The light weight of these planes makes them excellent jointer and fore planes. They are easy to wield, even if you have the arms of a little child (of which I am guilty).

And you don't have to create a perfect surface with these two classes of tools – that's the job of the smoothing plane. So if you have a jointer plane iron with a few pits in it that leaves a few plane tracks behind, then so be it. The smoothing plane (or Fein sander, or Timesaver wide-belt sander, or the abject blindness of your loved ones) will fix that.

But here is why you really should buy these planes. They are dirt, dirt cheap. The No. 32 shown in these photos was $35, and I overpaid. You can get transitionals really cheap. In fact, some tool dealers think they are too lame to even sell them.

Some people give them away like Yugos.

Purists are flinching right now, *but I find this a great way to true the sole of a wonky transitional plane. Take a light cut.*

It's best to have the *metallic frog in line with the wooden bed of the tool. Otherwise, bad things happen, such as chatter.*

Plow Planes: Metal vs. Wood

Though both planes cut grooves, there are important functional differences.

In my kindergarten class, someone was snitching cookies from the lunchboxes of the rest of the class. (Spoiler alert: It was the fat kid.) While the teacher's investigation was ongoing, she gave us a speech that I still remember.

"I once had a student who stole cookies," she said. "Then he stole lunch money. Then he stole money from his parent's wallets…."

Long pause. "Then he robbed a gas station."

If you are still in the "smoothing plane" (stealing cookies) stage of your slide into handtools, let me give you a peek at some of bad deeds you'll be committing against your family's checkbook in the years ahead. First stop: plow planes.

Plow planes make grooves in the edges and faces of stock, which is great for frame-and-panel work or making grooves for a drawer bottom. They also can be adjusted to make the tongue on a tongue-and-groove joint. And they are great for wasting away stock when you are making decorative moulding with moulding planes.

There are many different kids of plow planes, but I think there really are two families: the wooden plows and the metal plows. And their differences are in more than the raw materials used to make them.

Because that's the most obvious difference, however, let's start there.

METAL VS. WOODEN BODIES

If you're buying a used plow, the metal ones are usually in better shape than the wooden ones. And the metal ones can usually be resurrected a little more easily. That's because the wooden body

THE SHAVINGS IN A METAL *plow tend to bunch up between the fence and the tool's body.*

of a plow can warp (very difficult to fix), and the wooden wedge that secures the iron can be frozen in its mortise or can be so modified that it is useless.

That said, I always prefer a wooden grip on a plane, so the metal grips aren't my favorite. Heck – I've thought about wrapping some friction tape around the handles to improve the feedback.

WHERE THE SHAVINGS GO

In use, the biggest difference for me is where each tool's shavings go. On the metal plows, the shavings eject into the fence and the user's hand.

MOST WOODEN-BODIED PLOWS EJECT THEIR *shavings onto the benchtop. This is a good thing.*

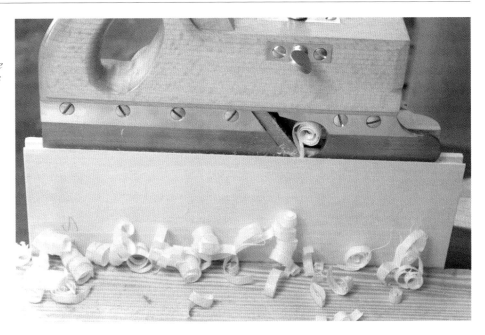

THE WOODEN SCREWS CAN BE *fragile and difficult to adjust accurately. They are, however, quite cool.*

This is annoying because many times the shavings bunch up like a wad of toilet paper in the fence and you have to stop your work and clear things out.

On many wooden plows, the shavings are ejected away from the user and onto the benchtop. I have yet to find a disadvantage to this way of work – except that you have to sweep off your bench once in a while.

ABOUT THAT FENCE

The fence on a metal plow is usually secured with two thumbscrews. Because of the tight toler-ances when the tool is made, it's usually simple for the user to get the fence parallel to the tool's skate – a critical detail.

With wooden plows, it's all over the map. Fences can be fantastic or one step above semi-adjustable firewood. The bridle mechanism on my D.L. Barrett & Sons plow is perfection. It's better than a metal plow. One thumbscrew locks every-thing, and it's always parallel to the skate.

However, most of the wooden plows you'll find have two wooden screws that adjust the fence (or sometimes wedges do the job). With the two wooden screws, it's a bit more of a hassle to get things parallel. Plus, sometimes these screws are damaged beyond saving.

DIFFERENT DEPTH STOPS

On a metal plow, the depth stop is on the side of the skate that is opposite the fence. On the wooden plow, the depth stop is typically between the fence and skate. I haven't found either arrangement to be troublesome, but you do have to pay attention to your work. You don't want to waste away part of the wood that you are going to need your depth stop to contact on a later cut.

I work with both tools and find that they both do everything a woodworker needs. The choice of tool comes down to:

■ How much you can spend
■ What is available in your area
■ How much work you want to put into the tool
■ And which form makes you drive by gas sta-tions that aren't on your way home.

HERE'S THE DEPTH STOP ON *the metal plow. It's on the side of the tool that's opposite the fence.*

THE DEPTH STOP ON A *wooden plow is traditionally between the fence and skate.*

The Moving Fillister

*A quick introduction
to one of the most important
joinery planes.*

As woodworkers dive into handwork, they usually start with a block plane, then they move on to bench planes, the saws and graduate to the joinery planes.

Joinery planes – such as plow planes, router planes, shoulder planes and rabbeting planes – are some of the easiest planes to set up and use. Their irons are straightforward to sharpen (no curves needed), and because the tool doesn't produce a show surface, you don't need to be a maniac about the keenness of your cutting edges.

One of the most essential joinery planes is the moving fillister. It cuts a rabbet either across the grain or with the grain. And it can make a rabbet of almost any size thanks to its adjustable fence.

A moving fillister is different than other planes in the rabbeting family in that its fence is adjustable (planes with a fixed fence are called standing fillisters), plus it can work across the grain because it has retractable nickers (planes without the nickers are just plain old rabbet planes).

The iron Stanley No. 78 is the most common vintage version of this tool, however I'm not fond of it. The fence wobbles because of the way it is attached to the body, so the plane does a poor job in hard woods (in my experience). Record, by the way, fixed this problem with its metal version of this plane, though it's a tough tool to find in North America. The Record No. 778 has two posts that secure the fence to the body. Veritas's new moving fillister also uses two rods, which makes the tool quite stable.

What do you do if you want a wooden tool? Wooden-stock moving fillisters are fairly common in the secondary market, though they usually require some rehabbing to be usable. So what do you do?

You could ask Clark & Williams to make you one – they make an excellent moving fillister. You could buy an ECE from toolsforworkingwood.com. Or you could buy a new traditional one from Philip Edwards at Philly Planes in England.

Philip's planes are excellent. I recently reviewed his miter plane plus a plane designed for raising panels for drawer bottoms. They both work like a charm. So it's very exciting to me (and a good sign for hand work in general) that there is a new moving fillister on the market from Philip's shop.

P.S. Want to learn more about joinery planes? Then definitely pick up a copy of "The Wooden Plane" by John M. Whelan.

FOR MORE INFORMATION

Clark & Williams
planemaker.com, 479-253-7416

Tools for Working Wood
toolsforworkingwood.com, 800-426-6313

Philly Planes
phillyplanes.co.uk

Rethinking the Block Plane

Should its iron be sharpened straight or curved?

When I learned to sharpen planes, the mantra was: Bench planes need a curved cutting edge, joinery and block planes need a straight cutting edge. And in a lapse of journalistic crotchetiness, I never questioned that rationale through four presidential administrations.

Several years ago David Charlesworth, a British craftsman, author and teacher, called to help me with another story I was working on and mentioned offhandedly how he would sharpen block planes with a curved iron. I briefly raised an eyebrow and then we plunged into some other topic.

Somehow his comment got stuck in my head (or I believe absolutely anything that is told to me in a British accent). So I began experimenting with using a curved iron in one of my block planes. And what I've found is that a gentle curve in a block plane iron is a nice thing in some instances. When flushing up joints, a curved iron leaves a slightly scalloped surface like that of a smoothing plane, so there's less (or no) follow-up scraping or sanding to do. No plane tracks.

Another advantage when flushing up joints is that you can use the curve to sneak up on an intersection of a rail and stile. In essence, you are using the fact that the tool is taking a very light cut at the edges of the shaving, which is a powerful tool.

Here's how. Let's say that you are trimming a proud stile to be flush with its mating rail. By paying attention to the width of the shaving you can position the plane so the thinnest part of the shaving will cross the joint line between the rail and stile.

This approach puts the heaviest part of the cut on the stile and just barely touches the rail, which is cross-grain to the stile. So there is much less clean up (if any) to do once the joint is flush.

When doing this operation, it also is helpful to skew the plane (if possible). When a skewed iron planes across the grain, it is much less likely to leave a woolly surface that is the result of planing directly across the grain.

I found the same advantage when trimming proud end grain (such as the proud end of a rabbet) so it's flush with the surrounding face grain. Also, the curved iron is helpful when trimming miters. You can plane away wood from a very small area of the miter while keeping more of the plane's sole against the wood.

When not to Curve

There are times, however, when the curved edge isn't so ideal. I do a lot of shooting of small muntins for divided-light doors. And I really like a straight cut for the shooting process. It keeps the edges true through their thickness.

I have a few block planes, so having two different shapes of irons isn't a big deal. I sharpened one of my little block planes with a coffin-shaped body with a curve. Coffin-shaped planes are no good for shooting anyway so I won't ever mistakenly grab a curved-iron plane for a straight-iron job.

So how much curve is correct? I sharpened it like I sharpen a smoothing plane. First I clipped the corners with a file, rounding them over. Then I sharpened the iron in a honing guide using finger pressure at different points along the edge. I took six firm strokes with my fingers at each corner. Then I took three medium-pressure strokes at points between the middle of the iron and the corners. Then I checked my work to make sure the curve looked good.

If the curve is too pronounced, take additional strokes with finger pressure in the middle. If it's not enough, apply more pressure at the corners while sharpening.

Next sacred cow, please.

Chisel Planes: The Bacon Saver?

This unusual tool may sit idle until just the right moment.

The first time I saw a chisel plane was at an antique market in Kentucky. It was sitting out on a table with a bunch of common planes. Every person who walked up to the table picked it up to check its price tag, but the seller knew what he had. The original Stanley No. 97 "Cabinet Makers' Edge Plane" is a fairly rare bird.

It turns out that wooden-bodied chisel planes are also uncommon, according to John M. Whelan's essential book "The Wooden Plane." As a result, I've always been a bit skeptical as to how useful the form is.

One user told me that he used it for trimming plugs flush to the surrounding surface. I haven't had much luck with using a chisel plane for this purpose. Most of my plugs are a tough species, such as oak. And no matter how closely I saw them, there's still too much wood left to pare with a chisel plane. Instead, I've had far more success using a plain old smoothing plane for trimming plugs flush.

Lately, however, I have found a few instances for the small Lie-Nielsen chisel plane where the chisel plane earned its keep. (Note: Veritas also makes an inexpensive one you can experiment with.)

■ FAIRING ONE SURFACE TO ANOTHER. Recently I had to extend the slot on my bench's top to install some new vise hardware. I sawed out the waste then used the chisel plane to bring the sawn surface into the same plane as the existing slot. It worked brilliantly. The sole of the chisel plane rode the existing slot and pared the face grain with ease. And because there was no mouth on the tool I could work right up to the end of the slot. This operation could have been done with a paring chisel, but it was much eas-

ier with the chisel plane. Similarly, the chisel plane helps me fair up the corners of rabbets after I've chopped out the waste with a chisel. Again, this can also be done with a chisel, but the chisel plane makes for tidier results.

■ REMOVING GLUE. I've been turning to the chisel plane to remove the globs of glue that remain after a panel glue-up. I pare these globs away by working across the grain. The chisel plane works well at this because it doesn't have a mouth. When I'd do this with a block plane, softer globs of glue would get squished by the tool and make a mess of things. I also prefer the chisel plane to a glue scraper because it is less likely to damage the panel.

■ REMOVING FINISH SAGS. When I get sags on my film finish, I like to cut them away before adding another coat. I used to use an old block plane iron for this, but it can be hard to hold on vertical surfaces. The chisel plane makes quick work of sags.

In the end, I don't think the chisel plane is an essential tool for your kit – all of the operations above could be handled by other edge tools. But they are handy.

WHEN I FIRST BOUGHT MY *chisel plane I tried using it to trim some oak plugs flush. It was not ideal.*

How I Set a Bench Plane

*How to get the iron centered perfectly in the mouth using
your eyes, a scrap of wood and a baby hammer.*

There is no single best way to set a bench plane to take a proper shaving. I've seen people do it by eye, with their fingertips, using scraps of wood and even working on live stock and making adjustments on the fly. This last technique takes guts. It's like working on a car while the engine's running.

I've tried every single method above and can do them all with great ease. There is no secret to unlock any particular method. Only practice.

The following is how I prefer to set a bench plane to take a shaving with any plane, from a block plane to a moving fillister.

Before we get to the good part, let me shove a little dogma down the disposal with the evening's chicken bones. All of my bench planes (the fore, jointer and smoothing planes) have irons with curved cutting edges (so does my block plane, but that's another story in this book). I camber the cutting edge to keep the corners from digging into the work and to allow me to remove material from selective areas on a board. People who disagree with my approach are encouraged to visit the shop with their torches and pitchforks.

The good news is that the way I set a bench plane works for any plane, even ones that are sharpened straight across. So don't flee yet.

STEP ONE: KENTUCKY WINDAGE

The goal is to first get the iron centered in the mouth of the plane. The strongest part of the curved edge should be in the middle of the mouth, and the corners of the iron should be tucked safely into the body of the plane. If your curve is too pronounced, you'll take too narrow a shaving. If your curve is too flat, the corners will still dig in.

First you want to sight down the sole of the plane. Gaze at the toe of the sole and advance the iron until it appears as a black line across the sole. If your bench is light in color, you can use the benchtop as a background. If your bench is bubinga or

I<small>F YOUR BENCH IS A</small> *dark color, sight along the sole with a sheet of typing paper on the bench.*

purpleheart (you poor soul), do this against a sheet of white paper.

Adjust the iron laterally until the black line appears consistent across the mouth. With both Bailey-style adjusters and Norris-style adjusters here's how it works: Push the lever to the left and the iron will pivot so the right corner sticks out of the mouth more. Push the lever to the right and the opposite thing will occur.

Y<small>OU WANT TO</small> C<small>ENTER THE</small> *curve in the mouth of your tool. If it's too far left or right, the corners could dig into your work or produce unpredictable results.*

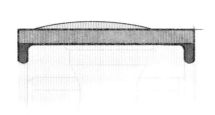

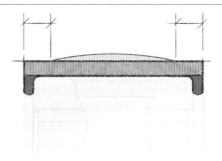

USE A SMALL OFFCUT TO *determine if your curve is centered. You can feel and hear the iron where it projects from the mouth.*

The camber on a smoothing plane and jointer plane isn't really visible, so you're looking for a line that is consistent in thickness. On fore, jack and scrub planes the camber will be obvious. Once you center these by eye you can go right to work. For all other planes, proceed to the next step.

USE A SCRAP TO REFINE

Retract the iron into the body of the plane and start advancing it (this removes backlash in the tool's mechanism. Use a small shim ($\frac{1}{16}$" x $\frac{3}{4}$" x $1\frac{1}{4}$" is nice) and run it across the mouth of the plane as you advance the iron a bit. Where the iron is cut-

ting, you'll feel it drag against the shim. It's not dramatic – more like a tug. I first got this trick from David Charlesworth. Thank you, David.

Where do I get my shims? Well you could send me $20 and I'll send you a bag of them. Or you could look in your garbage can for waste that has fallen off from your rip cuts.

The end result is that you want to feel zero drag at the corners of the mouth and a little drag right at the center. You can adjust the iron using the lateral adjustment lever (if your tool has one), but I prefer hammer taps using a small Warrington or tack hammer. These are love taps and are unlikely to mushroom your iron. I've been tapping one iron on one smoothing plane for about five years. I've almost used up the entire iron and have yet to find a mark from my tapping.

FINAL ADJUSTMENTS

Then I start planing – either on scrap or live stock. Likely the shaving is too thin. And that's OK. Advance the iron until you get the shaving you want from the plane. Then take a quick look at the shaving and where it is coming from in the mouth.

The shaving should be centered in the plane's mouth. And the shaving should look like this: It should be thickest in the center and fade away to nothing at the edges. And it should be as wide as possible. That's the sweet spot.

If I'm a little off-center at this point, I simply tap the iron with my baby hammer to move the shaving into the center of the mouth. Then I get busy.

A SMALL HAMMER CAN MAKE *fine adjustments to the iron's position in the mouth. You can use any small hammer – the taps are so light that it won't mushroom the back of the iron. Promise.*

Corrugations on Soles

Stopping stiction? Or for suckers?

Handplanes with corrugated soles vex many beginning woodworkers. If you find them on a vintage plane, should you grab it or should you shun it? If you order a bench plane from Lie-Nielsen Toolworks, should you spend the extra $35 to get a corrugated sole or is that money better spent on some Lehman Brothers stock?

Corrugated soles started showing up on planes in the late 19th century. Craftsmen noticed that their newfangled metal planes were harder to push than their old-fashioned wooden-bodied planes, according to period accounts and patent papers.

So manufacturers began to mill corrugations in the soles of their planes. For a peek at their reasoning, check out this 1869 patent by E.G. Storke:

"… (E)xcessive friction was caused by their exact and even faces (of their soles), which were not materially varied by use or atmospheric changes.

"When used on very level surfaces, there were so many points of contact that the friction was troublesome, and the adhesion was further increased by atmospheric pressure, as partial vacuums would thus be formed."

In other words, the planes were sticking to the work when the boards became really flat. I've encountered this when working with closed-grain woods, especially poplar and maple. In fact, if the board isn't too large, I can occasionally lift the board off the bench because it is stuck to the tool's sole. It's a neat trick.

"The ability to simplify means to eliminate the unnecessary so that the necessary may speak."

— Hans Hofmann
"Introduction to the Bootstrap," 1993

So many manufacturers began milling corrugations into the soles. The corrugations on Stanley planes were straight and boring. Other manufacturers used wild wiggly lines. And a few even milled the name of their company into the sole.

(I've even seen one set of planes where the guy milled his own corrugations – across the width of the soles. This is not advisable.)

But is the plane harder to push if it doesn't have corrugations? Many pointy heads I've talked to about this are dubious. Friction, they explain, is a function of force – not the surface area of the sole.

I have planes with both smooth soles and corrugated ones, and if there is a difference in effort required to wield them, I cannot discern it.

But there are some practical differences you should be aware of:

1. Corrugated soles on vintage planes are easier to flatten because there is less metal to remove. So if you have an old sole that needs work, corrugations are a plus.

2. The corrugations hold paraffin or wax. This wax wears away completely during use, so I assume it is lubricating the sole.

3. Corrugations on some sizes of vintage tools are rare. So if you are a collector, keep an eye out for them.

So here's my bottom line: Corrugations don't change the function of the plane for better or for worse, so it doesn't really matter either way. I wouldn't spend extra money to have them added, but I wouldn't kick them out of bed for eating crackers, either.

Get a Flat Frog Sandwich

The frog of the tool should be more aptly be called the 'heart.' In many cases, it determines how stable the tool is in use.

Reader Tim Williams writes: "I have a number of old Stanley planes that I've spent a lot of hours cleaning and refurbishing. I've read multiple places about how when tuning up a plane, it's a good idea to flatten the mating surfaces of the frog so the iron beds well, with lots of contact, to avoid chattering.

"However, I find that whenever I take a flat iron and attach a chipbreaker to it, the tension of the chipbreaker on the iron puts a very gentle curve on the iron. So, when I attach the chipbreaker and iron to the frog, there's a very slight gap under the middle of the iron (just enough to see light through if I hold it up to a light). I've tried loosening the bolt holding the chipbreaker and iron together to reduce the tension, but if I loosen it enough to remove the tension, the iron slides against chipbreaker.

"On one plane, I'm using a Hock chipbreaker. It mates more fully against the iron and doesn't curve the iron, so it appears to bed better on the frog. Finally, I've not really used these enough to notice much chattering. Should I even be worrying about this?"

A CURVING CHIPBREAKER

The answer: What's happening here is that you have too much curvature in your chipbreaker. When you cinch down the iron, it bends to match the shape of the breaker. There are several solutions to this: You can remove some of the curvature in your chipbreaker. Place one end of the breaker in a vise and push against it gently. It will bend easily. Then try setting up the iron and chipbreaker again. The chipbreaker should mate completely at the iron's cutting edge, the iron should be flat and the chipbreaker should be securely attached.

Another solution is to replace the iron with a thicker aftermarket iron. This is always a good idea. A thicker iron will resist bending.

If you do this, there are some pitfalls to watch out for. Some planes (of every make) are not compatible with thicker irons. The small dog in the frog that reaches through the iron to engage the chipbreaker might not be long enough. If this is the case, you can't use a thicker iron.

The other potential pitfall is that a thick iron might ram into the front of the mouth of the plane – even with the frog backed up all the way. If this happens, you can file the front of the mouth of the tool to allow the iron to pass.

Another option is to replace both the iron and the chipbreaker, which is what I like to do with vintage handplanes that I'm going to use for high-tolerance planing (jointing or smoothing). Aftermarket chipbreakers are thick and flat. They won't bend the iron and they won't themselves bend.

Of course, the bigger question here is if the bending is even a problem. It depends. With some forms of planes (such as infill planes) the lever cap puts so much pressure on the iron and breaker right up by the mouth that it doesn't matter if the iron touches the frog or not. Heck, some plane designs intentionally bed the iron only at the mouth and not anywhere else on the body of the plane.

In Bailey-style planes, however, the more contact you get between the frog and iron the more stable the whole assembly will be and the less likely that bad things will happen, such chattering or the plane going out of adjustment while planing.

When I set up a Bailey plane, what I shoot for is a flat sandwich of frog, iron and breaker, as shown in the photo above. That works best.

Understand
Grain Direction

TOP OF TREE

PLANE IN THE
SAME DIRECTION AS
THE CATHEDRALS ON
THE HEART SIDE

PLANE INTO THE
POINTS OF THE
CATHEDRALS ON
THE BARK SIDE

BOTTOM OF TREE

BARK SIDE

HEART SIDE

*We show you two ways to read grain direction (even in
rough stock) that will help you get tear-out-free surfaces.*

I often tell people that the grain direction in a board is like the fur on a cat. Stroke the cat (or board) one way and the cat will purr, and your tool will produce a nice surface. Stroke the cat (or board) the wrong way, however, and the cat will bite you, and your board will be as smooth as rotgut bourbon.

While that seems simple enough, the thing I sometimes neglect to mention is that boards (like cats) can behave unpredictably. And sometimes you will get bit even when you think you are doing everything right.

Wood is a little more complex than just comparing it to a bundle of soda straws or the fur of a feline, but you can understand grain direction quite well if you think a little harder about how trees grow.

TREES ARE CONES

Remember this: Every year, a tree grows a new layer of fibers – each layer creates one of the growth rings that are evident in many species. Also, remember that trees are bigger at the ground than they are at the top of their trunks. Each layer of fiber is therefore slightly cone shaped. And so, a mature tree is merely a series of cones stacked up on top of one another – I like to think of trees as a stack of ice cream cones.

The first time I ever saw this idea explained so simply and brilliantly was in an article by Russell Jokela, a woodworker living in Japan. That

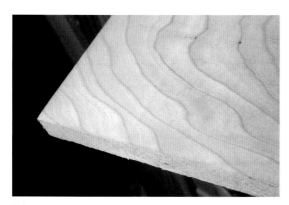

WANT TO KNOW HOW TO *plane or joint this edge? Read the grain direction on its adjacent face. This is usually foolproof, unless the edge runs through the middle of a cathedral.*

article changed the way I look at boards when I take them to the jointer, planer or workbench.

The grain direction in any board can be read using at least two different methods. Knowing both techniques will speed your work. You will be able to tell at a glance what direction the grain likely runs in almost any board, even if that board is rough-sawn and the grain lines are almost impossible to see.

These two techniques work well with domestic hardwoods and softwoods, but they aren't foolproof when it comes to exotic woods with interlocked grain, such as mahogany. What's interlocked grain? Well, we're getting ahead of ourselves now. First let's look at the way most people are taught to read the grain.

THE EDGES EXPLAIN THE FACES (AND VICE VERSA)

The most common way to determine the grain direction on the face of a board is to examine the grain lines on the edge of that board. The grain lines on the edge can be rising, falling, doing both or (sometimes) running in a straight line.

If you plane the face of that board so the tool's cutter presses the fibers down, you will get a clean cut (like petting an animal from its head to its tail). Plane the opposite way and the cutter will act like a wedge and lift up the fibers ahead of your cutter (like rubbing an animal the wrong way). This results in tear-out.

If the grain on the edge is straight, you sometimes can work the board's face in either direction with good results. If the grain reverses and goes up and down on the edge, sometimes you have to work in two directions, or you have to sand or scrape out the resulting tear-out.

This whole process also works if you want to know the direction that the grain runs on the edge of a board. Simply read the grain lines on the face of a board to determine how to plane or joint the board's edge.

SOME TROUBLES WITH THIS METHOD

Reading the grain on the edges works about 75 percent of the time for me.

Sometimes the edges can offer confusing or contradictory information, especially with plain-sawn boards that have quartersawn grain along the edges. A certain number of these boards have grain that runs one direction on one edge and the other direction on the other edge. What is typical with these miscreants is that you end up with a board that's separated into thirds: Two-thirds of the board has grain in one direction. And one-third of the grain runs the other way.

What gives? It's called spiral grain. This is when the fibers in a tree's growth ring don't run straight up and down in a tree. Instead, the fibers wrap around the trunk in a spiral. When this occurs, you can have a plain-sawn board with grain running one direction up the middle of the board and along one edge, and then grain running the opposite way on the other edge.

And when the grain spirals one direction one year (clockwise) and the other direction the next year (counterclockwise), that is called interlocked grain. And that is why they invented wide belt sanders. Nothing is more difficult to work with hand tools and basic machine tools.

Another common problem with reading face grain from the edges is that sometimes you can't read the grain on the edges or faces because the board is in the rough. When faced with this situation in my shop, I used to just guess at the grain direction. If I was wrong, I would turn the board around and hope I had enough material thickness remaining to remove the tear-out.

And that is why I learned to read grain direction by looking at the faces and the end grain of boards.

CATHEDRALS, HEARTS AND BARKING MUTTS

Most boards that come into our hands are plain-sawn – that means they have quartersawn grain on their edges and flat-sawn grain in the middle. It's this flat-sawn grain in the middle that creates the cathedrals (sometimes called peaks) on the face of a board.

If you understand that trees are cones, you can use this to your advantage.

The cathedrals on a board can point the way that the grain is running once you know if you are looking at the heart side of the board or the bark side of a board. (You can determine this easily by looking at the end grain.)

When looking at the heart side of a board, the grain direction generally goes the same direction as the cathedrals – think of the cathedrals as arrows that point the way that your handplane should travel or that the cutterhead should intersect the wood.

The way I like to remember this is: When planing the inside of the tree, plane inside the cathedrals.

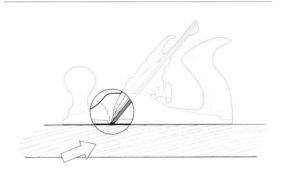

**PLANING AGAINST THE GRAIN —
TEAR-OUT**

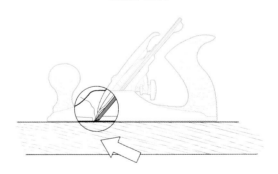

**PLANING WITH THE GRAIN —
NO TEAR-OUT**

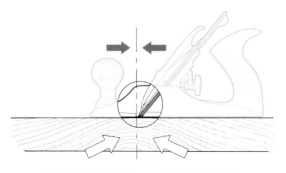

**REVERSE GRAIN — PLANE BOTH
DIRECTIONS TO AVOID TEAR-OUT**

THIS BOARD IS CUPPED ON *the bark side.*

When planing the bark side of a board, the grain is reversed. You plane into the tips of the cathedrals. The dumb way I remember this is that when I'm working on the bark side of a board I think of my plane as a dog (what is it with me and animals?). And the cathedrals are the barking noise coming from its mouth.

Knowing this trick won't save you from the agony of spiral or interlocked grain, but it will help you work boards that are in the rough. Though you might not be able to see every grain line on a rough board, you can usually pick out the cathedrals.

And this will help you get the wood surfaced quickly with less guessing and less tear-out. Here's how I proceed with a powered jointer and planer:

HERE I'M PLANING THE BARK *side of a board. Note that I'm planing into the peaks of the cathedrals. Can you hear the barking sound?*

"Many people never stop to realize that a tree is a living thing, not that different from a tall leafy dog that has roots and is very quiet."

— Jack Handy
"Saturday Night Live"

1. Check the board for cupping. Most boards cup on the bark side.

2. Check the face of the board for the direction the cathedrals are pointing.

3. Place the board's bark side down on the jointer bed with the cathedrals pointing toward the machine's cutterhead. Joint one face.

4. Take the board to the planer and insert it into the machine (bark-side-down again) with the cathedrals pointing away from the machine's cutterhead.

No Universal Solution

If I had the single secret to always knowing the grain direction on any board, I sure wouldn't put it in a book that sells for just $34.99 (wink). Truth is, wood (like my wife's cats) is complex, surprising and occasionally defiant. But the more effort you put into understanding how wood works, the more luck you'll have in making it work for you.

HERE I'M PLANING THE HEART *side of this board. The plane is following the cathedrals and the wood is behaving nicely.*

HERE YOU CAN SEE THE *cathedrals, even in the rough. When jointing one face and the bark side is on the table, the cathedrals usually should point to the cutterhead.*

WHEN PLANING THE BOARD, THE *heart-side cathedrals should point away from the cutterhead.*

Handplaned Surfaces

The beauty of imperfection.

A couple years ago I finally got to go to Winterthur, the DuPont's estate in Delaware that is a shrine to early American furniture. Right as our tour of the collection was about to begin, the docents segregated me from the gaggle of chattering blue-haired old ladies.

In retrospect, the docents were probably afraid I was going to mug them in the Marlboro Room.

In any case, it was a lucky turn of events. I and the two guys with me with were paired with our own personal docent for a tour. When she found out that two of us were furniture makers, she smiled and gave us little flashlights.

"I know your type," she said. "You're gonna crawl under the highboys."

And crawl like slugs we did. I learned a lot about casework that day, but the most lasting memory was getting to examine the sides of some of the grandest bonnet-top highboys I've ever seen. These were masterpieces of design. And yet, on almost all of them the side panels were split. Plus the panels would never pass muster in Ethan Allen. You could feel and see the regular scallops of the makers' smoothing planes. Heck – the undulations were so regular and obvious that you could tell what width the craftsman's smoothing plane was.

That was the most beautiful thing I saw all day.

Handplaned surfaces are not perfect. And thank goodness. They have a slight irregularity to them that I embrace. While it is entirely possible to tune a smoothing plane to produce a surface that looks like a machine dressed it (I'll do it at shows to impress the power-tool guys), that's not my goal. I aim to remove tear-out but to leave my mark.

So what does this look like?

Close up, it looks like crap. The photos on this page show every little detail of my work on a tabletop of the server in the final stages of completion. You can see how I angled my plane to begin my stroke, which reduces chatter at the beginning of a pass. You can see evidence of toolmarks everywhere when you get close enough.

When this top gets a finish on it (oil followed by lacquer), these hallmarks will become less obvious, but they will still be there for someone who knows how to look. For me, they are as telling about my work as my name that I'm going to stamp on the leg.

HERE YOU CAN SEE THE *light reflected off the surface of a cherry top that has just been planed. There's no finish on it.*

HERE'S THE SAME PROJECT FROM *a distance. Once there is finish on it you will be able to feel the subtle scallops left my the plane, but they won't be highly visible, except in some reflected light.*

Don't Work for the Pets and Pests

To work quickly, focus your attention on the show surfaces.

I quite enjoy looking at other woodworkers' work, but nothing makes me spit out my coffee faster than reading that a certain project took 300, 600 or even 900 hours of work. It makes me wonder: Are they boasting, admitting their shame or just stating fact?

If I worked for 600 hours on a single project I would probably be fired (and also be ready to check into a mental hospital). I mean, 600 hours is 15 straight weeks of eight-hour days. To be sure, there are some projects (anything with large amounts of marquetry) that could suck up the hours based on the sheer number of parts. But the projects I'm bemused by generally are quite nice, but not overwhelming in complexity. What I have found from examining work like this is that they are overwhelming in perfection.

This is the part of the story where you can start calling me a hack.

When I build, I log my hours of shop time on my cutlist. I don't log the time I wait for glue to dry overnight or time waiting for lacquer to set up – just the time I'm in the shop and putting tool to wood. And building for the magazine slows me down – I have to stop and take lots of photos regularly (about half of the photos I take get thrown out for space considerations). So I know what I spend on a table when it comes to time.

For example, a simple Shaker end table with one dovetailed drawer took me about 20 hours to build the first time. The second and third tables took me 17 hours each, and each table has a hand-cut dovetailed drawer.

Part of my time savings is due to the fact that I don't fuss over interior surfaces. All of the interior parts are trued by a jointer plane (this speeds assembly) but they never see a smoothing plane or scraper or sandpaper. I speed the fitting of mortise-and-tenon joints by always undercutting the tenon shoulders so they'll close tight the first time.

And I never do anything until I absolutely have to. I don't assemble a joint until it's do-or-die assembly time. Assembling and disassembling will slow you down and sometimes increase the chance that you'll damage a part. I don't break down a tool setup until I have to (this saves tons of shop time). And I keep many tools set up to do one thing only. My jointer plane is never set up as an oversized smoothing plane – it's always set up like a jointer plane. I don't use my powered jointer for rabbeting or bevels or other things that I have tools for. The powered jointer trues the faces and edges. Period.

Having a complete set of tools helps, obviously. And beginners are going to struggle and spend a lot of time setting and changing tools because of their financial and tool limitations. I understand that and empathize – I was there myself.

The point I'm trying to make is that you shouldn't feel like a hack if you don't spend eleventy-billion hours on a project. You shouldn't feel bad if there's tear-out on the underside of a shelf. The pets and insectoid pests in your home don't much care when they spot it. If you get pleasure from treating every surface like it's a show surface, that's fine; woodworking is more of a hobby than a profession for most. But know that there is also great virtue in getting things done so they can be used and enjoyed.

Handplane Cabinet

Hard-working tools deserve a decent place to rest.

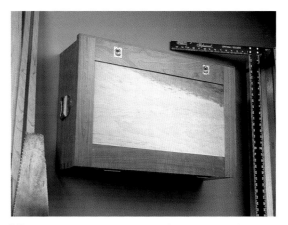

WITH THE LID CLOSED, YOUR *tools are protected.*

On certain holidays, such as New Year's Day, craftsmen in Japan clean their tools, put them on a shrine and offer them gifts such as sake and rice cakes. It is their way of thanking the tools for the service they have provided and will provide in future days.

As my own collection of handplanes grew from a few rusty specimens handed down from my great-grandfather to a small arsenal of new high-quality instruments, this Japanese tradition began to weigh heavily on my mind. My planes generally squatted on my workbench when not in use, and I had to constantly move them around to avoid knocking them to the floor as I worked.

After some thought, I decided that a cabinet dedicated to my planes was the best way to protect them from dings and to thank them for the service they provide almost every day of the year.

This piece is designed to be used either as a traditional tool chest that sits on a bench or as a cabinet that hangs on the wall on a tough French cleat. Because planes are heavy tools, the case is joined using through-dovetails. The lid is a flat-panel door assembled using mortise-and-tenon construction. And the dividers inside the cabinet are screwed together so the configuration can be rearranged easily as my collection (or needs) change.

As you design your own version of this cabinet, you should measure your planes to ensure there's enough space for everything you own, or plan to own. This cabinet should provide plenty of room for all but the largest collections.

DOVETAILS WITH THE PINS FIRST

Because of all the cast iron and steel in handplanes, the cabinet's carcase needs to be as stout as possible to resist the stress that all this weight will put on the corners. In my opinion, the through-dovetail is the only joint for this job.

Whether you choose to cut pins or tails first (or use a dovetail jig and a router) is up to you. Usually I cut the tails first, but I try to keep an open mind about different techniques. So for a year I built as many things as I could by cutting the pins first – this is one of those projects.

Lay out the joints using the illustration at right, a marking gauge, a square and a sliding bevel square set for 7°. I strike the lines with a marking knife and color them in a bit with a mechanical pencil. The pencil marks help me see the line and the knife lines keep me accurate. In fact, once you get some practice sawing, you should be able to easily remove the pencil marks from only one side of your knife lines. It sounds crazy, but it's actually not that hard.

There are many ways to remove the waste from between your saw's kerf lines. Some just chop it away directly with a chisel and a sharp blow from a mallet. I find that I'm sharpening my chisels less if I saw out most of the waste and chop out the little bit that's left. A coping saw with a fine-tooth blade works well, as does a jeweler's fret saw.

When you chop out the waste, be sure to stand so you can see the profile of your chisel – it must be perpendicular to the work. I use a standard bevel-edge chisel for this operation. Just make sure that if

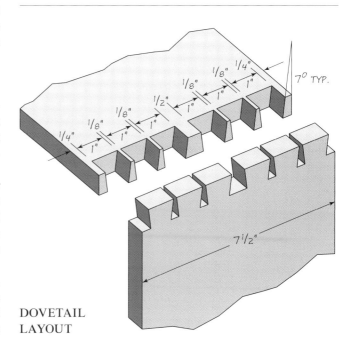

DOVETAIL
LAYOUT

you do the same that your chisel can be struck by a mallet without splitting the handle.

Next you need to mark out the mating part of the joint by using the first half of the joint as a template. Here's the main difficulty you'll encounter by cutting the pins first: You have to balance the pin board on edge to mark out the tail portion of the joint. With a small case it's manageable. But with a dresser it can be tricky.

Mark the joints with a sharp knife followed by a pencil. Then cut the tails. For this project I tried a technique you might want to take for a spin: As you can see from the photo at right, I skewed the tail board in my vise so I was sawing straight down

instead of at a 7° angle. I think this is a good trick for beginners as it makes it easier to track your lines. However, you have to shift the board 7° the other way for the other half of your cuts, so it's a bit more work.

At this point you have to pay close attention to your lines or your joint will have a sloppy fit. Saw on the waste side of the line, leaving the pencil line intact. This makes the joint just a little tight – something you can tweak by paring with a chisel.

Use a coping saw to remove most of the waste between the tails and chop the rest of the waste away with a chisel. Now you're ready for a dry run. Ease the inside edges of the tails just a bit with a

MARK THE LENGTH OF YOUR *pins and tails. There's a debate as to whether you should mark exactly how long you want them, a little less or a little more. I prefer to mark them $^1/_{32}$" longer so the ends are proud when assembled. Then I plane them flush after gluing.*

ONCE THE CUT IS STARTED, *hold the saw like you would hold a small bird that you're trying to prevent from flying away. Don't clench the handle; just keep enough pressure to avoid losing control. And never apply much downward pressure as you saw – this will cause your blade to drift.*

WITH THE PINS DEFINED, GET *out a coping saw with a fine-tooth blade and remove as much waste as you can. The closer you get to the scribed line at the bottom of the joint, the less cleanup you'll have with a chisel. But if you overshoot your line, you're cooked.*

CLAMP YOUR PIN BOARD TO *a piece of scrap and remove the rest of the waste using a sharp chisel and a mallet. I sneak up on the line on one side, then on the other, then clean up any junk in the middle. Clean out the corners of the pins using a sharp knife.*

knife. If the joint is too tight, try shaving off a bit on the inside faces of the pins – parts that won't show in the completed joint.

BOTTOM AND ASSEMBLY

Cut the remainder of your dovetails and mill the ¼"-deep x ½" groove for the plywood back/bottom. I milled this groove using a plunge router, a straight bit and an edge guide. Make sure you put the groove ½" in from the bottom edge of the sides to make room for the French cleat that attaches the cabinet to the wall (if you're hanging this cabinet on a wall).

Before you assemble the case with glue, use a smoothing plane to prepare all the inside surfaces of the carcase for finishing – including the bottom

PUT YOUR TAIL BOARD ON *the bench with its inside face pointing up. Position its mate on top of it and mark the locations of the tails using a knife, followed by a mechanical pencil. Be careful not to shift either board during this step. If you do, erase your lines and start anew.*

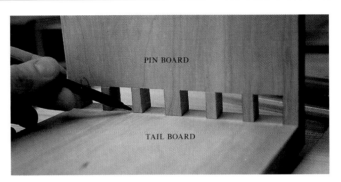

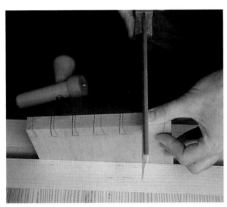

TRANSFER THE LINES ON YOUR *tail board across the end using a square. Clamp the tail board in a vise. You can see how I skewed the board in my vise so I'm actually cutting straight down. Angle the board one direction and make half of the tail cuts, then reverse the angle for the other cuts. Remember to cut ever-so-slightly outside of the lines.*

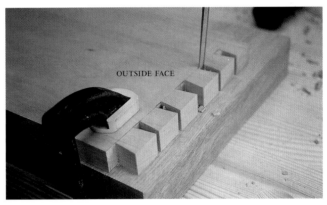

REMOVE THE WASTE FROM THE *outside face of the board first, then remove the rest from the inside face. This will result in a neater joint if the grain buckles while you are chopping it. Again, clean up your corners with a knife.*

NOW IT'S TIME FOR A *test fit. Assemble the joint using a deadblow mallet and a backing block to distribute your blows across the entire joint. You should be able to push the mating pieces together most of the way using only hand pressure, plus a few taps to seat it in place.*

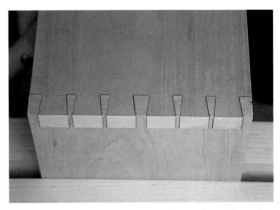

YOU CAN SEE THE PENCIL *lines on the tails and how the ends of the pins and tails stick up a bit on the completed joint. This makes it easier to trim them flush, but more difficult to clamp during glue-up.*

piece. I sharpen a gentle camber on the cutting edge of the blade (about .002") and set the plane to take a very fine shaving, about .001" thick. This creates a surface that generally needs little or no sanding, especially with wood that has mild, easy-to-plane grain.

Once you glue up the case, trim the dovetail joints flush to the outside and use a smoothing plane to prepare the exterior of the case for finishing.

BUILD THE DOOR

With the glue dry and the case complete, measure its width and length to determine exactly how big your door should be. You want the door to overhang the case by $1/16$" on either end and $1/16$" on the front, so size your door's rails and stiles accordingly.

As much as I enjoy handwork, I decided to cut the mortise-and-tenon joints for the frame-

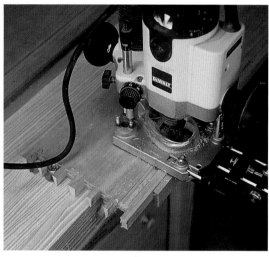

CUT THE GROOVE FOR THE $1/2$"-thick bottom in two passes using a plunge router outfitted with a straight bit and an edge guide. On the pin boards, you can cut the groove through the ends because it won't show.

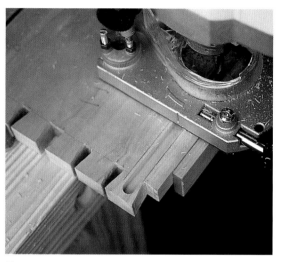

ON THE TAIL BOARDS, YOU need to stop the groove in one of the tails as shown. The dovetail layout shown in the illustration allows you to put the groove solidly into a tail.

I DON'T LIKE TO CLAMP carcase pieces between dogs unless I have to – the clamp pressure can bow the pieces as I'm working them. I prefer a stop on my bench, as shown. After planing the case pieces, I'll hit them with some #220-grit sandpaper to remove any ridges left by the plane if necessary.

I USE SIMPLE CLAMPING BLOCKS to clamp the tail boards firmly against the pin boards. These are easy to make using a hand saw or band saw. Apply a consistent but thin layer of glue to the tails and knock the case together with the bottom in its groove. Clamp up the case using the clamping blocks and let it sit for at least 30 minutes.

and-panel door using my "tailed apprentices" (my power tools). I begin making this classic housed joint by cutting a sample mortise with my mortising machine. Then I cut all the tenons using a dado stack installed in my table saw.

The rule of thumb is that your tenons' thickness should be one-half the thickness of your stock. The doors are ¾" thick, so the tenons are ⅜" thick with ³⁄₁₆" shoulders on the face cheeks.

Now install a dado stack in your table saw. These tenons are 1" long, so I like to put in enough chippers to make a ⅝"-wide cut in one pass. Set the height of the dado stack to ³⁄₁₆" and set the fence so it's 1" away from the left-most tooth of your dado stack. Make several passes over the blade to remove the waste from the face cheeks, then remove the waste from the edge cheeks and test the fit in your sample mortise.

A DADO STACK MAKES QUICK *work of tenons for the door. The table saw's miter gauge guides the rails over the dado blades to cut the face and edge cheeks.*

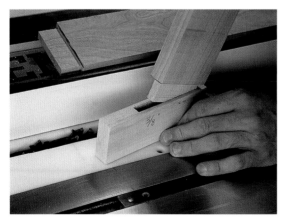

TEST THE FIT OF YOUR *tenon in a test mortise. When you're satisfied with the fit, cut the tenons on all the rails this way, being sure to check the fit after cutting each one.*

Planes at Rest: On Their Soles or On Their Sides?

One of the big debates among plane users is whether to place the tools on their soles or their sides when they are not in use. Traditional carpenters place the tools on their sides to protect the iron from getting dinged. Many woodworkers have picked up this tradition and it's frequently passed on from teacher to student (as it was to me).

But it might not be necessary.

A decade ago I was convinced by a fellow craftsman that it's better to place planes on their soles when you are working at your bench. Here's the rationale. The old carpenter's rule applied to work on the job site, where you could never be certain about where you were setting your plane (this was back when you might actually see planes on a job site). So placing the plane on its side protected the iron from grit and gravel that could cover any flat surface in a newly built home. Also, carpenters say that putting planes on their sides prevents the iron from being pushed back into the plane's body, which is what could happen when a plane is rested on its sole.

Woodworkers, however, work on a wooden bench – far away from mortar dust and gravel. So they say it's best to place an unused plane on its sole to prevent the iron from getting dinged by another tool on the bench. What about the iron getting pushed up into the plane's body? If you think about this statement for a moment, you'll see how ridiculous it is. The plane's iron is secured tightly enough in the plane's body to withstand enormous pressure as the plane is pushed through the work. It should be child's play for the iron to stay in one place with only the weight of the plane pushing it down.

Other woodworkers have come up with other solutions that work, too, including placing the planes soledown over the tool well of their bench. Or they rest the sole on a thin wooden strip that holds the iron slightly above the bench. But I don't mess with that. After unlearning years of training, I now put my planes sole-down on the bench.

Raise the dado stack to $^3/_8$" and remove the remainder of the waste on the edge cheeks. The bigger edge shoulders ensure that you won't blow out the ends of your mortises at glue-up.

Mark the location of your mortises using your tenons as a guide, as shown in the photo at right. Cut the $^3/_8$"-wide x $1^1/_{16}$"-deep mortises in the stiles using a hollow-chisel mortiser.

Next cut the $^3/_8$"-wide x $^1/_2$"-deep groove on the door parts that will hold the panel. I use a rip blade in my table saw. Don't worry about stopping the groove in the stiles; the hole won't show on the front because it will be covered by moulding. On the back you'll almost never see it because that is where the hinges go. If the hole offends you, by all means patch it with a scrap.

Assemble the door and make sure it fits on the case. When all is well, plane or sand the panel for the door and glue up the door – making sure not to put glue in the panel's groove.

With the door complete, mill the moulding that surrounds the door on three edges. Miter, glue and nail it in place. Then install the hardware: the butt hinges, catches, pulls and handles.

USE THE TENONS TO MARK *where the mortises should go on the stiles. I like this method because there is less measuring and therefore less room for error.*

Handplane Cabinet

	NO.	LET.	ITEM	DIMENSIONS (INCHES)			MATERIAL	COMMENTS
				T	W	L		
CARCASE								
❏	2	A	Top, bottom	$^3/_4$	$7^1/_2$	$26^3/_8$	Cherry	Cut $^1/_{16}$" long
❏	2	B	Sides	$^3/_4$	$7^1/_2$	17	Cherry	Cut $^1/_{16}$" long
❏	1	C	Back/bottom	$^1/_2$	16	$25^3/_8$	Plywood	In $^1/_4$"-deep groove
❏	1	D	French cleat for case	$^1/_2$	$2^1/_2$	$24^7/_8$	Maple	45° bevel on one edge
❏	1	E	French cleat for wall	$^1/_2$	$2^1/_2$	$22^7/_8$	Maple	45° bevel on one edge
DIVIDERS								
❏	2	F	Top, bottom	$^1/_2$	$2^1/_2$	$23^7/_8$	Maple	
❏	2	G	Sides	$^1/_2$	$2^1/_2$	$15^1/_2$	Maple	
❏	3	H	Horizontal dividers	$^1/_2$	$2^1/_2$	$23^7/_8$	Maple	
❏	1	J	Horizontal divider	$^1/_2$	$2^1/_2$	$10^3/_8$	Maple	
❏	1	K	Horizontal divider	$^1/_2$	$2^1/_2$	13	Maple	
❏	2	L	Vertical dividers	$^1/_2$	$2^1/_2$	$2^1/_2$	Maple	
❏	1	M	Vertical divider	$^1/_2$	$2^1/_2$	$4^7/_8$	Maple	
DOOR								
❏	2	N	Rails	$^3/_4$	3	$24^3/_8$	Cherry	Cut long to fit cabinet
❏	2	P	Stiles	$^3/_4$	2	17	Cherry	Cut long to fit cabinet
❏	1	Q	Panel	$^3/_8$	12	$23^3/_8$	Poplar	In $^3/_8$" x $^1/_2$" groove
❏			Moulding	$^3/_8$	1	65	Cherry	$^1/_4$" roundover on one edge

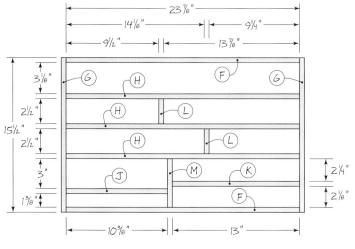

ELEVATION — INTERNAL DIVIDERS

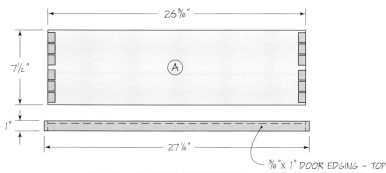

PLAN — DOOR REMOVED

³⁄₈" X 1" DOOR EDGING – TOP AND TWO SIDES ONLY

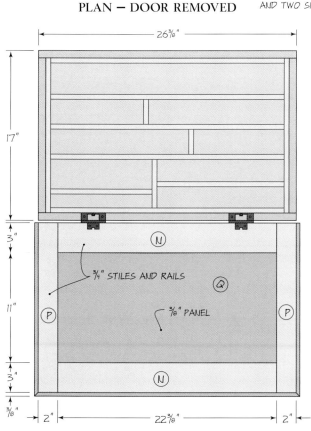

¾" STILES AND RAILS

³⁄₈" PANEL

ELEVATION

Slick Sole for Smoothing

When using a smoothing plane to prepare wood for finishing, you'll get better results if the plane's sole is waxed. The wax lubricates the sole and allows the plane to skim over the work. You'll use less effort and the end result looks better because you're less likely to stall during the cut. I use inexpensive canning wax (just a few dollars for a box) found at any grocery store. Apply the wax in the pattern shown below (keep it off the iron; that will change how the plane cuts). Then start working until you feel the plane becoming harder to move. Just reapply the wax and get back to work.

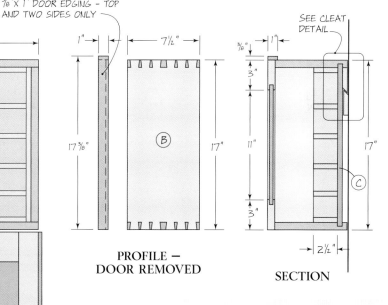

SEE CLEAT DETAIL

PROFILE — DOOR REMOVED

SECTION

SUPPLIES

Lee Valley Tools
leevalley.com, 800-871-8158
2 ■ Forged flush rings, 1¹⁄₂" x 2", #00L02.02
2 ■ Colonial chest handles, #06W02.01
2 ■ 2¹⁄₂" non-mortise hinges, #00H51.13
Local home-supply store
2 ■ Magnetic catches

DIVIDE AND ORGANIZE

Finally it's time to make the dividers for the planes. This is the easy part. I fastened the dividers using screws to make sure I could change the configuration in case my plane collection ever changed. The first step when building the dividers is to screw the four outermost pieces together and plane them down so they fit snugly inside the case.

Then divide up the rest of your space and screw everything in place. Secure the assembled divider in the case with a couple 1"-long screws. As this is shop furniture, I didn't choose a fancy finish. A few coats of clear lacquer is enough protection.

I hung my cabinet on the wall using a French cleat system, shown below. When installing the cleats, be sure to use 3"-long screws to fasten the cleat to the studs in the wall. This cabinet, when full, is quite weighty.

With this project complete and hung on my shop wall, I loaded the tools into their slots and thought for a moment about offering my planes some sake in the Japanese tradition. But then, coming to my senses, I offered myself a cold beer instead.

WHEN CUTTING THE MORTISE, CUT *one hole, skip a space, then cut the next one. Then come back and clean up the area in between. If you cut all your holes in a row, the mortiser's chisel can bend or snap because it wants to follow the path of least resistance.*

THE ³⁄₈" x 1" MOULDING *creates a dust seal around the edge of your cabinet and gives the piece a nice finished look. I cut a ¹⁄₄" roundover on the inside edge of the moulding. Miter the ends, then glue and nail the moulding to the door's edges.*

The Genius of French Cleats

When you hang a cabinet that will be loaded with heavy objects, I recommend a French cleat to fasten it to the wall. These cleats take a little more work than metal cabinet hangers, but they are well worth it because the cabinet will be more secure and it will be easy to put on the wall and remove.

To make a French cleat, take some of the ¹⁄₂" stock left over from building the dividers for the interior of your cabinet. You'll need one piece that's 24⁷⁄₈" long, which you'll attach to the backside of the cabinet. And you'll need a second piece that's a couple inches shorter than the first. Set your table saw to cut a 45° bevel and rip one long edge of each piece at 45°.

Glue and screw the long cleat to the top edge of the backside of the cabinet with the bevel facing in. Now screw the second cleat to the wall where your cabinet will go – with the bevel facing the wall. Be sure to use big screws (I used #12 x 3") and anchor the screws in the studs in your wall.

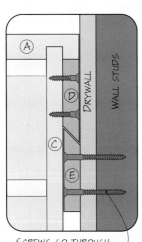

SCREWS GO THROUGH
CLEAT AND INTO STUDS

AS YOU INSTALL THE INTERIOR *dividers, it's a good idea to double-check your initial measurements against the real thing. I had a rude shock when my No. 4 plane was wider than I had anticipated. When everything looks good, screw all the parts together using #8 x 1" screws. Then screw the whole thing into the cabinet. I ran the screws in from the backside of the cabinet.*

SHARPENING

FUNDAMENTALS

TECHNICAL

EQUIPMENT

SCRAPERS

DETAILS

Sharpening
Plane Irons & Chisels

I've tried just about every sharpening system there is —
from sandpaper to ceramics to waterstones. Here's how
to get the best possible edge with the least fuss.

W hen I took my first class in woodworking some years ago, the first thing the instructor showed us was his shop-made waterstone pond.

With a reverence and care usually reserved for religious artifacts and small injured animals, the teacher brought the pond out from its special place in his cabinet. For more than an hour he talked with a furrowed brow about secondary bevels, wire edges and polishing the backs of our edge tools.

All of us in the class did our best to stifle our yawns. I kept looking at the rows of chisels and backsaws and wondered when we were going to get to the important part.

Within a week we all realized that we should have paid more attention to the sharpening lecture. Soon there were only two sharp chisels in the shop for a class of 10 students, and we quarreled over them. Trimming tenons with the equivalent of a butter knife was no fun.

So I made it a point to learn to sharpen well. And I've been fortunate to be able to use a variety of methods, including: oilstones, diamond stones, waterstones, ceramic stones, sandpaper, electric grinders and the Tormek system.

Each system has its good and bad points. Some are simple, others don't make a mess, some are less expensive and most systems can put an astoundingly good edge on tool steel.

For me, the two most important qualities a sharpening system needs are that it must be fast and it must produce the keenest edge. I'll pay a little more and suffer a little mess to get a good edge in a hurry and get back to the bench.

That's because I'm more interested in woodworking than I am in the act of sharpening. I have no desire to look at my edges under a microscope or fret about tiny imperfections in the metal. I'm not the kind of guy who wants to meditate on my "power animal" as I proceed up to #500,000 grit. I want to be done and get back to the good part.

FAMILIARITY BREEDS A KEEN EDGE

The steps I'm about to describe will work with every sharpening and honing system I know of on the market. That's because no matter what system you use, sharpening is about one thing: Grinding and polishing the two intersecting planes of a cutting edge to as fine a point as possible.

The tools you use to get there are up to you. But here are a few words of advice: Pick a sharpening system and stick with it for a good long time before giving it up. Many woodworkers who I've talked to jump around from system to system, trying to find the best thing (and spending a lot of money).

If you stick with one system, your edges will improve gradually as you get better and better at using your particular set of stones or sandpaper. Skipping around from one system to the next will only stunt your sharpening skills.

Second, please buy a honing guide to try. It's a big old lie that these things slow you down. In fact, these simple and inexpensive guides are quick to set up and ensure your edge will be perfect every time you sharpen.

However, don't buy a whole rolling army of honing guides. I use a $14 Eclipse-style guide (the gray-colored side-clamp contraption shown in most of the photos) for sharpening my chisels and most plane irons. I also own a Veritas Mark II honing guide. It excels at sharpening skew chisels and specialty plane irons that won't fit in the Eclipse guide, such as irons for shoulder planes.

Each honing guide holds the blade a little differently, and few of them are ever perfectly square. That's OK because what you're after with a honing guide is repeatability. Use the same guide over and over, and your edges will come out the same.

IF YOU DON'T POLISH THE *backside of your newly acquired chisels and plane irons, your cutting edges will always be jagged and easily dulled. You need to polish just the area up by the cutting edge. This is a process you'll only have to do once.*

POLISH YOUR BACKSIDE

There are three sharpening operations that must be performed on all chisels and plane irons that are new to you. First you must polish the flat backside (sometimes called the "cutting face") of the tool. Next you grind the cutting bevel. Finally you hone and polish a small part of that cutting bevel, which most people call the "secondary bevel."

Keep in mind that these three steps are only for tools that you have newly acquired. Once you do these three things, maintaining an edge is much easier. You'll probably only have to polish the backside once. You'll have to regrind an edge mostly when you hit a nail or your secondary bevel becomes too large. Most sharpening is just honing and polishing the secondary bevel so you can get back to work.

Begin with the backside of the tool. This is the side of the tool that doesn't have a bevel ground into it. It's one-half of your cutting edge so you need to get it right.

Start sharpening by rubbing the backside back and forth across a medium-grit sharpening stone or sandpaper. You don't need to polish the entire back,

WHEN HONING NARROW TOOLS, THIS *is the best way I've found to keep things steady and square. Put one finger on the cutting edge; put the other behind the jig to move it.*

just the area up by the cutting edge. I begin this process with a #1,000-grit waterstone, then do the same operation with the #4,000-grit and then the #8,000-grit stone. The backside should look like a mirror when you're finished.

Grinding the Edge

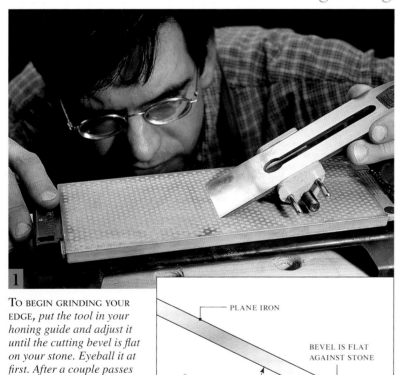

1

TO BEGIN GRINDING YOUR EDGE, *put the tool in your honing guide and adjust it until the cutting bevel is flat on your stone. Eyeball it at first. After a couple passes on the stone you'll know if you're off or not.*

PLANE IRON

BEVEL IS FLAT AGAINST STONE

25° BEVEL TYPICAL

COARSE-GRIT DIAMOND STONE

2

FLAT-GRINDING YOUR CUTTING BEVEL SHOULD *not take long on a coarse diamond stone. If you're having trouble gauging your progress, color the cutting bevel with a permanent marker and you'll get a quick snapshot of where you stand.*

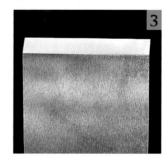

3

WHEN YOU'RE DONE GRINDING, THIS *is what your edge should look like.*

THE NOT-SO-DAILY GRIND

The next step is to grind the cutting bevel of the tool. You can do this on an electric grinder that has a tool rest, which will produce a slightly dished cutting bevel called a hollow-ground edge. Or you can do it on a coarse sharpening stone, which will produce a flat-ground edge.

Lots has been written about the advantages and disadvantages of each system. In comparing my hollow-ground edges vs. flat-ground edges I personally have found little difference between them in terms of edge durability.

I typically grind using a diamond stone for three reasons. First, it will never destroy a tool due to overheating (which can happen with electric grinders). Second, I use the diamond stone to flatten the waterstones. And third, the diamond stone is great for touching up my router bits.

I use DMT's extra-coarse stone for grinding my edges unless I have a lot of metal to remove (800-666-4368 or dmtsharp.com). Put the tool in your honing guide and set it so the cutting bevel is dead flat against the stone. Most tools come ground at a 25° bevel, which is good for most tasks. Mortising chisels should be ground at 30°; tools for light paring only can be set for 20°.

Shapton Stones: The Latest Thing In Sharpening

If you think white-lab-coat wizardry is reserved for the manufacturers of power tools, think again. Some of the highest-tech science-fiction stuff happens in the knuckle-dragging hand-tool industry: think unbreakable "nodular" cast iron, cryogenically treated tool steel and super-strong "rare earth" magnets that are incorporated into both tools and jigs.

And now the latest innovation is in sharpening. Shapton waterstones from Japan are all the rage among the sharpening gurus, who say the stones cut faster and wear longer than other stones. They also are expensive. There are several grades of the Shapton stones, and a basic setup of three stones can cost more than $200 – plus you'll need some way to flatten them.

We use the stones in our shop now and are impressed. They do cut faster and stay true longer than other waterstones.

FOR MORE INFORMATION
shaptonstones.com or
japanesetools.com, 877-692-3624

Why I Switched to Waterstones

There are a lot of sharpening systems out there. And while I haven't tried every one of them, I've tried most. After much experimentation, I settled about 12 years ago on a system that used DMT diamond stones and oilstones. My system worked pretty well, but the oilstone part was slow, and my final cutting edge was always "almost" perfect.

A few years ago, I got my hands on a set of Norton's American-made waterstones and it was like a door had been opened for me. These things cut wicked fast. And the edge they produce is darn-near perfect.

They feel different than many Japanese waterstones I've used. The best way to describe the difference is that the Norton stones give you different "feedback" as you sharpen. The #4,000-grit Norton actually feels like it is cutting (it is). The #4,000-grit Japanese stones I've used have a more rubbery feel to them in use in my opinion. And they didn't seem to cut as fast at that level. The #8,000-grit Norton waterstone also provides great feedback to the user.

The downside to all waterstones is that they need to be flattened regularly. For this job, I use a DMT DuoSharp stone with the coarse grit on one side and the extra-coarse on the other. I also use this same diamond stone for grinding the cutting edge of all my chisels and plane irons.

The most economical way to get started with this system is to buy a Norton combination waterstone that has #1,000 grit on one side and #4,000 grit on the other. Then buy an #8,000-grit Norton waterstone for polishing. Norton also makes a #220-grit waterstone, but if you buy the DMT diamond stone you won't need it.

FOR MORE INFORMATION
nortonabrasives.com, 800-446-1119

NORTON WATERSTONES AND THE **DMT** *DuoSharp stone are a great combination. The DMT handles the grinding jobs and flattens the Norton waterstones.*

Don't get too worked up about angles as you begin sharpening. Somewhere in the 25° neighborhood will be fine for most tools.

I use mineral spirits to lubricate my diamond stone. Most people use water, but a sharpening guru at DMT turned me on to mineral spirits. It evaporates more slowly than water and won't allow rust to build up easily on the stone.

Rub the cutting bevel against the diamond stone then check your progress. You want to grind the entire cutting bevel of the chisel or plane iron all the way across. If you set the tool properly in the jig, this should be approximately five to 10 minutes of work.

As you progress on this coarse stone, you should make a substantial burr on the backside of the tool. This is called a "wire edge," and you'll

Honing the Edge

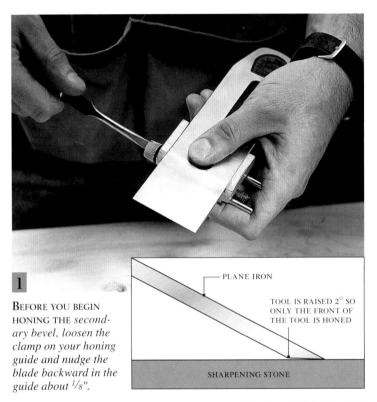

1 BEFORE YOU BEGIN HONING THE *secondary bevel, loosen the clamp on your honing guide and nudge the blade backward in the guide about* ⅛".

PLANE IRON

TOOL IS RAISED 2° SO ONLY THE FRONT OF THE TOOL IS HONED

SHARPENING STONE

2 BEGIN WITH A **#1,000**-GRIT STONE *and rub the tool back and forth across the work. Try to wear the stone evenly by moving the tool in a regular pattern.*

3 AFTER A DOZEN LICKS, TURN *the tool over and remove the burr from the backside by rubbing it a couple times over the #8,000-grit stone.*

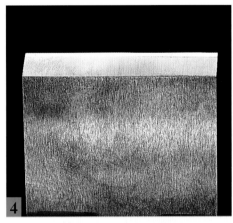

4 AFTER HONING THE TOOL ON *the #1,000-grit stone, this is what the secondary bevel should look like.*

want to remove it by rubbing the backside on your finest-grit stone a couple times. Never rub the backside on your coarse stone. That just undoes all your polishing work there.

How you hold the jig is important, too. For plane irons and wide chisels, put a finger on each corner of the tool up near the cutting bevel and use your thumbs to push the jig. For narrower chisels, put one finger on the tool by the cutting bevel and push the jig from behind with one finger.

With the cutting bevel ground, it's time to refine the leading edge to a keen sharpness.

HONING: THE FUN PART

Honing is quick and painless if your stones are flat and you've done the first two steps correctly.

More Honing & Polishing

CONTINUE HONING THE EDGE BY *switching to a #4,000-grit stone. Remove the burr on the backside with the #8,000-grit stone. Note that some woodworkers skip this intermediate #4,000-grit stage when honing. I have found this trick works best with waterstones and when the secondary bevel is small.*

AFTER WORKING THE #4,000-GRIT STONE, *here's what the secondary bevel should look like. It got a little bigger and it is more polished.*

REPEAT THE SAME PROCESS ON *the #8,000-grit stone. You are almost finished. Tip: You can move the tool back ¹⁄₃₂" in the jig and hone a third bevel, another trick used by some sharpeners. If your entire bevel isn't getting polished after a few strokes, your stone likely needs to be trued.*

POLISH THE SECONDARY BEVEL ON *the #8,000-grit stone until it is a mirror.*

HERE'S HOW TO TEST YOUR *edge without flaying your finger open. Pull your thumbnail across the edge at about a 90° angle. If the edge catches and digs in immediately, you're sharp. If it skids across your thumbnail, you have more work to do.*

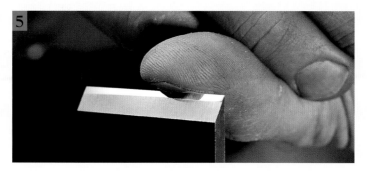

The first thing to do is to reset the tool in your honing guide. Loosen the screw that clamps the tool and slide the tool backward about ⅛". Retighten the screw of the honing guide.

This will set the tool so only a small part of the cutting bevel will get honed. This speeds your sharpening greatly.

Start honing with a #1,000-grit waterstone, soft Arkansas oilstone or #320-grit sandpaper. I use the #1,000-grit Norton waterstone. Lubricate your stones as recommended by the manufacturer. Rub the tool back and forth on the stone. Turn it over and check your progress. You should see a secondary bevel appear up at the cutting edge. Rub your thumb along the backside; you should feel a small burr all the way across the cutting edge. If there's no burr, then you're not sharpening up at the edge; so continue honing until you feel that burr.

Once you have that burr, remove it by rubbing the backside across your #8,000-grit stone. Go back to your #1,000-grit stone and refine the secondary bevel some more until all the scratches on your secondary bevel look consistent. This is the stage where you can introduce a camber to the iron if you are sharpening a bench plane. Add a little additional finger pressure to each corner of the iron to start cambering the iron.

Put the #1,000-grit stone away and get out a #4,000-grit waterstone, a hard black Arkansas oil-stone or #600-grit sandpaper. Go through the same process you did with the #1,000-grit stone. Remove the wire edge on the back with your #8,000-grit stone. The bevel should look a bit polished.

Finally, you want to polish the secondary bevel with your finest-grit stone or #1,500-grit sandpaper. I use an #8,000-grit Norton waterstone. There are Japanese waterstones at this grit level, too. However there are no comparable oilstones. A translucent oilstone is somewhat close.

Polishing is a little different. You're not likely going to feel a wire edge on the backside of the tool after polishing the bevel. Work both the secondary bevel and the backside of the tool on the #8,000-grit stone and watch the scratches disappear. And when they're gone, you're done.

Test the edge using your fingernail – see the photo on the previous page for details. Some people finish up by stropping their edges at this point with a piece of hard leather that has been charged with honing compound. I don't find it necessary. In fact, if you're not careful, you will round over your cutting edge while stropping.

Remove the tool from your honing guide, wipe it down with a little oil to prevent rusting and go to work on some end grain.

The tool should slice through the wood with little effort. And if that doesn't convince you of the value of sharpening, I don't know what will.

Sharpening Jigs for Almost Every Job

There are a lot of honing guides on the market these days. After trying most of them, I'm convinced that two will handle most edge tools.

The gray side-clamp jig you see at woodworking shows is the workhorse in my kit. You can find this tool for about $12 to $14. None of these gray jigs I've inspected grinds a perfectly square edge, but they're close. Be sure to tighten the jig's clamp with a screwdriver when you fix a tool in the guide.

Veritas has two guides. The original guide at right handles many oddball tools, including skew chisels, shoulder-plane blades and irons that are tapered in width. The Veritas Mk. II jig does all this and comes with a special registration guide that allows you to set your honing angle with amazing precision. Plus, you can even hone back-bevels on your tools. It's fantastic for sharpening any tool with a straight cutting edge. For sharpening curved edges, you'll need something else.

THE ORIGINAL VERITAS JIG WILL *help you hone tools that would normally have to be sharpened freehand. It's a good investment.*

FOR MORE INFORMATION
Lee Valley Tools
leevalley.com, 800-871-8158

Sharpen a Fore Plane

Some short work with a grinder makes a smooth, keen curve.

The fore plane is a traditional English tool used to get rough boards fairly flat so that you can then make them really flat with a jointer plane and ready to finish with a smoothing plane, scrapers and (sometimes) sandpaper.

Fore planes are supposed to be about 14" to 18" long. If you want to use an old metal plane as a fore plane, a No. 5 jack plane or No. 6 fore plane would be a good choice. I use a Hock Tools A2-steel replacement blade in my fore plane. The A2 is a little harder to sharpen for me, but this modern steel takes a heck of a beating before it gives up, so it's perfect for a fore plane. I also have a couple wooden-bodied fore planes that are nice because their light weight makes them less tiring to use.

Fore planes are supposed to have a curved cutting edge and are used directly across and diagonal to the grain of your board. Most people understand the idea of working across the grain (it allows you to take a deeper cut without tear-out). But many people are flummoxed by sharpening the curve on the edge. In fact, I've had about a half dozen readers send me their irons and ask me to do it for them.

Because I don't want to open a sharpening service, here is how I grind and hone the curved edge of a fore plane's iron. It's a simple process. And if you take your time the first time you do it, I know that you will succeed.

MARK THE CURVE

This week I noticed that the edge of my metal fore plane was chipped up and the tool was getting quite hard to push. It was time to grind and hone a fresh edge. The first thing to do is mark the shape of the curve on the iron so I can replicate that shape. I use a curve that is an 8" radius. I've experimented with lots of curves between 10" and 6" radii. I like 8".

I have a wooden template that is the same width as my iron and has the curve shaped on one end. I place the template on flat face of the iron and mark the curve with an "extra fine" point Sharpie.

Then I go to my grinder to remove all the nasty chipped-up metal. I keep my grinder's tool rest set to always grind a 25° bevel. I don't futz around with the tool rest. The first thing to do is to grind away the excess metal right up to your marked curve. This is done with the iron at 90° to the stone. I just balance the iron on the tool rest and go to town.

Grinding at 90° to the stone removes metal quickly to the shape you want and it creates a small flat on the end of your iron. This is a good thing. The flat helps prevent your steel from overheating while you grind away the bevel at 25°. Thin steel heats up really quickly.

When you reach the Sharpie line, put the iron flat on your tool rest and grind the bevel until the flat spot on the end is almost – repeat almost – gone. You remove the flat on the sharpening stones.

PLACE THE TEMPLATE ON YOUR *iron and trace its edge on your iron. A thin, consistent line is best.*

Hold the iron 90° to *the wheel and show the edge to the iron. Remove all the steel right up to your Sharpie line. The first time you do this, take your time. It gets easy real quick.*

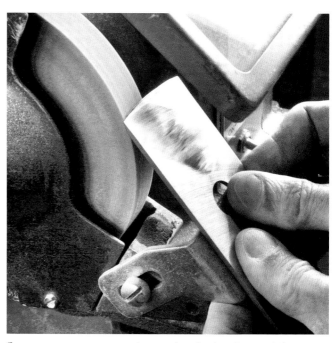

Show the center of the *iron to the wheel and sweep left or right. Here I'm sweeping right to grind to the left corner.*

Here is my completed edge, *ready for honing.*

Here is the flat left *on the tip of that edge. The reflection makes it look bigger than it really is. It's a little less than $\frac{1}{64}''$.*

When sharpening with a honing *guide, the stone should wear in the shape of an X.*

Start by showing the middle of the iron to the grinder wheel. You'll feel when the bevel is flat on the stone. Then sweep the iron right to grind up to the left corner. Try to keep the bevel in full contact with the wheel the entire time. Then repeat this process and sweep left.

Continue to grind and watch the flat shrink. Don't use a lot of pressure when applying the iron to the wheel or you will cook your edge (it will get rainbow colored like an oil slick).

THEN THE HONING

You can then hone the edge freehand. The edge doesn't have to be perfect because the fore plane never produces a finished surface. However, you can use a cheap side-clamp honing guide to help you (and your edge will look a lot sweeter, as well).

Put the iron in your honing guide and set the iron to hone a 30° secondary bevel. Place the iron on your coarse stone (#1,000-grit or coarser if you've got it). Put finger pressure hard on one corner of the iron and press that to the stone. Pull the guide toward you and shift your pressure to the other corner. This will feel awkward at first. But eventually you'll rock it smoothly and naturally.

Repeat this process by starting with all your finger pressure on the other corner. If you are doing this correctly you should see an X-shape appear on your stone. Then it's just like sharpening any tool.

Rock the edge back and forth as you move the jig. This might look hard. It's not. It also tends to shape the wheel of your honing guide into a slight barrel shape – which is a good thing.

Remove the flat on the end of the iron – you'll know it's gone when you can feel a burr on the other face of the iron. Then move up the grits and polish the burr off the flat side.

Now reassemble your chipbreaker and your plane. Sight down the sole of the plane and tweak the lateral-adjustment lever until the curve of the iron is in the center of the sole. This is easy to see.

Then work directly across the grain of a board. Increase the projection of the iron until you are removing material quickly and can easily push the plane. The shavings should be thick – I shoot for $1/32$"-thick with most woods.

The fore plane is really useful, even though I have a nice powered planing machine. It allows me to remove material in a localized area with ease or to peel the edge off a rough board faster than my jointer (because I can work only the high spots). And it allows me to flatten boards and panels that are too wide for my jointer and planer.

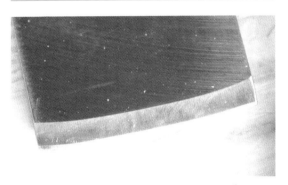

WHEN YOU ARE DONE SHARPENING *you should have a nice even secondary bevel.*

YOU CAN PROBABLY TAKE A *larger shaving in a softwood, but I usually poop out if I try to take a shaving thicker than $1/32$" – but still, that's a lot of material for one stroke of a plane.*

Rotary Lapping Machines

*A surprising advancement in making hand tools
ready to work right out of the box.*

One of the first rules in setting up hand tools (and in medicine, I think) is this: First, do no harm. But this is also one of the first rules to be broken because of ignorance, ham-handedness or just bad luck.

I've taught a fair number of people to sharpen their edge tools during the last 13 years, and I see the same problems among most beginners. They don't know what "sharp" really is. And they don't know how to get to "sharp." And so they do all the activities that resemble sharpening – it's a bit like seeing the monkeys imitate the visitors at the zoo.

They rub both sides of the tool (the bevel and the flat side) on the stones vigorously. They examine their progress (sometimes after hours of work). The result is that most edges from beginners look like they have been sharpened by, well, a monkey.

Of course, I should talk, my first edges looked just as bad. But that's little consolation when I tell that story to a beginning sharpener who has just ruined a perfectly fine steel tool.

The problem is, in part, technique. But the other part of the problem is in the manufacture of modern edge tools. Knowledge of metallurgy and heat-treating has been discarded by some manufacturers. As a result, some new tools can be almost impossible to sharpen.

Now I know I will take some grief for that statement, but I have set up hundreds and hundreds

I HAVE TWO RECURRING NIGHTMARES. *One is where I've forgotten to study for a test (decades after leaving high school!) and the second nightmare involves a whole day of lapping. Sadly, I have lived through this second nightmare in my waking hours as a tool reviewer at* Popular Woodworking.

of new and vintage edge tools as an editor for a woodworking magazine. Not a week goes by that someone doesn't send me something for evaluation that has to be sharpened, set up and used. I have lapped more brand-new chisel backs than I care to remember.

The defect I find in edge tools is related to the problem I see beginners struggle with, and that's in truing up the unbeveled surface of an edge tool, which is sometimes called the face or the back of the tool. (For this article, I'll call the bevel the bevel

HERE'S THE LEE VALLEY "LITTLE *Victor" plane disassembled. Note the shiny face up by the cutting edge. That blinding perfection was achieved with only 13 strokes on my sharpening stones. A new record among planes that I've lapped.*

NOT ONLY DID LEE VALLEY *lap the face of the iron, but employees also lapped the sole of the tool. The result is a little block plane that is made in Canada, costs less than a bottle of whisky and performs like a tool that costs as much as a bottle of single-malt scotch.*

and the unbeveled side the face.) So it's the face that's messed up. The steel is bowed or twisted into such a banana shape that it would take hours (perhaps days) to true up the edge enough to actually sharpen the darn thing.

Of course, I've found other tools that are warped in ways that are actually useful – the warp helps you dress the face. The face is concave, so rubbing it on a stone sharpens it up at the edge immediately. That is a good day.

In fact, I think you can tell when you are working with a set of tools that was shepherded by a manufacturer who knows what they are doing. A few years ago I set up an entire set of plow plane blades for a Record 044. It took about an hour to lap and sharpen the entire set (that's a record for a Record). The reason was that all of the irons were warped so that the face was worked immediately up at the edge. I was in heaven.

A chisel with a hollow behind the edge is a breeze to sharpen (which is one reason the Japanese toolmakers add a hollow to the face of their tools). Trying to sharpen out a belly on an edge tool is a lesson in frustration.

On the other hand, I have sharpened too many tools that have a pronounced belly on the face, a situation that is difficult to remedy at home. There are tricks to fix the tool, of course, but that's not the subject of this article.

"Have patience! In time, even grass becomes milk."

— Charan Singh (1916-1990)
mystic

Instead, I'd like to tell you about the $30 tool that has really changed my outlook on the future of hand tools in woodworking. In 2007, Lee Valley Tools introduced a new little block plane based on Leonard Bailey's "Little Victor" tool. It's a cute thing with the heart of a premium beast. The body is investment-cast steel. The iron is a well heat-treated chunk of oil-hardened high-carbon steel.

The plane showed up in the morning mail and sat on my desk most of the day. Late that afternoon, I decided to set up the tool. Perhaps, I thought, I could get the face of the iron pretty flat and then finish the sharpening the next morning.

So I pulled the maroon plane from its box, removed the iron and put it on my #1,000 waterstone. I rubbed it once along the stone and turned it over to see just how much work lay ahead. It was, to my surprise, done. The #1,000-grit stone

had removed the gray scratches on the face and left behind the beginnings of a polish.

For the next five minutes I showed every editor in our shop the iron. I explained that this was one fell stroke on one stone. Perhaps I had a wild look in my eye because I encountered a fair amount of eye-rolling. So I retreated back to my bench and put the iron on my #4,000-grit stone. After four strokes, I was done there and ready to work on the bevel. Five strokes is a new personal best. Since I'd spent only five minutes or so, I went to the #8,000 grit on the face. After eight strokes, the face was a mirror that I could shave in (not that I will be shaving anytime soon). I sharpened the bevel and went to work.

Within 10 minutes of opening the plane's box I was making gossamer shavings of jatoba and mahogany.

REWIND ONE YEAR

Though I was elated by the iron of the Little Victor (which works quite well, by the way), I could see this moment was coming. In February 2006, my magazine hosted a conference of toolmakers in our offices in Cincinnati. During the event, John Economaki, the founder of Bridge City Tool Works, showed off several of his tools that had an optical polish on the face of the iron. They came from the factory looking like a mirror. It was so sweet a polish that anything that the user did to that face was only going to degrade its appearance.

This was the first time I'd ever heard of the mechanical lapping process. The other manufacturers and individual toolmakers were interested in the process. Many asked John a lot of questions.

"To my knowledge, we were the first company to introduce cryogenic tempering to plane irons in 1999 and in that same year we introduced an optical lapped surface to plane irons," John wrote in an e-mail. "We were also the first woodworking company to mail 1.3 million catalogs featuring the wrong toll-free phone number, but that is another story."

When these irons were first introduced by Bridge City, they were lapped on machines designed for lapping silicon wafers, and both sides were lapped. Today, Bridge City still laps all of its irons, except the ones with a profile, or irons narrower than 1" in width.

Six months after the conference of toolmakers, Wally Wilson at Lee Valley Tools sent me an e-mail asking if I'd like to try some new plane irons developed for the Veritas bevel-up handplanes. There was no other explanation. Of course I said yes.

The irons arrived and they looked a little different than usual. The shape of the iron was different

THERE ARE TWO KINDS OF *tools. The lower chisel will take minutes to set up. Note how the concavity of the blade allows me to lap right up at the cutting edge after about four strokes. The chisel above will require a long time on the diamond stone before I actually can get the face reasonably true at the cutting edge.*

than usual and the unbeveled side of the tool looked really gray, like someone had misted it with some gray spray paint. So I went to set them up in our shop that afternoon and it went remarkably fast.

So I chatted with Robin Lee, the president of Lee Valley Tools, about the new irons and asked how they were nearly dead flat. Robin says the company has purchased two rotary-style lapping machines, which are used to produce remarkably flat metal surfaces across many industries, from semiconductors to optics. And though the machines produce a remarkably flat surface, they are remarkably low-tech.

The principle the machines work on is a bit like a random-orbit sander. The machine has a large circular table that can be several feet in diameter. Resting on top of this table are three large metal rings, which also rotate. The object you want to lap flat is placed into a French-fitted compartment within the rings, and a special weight is placed on top of the tool – it could be a metal weight, a sandbag or a silicone gel. It just has to press in the right place without stressing the tool.

Then an abrasive slurry (silicon carbide in this case) is pumped onto the large circular table. The table rotates. The tools in the rings rotate separately. The metal gets very flat – the Lee Valley Tools catalog quotes a flatness tolerance on the working surfaces of the tool to plus or minus 0.0002" (and no, I didn't add an extra zero to that).

The parts are checked by an employee occasionally, Robin says. The tools are removed from the machine when they are done and taken to the other machine for a second, finer grit. The finer the grit, the higher the polish. The Lee Valley irons are gray because they don't go to the high polish grits like Bridge City.

"It's the equivalent of a rock tumbler," Robin says about the machine. "You load it up and walk away. Fit the parts in the rings and walk away. Come back in an hour, pick off the ones that are done and put the others back in until they're done."

The process isn't labor intensive (employees can work on other tasks while the machine runs), it doesn't require complex fixturing like some CNC machines, and it doesn't stress the metal as it flattens the tools. The downside is that the process is quite messy and it requires the parts get a sonic cleaning afterward.

A MEASURING ERROR OR USER ERROR?

So what inspired Robin to invest the capital of his Canadian catalog and manufacturing company into these two machines? Was it a simple desire to have the flattest surfaces on the market? Not exactly. Robin says the wheels were set in motion years ago with the influx of inexpensive Chinese measuring tools.

After these tools arrived in North America, every woodworker could afford machinist-quality measuring tools, such as dial calipers, micrometers and high tolerance straightedges. And these woodworkers started looking at their tools with these measuring tools and howling about what they found.

"They (the customers) didn't know how to measure or what to measure. But we started hearing that this is out by a thou or two thou – and most people don't even know what a thou is," Robin says. "There isn't a broad understanding about what tolerances are important or where the tolerances are important."

It's a tough situation faced by many woodworking manufacturers. Customers routinely demand

Here you can see Lee *Valley's lapping machine loaded with plane irons. The three rings rotate, as does the giant plate below. An abrasive slurry dresses the irons dead flat.*

These inserts hold the plane *irons inside the rings of the lapping machine. The weights press the work against the abrasive.*

NASA specs on tools designed to cut wood – a material that changes in size every day.

"From a manufacturing perspective." Robin says, "it's sometimes easier to give customers what they want rather than educate them about interpretation of measurement and tolerances. I think that most manufacturers are providing tolerances that a customer cannot improve. They will only degrade out of the box."

So Lee Valley Tools started lapping the face of its high-carbon plane irons. Then the company added the A2 steel plane irons to the list of tools it lapped. Then, early in 2007, Lee Valley took another step with lapping, it lapped the sole (and the iron) of the Little Victor block plane, an investment-cast steel tool. The sole looks unlike any other plane sole I've ever seen. It's a bit of a luminous gray, and you can alter the surface finish by pressing hard with your fingernail. But the thing is flat – flatter than anything my Chinese measuring tools can find fault with.

And Lee Valley is poised to use the technology in other ways, Robin says. The soles of other planes are next, including the sole of a small router plane. Maybe chisels.

And Lee Valley isn't alone in experimenting with this process. Thomas Lie-Nielsen, the owner of Lie-Nielsen Toolworks, says he has been working with a rotary lapping machine in his factory in Maine, and he thinks it will become part of the company's production process. First he has to overcome some technical details, including setting up a clean room to prevent grit contamination.

All three companies – Lie-Nielsen, Lee Valley Tools and Bridge City – serve an audience that is far more demanding than the people Stanley built

tools for before World War II. Collectors and lovers of old user tools frequently crow about how nice their vintage tools are, but those tools were made to rougher tolerances. A Stanley or Record casting with a few pits in it would be sent on down the line to be finished and sold to the customer. Today, customers would first measure the tool, gripe about its tolerances, get it replaced and then stick the thing on a shelf and let it sit, unused.

"Rarely are you judged on use," Robin says. "You are being judged on appearance or measurements. But the business is what it is. So all of this leads to us looking at how we can meet the market expectation. And still not price yourself to the moon."

I judge on use. I use my hand tools just about every day. And after putting many of these tools from the three manufacturers to wood since 1996, I can see that their tolerances have tightened up considerably.

My first Lie-Nielsen planes, a scrub plane and block plane, look much less finished compared to newer versions. The machining is more precise. The wood is more crisply shaped. Same goes for Bridge City. I got to use the company's first block plane and early sets of combination squares. They pale in comparison to the Bridge City Tools I have on my bench right now. And Veritas has come a tremendous distance since it entered the plane market with its No. 4^{1}/2 bench plane and a low-angle block plane. Everything detail is crisper. Every adjustment works more smoothly than its ancestors.

Some of this is the result of experience that's been tucked into the belt of each of the three men behind these companies. But some of it is also the technology and the everyday search for how the newest process can be harnessed to better build some of the oldest types of woodworking tools.

A New Golden Age? A Polished One at the Least

For years, the unbeveled face a plane iron was a whole-day project. Not anymore. Here's why.

I sometimes shudder to think about all of the chisels and plane irons I've set up in the last decade. Every review has involved hours and hours of setup time, most of that flattening the back, unbeveled side of the tools. I've worn out a half-dozen diamond stones, several coarse waterstones and even a fine polishing stone (it was a very thin King stone, by the way).

But a weekend in 2005 marked a new milestone. I brought home three Veritas bevel-up planes to set up for a forthcoming review – the jack and the new smoother and jointer. Normally, this would be five hours of work to flatten the backs, polish the backs and hone the cutting edge. But I was planning on using David Charlesworth's "ruler trick" to slash that time considerably. The trick, in a nutshell, is to position a steel ruler on your polishing stone that elevates the iron. This polishes a small back bevel right at the cutting edge, saving time.

So I got out an old steel ruler. But before I began in earnest, I took a couple swipes with the iron on my #1,000-grit stone. The unbeveled side of the iron was dead flat. Most of the machining marks on that unbeveled side were gone with that little bit of effort. I took a few more swipes for good mea-

sure then went to the #4,000-grit stone, anticipating trouble. No trouble found. Ten swipes and I was done there. Same with the #8,000-grit stone.

I thought I had gotten lucky with the first iron. So I did the other two irons. They were all perfect. I set up all three irons (and the planes, too) in less than an hour. This is a far cry from the effort involved in setting up an iron from Veritas or Lie-Nielsen in earlier days – and don't even get me started on Stanley, Record or other imported tools. (A test of jack planes a few years ago required more than 50 hours of setup time on my part.) Both of these premium plane-making companies have made steady progress on improving their irons, and both are now making tools that are virtually ready to go when you open the box, which is how it should be.

Some fans of vintage tools often chide me as an apologist for the modern plane makers. But you know what? I've served my time (and it was hard time) setting up a lot of messed-up old tools. It taught me a lot about plane mechanics, but it also took me away from my true love, woodworking. If you enjoy the metal filings, the drudgery of hours of lapping soles and the Lazarus-like satisfaction of resurrecting an old tool, I won't stand in your way when we reach for the same tool at the flea market. But if you like the smell of freshly cut wood, luminous planed surfaces and building furniture, there are new tools out there just for you. They work perfectly, precisely and predictably from the get-go. They are worth every cent.

As of that day, my friends, we were officially in a new golden age of hand tools.

'Blessed Are the Grinders'

If a tool is properly made, it should be easy to set up. Anything less is sloppiness.

Some days it's overwhelming to think about all the toolmaking knowledge that's been lost. At the 2005 Mid-West Tool Collectors Association national meeting it was astounding to see all of the quality tools that simply have vanished from the shelves of the hardware stores. And today, while tuning up a plow plane for an issue of *Woodworking Magazine*, I was reminded again of the amazing work that came out of Sheffield at one time.

For a good while I've been a fan of the Record 043 plow plane, a small metal plow that is sweet for drawer-bottom grooves and other small-scale work. So I also picked up a Record 044, its bigger brother. The Record 044 comes with seven irons and mine were neatly packaged in a blue cardboard sleeve.

I've been avoiding setting up all the irons because seven cutters can take a long time to flatten the faces, grind and hone. But today I had a spare couple hours and decided I could tweak one or two of the irons to get things rolling. I started with the widest irons in my set. I don't think were ever used; they looked completely untouched.

I took a deep breath and started flattening the unbeveled face. This part is usually drudgery because there's a lot of metal to be removed. The first iron was bowed a bit from heat-treating, but the bow worked in my favor – pressing the cutting edge against the stone so it polished up immediately. A lucky break.

So I did the next iron. Same exact bow; same luck! The next two were exactly the same. The grinder or heat-treater or both knew what the heck they were doing because they had oriented the tooling so the bow worked for the woodworker. In fact, in the entire set of seven cutters, only the smallest two were messed up. And that was because they had

been used and the face had been dubbed (rounded over) by a lazy sharpener. Within two hours, all seven cutters were polished, ground, honed and ready to use. That's a record (no pun intended).

This reminded me of a chapter from one of my favorite books about toolmaking: "Memories of a Sheffield Tool Maker" by Ashley Iles. Iles made two statements that have stuck with me to this day: "You sank or swam on your hardener; his reputation was always on the line, and he knew it." Iles then recalls a chisel maker who went out of business after one batch came back soft. And later in the chapter, Iles states: "Blessed are the grinders." (He says it's from Ecclesiastes chapter 10, but I can't find it.)

Both statements are so true. Even if your steel is great, it's no good if it's heat-treated, tempered or ground poorly. During a test of new chisels about six years ago I set up almost 100 chisels; probably more than half were warped so that the face was bellied. We've forgotten something.

One last postscript. The Record 044 is an excellent tool. And the nice kicker to the story is I had bought it from Ashley Iles's son, Ray Iles. Ray always has a few of these tools in stock.

WELL-MADE TOOLING IS DESIGNED TO *be set up easily. Steel warps when it is heat-treated. And it can either warp to help you or it makes your life difficult.*

Why Some New Tools Have Poor Edge Life

Is your iron dull after five minutes of use? It might not be your sharpening. It might be the new steel.

Sometimes brand-new chisels and planes (even from the best manufacturers) don't hold an edge well. I've seen some edges crumple like tin foil after two whacks with a mallet or two strokes on a board.

Weak edges aren't as common a problem as weak chin lines, but they do happen. When I teach a class of 18 people, for example, there's always one person with a spanking new tool that would crumble if you chopped a Moon Pie.

My solution to this problem has always been to take the tool to the grinder and create a new primary bevel. Then I grind off just a tad more. I take the tool back to the stones for honing and then (by magic) the tool holds its edge.

The strategy almost always works, but I've never known exactly why.

So I went to tool-steel guru Ron Hock, of Hock Tools (hocktools.com), looking for answers. As always, Ron set me straight. There could be two culprits: too much heat or too much oxygen during the manufacturing process.

"Should the blade be subjected to temperatures in excess of the steel's critical temperature (the temperature at which the iron crystals transform from ferrite to austenite) the steel will tend to form large grains, which don't stick to each other as well as

we'd like," Hock writes. "This will cause the resulting steel to be very brittle and crumbly, though it will test as properly hard with a Rockwell hardness test."

If a tool breaks, you can see evidence of this problem, according to Hock. In a well-treated tool the fracture should look a very fine-grained gray color (almost like gray primer paint).

"If you see sparklyness instead, it's been overheated," Hock writes, "Which is probably why it broke and you're looking at it."

Because the cutting edge of a tool is typically the thinnest part of the tool, it's the easiest part to overheat, even if the overheating is brief.

The other culprit is oxygen. As steel approaches its critical temperature, the carbon is released and is free to migrate about the steel. If there is air present when it reaches the surface (such as when heat-treating in air with a torch or forge) the carbon atom will run off with the oxygen atom to become carbon monoxide or carbon dioxide and the carbon is lost from the steel, according to Hock.

Most professional heat treaters use furnaces with atmosphere control (vacuum or inert or carbonaceous gas) to minimize this problem, which is called "decarburization."

"This creates a low-carbon skin on the steel," Hock writes. "This would not be a big deal except for the fact that the flat back of the tool is the cutting edge, and any loss of carbon results in a loss of hardness. Here again, the edge takes it in the shorts with the most to lose and the least to lose it from."

Both of these problems can completely ruin a piece of steel through-and-through. But usually the damage is localized, and you can get to the good stuff by grinding away some of the bad stuff.

Just tell your spouse you're exfoliating.

Why You Should Freeze Your Tools

*Cooling your tooling to -320° F can double or triple
the time between sharpenings.*

About 150 years ago, Swiss watchmakers noticed that extreme cold changed the properties of their metal clock parts for the better. So after manufacturing their gears or what have you, some watchmakers would then store the parts in caves during the cold Swiss winters and let them freeze.

Unwittingly, they had given birth to what is now commonly known as cryogenics.

During the last century, toolmakers and metal heat treaters have explored what extremely cold temperatures do to tooling, metals and other materials. And they have come to some remarkable conclusions. For certain types of metals, cooling them to -320° Fahrenheit can make them at least twice as resistant to wear as untreated metal.

The wear resistance is permanent. You have to treat your tooling only once, and it will remain that durable forever, experts say. And the price of cryogenically treating your tooling is becoming quite reasonable. We found that treating about four pounds of metal will cost you about $30 to $50. (If you treat a lot of items, the cost can be as little as $1 a pound – and prices continue to drop). Cryo labs themselves are also becoming more common because commercial heat treaters are investing in the technology so they can offer the service to their customers. If you live in an industrial area, you'll probably be able to find a cryo lab locally. But even if you live in the sticks, there are cryo labs you can ship your tooling to for treatment.

So what's the catch? If cryo is so amazing why doesn't anyone sell cryogenically treated planer knives or router bits? Many of the manufacturers we talked to, including Freud, had experimented with the process in its early days and found it had little or no effect.

That's not surprising, says Bill Bryson, author of the book "Cryogenics" (Hanser Gardner Publications) and the president of the company Advisor in Metals in Milton, N.H.

"Back in the 1970s it was a free-for-all, and it hurt the industry," Bryson says. "People were dumping tools in liquid nitrogen and they were cracking, or they weren't tempering the tools after the (cryogenic) process."

As a result, cryogenics got a bad rap in the steel and tooling industry, Bryson says. Not only for the early mistakes that were made but because some people thought that cryogenics would hurt sales. If tooling lasted twice as long, they might sell only half as many tools.

But during the last 30 years, heat treaters and cryogenic advocates began figuring out more about how, why and when cryogenics works. And today, most people in the industry acknowledge that it works well for certain types of metals, Bryson says, particularly the more complex alloys (more on that later).

In the home woodworking market, we've seen only a few cryogenically treated tools on the market. A few years ago, Vermont American announced it would sell "Ice Bits," cryogenically hardened screwdriver bits. Hock Tools, Bridge City Tool Works and Lie-Nielsen Toolworks now offer a line of cryogenically treated A2 plane blades. The cryo blades cost a little bit more than the same-size high-carbon steel blades.

But cryogenic treatment can help woodworkers with a lot more than plane blades or screwdriver bits, Bryson says. Just ask James Larry Poole of P&K Custom Cabinets in Lula, Ga.

A couple years ago Poole sent out his carbide-tipped sawblades, router bits and shaper cutters to a lab for treatment.

MANY CARBIDE TOOLS ARE GOOD *candidates for cryogenic treatment. Before you treat your carbide-tipped saw blade or router bits, check with the manufacturer to see if the carbide is new or recycled – some companies use carbide recovered from old tools. For some reason, recycled carbide doesn't improve after cryogenic treatment.*

"It really makes them last longer," he says. "I had one sawblade in particular that just would not wear out."

Poole used to be involved in car racing, and he had heard about the benefits of cryogenically treating some car parts, including crankshafts and pistons. So when a friend of his from the racing business started a cryo lab, Poole decided to see if it would help his tools.

"You really can tell the difference," he says. "I get twice the life at least … so it's worth the money."

But before you start gathering all the cutting tools in your shop to take to a lab, there are some things you need to know.

IN A NUTSHELL: WHAT CRYO DOES

There's a little science here, but it's easy to digest. When tooling is made, the manufacturer heats it to make it hold an edge. During heat treatment, the structure of the steel changes. As it is heated, the steel has a structure that is called "austenite," which is softer and has a coarse, irregular grain. When the blade is quenched (reduced quickly in temperature), the austenite changes into "martensite," which has a finer grain and is more resistant to wear.

The problem is that the transformation from austenite to martensite is never 100 percent. If a tool is carefully heat treated, it might end up with 90 percent martensite and 10 percent austenite. Commercial heat treating typically results in 75 percent martensite, Bryson says. In low-quality tooling, it can be as low as 50 percent martensite.

By carefully cooling the tooling to -320° then thoroughly retempering the metal, nearly all of the austenite is transformed into martensite. Bryson says it's proven to be a 99.9-percent transformation or more.

All tooling will benefit from cryogenics, Bryson says. But if the steel is an alloy containing cobalt or tungsten, the cryogenic process will create very fine micro-carbides, which add even more durability to the edge.

The alloy A2 steel, which is now found on some handplane blades, contains carbon and chrome, so it reacts well to cryogenic treatment. High speed steel (HSS) contains molybdenum (which makes the tool resistant to heat), chromium and sometimes tungsten, which makes it ideal for cryo treatment. You'll find HSS in your planer knives, your jointer knives and in other cutting tools. As a rule with metals, the higher the alloy content, the better the cryogenics will work.

But what about carbide tools? Will saw blades and router bits benefit from cryogenic freezing? According to Bryson, that depends.

If the carbide is newly manufactured and not recycled from old carbide tooling, cryogenic treatment works, Bryson says. Carbide that has been reclaimed or recycled is not improved.

"And we don't know why," he says.

In new carbide, cryogenic treatment strengthens the binder between the individual carbides, he says. Cryogenically treated bits should last twice as long between sharpenings, Bryson says, though some people report even longer times between sharpenings.

BEWARE OF THE THIN FILM

Perhaps one of the strangest aspects of cryogenic treatment is something that experts have yet to fully explain.

It seems that after a tool has been frozen then retempered, some report you won't get the added wear-resistance until the tool is resharpened.

Bryson says there's a layer of metal that's between .00007" and .0001" thick on the outside that remains untreated by the cryogenic bath. After you remove this layer by sharpening, the tool works great. Bryson calls this the "Thin Film Phenomenon," and he says it's one of the reasons some people thought cryogenics was a crock in the early days. People would treat their sharp new tools, put them to use and see almost no difference in the tool's life. But if you sharpen the tools after treatment, Bryson says, that's when you see the the full benefits of cryogenic treatment.

Cryo: It's Not Just for Tools Anymore

Sure, cryogenics can make your tools last longer, but it also has a lot of other benefits, some practical and some wild. Here's a short list of claims we've gathered from books, magazine articles and the Internet:

■ **PANTIHOSE.** Nylon stockings that have been cryogenically treated are less likely to develop runs.

■ **GOLFING.** Cryogenically treated golf clubs hit balls 3 percent to 5 percent farther. Cryogenically treated balls can be hit farther.

■ **RACING.** Hickson Engines has treated small-block Chevy engines and found significantly less cylinder wear during a racing season. Many other racing professionals have also used cryo.

■ **FIREARMS.** Treated rifles are more accurate.

■ **MUSICAL INSTRUMENTS.** Cryogenically treated brass instruments have a better tonal quality and the valves slide more easily.

■ **GUITAR STRINGS.** It doesn't even have to be the entire instrument. Some people treat guitar strings and say it improves their tone.

■ **SPORTS.** Baseball bats that have been frozen hit balls 2 percent to 4 percent farther.

TOOLS THAT ARE DIFFICULT OR *expensive to resharpen, such as this Forstner bit, are prime candidates for cryogenic treatment.*

HOW TO SHOP FOR CRYO

There are several ways to cryogenically treat tools, and experts say some are better than others.

WARMER CRYO

Some labs use dry ice to cool the tools. Dry ice will take the temperature down to -109° F. This process works, but you won't get a full transformation of austenite to martensite.

QUICK DIP

Some labs dip the tools into liquid nitrogen (-320° F), leave it there for a short period of time, remove the tools and let them return to room temperature. This process can cause the tools to shatter from thermal shock. It also can transform only the outer layer and leave the core untreated. Many of the experts we talked to do not recommend this procedure.

LONG BATH

Other cryo labs use gaseous nitrogen to reduce the temperature slowly; they keep it there for 20 hours or more (using either gas or liquid nitrogen), then slowly return the tools to room temperature. Bryson says he's tried a variety of methods, and the equipment he prefers (and sells to other cryo labs) takes the temperature down using gas then soaks the tools in liquid nitrogen. Either process works, however.

One of the keys to getting the best results is to choose a lab that has some knowledge of heat-treating and metallurgy and is willing to soak the tools for a long time, says Randall Barron, pro-

fessor emeritus at Louisiana Tech University's Department of Mechanical Engineering. Barron's pioneering research in the 1970s, 1980s and 1990s helped convince many industries to use the process in manufacturing.

Barron's studies showed that bringing the temperature down to -320° F created a more durable tool. Plus, his research showed that soaking the tools for hours was what led to the creation of the micro-carbides, which lend additional wear resistance.

No matter which process is used, after the tools return to room temperature, the tools need to be retempered because the new martensite is fragile and can shatter, experts say. This retempering process is almost always included in the price for the cryo treatment.

Bryson recommends that the tools be tempered at 300° to 350° F for two hours for every inch of thickness of the tool. He also says you should make sure that the items are not stacked on top of one another during tempering.

HOW WELL DOES IT WORK?

This, of course, is the big question. Some of the claims seem outright outrageous. A dowel maker claimed his A2 knives lasted 800 percent longer. A titanium aircraft bit that once lasted for 15 holes was replaced by a common bit that had been cryogenically treated that would last for 200 holes.

Most cryogenic labs will tell you it's reasonable to expect your tooling to last two or three times longer between sharpenings. Considering how inexpensive cryogenic treatment can be, you'll make your money back after one sharpening.

Several years ago, we sent a batch of tooling from our shop here at *Popular Woodworking* to a cryo lab for treatment — everything from a chisel to 12" jointer knives. We tried to compare the durability of these tools with the identical untreated tooling we recently installed in our machinery.

Truth is, it was hard to tell with the sawblade and router bit. It seemed to make a difference with the chisel. However even if cryogenic processing works like crazy, don't be surprised if you don't ever see cryogenic planer blades for sale in woodworking catalogs.

Professor Barron says that one of the studies he did in the early days was for a manufacturer of razor blades. The company wanted to see if the cryogenic process could improve the dies they used in making the blades.

"I asked if they wanted to treat the razor blades to make them last longer," he says with a chuckle. "They said no, because then they might not make as much money."

Understand Honing Guides

*Honing guides are not a one-size-fits-all affair. We examine
the weaknesses and strengths of four popular models.*

With the exception of your two hands, there is no such thing as the perfect honing guide for every shape and size of woodworking tool.

Some guides are great for short tools. Some are great for chisels. Others excel at gripping odd-shaped tools. But none of the guides handle all the tools all the time.

During the last decade, I've taught a lot of people to sharpen chisels and plane irons, so I've gotten to use many of the students' honing guides. Some of these guides I've purchased for our shop at *Popular Woodworking*. Other guides haven't impressed me much.

The honing guides in this article are four models that I've found to be useful and commonly available. Now, I don't think you need to buy four honing guides to get your tools sharp. Depending on your work, you might need one or maybe two.

Or, perhaps if your hands are willing, you might not need any of these guides at all.

THE CASE FOR GUIDES

More often than not, I use a honing guide when sharpening. Though I can (and do) sharpen without them, I find them to be brilliant at providing repeatable and quick results. And when I teach sharpening, I like to show students how to use a guide. Many woodworkers sharpen infrequently and have difficulty training their hands to do what they want every single time.

I'm not hostile to hand-sharpening. If you like the process and your results, please don't change. But I also bristle when hand-sharpeners run down people who use guides. The act of sharpening already causes enough anxiety among woodworkers.

ABOUT THE DULL TOOLS

Hand tools come in a wide variety of sizes and shapes, so I selected a broad range of shapes that have been both easy and difficult for me to secure in honing guides.

Some of the tools are common and are (usually) easy to secure in guides, such as 2"- and 2¼"-wide plane irons, a ½"-wide bevel-edge chisel and a 1"-wide Japanese chisel.

Other tools are tricky because of their shapes, such as a short spokeshave iron, a T-shaped shoulder-plane iron, a fishtail-shaped bench chisel and a skew chisel.

And I threw in one tool, a traditional English mortising chisel by Ray Iles, that gives almost all the honing guides a fit.

HERE ARE SOME OF THE tools I sharpened (or attempted to sharpen) with the four honing guides. From the left: plane irons for a block plane, spokeshave, bevel-up smoothing plane, bevel-down smoothing plane and shoulder plane. The chisels include: a dovetail, fishtail, Japanese, bevel-edge, skew and mortising tool.

ABOUT THE GUIDES

Honing guides have, in general, two ways of going about their job of holding the work. Some guides clamp a tool on its sides; the others clamp a tool from above and below.

Neither system is superior in all cases. The side-clamping guides excel at grabbing most common woodworking tools and holding them square, no matter how aggressively you work. But these jigs fail when trying to hold tools with an unusual shape or size.

The top-and-bottom clamping guides are best at holding the weird stuff that's thick, tapered or odd-shaped. These jigs aren't as good at holding the tool square as you work. The work can shift out of square, especially if you are removing a lot of metal or correcting an edge that isn't square – your finger pressure will force the tool to shift in the guide.

Let's take a look at each of the four guides and their weaknesses and strengths.

THE SIDE-CLAMP GUIDE

When I started sharpening woodworking tools, the first guide I bought (and the one I still use the most) is the common-as-dirt side-clamp honing guide. This is sometimes called the Eclipse guide after the name of a popular English brand. The guide is rugged, common and inexpensive (less than $20).

It grabs wide tools (up to 3¼" wide) using the two lips at the top of the guide, and it is designed to clamp bevel-edge chisels (up to 2" wide) in the dovetailed channels below.

This guide is great if you don't have a lot of unusual tools. It's my first choice for clamping my

HONING GUIDES CAN CLAMP THE *work from the sides of the tool (above) or from above and below (below). Neither tool-holding system is perfect.*

THE SIDE-CLAMP GUIDES HOLD WIDE *tools with the lips on top of the guide. It holds the bevel-edge chisels (and some other tools) using the dovetail-shaped channel below.*

2"-wide smoothing plane irons, block plane irons and (as long as they aren't too narrow) most chisels.

The guide's narrow, ½"-wide roller gives you lots of control over the shape of your cutting edge. If you apply uniform pressure on the tool's bevel, your cutting edges will be straight. If you want a slightly curved cutting edge, you can shift your finger pressure exactly where you want to remove metal, and you'll end up with a cambered cutting edge for a smoothing plane or other bench plane.

Where this jig fails is with tools that have sides that are some other shape than a straight line. A fishtail-shaped chisel is a nightmare with this jig, as are skew chisels.

The tool also doesn't like thick chisels without bevels on the sides – such as mortising or firmer chisels. The chisels' thick flanks won't nest in the guide's dovetailed ways.

It also doesn't like narrow block plane blades. Once a tool is skinnier than 1⅜", then you can't (easily) grip it with the lips on the top of the guide. And good luck getting much of anything unusual into the dovetailed-shaped channel below. The guide doesn't like tools thicker than 3/16" down there.

You can fiddle with the jig to get it to hold most spokeshave blades, some shoulder plane irons and some scraper plane irons (which have to be honed at a high angle).

What else do you need to know about this guide?

THE KELL JIG IS GREAT *for short tools that need straight edges, such as plow plane irons or this dovetail chisel. It's a versatile jig because you can also clamp things below the jig's guide bars, as shown.*

These jigs can be poorly made. I've seen more than 100 of these in my career, and I'm amazed at how some are perfect and others are covered in globs of paint. Use a triangular-shaped file to remove excess paint in the guide's dovetail channel. And keep the jig's wheel oiled. It's easy for the wheel to get clogged and stop turning. When that happens, you end up sharpening a flat spot on your wheel and the jig is worthless.

And finally, I recommend you always secure your work in this guide using a screwdriver. Hand pressure alone isn't enough to prevent your tools from slipping.

RICHARD KELL'S NO. 1 HONING GUIDE

Recently I've become enamored with this side-clamping jig because it handles some difficult tools with great aplomb. Plus, it's a beautifully made tool and rolls smoothly in use on its Ertalite TX low-friction wheels.

Richard Kell makes two versions of this guide. The No. 1, which handles tools up to 1¼" wide, and the No. 2, which handles tools up to 2⅝". The large guide isn't ideal for shops that sharpen on 3"-wide sharpening stones. That's because when you clamp a wide plane iron into the large guide, the wheels are pushed out so far that it's difficult (or impossible) to keep the jig and iron on your stone. You could build a sort of platform around your stone (or you could sharpen with sandpaper stuck to glass), but building a platform is more work than is reasonable in my opinion.

The smaller Kell guide, however, is ideal for narrow and unusual tools, and it is the only tool that easily holds the Ray Iles mortising chisel. The secret to the jig is, I think, the plastic washers that do the actual clamping. These clear plastic washers are tough but grippy, so they can hold a tool that has a slight irregular shape, such as a handmade Japanese chisel.

The other brilliant part of the Kell jig is that you can clamp your work either above or below its stainless steel guide bars. That makes gripping unusual

shoulder-plane irons and dovetail chisels an easy proposition.

So where are the warts? The small Kell won't clamp fishtail-shaped chisels or sharpen skew chisels. The small Kell guide also won't hold a standard spokeshave, smoothing plane or block plane blade.

Also, it will not allow you to create a blade with a curved cutting edge. The jig forces your edges to be straight, like it or not. The upside to this is that if your only hand tools are chisels (or you have mortising chisels that give you sharpening fits), the Kell is an excellent choice.

One final note: I'm also quite fond of the way you secure tools in the Kell. Unlike the other side-clamping honing guide, you don't need a screwdriver to torque the Kell down. Here, finger pressure is enough.

VERITAS MK. II HONING GUIDE

The second honing guide I bought was actually Veritas's ancestor to this jig. I bought that older jig – which also clamped tools from above and below – to handle my odd-shaped tools. That jig served me well, but tools would shift around more than I liked.

This improved version of that older guide is more complex, but the changes added accuracy, versatility and clamping power.

The Veritas is the only jig that allows you to set the sharpening angle with an included blade-registration jig.

You select the angle you want to sharpen at, then set that angle on the included blade-registration jig. Clip the jig to the front of your guide then insert your tool between the jig's two clamping

THE VERITAS MK. II HONING *guide sets your sharpening angle with an included blade-registration jig. The clamping bars allow you to grip a variety of shapes.*

bars (up to $2\frac{7}{8}$" wide). The blade-registration guide sets the sharpening angle and holds the tool square while you clamp it in place using two thumbscrews. Then you remove the blade-registration jig and start sharpening.

It's remarkable what tools the Veritas will hold. With the exception of the Ray Iles mortising chisel, the Veritas grabbed every tool securely without complaint.

And it's amazing the wide range of sharpening angles the jig can be used to achieve. Because it is so adjustable, you can use it to sharpen weird angles (such as 20° back bevels on handplane irons) that advanced sharpeners sometimes require.

What are the downsides to the jig? They are minor. The base model from the factory will sharpen your tools straight across only. Making a curved edge with this jig is nigh on impossible without modifying the jig – thanks to the $2\frac{1}{8}$"-long straight roller. Veritas makes a Camber Roller Assembly that replaces your straight roller with one that has a slight cigar shape. That allows you to camber your cutting edges with finger pressure – just like the side-clamp honing guide.

Veritas also makes a Skew Registration Jig that allows you to set all sorts of oddly skewed tools in the honing guide.

Like all honing guides that clamp from above and below, there is always the slight chance that your tool will shift in the guide, especially if the tool is narrow, if you are working aggressively or if you are fixing an out-of-square cutting edge. And this is something to be careful of with the Veritas.

One way to help prevent this is to take care when securing your tools. The two thumbscrews that control the jig's clamping bar should be advanced so each one is applying the same amount of pressure. If one of the thumbscrews is doing most of the work, the tool is more likely to shift.

The other thing to watch for on this jig is the position of its roller. The jig allows you to tweak the roller down a couple degrees so you can create a secondary bevel on your tools. You need to remember to return this roller to its highest position when you are done sharpening, or you will introduce some minor errors to your tools that can add some sharpening time later on to fix. It's a minor point, but it is something to which to pay attention.

THE SHARPSKATE

The newest honing guide is the SharpSkate, which was developed by sharpening guru Harrelson Stanley of JapaneseTools.com. Like the Veritas, the SharpSkate clamps blades from above and below. But other than that, the SharpSkate is different than all the other honing guides in this article.

Every other honing guide that I've used pushes the tool's cutting edge forward and back on the

Holding Power of Four Honing Guides

TOOL	VERITAS	SHARPSKATE	SIDE-CLAMP	NO. 1 KELL
CHISELS				
1" Japanese	Excellent	Excellent	Excellent	Excellent
$\frac{11}{16}$" fishtail	OK	OK [1]	Poor	Poor
$\frac{1}{4}$" dovetail	Excellent	Excellent	Excellent	Excellent
$\frac{1}{2}$" bevel edge	Excellent	Excellent	Excellent	Excellent
$\frac{1}{4}$" mortising	Poor [2]	OK [2]	Poor	Excellent
$\frac{3}{8}$" skew chisel	Excellent	Excellent	No	No
PLANE IRONS				
$2\frac{1}{4}$" bevel-up	Excellent	OK [3]	Excellent	No
2" bevel-down	Excellent	Excellent	Excellent	No
$1\frac{1}{4}$" block plane	Excellent	Excellent	Poor [4]	Excellent
$\frac{3}{4}$" shoulder plane	Excellent	OK [1]	OK	Excellent
$2\frac{1}{8}$" spokeshave	Excellent	Excellent	OK	No

NOTES:

[1] Fit in guide with some fiddling.

[2] Chisel repeatedly shifted out of square on tool's rounded surface.

[3] A steep position of tool in jig left little room for finger pressure for cambering edge.

[4] Iron had to be sharpened in chisel notch, which had a poor fit.

stone, like a snowplow. The SharpSkate works the edge side to side, more like a rollerblade. The jig rolls on nine ⅜"-diameter steel wheels.

The SharpSkate's blade-clamping mechanism is also unusual. It's a serrated V-shaped clamping pad. The serrations grab your tools (up to 2⁷⁄₁₆" wide) and squares them in the jig. The V-shape of the pad allows you to flex the pad slightly to generate serious clamping pressure.

This pad also can be rotated to grip skew tools of any angle and has three detents (left and right) for common skew angles.

The SharpSkate is the only honing guide that could grip all the tools in the test well enough to hone them reliably and repeatedly, though its hold on the fishtail chisel and mortising chisel weren't ideal.

The advantage of sharpening side-to-side (as opposed to forward-and-back) is that you can easily sharpen on all points of your stone to spread out the wear and reduce your stone-flattening chores. It takes a little practice, but you'll be an expert in less than an hour.

There are some quirks to the jig you should be aware of. I recommend you use a hex-head wrench to secure and release your blades. Hand pressure is not always enough to prevent the tool from shifting.

Also, you need to watch where you put your finger pressure with the SharpSkate. One of the advantages of this jig is that you can use finger pressure to create a cambered cutting edge. But that finger pressure can work against you when you don't want to create a cambered or skewed shape to your cutting edge.

Speaking of cambers, one of the great advantages to the jig is you can hold small blades at a variety of angles. The downside comes when sharpening at really steep angles for smoothing planes in bevel-up tools. As you get into the really high angles (more than 40°), it's difficult to get your fingers where they need to be to create the camber with pressure.

Also, just as with the Veritas, you need to take care that the tool doesn't shift slightly out of square when working. Though the serrations on its clamping pad work well, you can still move the tool a bit when working aggressively or correcting an edge.

One final note: Be sure to keep the nine wheels clean. There's some potential for sharpening grit to accumulate near the wheels. A quick spray of water keeps everything tidy. Also, there is a new version of this guide available that we haven't yet tested.

CONCLUSIONS

The jig or jigs you choose should match your set of tools today and what you might buy tomorrow. If

THE SHARPSKATE HONES YOUR TOOLS *side to side, which allows you to work all the corners of your stones, even to work off the stone if you like.*

you're a chisel-and-block-plane woodworker (and always will be), the side-clamping honing guide might be all you need.

The Kell is ideal for people with small-scale tools with straight edges, or it is an excellent second guide.

The Veritas is an excellent guide for beginning and advanced sharpeners because it allows you to hold a wide variety of tools and accurately set them at the right angle every time you pick up the jig.

The SharpSkate is also a good guide for people with tools of varied shapes. It might be the best guide for woodworkers who want to graduate to hand sharpening some day. The inventor rightly points out that his guide is a good set of training wheels for some kinds of hand sharpening.

For my work, I like having two guides. One that clamps tools on the sides so I can get a straight edge when I need it. And a second guide that clamps above and below so I can sharpen odd-shaped tools that I own now (and those I might own in the future). Exactly which guide or guides you purchase is up to your tools and your pocketbook.

FOR MORE INFORMATION
Woodcraft
woodcraft.com, 800-225-1153
Tools for Working Wood
toolsforworkingwood.com, 800-426-4613
Lee Valley Tools
leevalley.com, 800-871-8158
JapaneseTools.com
877-692-3624

Camber With A Honing Guide

Make curved cutting edges using finger pressure.

A curved cutting edge is critical to most operations with your bench planes. The curve prevents the corners of the iron from digging into your work, and it allows you to correct the flatness of the face or edge of a board.

But how do you create this curve, sometimes called a "camber" with a honing guide? There are lots of valid ways to create the curve. Here's how I do it.

I start with a #1,000-grit waterstone. This stone cuts quickly enough to shape an edge or remove small nicks. Clamp your cutter in your honing guide and then (mentally) divide its edge into five "positions" (see the photo above).

The trick to creating a curve is to put finger pressure at each position. At position "1," put your fingers firmly against the corner and sharpen the corner for 10 strokes.

Then move your fingers to the other corner (position "2") and go for another 10 strokes. Then, at positions "3" and "4," go for seven strokes. Then do a few strokes in the center at position "5." Now check your work with a square.

You need to learn what the curve should look like for each of your planes. Here are the basic principles: If the iron is bedded at a high angle greater than 45°, you need less curve. If the iron is bedded at a lower angle such as 12° or 20°, you need more curvature to get the same effect.

And what is the desired effect? You want to take the widest shaving possible without the corners of the cutter digging in. There is math here. Having a .005" arc-to-chord curve at 45° results in a curve of .0035" being exposed out of the mouth. (If you have a bevel-up plane bedded at 12°, the same .005" arc-to-chord curve will result in .001" curve being exposed in the mouth – thanks to woodworker Rob Porcaro for the formulas.)

The truth is you need to learn what the right curve looks like when you show the cutting edge to a straightedge. If there is too much curve, sharpen some more in the middle (position 5) to flatten the curve. If the curve is too flat, add more finger pressure or strokes at the corners.

When you have a satisfactory curve, advance to the polishing grits (#4,000 and then #8,000) and repeat the same regimen. The polishing grits will remove less metal, but you definitely can increase or decrease the curvature while polishing.

It takes a little practice to find the right curvature for your plane, but the rewards are enormous: Shimmering surfaces with a sensuous, scalloped and touchable texture. It's worth the effort.

Put finger pressure at each *station and count your strokes. Be sure to watch the sharpening stone – it will tell you where metal is being removed.*

The Speed Demons of Sharpening

We test three new machines that attempt
to replace grinders and traditional sharpening stones.

For hundreds of years, the best way to get the keenest edge on a woodworking tool was to rub it on a series of progressively finer abrasive stones. This hand skill is one of the last holdouts of woodworking from before the Industrial Revolution, which drove craftsmen to use their moulding planes as firewood when they traded up to electric routers and shapers.

Sharpening by hand has held on because traditional motorized grinders are – in general – too coarse and aggressive to get a truly keen edge for fine woodworking. And water-cooled grinders, such as the Tormek and Makita models, are slow and don't offer the full range of grits that waterstones, diamond stones, sandpaper or oilstones do.

So sharpening is generally a two-step process. Once you shape the tool's edge on a motorized grinder, you finish up by honing the tool on sharpening stones. As a result, proper sharpening is an expensive and time-consuming process.

But in the last few years, manufacturers have introduced machines that try to make sharpening simpler and faster. These machines both grind and hone the tool's edge using progressively finer grits of sandpaper. The coarse sandpaper shapes the tool's edge much like a grinder, while the fine grits polish it to a mirror, similar to a set of sharpening stones.

For several months, I sharpened dozens of tools on three machines and was impressed with their speed and accuracy. But each machine is radically different in the way it approaches its task. And each has strengths and weaknesses. If you're considering one of these machines, here's what you should know about the Australian Multitool, the Veritas Mk. II and Jooltool's Warrior.

JET GRINDER & MULTITOOL JIG

To create its sandpaper grinder, Jet combined a traditional Chinese-made grinder with a rugged Australian-made jig that spins a 2"-wide x 36"-long sandpaper belt. The jig part of this machine, called the Multitool, has been for sale for years as an aftermarket accessory in Australia and is now imported here by Multitool USA (ausmultitool.com or 800-660-0880). In Australia, the Multitool jig is popular with hobbyists and professionals who use it for a variety of woodworking and metalworking tasks. Jet has discontinued this model recently, but you can still buy the Multitool attachment for any grinder (Van Sant Enterprises, vansantent.com).

In fact, sharpening is one of this machine's side duties. It comes with a traditional 6" or 8" grinding wheel on one end of its arbor. On the other end is the Multitool jig and a disc sander. You can sand curved

JET JBGS-82

THE **JET JBGS-82** COMBINES THE *Multitool jig with an 8" grinding wheel and a 7" disc sander. It's a complete sanding and grinding station. The sharpening jig (shown at right) screws into place on the Multitool jig. Use a light touch when sharpening – this thing is aggressive.*

work, grind, polish and even clean up welds on the belt (we're told that auto enthusiasts love this machine).

To sharpen tools, you must purchase a separate $75 accessory tool rest from Multitool USA. This tool rest sets the angle of the bevel on your tool and holds it square against the belt as you sharpen.

One of this machine's virtues is how easy it is to change the belts to finer grits. It takes about five seconds total. Just press the front wheel forward until it locks in a retracted position. This slackens the belt. Then you remove one belt, slip the next one on and flip a switch to engage the tension. It's very smart.

Sharpening is also remarkably fast. The grinder's motor spins at 3,450 rpm, while the small 3½"-diameter wheel spins at 5,557 rpm, according to our tests. This translates into 4,280 feet of sandpaper passing under your tool every minute. In other words, you need to be careful about your tool heating up to the point where it turns blue and loses its temper, rendering it unable to hold a sharp edge. You need to use light finger pressure and touch the tool to the sandpaper for only a couple seconds at a time. If you bear down on the tool even a little bit, you will cook its edge instantly. We destroyed sev-

On the Jet JBGS-82, set *the angle of your tool's bevel by lining up its front edge with marks on the jig. Three common angles (25°, 35° and 40°) are called out.*

PUSH FRONT WHEEL TO
CHANGE BELTS

Changing the belts on the *Jet JBGS-82 is extraordinarily fast. Push the front wheel forward and it locks with the belt in a slack position. Replace the belt, push a switch and you're done.*

eral chisel edges before getting the hang of it.

The Multitool has a few drawbacks. There isn't a way to remove the burr on the backside of a tool's edge as you move to finer grits. It may be tempting to remove the burr by touching the backside to the flat platen of the jig, but because it's moving so quickly, I wouldn't recommend it. You'll have to remove the burr on a fine sharpening stone or when the machine isn't running.

Second, because the wheel you sharpen on has a small diameter, you will grind the edge quite hollow. In other words, the bevel is very concave, even compared to the hollow that's created on a 6" grinder. Sharpening experts assert that a hollow-ground edge isn't as durable as one that is ground with a flat bevel (which is what you get when grinding with a flat sharpening stone).

Also, the jig will hold most Western chisels and plane irons up to $2^7/_{16}$" wide. But it won't hold short-bladed tools such as Japanese chisels, butt chisels and spokeshave blades.

So how does the edge look? We sharpened several chisels on the Multitool using 3M's Trizact abrasive, available from Multitool USA. This high-tech sandpaper is made up of consistent pyramid-shaped structures instead of paper coated with randomly arranged grit, which is how traditional sandpaper is made.

We used the Trizact A6-grade paper as the final grit. This abrasive is equivalent to 6-micron sandpaper. In the world of abrasive grading, that puts it near a #2,000-grit Japanese waterstone. By way of comparison, most waterstone sharpeners finish chisels on a #4,000-grit stone. Some, like me, take their edges up to #8,000 for an ultimate polish.

Looking at the edge from the Multitool under a 30x jeweler's loupe (see "$10 Magnifier Improves

Edges" later on in this story) it was amazingly consistent, but it didn't look as polished as you'd get from a Japanese waterstone.

True Grit – The Different Systems

One of the difficulties in understanding sharpening is knowing how the size of the grit is measured. The Japanese have one system, sandpaper in the United States is measured using another system (called CAMI, the Coated Abrasives Manufacturers' Institute), and the abrasive in really fine sandpaper is measured in microns (one micron is equal to one millionth of a meter). It's all quite confusing.

Here are the rough equivalents for the three systems, from coarsest (at the top) to finest.

Japanese Grit	CAMI Grit	Microns
—	36	535
—	80	192
150	100	141
—	120	116
—	150	97
—	220	60
240	—	58
360	320	36
1,000	700	14
2,000	—	7.5
4,000	1,500	3
6,000	—	2
8,000	—	1.2
10,000	2,000	1

VERITAS MK. II
POWER SHARPENING SYSTEM

As the name implies, this is the second generation of this sharpening machine. The first version was bigger, more complex, more expensive and (some claimed) a bit underpowered.

Unlike the Jet Multitool, the Canadian-made Veritas Mk. II is designed for one operation: sharpening plane irons and chisels. And it excels at that.

To sharpen a tool, you first place it in a jig (included with the machine) that sets it square and positions it so that the proper amount of the tool is projected.

The jig rides on a tool rest that's suspended above a flat platter of sandpaper that spins at 678 rpm, according to our tests. That translates to 1,419 feet of abrasive passing under the tool's edge each minute – three times slower than the Jet. The height of the tool rest determines the angle you grind at – anywhere from 15° to 45° in 5° increments.

The machine comes with two platters. One is for grinding and has #80-grit Zirconia paper on one side and #150-grit aluminum oxide paper on the other. The other is for honing and has #320-grit aluminum oxide on one side and 9-micron paper on the other.

Other grits and additional platters are available as accessories for special applications.

One of the real strokes of genius with this machine is that the platter used for honing is 1 millimeter thinner than the platter for grinding. This creates a 1° microbevel on the edge of your tool, which greatly speeds sharpening.

Also, the jig holds a variety of tools, including short-bladed ones (as little as 1¾" long) and wide ones (up to 2½" wide). Plus there are retractable stops on the jig that allow you to wedge skew chisels in place for honing.

This is the only machine in our test that is designed to flatten the backside of the tool – the

VERITAS
MK. II

LIGHT FINGER PRESSURE IS ALL *it takes to hone a polished edge quickly and easily on the Veritas machine.*

THE MK. II ALSO ALLOWS *you to flatten and polish the backside of your tools and remove the burr on the tool's backside while sharpening.*

THE VERITAS MK. II POWER *Sharpening System is designed to do one thing extraordinarily well: sharpen woodworking tools. Just set your tool in the jig with a second easy-to-use jig (right).*

THIS JIG HOLDS THE TOOL

THIS JIG SETS THE PROJECTION OF THE TOOL

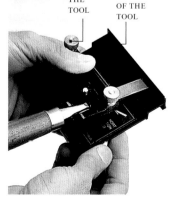

TOOL REST

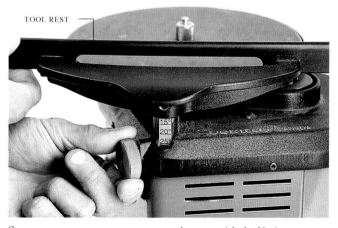

SET THE BEVEL ANGLE YOU *want to sharpen with the Veritas system by adjusting the tool rest up and down.*

critical first step to sharpening a new tool – and to remove the burr on the backside that develops during grinding and honing. The speed of the platter is just right for this: it's slow enough to keep the tool under control, but fast enough that you don't feel like you're wasting your time.

Also, while the machine is designed for sharpening tools with a flat edge, you can sharpen many carving tools freehand by resting them on the bar that the jig rides on. You also can sharpen the slightly cambered edge necessary for smoothing planes and jointer planes by alternately applying a little more pressure at the corners while grinding and honing.

In use, the machine is almost foolproof. Because of its slower speed, it's difficult to build up the heat necessary to destroy the temper of the tool (though it's still possible). And the completed edge looks good and polished under magnification, much like a hand-sharpened edge.

THE WARRIOR FROM JOOLTOOL

The most unusual machine in this test is the American-made Warrior, a system that utilizes an optical illusion.

Essentially, you sharpen your tools against a disc of spinning plastic covered in Trizact paper. The disc is shaped so that when it's spinning, you can see the tool's edge as it's being sharpened.

Like the other two machines, the Warrior comes with a variety of grits so you can hone a fine edge. The base model comes with grits from #80 up to 10 micron, very similar to what's available on the other two machines.

One downside to the base package is that it comes with only two of the plastic "backpads," which is what the sandpaper sticks to. It would be nice to have three or four to handle most woodworking tools. Additional backpads are available from Jooltool.

Unlike the other two machines, the Warrior has no jig to hold the tool square as you sharpen it. However, it was surprisingly easy to keep a reasonably square edge while sharpening freehand. Where

THE 3M TRIZACT SANDPAPER IS *attached to plastic discs (called Ninja Disc Backpads) that screw onto the machine's spindle. Swapping discs is fast and easy.*

THE PLASTIC DISCS' SHAPE ALLOW *you to see the tool's edge as you grind and hone it. Shaping unusual tools is remarkably easy.*

JOOLTOOL'S WARRIOR

the tool really excelled was with shaping my carving tools. It is astonishingly simple to shape the edge the way you want because you can see exactly where you are removing metal.

Another plus is that the Warrior tended to keep the edge cooler than the other two systems. We measured the heat generated by each system by holding a temperature sensor to the chisel (at $^3/_{16}$" behind the edge) then sharpening the tool in three separate three-second pulses with a three-second pause between each pulse. With the Warrior, the temperature of the tool went up to 77° Fahrenheit on average, only 5° F more than room temperature. Tools on the Jet heated up to 84° F and on the Veritas to 81° F.

You still can destroy the tool with the Warrior, however. The delicate edge of V-tools, particularly where the two sides of the "V" meet, was susceptible to heating up.

On the downside, the Warrior can't reliably remove the burr from the backside of your tool – that's something you'll have to do with a sharpening stone for flat tools and a slipstone for curved tools. Also, the widest blade you can reliably sharpen with the Warrior is slightly smaller (about $2^3/_8$") than the tools the other two machines can sharpen.

Another downside is the machine is lightweight, so you should screw it to a work surface to make sure you don't knock it over (holes are provided in the base specifically for this purpose).

Like the Jet, the Warrior has a lot of uses besides sharpening, including polishing, deburring and altering jewelry. You can even shape small wooden parts with it (there's a dust-collection port for your shop vacuum).

After some practice, our edges looked pretty good. They weren't as consistent as those on the Jet or as polished as those on the Veritas, but they were respectable. The more we worked with the Warrior, the more we began thinking about ways to add a jig that would hold the tool for us – perhaps an upside down tool rest from a traditional grinder.

$10 Magnifier Improves Edges

When someone suggested that I examine my sharpened edges "up close and personal" with a magnifying glass, I thought they were nuts. But once I tried it, I was hooked. You really can see how sharp your edge is and if your scratch pattern is consistent throughout.

I recommend a 30x magnifier, traditionally called a "loupe" by jewelers, which is used to examine gemstones for flaws. These are readily available through a number of web sites for about $10.

CONCLUSIONS

Because each machine is different, it's difficult to make a single recommendation for all woodworkers. If you're looking for a system that is dedicated to sharpening plane irons, chisels and other curved woodworking tools, the Veritas is the clear winner. But if you also need a sanding and grinding station, or you work entirely with turning or carving tools, you should look closely at the other two models.

The bigger question is, of course, if these systems replace hand sharpening. These three range in price from $350 for the Jooltool to $400 for the Veritas system.

All three systems replace a good-quality motorized grinder, which is a $65 to $200 expense, on average. Plus they replace some or all of the sharpening stones you need. A Japanese waterstone system can cost $40 to $220 (or more). If you finished up your edges with sandpaper, the additional cost would be negligible.

So these three machines are (on the whole) more expensive than most hand-sharpening systems. But they are undoubtedly faster – in some cases much faster. And the less time you spend sharpening means you can spend more time working wood, and that is something that's almost impossible to put a price tag on. So we think these machines are worth checking out.

Power Sharpening Systems

BRAND/MODEL	RPM AT TOOL	FEET/ MINUTE	AVG. TEMP. INCREASE	AMP. DRAW	MAX. TOOL WIDTH	COARSEST GRIT AVAILABLE	FINEST GRIT AVAILABLE	WEB SITE
Jet JBGS-82*	5,557	4,280	12° F	4.3	$2^7/_{16}$"	24 grit	5 micron	wmhtoolgroup.com
Veritas Mk. II	678	1,419	9° F	2.5	$2^1/_2$"	80 grit	9 micron	leevalley.com
Warrior M-2000-PKG	5,463	4,288	5° F	.25	$2^3/_8$"	80 grit	10 micron	jooltool.com

* The JBGS-62, a 6" model, was also available.

A Better Way
to Sharpen Scrapers

*We compared 14 methods to find the fastest way
to prepare this useful tool.*

S crapers are one of the most misunderstood but useful tools in a woodshop. A scraper in its basic form is simply a piece of hardened steel with a small hook that is created by pressing on the tool's edge with an even harder rod of steel. This tool is capable of making tear-out free cuts in hardwoods that no plane can manage.

But how to sharpen a scraper is a mysterious or confusing process for many woodworkers. One reason for the confusion is that there are many different techniques that offer conflicting advice.

So I compiled a list of 14 different techniques for sharpening this rectangle of steel that have been published since 1875. All of the 14 techniques basically agree that there are three steps to sharpening a scraper: Filing the edge of the tool, removing the file marks with a sharpening stone then creating the hook (sometimes called the burr) with a hardened rod of steel, usually called a burnisher.

But none of the accounts agree on the details. Should you file the edge of the scraper with the file parallel to the edge or at an angle (and if so, what angle)? What kind of file should you use? Should you stone both the edge and faces of the tool? To what grit? And how should this be done?

Do you have to burnish the faces of the tool before turning the burr of the scraper? If you do, what angle do you use? And how should you burnish the edge to create the hook? At what angle? Do you slide the burnisher as you turn the burr?

So one weekend I tried all these techniques then compared the results. I used high-quality scrapers from Lee Valley, Bahco and Lie-Nielsen. All of the published techniques worked and created a tool that made shavings. Yet some techniques were faster, some required fewer hand skills to master and some made a hook that really grabbed the work.

After trying these techniques and applying my own training, I think I've found a 15th way to sharpen the tool that doesn't require a lot of equipment, is fast and is easy for beginners.

LIKE ANY TOOL'S EDGE

What's important to understand is that a scraper is like any cutting tool and it responds to your sharpening efforts in the same, predictable way.

A sharp edge is the intersection of two steel surfaces (in a chisel, it's the bevel and the face, which is sometimes called the back of the tool). Any cutting edge is at its sharpest when these two surfaces meet at the smallest point possible.

The edge becomes more durable as it gets more

STEP ONE: *Filing the Edge*

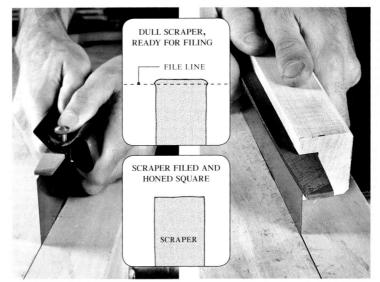

DULL SCRAPER, READY FOR FILING

FILE LINE

SCRAPER FILED AND HONED SQUARE

SCRAPER

A PERMANENT MARKER WILL HELP *you determine if you have filed the edge sufficiently. Once the color has been removed, you are ready to stone the edge of the scraper.*

TWO OR THREE PASSES WITH *a file is usually all it takes. Use only a push stroke with a file and use the fingers of both hands to keep your filing jig's fence flat against the scraper.*

YOU CAN MAKE A PERFECTLY *good filing jig from a scrap of hardwood as shown here. Cut a kerf in the block that allows the file to be held with a firm friction fit.*

AFTER TWO STROKES WITH THE *file, the color is almost gone from the edge.*

polished by higher grits. Polishing removes tiny scratches in the steel, and scratches are the places where the edge breaks down and becomes dull.

A harder steel can also contribute to a more long-lasting edge. However, if it is too hard it can be fragile and susceptible to shock.

All these rules apply to scrapers. The cutting edge of a scraper is two surfaces: the edge and the face. The more polished those two surfaces are, the more durable and sharp the edge is. So with that principle in mind, here's the thinking behind my scraper-sharpening technique.

STEP 1: FILE THE EDGE

The edge of the card scraper should be filed square to the tool's faces (all the sources agree on this). You should use a fine file. Look for one with single rows of parallel teeth (this is called a single-cut file) and teeth that are fine, usually labeled "second cut" or "smooth." Scrapers are soft and easy to file, so a coarse file will create deep scratches that are difficult to remove.

Color the edge of the tool with a permanent marker. This will allow you to see where you are cutting. When the color is gone, the filing is done.

How you hold the file in use is in dispute. You can work with the file parallel to the edge, perpendicular to the edge or anywhere in between. All can result in a square edge, but there is only one technique that gives perfect results every time regardless of your skill with filing: Use a jig, either commercial or shopmade.

Veritas makes an inexpensive jig that I like. You also can purchase a vintage saw jointer, which was used to file handsaw teeth down for reshaping. Or you can cut a kerf in a block of wood to hold your file. Freehand filing is great if you are skilled at it. Most of us are not, so I recommend a jig.

STEP 2: STONE THE TOOL

After filing, you smooth away those scratches with a sharpening stone or two. Some sources say you have to stone only the narrow edge of the scraper. Others say you stone both the edge and the faces. Because we now know that a good edge is the intersection of two polished surfaces, you should stone both the edge and face.

How do you stone the edge? You can rub the tool on edge on your stone, but this can make it difficult to balance the tool. Some published accounts recommend sandwiching the scraper between two blocks of wood for additional support, but you'll

STEP TWO: Stoning

THERE ARE MANY WAYS TO *stone an edge. This 2" x 2" x 5" block is what I prefer. You can move the block as you rub the scraper against the stone, which spreads the wear out on your stone. Alternately, with thick waterstones you can use the side of the stone and support the scraper with a block of wood.*

HOLD THE RULER WITH ONE *thumb or it will slide. Use your other hand to stroke the edge against the stone. The wood block improves control.*

THE RULER TRICK SHARPENS THE *scraper only at its cutting edge, saving much time and effort.*

STEP THREE: *Burnishing*

RUB YOUR
BURNISHER FLAT
AGAINST *the
scraper five or
six times. This
work-hardens
and consolidates
the material. And
it draws out the
steel at the edge,
making it easy to
turn the hook.*

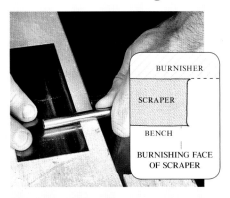

A JIG SUCH AS
THE *Veritas Vari-
able Burnisher
allows you to
turn a hook with
little chance for
error. If you are
having difficulty
with burnishing
freehand, this
is an excellent
option.*

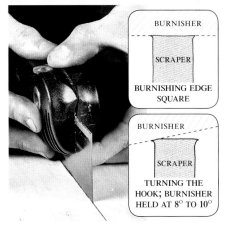

AFTER THREE
PASSES WITH THE
*burnisher using
mild downward
pressure, feel the
edge for a hook
as shown. It
should feel like a
tiny lip that your
fingernail could
almost grab.*

BURNISHING FREEHAND IS TRICKY FOR *some and a cakewalk for
others. Here's a tip: Rest one hand on the bench to control the
angle of burnishing. Use the other hand to draw the burnisher
along the edge of the scraper. This usually helps to increase
your control.*

usually end up abrading the wooden blocks more
than the tool.

Alternately, you can bow the scraper as you rub
it on the stone to spread the edge out over more of
the surface. This works well with flexible scrapers
but is quite difficult with the thicker ones.

Instead, I like to hone the edge of the scraper
on the sharpening stone with a single block of wood
supporting it from the side. I'll sharpen on the face
of the stone as shown on the previous page. This
allows you to spread the wear out across the stone's
face by moving the block of wood.

With the edge stoned, how do you stone the
two faces of the tool? Here is where the real trick-
ery begins. Every other technique that discusses this
has you rub the face of the tool to and fro on the
stone. This works, but it takes a while. The face of
a scraper is a lot of steel to deal with. Most woodworkers do what they can on the faces and give up
when they get bored. And that doesn't cut it.

Why sharpen a bunch of steel you aren't
using? So I took a page from the playbook of David
Charlesworth, a British craftsman. He sharpens the
unbeveled face of a plane iron by propping up the
back of the tool on a thin ruler set on the stone. This
technique, called the ruler trick, sharpens only the
section of steel up by the cutting edge.

Would this work with card scrapers, I wondered? It does. And brilliantly. You sharpen only the
metal up by the edge. It takes far fewer strokes. And
the slight change in edge geometry has no discern-
ible effect on the final cutting edge. Thanks David.

The other question is what grit of stones you
should use. This is honestly up to you. The more polished the edge, the more durable it will be in use.

I start by marking the face with a permanent
marker. First work the tool with a coarse stone, such
as a #1,000-grit waterstone. Then go directly to
any fine polishing stone, such as #4,000, #6,000 or
#8,000 grit. Oilstones or sandpaper are fine options
as well. To improve your grip on the tool, you can
affix a strip of ¼" x ¼" x 6" scrap to the scraper
with double-stick tape.

STEP 3: BURNISH THE TOOL

Of the 14 scraper-sharpening techniques I
tried, eight recommended burnishing the flat face
of the scraper before burnishing the edge to turn the
hook. The explanations for why you burnish the flat
face of the tool were varied: To soften the metal, to
harden it, to consolidate the metal, or to warp the
metal over the edge so you can turn it into a burr.

So I did what any mind-muddled journalist
does: I called an expert. Ron Hock runs Hock Tools
and sells a wide variety of replacement plane irons.

Here's what Hock concluded: Burnishing the flat face of a card scraper does two things: It work-hardens the metal by compressing the crystal structure of the steel. The burnisher is harder than the scraper. Burnishers will typically be of a Rockwell hardness (Rc) of 58 to 60. Modern scrapers are typically Rc 48 to 53. The harder burnisher will compress the steel of the softer scraper, making the steel harder and probably more durable in use. Burnishing the face is especially useful with old scrapers, which have a Rockwell hardness that is lower, more like in the mid-40s, Hock said. (Scrapers were typically made from old saw blades in the early days.)

The other thing that the burnisher does is to draw the steel off of the face of the scraper. Essentially, it moves the metal so the steel makes a small point where the face meets the edge. Why is this important? It makes the scraper's burr much easier to turn when you burnish the edge of the tool. You can turn the burr in fewer strokes and without much downward pressure on the tool.

Hock's points about steel fit in perfectly with my experience during the 13 years I've sharpened card scrapers. Must you burnish the face to get a burr? No. But if you don't burnish the face, the burr is more difficult to turn, and you must use more pressure or more strokes. Using more strokes or pressure can introduce error and create an irregular burr.

Point two: Burnishing the face creates (in my experience) a burr that lasts longer. Hock suggests that this is because the steel has been work-hardened by the burnisher before turning.

Once you burnish the face, you have to turn the hook with the burnisher by running the burnisher across the edge. Like with all things with card scrapers, there is debate. At what angle should the burnisher be held against the edge: 0°, 5°, 10°, 15°?

Should you use light pressure? Heavy pressure? How many times should you draw the burnisher across the edge? Some accounts say you burnish first at 0° and then burnish again at a slight angle. (I've done it this way for years. It works, but so does skipping the step. See what works for you.)

I have always been stymied by the question of the final hook angle, so I tried a little experiment and prepared a scraper with four different hooks (5°, 7°, 10° and 15°) made using the Veritas Variable Burnisher. Then I gave the scraper to Senior Editor Bob Lang and asked him to use it as I watched, and we then discussed the different working characteristics of the four hooks.

The conventional wisdom is that the steeper the hook, the more aggressive the tool (15° is supposed to be for removing paint; 0° is supposed to be for

marquetry). But the truth is, we could get excellent results with all the edges. You could get the wispiest shavings with a 15° hook if you used light pressure. In fact, the only scraper that seemed to perform significantly different is one that I prepared with no hook. That one took only light shavings.

So how much pressure should you use when burnishing? I use pressure that is similar to when you "spread butter on bread," an apt description by woodworking author Graham Blackburn.

Should you use one stoke? Two strokes? More? I stroke the edge until I can feel a burr. Then I stop. This takes two or three strokes.

I again recommend a jig for the burnishing, especially if you're a beginner. I'd never used a jig until a couple years ago, and I'd never had problems with freehand burnishing either (but I sharpen a lot). The jig gives you speed and consistency.

Most sources recommend adding a drop of oil to the edge before burnishing to prevent galling. What's galling? That's when you force metal parts together (screw threads are a common example) and there is so much friction that the high points heat up and cause tiny welds on the high points that then break off, making the corner feel rough. I've done this, but I had to try to do it to make it happen. I oil the edge because it makes the burnisher slide sweetly.

USING THE SCRAPER

To begin scraping, I flex the card scraper just a bit at the center and hold it at a angle to the work that's usually between 60° to 65° to the surface. I adjust my wrists until the scraper starts to cut shavings. If you are getting dust instead, adjust your angle first. Then check your hook to see if it is still there. A hook feels like a lip on the edge.

Scrapers are great for removing tear-out, but you do have to be careful not to create a depression that will show up after finishing. When you work a small area, it's best to then blend in that low spot with the area around by working the wood around your problem area with the scraper as well.

Scrapers are subtle tools and are capable of a great number of tasks. In fact, there are even more uses for a scraper than there are ways to sharpen it – and that's saying something.

FOR MORE INFORMATION
Lee Valley Tools
leevalley.com, 800-871-8158
Lie-Nielsen Toolworks
lie-nielsen.com, 800-327-2520
Woodcraft
woodcraft.com, 800-225-1153

Resharpening a Scraper Plane

Can you just reburnish the hook and get back to scraping? Or do you have to drop back to the coarse stones?

Reader David Raeside asks: I've noted that you've recently mentioned that you've been looking into scrapers, so I thought that maybe you could answer a question that I have about scraper-plane blades.

Recently I acquired a Stanley #12 scraper plane and the three Lie-Nielsen scraper planes (modern versions of the Stanley #112, #85, and #212). I am in the process of preparing and using these scraper planes to smooth the surfaces of the blanket chest that I made at Chris Gochnour's Marc Adams School of Woodworking course. I intend to thereby avoid sanding.

I intend to paint the chest (which is made of poplar) following the methods given in the painting article in a recent issue of *Woodworking Magazine*.

I am preparing the scraper plane blades just as I would plane blades: both back and bevel, five DMT plates of grits from #120 to #1,200 followed by four Shapton waterstones of grits from #2,000 to #16,000. The burnishing of the 45° bevels to produce a burr is being done with a Glen-Drake burnisher following the method of David Charlesworth (which is similar to the method given by Garrett Hack).

It is my understanding that when a scraper plane ceases to proceed shavings and starts to produce dust that I must go back to honing and redo the burnishing to produce a new burr.

Here is my question: How far back must I go in the honing sequence?

Certainly I need not go back to the DMT plates. But, do I need to go back to the #2,000 grit Shapton waterstone? And, can I get away with only re-hon-ing the bevel, or must I re-hone both the back and the bevel?

If you are able to help me understand how to do the refurbishing of defunct scraper plane burrs I would greatly appreciate it.

Answer: I have indeed been doing a lot of work on the care and feeding of scrapers. In brief: They are like any other edge tool. All the same rules apply. The burr is strongest when it is turned from the intersection of two highly polished planes.

And so resharpening of scrapers involves exactly the same regimen as it would for a plane or chisel.

1. If the edge of the scraper is only slightly degraded (this is, it is just begiining to make dust), then I'll begin with a polishing stone (#8,000), remove the wire edge then turn the burr again.

2. If the edge is mostly used up but still unchipped (that is, I have been making a combination of dust and shavings for a while), I'll begin with the #1,000 stone, then polish, then turn the burr.

3. If the edge is chipped or otherwise damaged, I drop back to the diamond stones, grinder or other coarse grinding abrasives. Then the #1,000, #8,000 and burnisher.

What I don't do much of is to try to resharpen with burnishing alone – which is a common remedy I read about from other craftsmen. My results with this technique have always been inconsistent.

Occasionally it works just fine. Usually, however, I get a burr that is OK in some places and weak in others. Other times I get nothing but a trip back to the grinder. No matter what, this "refurbished" burr never lasts as long as a new burr.

Seeing, Sawing & Other Tottering Principles

The real challenge to getting a keen edge is not in your hands — it's in your eyeball.

Whenever I attempt to teach a bit of woodworking I say things that don't come out quite right. Things like: "Sharpening is perhaps the most fundamental of hand skills." Or: "Handsawing is the most fundamental of joinery skills." Also: "Design is the most blah, blah skill." And finally: "I think it's time for a group hug."

When I say these things, what I'm really trying to say is that there's a basic skill beneath all the other high-level skills. But it's not sharpening, sawing, planing or design.

It's seeing.

In March 2007 I was at the Sterling Heights, Mich., Woodcraft store to teach two one-day classes. One class on planing and the other on sawing. So inevitably I made some grandiose sweeping statements like the ones above. But as I got into the down-and-dirty part of teaching these skills, I kept running into the problem of myopia.

Sharpening isn't about rubbing tools on abrasive as much as it is knowing when to stop rubbing the tool on the abrasive. And the way you know when to stop is by observing the cutting edge.

Planing isn't about making shavings, it's about seeing the resulting surface you are leaving. Is it flat, true and free of tear-out? And sawing is about muscle memory, but it's also about seeing a line and following it with your saw using subtle hand pressure.

The good news is that teaching one-on-one is the absolute best place to give the gift of sight. I don't know how many frustrating and circular phone conversations I've had with woodworkers who are trying to teach themselves to sharpen, plane or saw. They struggle longer than necessary because they don't know when they have a sharp saw, a flat board or a correctly cut tenon.

But when you can get that in-person feedback and observe what a really sharp edge, flat board and perfect sawcut looks like, your skills advance in great strides. I was amazed at how quickly all of the students caught on once the scales fell from their eyes and they could see the scratches, gaps of light and miscuts.

What I didn't really have the heart to say is that seeing is a blessing as well as a curse. Once you can see the scratches, you will work like heck to remove them. You won't settle for bowed stock. And you will correct miscuts. And learning to do those things quickly takes time and effort.

And there's one more curse. It's even worse, and it deals with design. Once you can truly see good design, you will never be able to walk into a furniture store or neighbor's house without the occasional wince.

HERE'S A WAY TO GET *a leg up on your seeing skills. Buy an inexpensive jeweler's loupe (this one cost me $10). It helps you see scratches.*

Woobie,
Beloved Wiper
(1996-2008)

The key to preventing rust is to wipe down your tools after every use. Here's a cautionary tale about what happens when you become too attached to your rag.

As a woodworking writer, I try not to "over-share" when it comes to personal information. I try not to talk about my exotic skin lesions, what I had for breakfast and the wide array of annoying personal habits of my co-workers.

But today is a sad day here in the shop. It's time to let go of the "woobie."

The woobie is actually a rag (there, I said it) that has been soaked with the lubricating juices of many plants, animals and petroleums. For more than a decade, the woobie has wiped down every tool when I put it away. It has wiped every plane sole to make it easier to push. It has cleaned off every edge after sharpening.

But today I think the woobie goes in the garbage.

Here's the problem: I think the woobie has been contaminated by some sort of abrasive grit. Here's the evidence: My handplane edges are deteriorating more rapidly.

One of the indicators that it's time to resharpen a plane iron is when the shaving from the plane's mouth isn't intact across its width. Instead it comes out as several smaller ribbons. What's happened to the iron is that it has suffered small nicks or fractures in its edge that prevent it from taking a full-width shaving. Plus, it leaves little plane tracks behind at these fractures.

I've noticed that my smoothing plane iron at work is now deteriorating much more rapidly than my smoothing plane at home (which is where I keep "son of woobie").

More evidence: When I was teaching at Kelly Mehler's School of Woodworking in September 2008 I left my woobie at home. And after crouching and whimpering in the corner a bit because of my forgetfulness, I noticed that my edges were lasting a long time again, even though I was loaning my planes to the students.

Hmmm. The woobie sees a lot of abrasive when it wipes off my tools from sharpening. And it sits by the drill press, where there are metal filings and other nastiness. The woobie could be the source of the problem. Embedded grit could be scratching the irons when I wipe them off.

I could launder the woobie, but I want to stay married. So here's what I'm going to do: I'm going to put the woobie at the bottom of my now-empty garbage can, start a new woobie and monitor the longevity of my plane irons. If my edges improve I'll let the woobie go to the dump with the next load of trash.

And judging by how quickly we move here, that should be about Christmas.

Afterward: The durability of my edges did improve. But the old woobie lives on. Managing Editor Megan Fitzpatrick has secreted it away to sell "shards of the true woobie" to readers. I think it goes without saying we have a lousy retirement plan here.

TECHNIQUES

Planing the Perfect Board

A common exercise from shop class will jump-start your planing skills.

Mr. Peel was shaped exactly like one of the Fisher-Price Little People, he jangled his keys in his pockets nonstop and he had a reputation as a tyrannical shop teacher at Chaffin Junior High School in Fort Smith, Ark.

My friends would talk in the school's lunchroom about how every student had to get a single board straight, square and flat using hand tools before they could proceed to building anything in shop class. Creating this "perfect board" was daunting for most students, and I was glad at the time that I was exempt from shop class (and Spanish class – whew) because I was in the journalism program.

Since junior high, I've heard about other shop class teachers who had a similar exercise, and the "perfect board" is part of the teaching at The College of the Redwoods and Rosewood Studios. In 2006, I added this exercise to the classes I teach

on handplaning and it has been illuminating for me – and I hope for the students.

We don't start with rough wood (these are one- or two-day seminars). Instead I start with pieces of mild cherry or walnut that is ¾" x 6" x 14" and has been accurately jointed and planed on both faces. I quite like using machined wood for the exercise because it points out how machining a board might not make it flat enough for some work.

We begin by discussing how wood is structured and how it warps and cups – these are key to understanding how to plane it flat. Then I show them the different techniques for flattening a cupped surface through traversing. And how to flatted a bowed surface by creating a slight cup then removing it.

I instruct the students how to refine the face using a cambered iron in a jointer plane and diagonal strokes. And then how to use the camber to true both edges to the true face without creating a big hump in the middle. They don't have to smooth the faces and edges to perfection (though extra points are awarded for those who do) – so it's a good exercise even if you have only a jointer or jack plane.

Then the students submit the board to my straightedge and ruler. I show them the problem areas – where the light is leaking under the measuring equipment– I mark the high spots in chalk and send them back to the bench. It usually takes them a few attempts, but I'm always amazed that they manage to correct the problems once they can see them marked in chalk on the board.

If you've never tried this exercise, I think you should.

Now I'm not yet shaped like Mr. Peel; though after a recent bout with pizza and the some endless web site coding I am heavier and balder. And I hope never to twitch like he does, which was why he kept his hand on his keys I suppose. But I am entirely sympathetic to his "perfect board" exercise.

I just hope my students aren't talking about me in the lunchroom.

GET IT FLAT, SQUARE AND *looking good. If you can get one board to behave, you are on your way to planing panels and entire projects.*

Tricking the Banana

One of the most common errors when planing is to create a gentle banana shape on one face — where the length is curved instead of flat.

One of the most common errors when planing is to create a gentle banana shape on one face – where the ends of the board end up thinner than the middle.

The cause of this problem resides both in you and in your tool. First off, divide the sole of your plane into two regions: The infeed side of the sole before the blade (the toe). And the outfeed side of the sole behind the blade (the heel). And remember this: The blade of your plane isn't co-planar with the outfeed side of your handplane.

This feature makes it different than your power jointer. As a result, a handplane has more of a tendency to make bananas. (By the way, you can make bananas – and wedges – with a power jointer as well). What tends to happen is the tool takes a heavier cut at the beginning of the stroke when you have only a small amount of the sole planted on the work. And the tool can take a slightly heavier cut at the end of a stroke as the toe runs off the board.

But I think the tool's role in banana-making is a minor problem. The bigger problem is you and where you are putting pressure on the tool as you plane. Here's how it's supposed to work:

At the beginning of the cut, plant the toe of your tool firmly against the work. With the hand on the front knob, put all of your downward pressure right there. Your other hand (on the tote) should only push the tool forward. This is mostly to keep the plane from skittering at the beginning of the cut – a common problem in hardwoods.

As soon as the entire sole is on the work, you should shift your pressure: Use equal and forceful downward pressure with both of your hands.

As soon as the toe approaches the end of the board, release the pressure on the front knob but continue to exert downward and forward pressure at the tote. Heck, sometimes I remove my hand from the front knob entirely.

The procedure above works, but it can be a trick to remember all the pressure points for beginning planers. It's hard to get all your muscles lined up. So I tell them this simple mental trick: Just try your darndest to plane a big old valley in the middle of each board by scooping out the center.

Planing a hollow in this manner is almost impossible to do with a handplane that has a flat sole. So what you wind up with is a board that is fairly consistent in its thickness.

I cannot take credit for this mental trick, but I also can't remember who told it to me years ago. But it works like crazy. And with that aspect of planing under control, you can then turn your attention to removing cupping and twisting in your boards.

THE OTHER BANANA

There's a second banana problem for beginning planers: They create a gentle curve across the width of the board. This is caused by using a plane with a cambered iron and starting the tool in the wrong place on the board.

If you start the plane on a board with the middle of the tool directly over the edge of the board, you will end up making this type of curve. Instead, start the tool so the thin edge of your shaving begins on the edge of the board. This will encourage a flatter surface across the width of the board. Then check your work – you'll get the hang of it.

Squaring Boards Using Handplanes & An Historic Book

The methods and the tools for getting a board flat haven't changed much since the 17th century. Here's a quick lesson in traditional technique.

Squaring up a board using handplanes alone is more than an academic exercise. Anyone who appreciates wide boards knows the heartbreak of ripping them into smaller pieces to get them into their machines.

In my book, that is a cardinal sin.

Armed with only three bench planes, you can convert a rough-as-a-cob board to something ready to finish. The techniques to do this are so well prescribed that they were written down in the first English-language woodworking book, Joseph Moxon's "Mechanick Exercises," first published serially in 1678.

The most notable thing about Moxon's book is that the tools and techniques are the same now as they were in 17th-century England. The only difference is that these techniques and skills were once common – now they are quite rare. So, let's follow Moxon's instructions on truing a board that is 2" x 6½" x 48" to understand how simple it really is.

THE NECESSARY TOOLS

To convert rough stock into something suitable for furniture, you need three handplanes: a fore plane, a jointer plane and a smoother. The fore plane removes material quickly, the jointer plane makes the work flat and the smoothing plane prepares it for finish.

The fore plane is about 14" to 18" long (a jack plane will do the trick) and has a cutting edge with a thumbnail shape. This shape allows it to remove lots of wood. The jointer plane is 22" or longer and has a cutter that is either straight or slightly curved. The smoothing plane is 10" or shorter and has a cutter that is either slightly curved or has its corners relieved to keep them from digging into the work.

PLANING ACROSS THE GRAIN IS *easy to do. Work the high spots until they're the same as the low spots on one face of the board.*

WORK NARROWER STOCK AT AN *angle using the jointer, Moxon writes, to ensure flatness.*

Use your fore, jointer and *smoother to true and finish one edge. Check your work with a square and 2' rule.*

A marking gauge marks the *board's finished width. Make this mark on both faces – the finished and unfinished one.*

Step One: True One Face

Begin with the fore plane, setting it so it will take a shaving that is the thickness "of an old coined shilling," a bit more than $^1/_{32}$" thick. If the grain is difficult, reduce the cut to "the thickness of an old groat," or less than $^1/_{32}$". If the board is warped or cupped, plane across the grain – what Moxon calls "traversing" – to bring the high spots down to the low spots on your first face.

Moxon says you should check your work by sighting down the face of the board either with one eye, with a 2'-long ruler, or with a piece of straight stock that is as long as the piece you are working. When the first face is flat, you should refine it further. Set the fore plane to a lighter shaving and plane the board. Then use a jointer plane. Traverse across the grain for wide panels, or work at angles – corner-to-corner – for narrower stock.

Finish up that first face using a smoothing plane, if necessary. With this plane you should work with the grain and overlap your strokes.

Step Two: Straighten One Long Edge

Use a try square to find the high spots on one of the long edges of your board. Reduce these using a fore plane or (in extreme cases) using a hatchet, Moxon writes. Follow this up with a jointer plane and smoothing plane.

USE "LADDER CUTS" TO REMOVE *wood in a hurry. Chop down to your scribe lines, then remove the wood with plane-like passes as shown.*

WHEN WORKING WOOD BY HAND, *remove as little material as necessary. Scribe the finished thickness on your two long edges. Then work to these marks.*

STEP THREE:
WORK THE OTHER EDGE

Use a marking gauge or panel gauge to scribe the finished width of the board. The gauge's head rides on the finished edge and marks parallel to the rough edge. You also should strike this same line on the rough face.

Now work this edge down to your scribe line. Use a hatchet or a drawknife if you have lots of material to remove. The photo above shows how I was taught by a chairmaker to remove the material using "ladder cuts." Other woodworkers just chop away at the waste with the hatchet. Both techniques work. If there isn't much waste, use a fore, jointer and smoothing plane to dress the edge and get it true.

STEP FOUR:
THE SECOND FACE

With one face and two edges completed, use your marking gauge to scribe the finished thickness on your two completed edges. Press the gauge firmly against your first face to make these marks. Then use a hatchet, fore, jointer and smoothing plane to dress the fourth face.

Despite all the modern advances in tool technology, working wood by hand hasn't changed significantly. The workshop practices chronicled by Moxon are just as useful today as they were when every board was processed by hand. The only real difference is that processing lumber by hand today is an interesting exercise, whereas in the 17th century, it was a grueling necessity.

Make Plane-friendly Panels

*If you are going to plane a panel by hand, a little planning
can save you hours of frustration and scraping.*

Using a handplane to dress an assembled tabletop or carcase side frustrates many woodworkers. Because you have several boards with sometimes differing grain directions, there's a greater risk of tear-out. Also, getting a large panel really flat seems to require hundreds of strokes with a smoothing plane.

Some woodworkers solve the tear-out problem with high-angle planes or scrapers. And they have also resigned themselves to long planing sessions with their panels.

However, you can greatly reduce frustration when dealing with panels by paying close attention to your material and borrowing tricks from our ancestors.

LOOKS ARE FIRST

Whenever you create a panel from several narrow boards that will be visible in the finished project, the No. 1 consideration is the appearance of the completed panel. Other concerns are secondary. Alternating the growth rings in a panel (heart-side-up then bark-side-up then heart-side-up) is fairly modern advice. Early joiners and cabinetmakers rarely did this, according to texts and the surviving furniture record.

So arrange your boards with the most attractive sides facing up. Then mark on every face (including the undersides) the direction that the grain runs in each board. Use arrows to indicate which direction the handplane should travel to surface that board.

Sometimes a board can have grain that reverses – or it runs in two different directions in two places. Mark each area with its own arrow; sometimes you can trim a panel to remove a section of squirrelly grain.

The best-looking panels are those where the appearance of the grain is similar at the seams. That means putting quartersawn grain next to quartersawn grain. I avoid using boards that have an edge that occurs in the middle of a plainsawn cathedral. It's difficult to incorporate that figure into a good-looking panel.

EDGES AND ASSEMBLY

If you are going to dress your completed panel by hand, lining up your boards at the seams is critical. If just one board ends up lower that its mates it can result in a lot of unnecessary planing of the others to get it flush.

With small panels, you can usually just plane the long edges flat then manipulate the edges at glue-up. However, for large tabletops, I recommend a traditional tongue-and-groove joint or spline. (Some woodworkers prefer biscuits or dowels.) A well-made tongue-and-groove joint can result in a near-perfect panel and a stress-free glue-up.

When you glue up your panel, start by clamping in the middle of the panel. Apply pressure and touch each seam. Manipulate your boards until they are flush. Then clamp toward the ends. To keep the boards lined up, I'll apply an F-style clamp across each seam then cinch the bar clamps.

I USE LARGE ARROWS TO *indicate the grain direction on the faces of all the boards. Bold marks help ensure you won't make a mistake at assembly.*

WITH SMALL PANELS (THIS ONE *is 42" long) you can join the edges using glue and clamps alone. For longer panels, consider a spline joint or a tongue-and-groove.*

DRESSING THE PANEL

If you have prepared your panel with care, dressing the panel with your planes should be as easy as planing a single board. Use a jointer plane and diagonal strokes to remove any twist or slight cupping. Then follow that with the smoothing plane.

However, if you do have a lot of material to remove, there is a traditional strategy that can help. If you plane directly across the grain of a panel you can take a thicker shaving with less effort – this is called "traversing."

If my panel's seams are misaligned by 1/32" or so, I will traverse the panel with my jointer plane. If my seams are out by more than that, I will traverse the panel first with a plane designed to take a thick shaving (such as a fore, jack or scrub plane). Then I will follow up that work with a jointer plane.

All this is followed by strokes with a fine-set smoothing plane. (Usually set to cut a .002" shaving.) If I have taken care through every step of the process of constructing the panel, then this part of the work is brief and enjoyable.

BEGIN CLAMPING IN THE MIDDLE *of the panel. Apply pressure and check each seam with your finger. Adjust the boards until they line up.*

AN F-STYLE CLAMP ACROSS EACH *seam can help bring your seams into alignment.*

BEFORE YOU TRAVERSE ANY BOARD, *be sure to plane a small chamfer on the out-feed edge. Otherwise, the edge will splinter (this is called "spelching").*

A WELL-PREPARED PANEL SHOULDN'T REQUIRE *more than a few minutes with the smoothing plane to dress. As a bonus, you won't have to sharpen or adjust your smoothing plane as much.*

Flatten a Workbench's Top

Is it necessary? And if so, what are the best techniques?

L ike any tool or machine, a workbench requires accessories (jigs, fixtures, appliances) and occasional maintenance to actually do anything of great value. A bench without a bench hook is a heavy-duty dining table. A bench with a cupped work surface is an exercise in bewilderment and wasted effort.

There are a variety of ways to go about flattening a workbench top, including some that are patently nuts. But before I march down that list of your options, I ask: Does the top need to be flat?

Whenever I'm in an old barn, workshop or even an antique mall, I can't resist poking around the guts of any old workbenches I find. When my wife and I take the kids on a hayride, I end up in the chicken house checking out the 18th-century wooden screws on a face vise. When we visit living history museums, the kids are chasing the animals, and I'm asking the guy dressed as a cooper if I can poke around the undercarriage of his bench.

I've found little evidence that these benches were flattened regularly. Many of them bear toolmarks that are deep and of varying ages. I've seen benches that are so worn from use that the edges look as round as a pillow. One bench I saw in Columbus, Ohio, was so worn away in one spot that its 3"-thick top was less than an inch thick.

And when I check the 19th- and early 20th-century books, there's very little attention given to the workbench top. While there is detailed instruction on sharpening, tool maintenance and the act of building a bench, flattening its top isn't often listed as routine shop maintenance. At most, they'll note that the top should be flat.

There are several explanations for this:

1. Workbench flatness is overrated and a product of our modern obsession with granite surface plates and dial calipers.

2. Early woodworkers would use "planing trays" – a disposable workshop appliance that attached to the bench and allowed woodworkers to plane cabinet-scale parts at a variety of angles.

3. Or a flat workbench was so important to those who handplaned panels and furniture components that its flatness was a given.

I don't have the answer, but I suspect that all three are true to some degree. If you've ever done any handwork on a bench that was cupped, bowed

MOVE YOUR BENCH SO THAT *one end points to a window. This makes it easier to read your winding sticks as you look for gaps underneath them and for alignment across their lengths.*

MY WINDING STICKS HERE ARE *36"-long aluminum angle. Place one winding stick at the far end of your bench and the other one about 24" away. Sight across them both, looking for high and low spots. Move the far winding stick to the other end of the benchtop and repeat.*

or twisted, then you know that it's not a good way to work. The downward pressure from a handplane (particularly wooden-bodied planes) can bend your work into a low spot in the bench. When using long planes in particular, a low spot will prevent you from ever planing the board flat.

You can use small wooden wedges under your stock to support it and prevent it from bending into a low spot on your bench, but the problem is that you will have difficulty knowing when your board is flat. A workbench top that is fairly flat is also a fair way to gauge of the flatness of other boards.

TWO SOLUTIONS FOR TOPS

So my recommendation is that if you can wield a handplane (even just enough to be trouble), then you should either use a planing tray or strive to keep your top fairly flat. You can overdo this. It's not necessary to flatten the top using methods that involve a machinist's straightedge and feeler gauges. And I would ward you away from methods that use a router that runs on a carriage suspended over your bench. I've watched people do this, and it is a lot of trouble to build these devices.

I think there are two smart paths: Learn to use a jointer plane (flattening a workbench top is the best practice for this) or remove your benchtop and take it to a cabinetshop that has a wide-belt sander.

(Side note: Some workbench designs can be flattened using home woodworking machines. One such design has a benchtop that is made of two thick 10"-wide slabs with a 4"-wide tool tray screwed between them. Simply remove the screws and run each 10"-wide slab through your portable planer. Reassemble! Side, side note: I dislike tool trays, a.k.a. hamster beds.)

I can hear the workbench purists squirming from where I perch. Won't sending a workbench top through a wide-belt sander embed it with grit that will mar the workpieces of future projects? Not in my experience. Once you dust off the top and put a finish on it, such as an oil/varnish blend, the grit becomes part of the finish.

Plus, even if there is a little #220-grit in my benchtop, that fine grit is a lot kinder to my workpieces than what else gets embedded in my bench during my normal work: bits of dried glue, dyes, pigments and occasional stray metal filings.

NOW THAT I KNOW THE *geography of the top, I'll drag one stick all along the top and watch the gap under the winding stick. This quick check confirms my suspicions about where the high spots are (and they are usually along the long edges of the top).*

BEFORE I GET DOWN TO *business, I'll cut a small chamfer ($^1/_{16}$" to $^1/_8$") on the long edges of the top. This will prevent the grain from blowing out (the British call this spelching) when I plane cross-grain.*

FLATTEN IT WITH A HANDPLANE

Because I don't have a wide-belt sander, I prefer to use a handplane to do the job. Once you do this a couple times, you'll find that it's a 30-minute job – and a lot less lifting than carting a top across town to a local cabinetshop. The first time I ever tried to flatten a benchtop with a handplane (years ago) I was 100 percent successful, and I just barely knew what I was doing.

Flattening a benchtop is like flattening a board on one face. First you remove the high spots. These high spots could be at the corners or there could be a hump all along the middle (though I have never had one of these in my benchtop). Find the high spots using two winding sticks – parallel lengths of hardwood or aluminum angle that are longer than your bench is wide.

Mark any high spots in chalk or pencil and work them down with a bit of spirited planing using a jack, fore or jointer plane set to take an aggressive cut and equipped with a cambered iron. Get things close. Check your results with your winding sticks.

Fetch your jointer plane and work the entire top using diagonal strokes that overlap. Repeat that process by going diagonally back the other way across the top. After each pass, your shavings will become more and more regular. When your shavings are full length, your top is flat (enough). Now plane the entire top with the grain and use slightly overlapping strokes. It should take two or three passes to produce regular full-length shavings. You are finished. So finish it with some oil/varnish blend and get back to work.

Need details? Visuals? I've prepared a pictorial essay of the process that should help you get started. My digital camera codes each photo with the time it was taken. The first photo was snapped at 10:46 a.m. By 11:44 a.m. I was done. And remember: I'd stopped to take photos about the process, and each photo had to be illuminated with our photographic lights. I think the photography took longer than the actual work.

IN GENERAL, MY TOPS BECOME *cupped in use. So I remove the two high hills by working directly across the grain. In this instance the cup is slight, so I started with a jointer plane. If the cup is severe, start with a jack plane so you can take a thicker shaving.*

EVERY STROKE ACROSS THE TOP *should overlap the stroke before. The shavings will give up easily (though I am told that the iron will dull more quickly). Work from one end of the top to the other. Then back down. Repeat until the plane's cutter can touch the hollow in the middle.*

WORK ACROSS THE TOP DIAGONALLY *now, overlapping your strokes as before. Take care at the starting corner and stopping corner – your plane's sole won't have much support. You can proceed with speed during the middle strokes.*

Sᴡɪᴛᴄʜ ᴅɪʀᴇᴄᴛɪᴏɴs ᴀɴᴅ ᴡᴏʀᴋ ᴅɪᴀɢᴏ-
ɴᴀʟʟʏ *the other way across the top. Repeat
these two types of passes until you can
make shavings at every point in a pass.*

Nᴏᴡ ʀᴇᴅᴜᴄᴇ ʏᴏᴜʀ ᴅᴇᴘᴛʜ ᴏꜰ *cut and use
your jointer plane along the grain of the
top. Overlap your stokes and repeat your
passes until you are getting full-length
shavings.*

Yᴏᴜ ᴅᴏɴ'ᴛ ʜᴀᴠᴇ ᴛᴏ ꜱᴍᴏᴏᴛʜ-ᴘʟᴀɴᴇ *your
benchtop, but it's good practice with a
large laminated surface. You can begin
smooth-planing with the grain; there is no
need for cross-grain or diagonal strokes.*

Wʜᴇɴ ᴡᴏʀᴋ-
ɪɴɢ ᴀᴄʀᴏss
ᴛʜᴇ ɢʀᴀɪɴ, *this
is what your
shavings should
look like. Take
the heaviest cut
you can manage
and keep your
handplane under
control.*

Fᴜʟʟ-ʟᴇɴɢᴛʜ
sʜᴀᴠɪɴɢs ᴛᴀᴋᴇɴ
ᴀᴛ **45°** *will look
like thick ribbon.
Shoot for a thick-
ness of .005",
or perhaps a bit
more.*

Iꜰ ʏᴏᴜ ꜱᴍᴏᴏᴛʜ-
ᴘʟᴀɴᴇ ʏᴏᴜʀ
ʙᴇɴᴄʜᴛᴏᴘ, *set
your tool to take
a shaving that
is .002" or less.
You can take even
more if your top is
behaving and it is
a mild wood.*

Rᴀɢ ᴏɴ ᴛᴡᴏ ᴄᴏᴀᴛs ᴏꜰ *an oil/varnish blend. When everything is dry, a coat of wax will
help your top resist glue, but it will make it slippery (a bad thing – hand-tool users don't
want their stock sliding everywhere).*

9 Ways to Plane for Longer Periods

Planing can be strenuous, but if you change the way you work (and the tools you select) you can make life a lot easier.

When I teach classes about handplanes, the climax is a contest where we see who can plane a ¾" x 6" x 12" board to perfection – both to the try square and to the eye.

Last year at one of the classes, one of the young students in the front row took the contest to heart. When he brought his board up to me to evaluate he was out of breath and as wet as a Louisiana underarm.

I thought he had dunked his head in the toilet and was playing a joke on me. Or perhaps he was having a coronary event.

Neither turned out to be true. He was ragged out from planing. It's a common complaint among readers: Planing is hard work. However, I can generally work all day in the shop without increasing my heart rate beyond what it is during a horror movie. You might think it's my age (I'm 40), but I think it's more than that. Over the years I've developed some habits that allow me to work steadily all day. Here are a few:

1. Make sure your bench is low enough. A high bench requires you to use the shorter muscles in your arms, which tire rapidly. A lower bench allows you to use your legs and abdomen more. When I finally lowered my bench to 34" it made a huge difference in my work.

2. Step forward during your planing stroke. When planing a longer board (36" or more), I begin the stroke with one foot in the air and step forward.

The act of dropping my foot begins the stroke. This puts gravity on your side. It looks funny (like a Monty Python Silly Walk). But boy does it work.

3. Traverse as much as possible. Planing across the grain allows you to remove more material with less effort. I'll traverse with my fore plane and my jointer plane. Then a few diagonal strokes with the jointer plane and I'm off to the smoother. The longer I can traverse, the longer I can work.

4. Plan your work around fatigue. One of the great things about hand-tool woodworking is that you can work in short bursts at different tasks and use different muscle groups. For example, I'm building web frames this week. I'll jointer plane the components. Then I'll cut the tenons. Then the mortises. Then I might smooth plane them and assemble them. Then I'll move onto the next web frame.

5. Wax your tools. Paraffin wax on the sole of your tool (or a wipe with a non-drying vegetable oil such as jojoba oil) can do wonders. It reduces the effort to push the tool. And – if you apply it to your tools between each board you plane – you also get a short breather.

6. Sharpen. I'm always amazed at how a sharp tool is easier to push than one that is approaching dull. Sharpening is also a break that can allow you to recover.

7. Use different secondary woods. For the internal guts of your project, consider using Eastern white pine or basswood instead of using poplar or lower-

grade boards of your project's primary wood (i.e. don't use rock maple for your drawer bottoms).

8. Don't smooth plane the inside components. When I plane a carcase side or some internal components, I typically stop with the jointer plane. Sometimes I'll stop with the fore plane (such as on the underside of a large tabletop). Only the surfaces that show will be smooth-planed. This can cut your planing time dramatically.

9. Always use the coarsest tool possible and take the thickest cut that does not cause tear-out. One 6-thou-thick shaving saves time and effort compared to 12 half-thou shavings. If your wood is mild, take a thick shaving.

So how about you? Any suggestions (besides indenturing an apprentice or chugging Red Bull) for increasing your working time?

READER TIPS

■ I would add: Use a narrower and more crowned blade, the rougher the work.

Jeremy Kriewaldt

■ Green red oak … if that makes any sense. Freshly cut, riven quartered red oak. There, that's more specific.

Peter Follansbee

■ One thing that will without a doubt reduce the effort of dimensioning stock, especially larger pieces, is to use wooden planes to start with. I use a jack plane with a 2⅛" blade that has the iron cambered, then a 22" fore plane with a 2½" iron. They are less work for two reasons: One is that they are lighter than a metal plane. Two is that the wood soles will glide over a board with much less effort than a metal plane, no matter how much paraffin is used on the bottom. If you use an antique plane, I firmly believe there is a third reason – that the old tapered irons will stay sharper much longer than a metal plane blade, new or old. And as Chris said, a sharp iron means much less effort than one that isn't. I suppose a fourth reason, if you use antique woodies, is that they can be had so cheaply that it sure will take less time and effort at work to make the money to buy them instead of good metal planes.

That said, I use infilled planes after the woodies to remove and prevent tear-out, and I know through much use that these heavy planes require much less effort than a Bailey-type metal plane on hard and figured wood.

John Walkowiak

■ For certain tasks, wood can be hogged off more quickly and with less effort using tools such as a drawknife or a large chisel before finishing with a plane. For example, I recently needed to put a large chamfer (about ¾" x 1½") on the underside of a cherry tabletop. Once I had marked my lines, I was able to hog off wood very quickly close to the lines, then finish with a few passes with a plane. A good drawknife, sharpened well, is a great asset.

Dave Fisher

■ I too prefer wooden planes and for the reasons John Walkowiak offered above. But I could add one more reason: I find metal planes restrictive in the way you hold them. Wooden planes offer my hands more places to grip the tool. I often hold my jack plane's body, hooking my thumb around the tote. I also pull my planes, especially smoothers, hooking my fingers inside the escapement. I think this staves off fatigue by subtly changing which muscles I'm using.

I've heard the physical fitness benefit of working with hand tools made fun of. If you want a workout, some say, go to a gym. Some say physical fitness is the wrong reason to select a woodworking tool. I disagree. You take the stairs for a bit of exercise. They take longer. Though I understand why some cannot go that route. I actually look at it the other way around. I try to stay in shape so I can work wood the way I want to. If you only work for a few hours per month, consider supplementing your woodworking in the gym or tennis court. Upper body strength is certainly helpful for a woodworker. But not as helpful as "core" strength, the strength of the muscles around your spine (including your stomach). Many athletes are focusing on "core" strength and many exercises and activities are "in" right now for core strengthening.

Maybe the best thing you can do to stave off fatigue is work, or work out, more. Look at it this way: You're not just completing projects faster, you may be saving your life.

Adam Cherubini

"Equating time spent and quality may in fact be empirically false. Painting teachers encourage students not to overpaint a picture, continuing to put paint on the canvas until an initially good idea is buried in a muddy mess."

— Howie Becker (1928 -)
from "Writing for Social Scientists:
How to Start and Finish Your Thesis, Book, or Article"

Taming Handplane Tear-out

*One of the biggest frustrations is when
the grain tears out instead of slicing clean.*

N othing in handplaning is more frustrating than tear-out – which is when the wood rips up in small chunks instead of being sliced clean away. Over the years, I've collected solutions to eliminate it and found the following ones to be the most useful.

No 1: The Answer is in the Branches

Whenever I'm working a booth at a woodworking show, there's a fair chance that some power-tool-only woodworkers will give me some grief. Usually it starts with a few taunts during a handplaning demonstration ("Hey buddy where do you plug that thing in?").

But I always relish the moments when they start to ask real questions. Here's my favorite question (slightly edited to make it saucier):

"So Mr. Handplane guy," they'd say. "Let's say you have a hickory board that's 8' long from a tree that grew on a hill. The board's in wind, and it's got a good crook in it as well. How would you deal with that board?"

"Oh that's easy," I'd reply. "I'd start with my broad axe."

"Axe?" they'd say, confusion spreading across their brow.

"Yup, I'd chop the board into 12" lengths and feed them to the wood-burning stove."

I know this sounds like Southern hyperbole (to which I am prone), but I'm serious when I say that the best way to reduce your tear-out problems (with both hand and machine tools) is through careful stock selection.

About seven years ago I worked with Sam Sherrill and Michael Romano on a project to encourage woodworkers to use lumber in their projects that woodworkers harvested from downed or doomed urban trees.

One of these projects was a large dining table that Sherrill had built using a gargantuan pin oak. The table was nice, but the story behind it was not.

The lumber for the table had come from the enormous, Jurassic-scale branches of the pin oak. The boards were wide (like those from a bole) but they were still reaction wood. Branch wood. Junk wood.

When Sherrill and Romano went to dry the wood and surface it, the wood self-destructed. It

Everybody must get stoned. *When I have some tear-out that I cannot tame, the first place I turn is my sharpening stones. A sharp iron greatly reduces tearing.*

warped, split, you name it. They told wild tales of how it exploded (yes, exploded) in the planer. They lost the majority of what they had cut, according to Sherrill.

That story sticks with me to this day. When I pick my boards for any project. I stay tuned to the grain of the boards at hand. If the grain reverses on itself through the plank a good deal, then I skip the board or saw it into short lengths, which might not give me trouble.

That sounds wasteful. But the most precious commodity in woodworking is not the wood, but the time we spend working (or butchering) it. You can make your work faster and easier just by being a lot more choosy.

No. 2: Look Sharp

For me, sharpening is like changing the oil in my car. It's messy and time-consuming, but you do it regularly or disaster will befall you eventually.

So I'm not a sharpening fascist. I'm a good sharpener, but I don't take more than five to 10 minutes to renew a micro-bevel. But I firmly believe that a sharp iron is the second-best way to reduce tear-out when handplaning.

This belief guides me when I sharpen my tools and regulates the attention I pay to each tool's edge. Here is what my typical sharpening chores look like in my shop:

For me, sharpening begins at the end of a project. With the piece of furniture complete and the deadline pressure off, I take a few hours to sharpen my tools. I always sharpen the iron of my jointer, smoothing and block planes. If I used any chisels for more than a quick pare, I hone them. Then I move through the rest of the tool box. Any joinery planes (such as router, shoulder, fillister and plow planes) and moulding planes that I used get sharpened. I'll also examine my marking knives, jack plane, auger bits and marking gauges. If they're dull, I touch them up.

I do this at the conclusion of the project so when I start a new piece of furniture, everything is ready to go. Anal-retentive? Perhaps. But as I build the next project I don't stop to sharpen unless I damage a tool by dropping it or hitting a nail, or my smoothing plane leaves tear-out.

If my other planes give me tear-out, I can usually wait it out. But tear-out at the smoothing stage of a project is a frustrating battle to fight. You can try a bunch of different strategies to eliminate the tear-out, but the first one should be to hone up your smoothing plane's iron and try again.

No. 3: Think Small

Most handplane geeks know that across the Pacific Ocean there is a culture that is even more obsessed than we are with the mechanics of cutting wood with a plane.

I'm speaking, of course, about the Japanese, who hold handplaning contests where competitors see who can make the longest and thinnest full-width shaving.

They measure the thickness of these champion shavings in microns. And the results are often affected by the weather. A wet day will swell the shavings by a few microns.

Sadly, Western woodworkers have become obsessed by creating ultra-thin shavings, which requires planes to be tuned to a very high note. What's wrong with this philosophy is that it focuses on the garbage instead of the good stuff. The shavings get thrown away, remember? It's the resulting work surface that we keep.

You want to be able to take the thickest shaving you can without tear-out, chatter or requiring you to bulk up like Conan the Barbarian. A thick shaving will get you done with fewer passes of the smoothing plane over your workpiece.

So how thick should your shaving be? Good question. Most people talk about getting shavings that are less than .002" thick. Or they talk about "sub-thou" shavings. Yes, it's all very empirical, except for the fact that few woodworkers really know how to measure shaving thickness. Squeeze a dial caliper hard enough and you can make almost any shaving into a "sub-thou" shaving. Wood compresses. Metal bends.

So I go for visual cues instead.

If the wood is well-behaved, I go for an opaque shaving – that is, as long as the curvature of the cutting edge of my iron is significant enough to keep the corners of my iron from digging into my work.

A SUBSTANTIAL SHAVING SUCH AS *this one reduces the number of passes you take, but it can increase your chances of getting tear-out.*

THIS SHAVING IS ABOUT HALF *the thickness of the thick one. Use this size shaving if you start to see tearing on the surface of your project.*

BEFORE I BREAK OUT THE *sander I try cutting a shaving such as this one. It takes more passes than I like, but it is less likely to tear the grain.*

ALL THREE OF THESE TOOLS *have their bevels facing up. This fact makes them easy to configure to a high angle of attack. It just takes a little sharpening.*

See the photo at bottom left to see what this shaving looks like. This shaving gets the work done fast. If the surface has been flattened by a jointer plane, a shaving like this will dress a surface for final finishing in one or two passes.

If I get tear-out with a beefy shaving, I retract the iron into the mouth of the handplane and extend it until the shaving looks like the photo in the center at left.

This shaving will clean up my surfaces in three of four passes. It usually eliminates tear-out more than the shaving above. But sometimes I need to get nuttier.

And that's when I push my tool to get a shaving even thinner (see the photos at left). This thing is about to fall apart. In fact, it sometimes will fall apart when you remove it from the mouth. Usually, this shaving requires a persnickety setup to achieve. I can't get this shaving with an Anant, new Stanley or Groz plane. They are just too coarse to tune to this high level. This is what you are paying your money for when you buy a premium tool. Premium tools will do this with little fettling. My vintage planes that I've fussed over will do this as well.

The downside to this shaving is that you will be making a lot of them to remove the tear-out on the board. About 10 cycles or more is typical for some small tear-out.

Can you get nuttier? Sure. If all else fails, I can set my plane to remove something between a shaving and dust. These "shavings" don't really look like much. How do you get them? That's easy. When I get my thinnest smoothing-plane shaving possible, I'll rub some paraffin on the sole of the tool. This actually reduces the depth of cut just enough to get the furry, dusty stuff. Beware: Taking a shaving that small will force you into a lot of work. Lots of passes.

But when you need it, you need it.

NO. 4: PERFECT PITCH

After taking a recent course in handwork, Rick Gayle, a reader and professional painter, visited our shop at the magazine and looked over some of the planes in my wall-hung toolbox. He reached up and pulled out the Veritas Bevel-Up Smoother Plane.

"This plane has made all other planes obsolete," Rick said. "Well, that's what my instructor said."

It's a strong statement to say that hundreds of years of handplane manufacturing have been eclipsed by one tool, but I know what Rick's instructor was getting at. When it comes to reducing tear-out, one of the most important weapons is the angle of the tool's cutter – a.k.a. the "cutting angle." And no other tool gets you to a high planing angle as easily.

The higher the cutting angle, the less likely the wood fibers will lift up and tear out. Sounds good, right? What's the catch?

The only practical downside to a high cutting angle is that the tool is harder to push. And that's not too much of a factor when your shavings are tissue-thin. Plus, the high cutting angle works great with well-behaved hardwoods, too.

So what does the Veritas plane have to do with the cutting angle? After all, its cutter seems slung a lot lower than the cutter on a traditional plane. Well, the difference is that the Veritas (and some other block-plane-like tools such as the Lie-Nielsen No. 164) work with the cutter's bevel facing up, while traditional planes cut with the bevel facing down.

This makes a huge difference.

In a traditional plane with the bevel facing down, the cutting angle is almost always set by the frog (the casting that holds the cutter). In almost all vintage metal planes, this angle is 45° (new planes by Lie-Nielsen let you pick a 50° or 55° frog, however).

When you flip the cutter over, the angle the bevel is sharpened at comes into the equation when figuring out the cutting angle. Here's how: The cutter in a bevel-up plane is usually bedded at 12° or 20° to the sole of the plane. Let's use 12° for our example. If you sharpen the cutter so it has a 30° microbevel on it, then you add the angle of the bed (12°) to the angle sharpened on your cutter (30°) to get the cutting angle (42°).

So this configuration would make a bevel-up plane behave much like a traditional bevel-down plane – or perhaps even a bit worse.

But if you sharpen the cutter at 45° instead of 30°, then the world changes. You add the 45° to the 12° and suddenly you have a cutting angle that is 57° – that's fairly steep. And you can achieve that angle (and remove it) with just one quick sharpening.

So what's the best cutting angle for gnarly woods? I've found that with almost all woods, tear-out tends to disappear with a 62° cutting angle – that means sharpening a 50° bevel on your cutter and putting it on a 12° bed in our example.

If you have a bevel-down plane, you get to this high angle by sharpening your iron with a knife edge, which is more work.

No. 5: Button Your Lip

I have held (and used) three of Karl Holtey's revolutionary No. 98 planes. The first thing you notice about these tools is that they are flawless. Holtey lavishes attention on his planes like Gollum on the Precious. Every surface, inside and out, is perfect. Once you take that in, the next thing you notice is the non-adjustable mouth of the tool. It is, by most tool snob standards, big enough to drive a scrub plane shaving through. What gives?

To find out, I sharpened up two planes: My trusty Lie-Nielsen No. 4 with a 50° frog and a mouth aperture between .002" and .0025" wide. Then I sharpened up the Holtey so its angle of attack was also 50°. Then I took a board of nasty, surly Jatoba (it's almost as mean as coconut) and planed it with both tools. Then I turned that board around and planed it against the grain with both tools.

I know this board, and it's about as bad a board as I ever want to work. Most standard-pitch planes tear it out. But both the Holtey and the Lie-Nielsen cleaned it up with no problems – both with the grain and against the grain.

This little experiment calls into question the plane snob's obsession with tiny mouth apertures. (By the way, I'm the chapter president of the local plane snob club.) After planing that Jatoba, I had to ask myself: Do you need a fine mouth for high-tolerance work?

I think the answer is: It depends. I think tightening up the mouth aperture of your plane is just one of the weapons you have in your battle against tear-out. But I don't think it's the doomsday weapon.

The long-held theory about the plane's mouth is that a small aperture is preferred because it will press down the grain of the wood as the cutter slices it. If the mouth is tight, then the cutter will be unable to get under the grain and lever it up ahead of your cut, tearing out the grain. This sounds reasonable, but there's more to it.

The sometimes-forgotten problem with a fine aperture is that it makes your tool more likely to clog, especially if you have the chipbreaker set close. So a tight mouth is usually a time-consuming set-up, unless you have a smoothing plane dedicated to fine cuts.

I start closing up the mouth of a tool only when my other efforts fail: I've sharpened the iron, I've set it to take a fine cut, and I'm using the tool that has a high (62°) angle of attack. If all those efforts fail, then I'll weigh my choices: Tighten up the mouth and face some clogging issues, or get out the card scraper or sandpaper and call it a day.

No 6: Chipbreakers

If you follow the conventional wisdom for setting your chipbreaker, you might hate your handplane.

What's the conventional wisdom on chipbreakers? According to Charles Holtzapffel's seminal 19th-century work on the cutting action of tools, you should set your smoothing plane's chipbreaker .02" from the cutting edge of your iron (other respected sources say to set it even closer) and to have an extremely tight mouth.

This, Holtzapffel says, prevents tear-out.

TIGHTENING UP THE MOUTH APERTURE *of your plane can help in some cases, but you are likely to increase the chance of clogging up the works.*

This, says your neighborhood magazine editor, makes your plane choke.

Chipbreakers can do more harm than good in a handplane. Whenever I'm having trouble with a plane (especially if the plane is choking or refuses to cut), the first place I look is the chipbreaker. Whenever I fettle a new or vintage handplane and the thing won't behave, the first thing I'll do is swap out its chipbreaker with another plane that has a working chipbreaker. In almost all cases, this solves my problem.

So what is the purpose of the chipbreaker? My cynical view is that it became widely used so toolmakers could use a cheap, thin steel cutter and reinforce it with an inexpensive iron or soft-steel plate. This is supported by the odd names given to chipbreakers. Some early sources call them cap irons, double irons, break irons or top irons. In other words, not everyone agrees that they were designed to break chips.

Early planes had thick irons and didn't have chipbreakers, even during the age of mahogany, which is hard to plane well.

In my view, the chipbreaker's primary purpose in a modern plane is to mate with the tool's blade-adjustment mechanism and to aid in chip ejection. Oh, and it exists to frustrate you.

So in what position should you place your chipbreaker? I set mine back about 3/32" in a smoothing plane – sometimes even a little farther back if the mouth is tight. All I'm really trying to do is to prevent clogging.

Which begs the question: Why did I list a chipbreaker as one of the ways to reduce tear-out? Well, I did mention one use for the chipbreaker in a modern Bailey-style plane – it mates with the tool's depth-adjustment mechanism. This mechanism allows you to easily set your tool to take the finest cut possible, which really will reduce tear-out.

No. 7: Skewing

I keep a list in my head of what I call "The Woodworking Mysteries" – things I pretend to understand but are outside my grasp.

One mystery is how a tree can pump water to the furthest reaches of its branches. There are many clues as to how it works, but a complete picture eluded me until recently. Another mystery is about how yellow glue actually works. Again, I've never read a complete and satisfying explanation.

A third mystery relates to handplanes and basic geometry. One common strategy for reducing tear-out in a board is to skew the plane as you make the cut. This strategy was beaten into my head by all my teachers both dead and living. It's repeated on the

LEVER CAP

CHIPBREAKER

THE CHIPBREAKER IS SUPPOSED TO *reduce tear-out, but if it is set too closely, it will clog your plane. When you have a problem with your tool, investigate the chipbreaker first.*

Internet by people I deeply respect and trust. And I do it myself in my work.

But if you do the math, you see how this strategy doesn't make much sense.

Let's start with a fact: The higher the angle of attack when you plane a board, the less likely you are to experience tear-out. Another fact: Skewing a plane in use reduces your angle of attack. Mike Dunbar, the founder of The Windsor Institute, explains this in the clearest way possible. When a shaving encounters a plane iron, the angle of attack is like a hill that the shaving has to walk up. If you walk straight up that 45° hill, that's a lot of work. When you skew the tool, it's like the shaving is walking up the hill at a lower angle. Or put another way, it's a bit like building a road up a steep mountain. You don't make the road go straight up the mountain, you build switchbacks so the vehicles can actually make it up the incline. Skewing reduces the amount of work required – both to plane a board and to climb a hill.

How much does skewing reduce your angle of attack? Skewing a 45°-pitch handplane by 30° will reduce your effective cutting angle to 40.9° – that's significant.

So here's the problem: If high planing angles reduce tear-out, and skewing a plane reduces your cutting angle, then how can skewing the plane reduce tear-out?

Hint: The answer is in the branches.

To explore this seeming contradiction, I did a little experiment. I took a short piece of ash with pronounced grain direction – that is, there was no question about which way the grain was traveling in the board.

I cleaned up one face with a smoothing plane then turned the board around so that I planed against the grain, which is when you are more likely to encounter tear-out. Then I planed the board with a bevel-up block plane. This plane is bedded at 12° and the iron is sharpened with a 35° micro-bevel, so its cutting angle is 47°. The mouth on the plane is wide open, so it's not much of a factor. The tool is set to take a shaving that is about .002" thick.

First I planed the board against the grain without skewing the tool. This cleaned up the board just fine with no tear-out. Then I skewed the tool by 30° (which lowered my effective cutting angle to about 43°) and did the same operation. I tried skewing both to the left and to the right. Two areas of the board tore out grotesquely.

Then I cleaned up the board again and tried skewing the plane at 20°. Tear-out occurred at the same two places but not as badly. So I tried skewing the plane at a variety of angles. And without fail, the more I skewed the plane, the more tear-out occurred.

So how can skewing reduce tear-out?

You have to remember that trees are not manufactured items. They are giant cones made of fibers that grow in different directions as the tree responds to its environment: a hill, a disease, a wind storm. Then we slice them up into shapes suitable for building things, regardless of how the fibers are traveling through the tree.

In some boards, grain can change directions on you a couple times. And the grain can be at odd angles – you cannot assume that all your boards will have grain running from one end to the other – the grain may be traveling at a 20° direction along the face of the board and 10° along the edge. And the grain might be in the shape of a shallow wave.

So there are times when skewing the plane puts the edge in the right position at the right time to deal with that patch of grain.

In my example board above, the two places where the tear-out occurred were at places where the grain rose quickly. So how did I deal with this board? As I encountered the areas that tore out, I straightened out the tool – no skew. When I worked the areas that didn't tear out, I skewed the tool to reduce the effort required for planing.

So the trick with skewing takes us back to the No. 1 way to reduce tear-out: The best strategy is to select the best wood possible and learn to read the grain so you can begin to predict how your tools will behave. Sometimes, the best strategy is to not skew the tool.

PLANING WITH NO SKEW RESULTED *in no tear-out on this ash board.*

PLANING WITH A **30°** SKEW *(both skewing left and skewing right) created this ugly patch of torn grain.*

PLANING AT A **20°** SKEW *(both skewing left and skewing right) created a little tear-out.*

Or put another way: Because grain is irregular, sometimes skewing the plane allows the blade to encounter the grain at a non-skewed angle – and therefore you can plane it without tear-out.

Two Addendums

There is something deeply and dangerously ingrained in our culture about the expression "going with the grain."

Not to get philosophical, but I consider that expression to be the embodiment of our civil culture. That is, if we cooperate with the other people around us, then everything will be OK (taxes get paid, kids go to school, wooden boards get smooth). And If you go "against the grain," then bad things happen (cats and dogs living together, mass hysteria, tear-out).

Here's why this thinking is dangerous: It assumes there are only two ways to accomplish things – either you work with the grain or against it. That's ridiculous.

Some of a handplane's most awesome powers can be unlocked by working across the grain of the board. Working across the grain – what Joesph Moxon calls "traversing" – allows you to easily remove the cup out of a board. Think about that for a second. If you take a cupped cabinet side and plane it "with the grain" all across the board then you will end up with a nicely planed cabinet side that is still cupped.

Working across the grain has another amazing and distinct power: It can eliminate tear-out. Working cross-grained means that your cutting edge is not going to lift up the grain, lever it upwards and tear the wood fibers ahead of your cutting edge (that's the long-winded description of how tear-out occurs). Instead, working across the grain simply severs the fibers. They don't get lifted.

Now, the resulting surface isn't ready to finish. It looks wooly and dull. But it isn't torn out. And your board will be flat.

That's an ideal place to be when you are working difficult woods. To understand why, let's look at how I worked the slightly cupped front of a curly maple blanket chest. First, let's plane this board "with the grain."

WORKING WITH THE GRAIN

First take your jack or fore plane and work the high edges down so the panel is fairly flat. Working with the grain on curly maple will produce some tear-out. Then work the panel with the jointer plane to remove the rough surface left behind by the fore plane. Working with the grain will continue to leave tear-out behind over the entire surface of the board. Then take your smoothing plane and remove the tear-out and tool marks left by the jointer plane. If the tear-out is deep, you will typically need to make 10 to 15 passes over the panel to get most of the tear-out removed. Deep patches will have to be scraped or sanded.

WORKING ACROSS THE GRAIN

Flatten the panel with cross-grain strokes of your fore plane. No tear-out will be left behind. Now follow up with cross-grain strokes with your jointer plane. Begin to work diagonally across the grain, but take care not to work at an angle where tear-out appears. Again, done correctly, you will have no tear-out. Then follow up with your smooth-

ing plane and plane "with the grain." Because there is no tear-out to remove, you only have to remove the hollows and high spots left behind by the jointer plane. With my tools, that typically will be four or five passes over the board.

Working across the grain reduces the amount of work I have to do on a board and it reduces the amount of sharpening I have to do on my smoothing plane. Both are good things.

Now, I would be remiss if I didn't mention the two disadvantages of working across the grain. First, you will splinter the far edge of your board or panel. To remedy this, you can plane a small 45° bevel on the far edge, or leave your board over-wide and rip it to final width after planing. The other disadvantage is that working cross-grain tends to dull your tools faster. But this isn't as big a deal because you are dulling the fore plane and the jointer plane, which don't have to be hair-splitting sharp anyway.

In addition to working across the grain, here's the other weapon you should consider: a small high-angled smoothing plane (as shown above). Tear-out can be localized on a panel. If that occurs, you have several choices: Plane the entire panel some more to remove the tear-out (laborious), scrape or sand the torn-out area (then you'll have to sand the entire panel to make the panel look right), or plane out that small area by working localized.

Short and narrow smoothing planes allow you to sneak into these areas without a lot of extra work. I like to use my little Wayne Anderson high-angle smoothing plane for this job (it's about as big as a block plane). You don't have to invest in a beautiful plane like this one to do the job, however. Any low-angle block plane that has been sharpened with a high angle and a curved cutting edge will work wonders.

The 17-degree Difference

The best weapon in the fight against tear-out: a 62° cutting angle.

When I was first learning to use a handplane, I was both intimidated and skeptical of some of the claims made by the "handplane gods."

The gods claimed they could plane any species of wood, with any grain direction and with any sort of figure in the wood without the wood tearing out. So what was the secret of the gods?

Sometimes it was the tool (usually an infill plane, but sometimes a Bed Rock that had spent some time in a peyote hut in New Mexico getting in touch with its inner frog). Or sometimes it was their sharpening skill and waterstones (#100,000-grit stones, or perhaps the trail of split hydrogen atoms they left in their wake.) Sometimes the secret was their skill – they could plane any board with a piece of tin foil taped to a Monchhichi doll.

But I was skeptical, because these boasts were never accompanied by photographic evidence.

So here's a bit of truth about my own work. I've been handplaning boards for more than 15 years now, and I still fight and struggle with tear-out, even in some domestic species. Usually, the way I deal with tear-out is to choose my wood with extra care and stay away from boards that are going to give me trouble. Careful planning makes for easy planing.

After that, I must say that I have the most success in removing tear-out by using a plane with an iron pitched at a high angle (usually 60° to 62° – whatever my honing guide can manage).

Here's an example: While building a blanket chest for the Summer 2008 issue of *Woodworking Magazine*, I used some kicking tiger maple that I bought from a fellow woodworker's private stash. While machining all the boards, the grain tore out in some critical spots.

Then I flattened all the boards and assembled panels with my jointer plane. It was freshly sharp-ened, pitched at 45° and set for a fairly light cut – .003" or .004" I'd say. The tear-out didn't recede much, but I didn't panic.

That's because I have a plane with a 62° angle of attack that is for just this purpose. The one shown on my bench is the Veritas Bevel-up Smoothing Plane, but don't take that as an endorsement of that single brand. I have a Lie-Nielsen version at home (the low-angle jack) set up identically. And I can even get this 62° angle on a standard old-school handplane by honing a back-bevel on the iron.

I guess what I'm trying to say here is that it's not the tool as much as it is the angle.

The photos below show the results of the high-pitch plane. The tear-out took about eight passes to remove with the tool set to take an extremely thin shaving. I don't think I've entered the realm of the handplaning gods, but when you have small victories like this, it sure makes you feel like one.

HERE IS A SECTION OF *torn grain left by a 45° angle plane in some curly maple.*

HERE IS THAT SAME SECTION *of curly maple after planing it with a tool pitched at 62°.*

Removing Plane Tracks

Here's how to diagnose the problem and the steps to fix it.

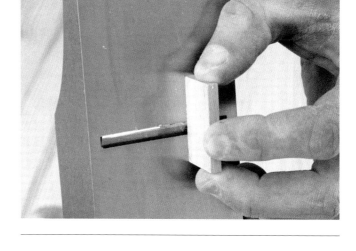

Chris Sundstrom writes: I recently finished smoothing a tabletop with my smoothing plane and if the light hits the top right, I can see lots of lines. I tried to camber the blade before smoothing the top, but I still have the plane marks. Any suggestions on getting the top mark-free?

Answer: This is hard to teach remotely. But it's very easy to show in person. Here are the questions you have to ask yourself and the things you must check to get good results.

■ Is your blade indeed cambered? By how much? And is the camber in the dead center of the cutting edge? Check the camber by holding the cutter up to a strong backlight and balancing something perfectly straight on the edge (I use the edge of a piece of wood that has been freshly planed). To determine if your camber is in the center of your plane's mouth, rub a small shim of wood over the mouth. Where the block grabs is where the camber is.

■ Is the cambered section of the iron in the middle of the mouth of the plane? If the camber is off-center, this usually makes one of the corners of the iron dig into the work, creating a plane track.

■ How thick a shaving are you taking? If you are taking a heavy shaving, that can cause plane tracks. If, for example, your camber is about .002" at the corners and you are taking a .004"-thick shaving, then the corners of the iron will dig in.

■ Are the mouth and sole of the tool free of metallic burrs that could be marring your wood? This is a woefully overlooked problem. Small burrs on the tool (usually on the edges of the sole or on the tool's mouth) create scars in the work that look like plane tracks. And it doesn't take a big burr to make a big problem. If all the other things above check out, feel the edge of sole and behind the mouth. If you can feel any burr you can remove it one of several ways. I like to use a fine file, followed

by sandpaper. Others like to use a sheet of #400-grit wet/dry sandpaper stuck to a dead-flat surface.

When your tool is working right and producing a perfect surface, here are the setup characteristics.

■ The iron should have a camber that is about .002" to .004" at each corner.

■ You should have the iron adjusted laterally in the mouth of the tool so the camber is in the middle. Use a small scrap of wood to confirm where the iron is cutting. Run the scrap of wood over the mouth. It should not cut at the corners and cut only in the middle of the mouth – where the camber is.

■ You should be making a shaving that is .001" to .0015" thick at the center and tapering to nothing at the edges.

■ Your sole and the back of the mouth should be completely smooth and free of burrs.

■ When you use the plane, your strokes should be regular and overlap each other slightly.

Try these things – it takes practice. When you can set up your plane to those parameters, it will leave a nice clean surface. Until you get there, don't be ashamed to scrape or hand sand out the plane tracks.

YOU CAN CREATE A PROPER *camber by using finger pressure at the corners of the iron while sharpening.*

Shooting
Board:
A Review
& Primer

These workshop appliances are used for squaring edges and ends. We review one design and walk you through the basic strokes.

S hooting boards are one of those hand-tool jigs that people talk about (a lot) but few people actually know much about. Whenever I teach, students always clamor for a demonstration of the device, even when I'm teaching something that doesn't directly relate (sawing tenons, sharpening, steaming salmon).

Recently, Bill Kohr at Craftsman Studios (craftsmanstudio.com) in San Diego loaned me a ramped shooting board that he sells in his catalog and store to try. So here's a short review and a brief tutorial on using it to trim end grain.

First things first: Why do you need one? Shooting boards are one of the most powerful trimming tools in my shop. They are the only tool, machine or jig that I have that reduces the length of a board in .001" increments. They adjust the ends of boards so they are square, even if you have only $\frac{1}{32}$" or less to remove. Trimming cuts like this can be tricky on power equipment because the spinning saw blade can deflect in the cut, giving you an inconsistent cut through the thickness.

The shooting board (some call it a "chute board") holds your work in position and 90° to a track that a handplane rides in. Push the plane in the track and it will trim the end of the board until

it is square. (Note: There also are shooting boards designed for long grain, but I generally plane these freehand or use the tail vise and dogs to do the job – but that's a story for another day.)

The shooting board shown here is made by Micheal Connor in Australia from New Guinea Rosewood, a dense and stable material. This shooting board is unusual in that the area that holds the work is ramped about 4° along its length. This ramping spreads out the wear on your plane's iron a little. For example, a $\frac{3}{4}$" x 6"-wide piece of stock will wear an area of your iron that's $1\frac{3}{32}$" instead of a $\frac{3}{4}$"-wide area of your iron.

Having the ramp is nice, but I wouldn't call it a do-or-die feature. My shop-made shooting board is

HERE YOU CAN SEE AN *out-of square board on the shooting board. By showing it to the plane's sole you can see immediately where material needs to be removed.*

flat and made from plywood. It's fine. I just have to hold the stock more firmly and sharpen more often.

The downside to the ramp is that you have to do some extra rigging to support long workpieces that stick out off the shooting board. I have an adjustable planing stop on one of our benches that can be angled to support the work at 4°. Another option is to make a block of wood that has a 4° ramp – easy work on a band saw.

The Connor shooting board is well made and dead-nuts accurate. The fence, which is the most critical component of the jig, is secured in a dado in the ramp, so it's not ever going to move. My only real quibble with the jig is that the finish on the fence and ramp allow your work to slide around more than I like. I'd put a layer of stick-on sandpaper on the fence, which is what I have on my shop-ade shooting board.

SHOOTING BOARD USE

There are many ways to go about using a shooting board. David Charlesworth has an excellent DVD on the topic that explores his simple shooting board and the techniques to use it. I've used his shooting board and his techniques with excellent results. But perhaps because of my American-ness,

I do it differently. Charlesworth takes a pass with the plane, then pushes the work up against the sole of the tool and makes another pass. He repeats this until he makes a full-width cut and is at his destination length. I usually use his technique when reducing boards in length, but do it a bit differently when correcting the angle on the end of a board.

So I start out with a board I've trimmed on our out-of-whack miter saw. It's out by a couple degrees. I put plane in the track (I always use a heavy plane with an iron that is sharpened straight across). Then I put the jointed edge of the board against the shooting board's fence and show the wonky end to the plane's sole. That shows me which corner is high and which corner is low.

Now relieve the corner of the work that will go against the fence. Cut a tiny bevel with a chisel to reduce blow-out on the end. If I am working to a knife line I'll chisel the corner to that line.

I take the plane off the track and position the board so the low corner is flush to the track and the high corner sticks out over the track. Then I push the work against the fence (push hard!) and then place the plane in the track and begin planing. Focus on pushing the plane down and forward. Use just enough force against your workpiece to keep the tool in the cut. If you push too much to the side you'll push the work out of position instead of cutting it.

When the plane stops cutting, the edge is square. Check your work to confirm.

The Connor shooting board is available in both left- and right-hand versions and is $95. For woodworkers who don't want to build one (or question their ability to do so), I think it's an excellent way to get a jump-start on shooting.

TO AVOID BLOWING OUT THE *corner on the outfeed side of your work, chisel a small chamfer there.*

I USE MY FINGERS TO *flush up the board on the shooting board with the waste area hanging out over the ramp.*

HERE'S THE SHOOTING BOARD IN *use. You don't want your work to slide left or right during the cut, so put your back into it.*

Cheating at Jointing Edges

If your skills aren't up to freehanding an edge with a jointer plane, these 'training wheels' are definitely helpful – if you know how to use them.

When I glue up panels from several narrow boards, I use my jointer plane to dress all the mating edges. While our power jointer is fairly well tuned, it's rarely perfect – we have a busy shop. So I find it easier to dress my edges by hand than to fuss with the powered jointer.

My jointer plane has a cambered iron, which allows me to correct an out-of-square edge. (You move the camber over the high spots on the board's edge.)

Until I mastered using a cambered iron in my jointer plane, I used to use a straight iron and a jointer plane fence to dress my edges. Even now, I still use a jointer plane fence on occasion when I only have one or two chances at getting an edge dead-nuts square.

There are two kinds of commercial jointer plane fences. The more common one now is the Veritas Jointer Fence, which attaches to the plane with two rare earth magnets and a post that wedges the whole thing on your plane's sidewall. This fence works with almost any bench plane, though I usually use it with a plane the size of a jack or a jointer (14" to 22" long).

The other kind of fence is like the discontinued Stanley No. 386. This fence attaches to the plane using thumbscrews. The nice thing about the No. 386 is that you can set it for a wide range of angles and it has a knob that I find useful for the edge-jointing process. The other nice thing about the No. 386 is that I can use it with a cambered iron because the fence is under the sole of the tool. The fence centers the plane over a typical edge, where the cambered iron is basically straight. (You can do this with the Veritas fence by adding a wooden block to the fence.)

The No. 386 can be tough to find in the wild. St. James Bay Tool Co. makes one that is similar, but I haven't yet tried it.

HOW TO JOINT EDGES WITH A FENCE

Just like with using a power jointer, there is some technique involved in using a jointer plane fence.

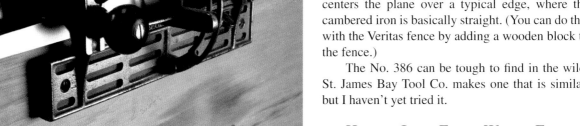

HERE'S THE STANLEY NO. 386 *on a Bailey-style plane. It is robust, accurate but difficult to find.*

Things to watch: The cutter has to be sticking out of the tool dead square. This is why I learned to use a curved iron in my jointer plane – it's actually a more forgiving setup than using a straight iron.

Second: Use your dominant hand to push the plane forward and your off-hand to control the fence. With your off-hand, use your thumb to push the toe down against the edge and use your fingers to push the fence against the face of your board.

Third: What you have to understand about hand-planes is that the tool's cutter sticks out below the sole of the tool. As a result, the tool takes a slightly heavier cut at the beginning of the pass when only part of the plane is on the edge.

I tried to measure this by edge jointing a 30"-long board then measuring the shaving's thickness at five points along its length. At the beginning of the cut (toe engaged only) my cuts were consistently .0055" thick. In the middle and end of the cut the shaving was .005" thick.

That is not much difference. But it can add up. After several strokes the edge develops a gentle curve to it. And that's no good for gluing.

So here's what I do: First remove some of the middle section of the edge. I start the cut a few inches in from the end of the board, and I end the cut a few inches from the end. I'll usually take two passes like this. (This is similar to what David Charlesworth does, though I believe he continues to make passes until the plane stops cutting.)

Then I take a pass all the way through the edge. If I get one perfect unbroken shaving, I'll test the edge with a straightedge or the board's mating edge. If the edge is perfect or is a little hollow in the middle, I'll get the glue and the clamps. If the edge still bulges, I'll remove another shaving in the middle.

One more thing: Some woodworkers poo-poo the jointer plane fence. As Senior Editor Robert W. Lang might say: "You might as well show up on the job site wearing a dress."

IF YOU PUT AN ACCESSORY *face on your jointer fence you can shift the cutting action to the center of the plane, which allows you to use a cambered iron.*

HERE'S THE PROPER HAND POSITION *for jointing with a fence. Your off-hand should push the tool down and against the work. Your dominant hand pushes the tool forward.*

TO REMOVE THE MIDDLE OF *the edge, start the tool a few inches from the end. End the cut a few inches before reaching the far edge of the board.*

Coming Around to Square Edges

The edge-trimming plane excels at creating square and clean edges — if you know how to set up and use the tool.

Thanks to my job and the freelance work I do for *The Fine Tool Journal*, I get to see a lot of specialty handplanes that most people see only in the catalogs or in one of the lusty tomes by Sandor Nagyszalanczy.

But despite getting to actually use a corebox plane and dozens of other unusual and cool forms, I tend to stick with the basics when I build. I use the jointer plane more than any other bench plane, followed by the smoothing plane and block plane. A few other specialty tools – router planes, a moving fillister and a plow plane – round out my personal set.

One plane I've never quite made nice with is the Stanley No. 95, the edge-trimming block plane. This tool is now made by both Veritas and Lie-Nielsen Toolworks in iron or bronze. And though the two brands have some significant differences, the basic form is the same.

The No. 95 is a block plane with a skewed blade and an integral and fixed 90° fence. The idea is that you press the fence against the face of your work and the tool planes the adjacent edge perfectly square to the face.

I've never been fond of the tool – I tend to use my jointer plane to dress edges square to the faces. But during the last few projects I've built I've found the tool in my hand a surprising number of times. I've been using it to plane solid-wood edging square and flush to plywood. I've been trimming face frames flush to carcases. And I've been dressing rails and stiles of doors and face frames before assembly.

That last task finally convinced me that the tool is a gem for a shop that blends power and hand tools. Here's why: When I dress stock by hand, all the edges of my rails and stiles end up planed square from the jointer plane. So the No. 95 sits idle.

But when I dress my rails and stiles with a powered jointer (as I'm doing this week), the edge-trimming plane shines. The goal there is to remove the toolmarks, to keep the edges perfectly square and to not remove a lot of material. The No. 95 accomplishes all three goals with aplomb. Typically, one or two light passes is all it takes to get crisp inside and outside edges on the parts for a frame-and-panel construction.

Here are a few tips for use: First, the setup is key. The iron has to project evenly from the mouth or your edge won't be square. Take some test passes and examine the shavings. Their thickness should be the same on both long edges. Shift the iron around until the tool makes a consistent shaving and a square edge.

Second, press down on the toe of the tool with more force than you would use with a block plane. The plane tends to want to rise out of the cut in softer woods. Also, use one hand to press the tool's fence against the work and use the other hand to press the work against the fence on the opposite side. All this pressure ensures your cut won't go astray, which can be trouble.

Now, despite my crush on this tool, I haven't been able to justify getting both a left- and right-hand version, however. Because my stock is dressed with a planer, it's true on both faces, so I can work with the No. 95's fence on either face of the stock without worrying about grain direction. The tool can be pushed or pulled with ease.

Now if I could just find the same love for my antique chamfer plane I wouldn't feel so guilty every time I open a certain drawer in my toolbox.

Using Router Planes

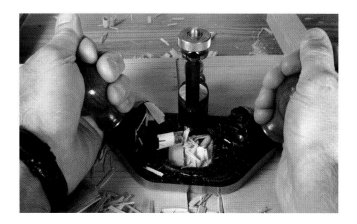

These tools are one of the most useful trimming tools in your shop. Here's how to set them up and use them.

For those unfamiliar with router planes, the tool might seem easy to dismiss when compared to the ubiquitous power tool of the same name. At first glance, the electric router would seem to be superior in all respects because of the wide range of bits and accessories available for it.

But once you understand how to use a router plane, you'll see how it can be used to create and refine your joinery with a precision and control that is difficult to achieve with its electrified cousin.

ROUTER PLANE BASICS

The word "router" comes from the verb "root," and the tool works much like a pig rooting about in the dirt. The router plane excels at cutting joints that are trenches, such as grooves, dadoes and rabbets, and at adjusting joints, such as tenons.

THE CUTTER IS "L"-SHAPED AND *in most cases must be sharpened with its shank hanging off the stone. (Some routers allow you to remove the cutter from its shank to make sharpening easier.) Note that I'm plunging forward and back on the stone – not rubbing side-to-side. This helps ensure my cutting edge will be sharpened straight across.*

Unlike a bench plane, a router plane is simple to sharpen and use. You'll be an expert after your first attempt. Router planes have two kinds of cutters: a flat cutter that can be in a variety of widths, and a spear-point cutter that is designed to sneak the tool into tight corners.

Sharpening these cutters is like sharpening a chisel. Polish the unbeveled part on your sharpening stones then flip the cutter over and polish the bevel flat on your stones. Some woodworkers add a secondary bevel and some don't. Either way, the work is quick because there is not much metal involved. Then insert the cutter into the tool and you are ready to work.

TRENCHING: DADOS AND GROOVES

To make a dado or groove by hand, routers are used in conjunction with other tools. Typically, you saw the sidewalls of the trench, hog out the waste between with a chisel and finish the joint with a router plane. While some woodworkers will simply saw and chisel the joint, using a router plane is superior because it lets you to achieve an exact and repeatable depth. This is important in casework construction because it helps ensure your openings for your doors and drawers also will be square.

STOPPED DADOS

Making stopped dados is simple work for a router plane. First drill a hole that is the diameter of your dado at the location where the dado will stop. Then saw out the sidewalls of your trench, connecting them to the hole. Then remove the waste with a chisel and your router plane.

HALF-LAP JOINTS

When making lap joints, the router plane excels because you can work on both components at once if you like and fine-tune the fit with ease. Making this joint using power equipment is time-consuming and requires wasting several test pieces to get a good fit. With a router plane, you can skip the test pieces. And once you have the depth set on your first joint, its simple to make many of these joints (if your router plane has a depth stop).

FITTING TENONS

One of my favorite tasks for using a router plane is to fit oversized tenons into their mortises. The procedure is similar to cutting a half-lap joint. Clamp your tenon to your bench and place a piece of scrap at the end of the tenon that is the same thickness as your workpiece. Then use the router plane to thin the tenon cheek. Flip the piece over and thin the other cheek using the same setting. Test your fit.

CASEWORK DOVETAIL SOCKETS

Joining a leg and a rail is a classic casework joint. You cut a single dovetail on the end of each rail then make a matching socket in the top of each leg. This joint is difficult or dangerous to make with power equipment because the top of the leg has little surface area to work on. It's also tough to do with a chisel alone because you want the socket to be an exact depth. The router plane is small enough to balance on the top of a leg and is capable of the precision you need.

To make a dovetail socket, cut the sides of the socket with a dovetail saw. Remove the bulk of the waste with a chisel, then clean up the floor of the socket with your router plane – small router planes work best here.

OTHER USES

Once you understand that a router plane is a trenching tool, you can see how it can be used elsewhere in your work: adjusting the depth of grooves

MARK YOUR FINISHED DEPTH WITH *a knife and take small bites until you reach your finished depth. Note that you should work from the edges and into the center to avoid blowing out your edge grain when the tool exits the work.*

MAKING A STOPPED DADO IS *dangerous with a table saw and stack dado cutter. The better choice is a saw, chisel and router plane – or a plunge router and spiral bit.*

in a frame-and-panel door, removing background waste in a carving, making recesses to receive inlay or banding and lots more.

In fact, the router plane is like its electric counterpart in one important regard: Once you've used the tool you'll wonder how you ever worked without it.

HALF-LAPS ARE TOUGH TO CUT *with machinery such as a table saw. It's easy to overshoot your mark because the adjustment mechanism is coarse. Not so with a router plane, which is simple to dial in correctly.*

ADJUSTING YOUR TENONS WITH A *router plane has the added benefit of ensuring that your tenon will be centered on your stock – something you cannot easily achieve with a shoulder plane.*

IF YOUR ROUTER PLANE HAS *a spear-point cutter, it's ideal for getting into the acute corners of the joint. If you don't have a spear-point cutter, clean out what you can with your router plane and finish the corner with a chisel.*

Better Methods of Mating

Making two flat surfaces completely flush is do-able with a plane.

One of the most powerful things about hand-planes is that they allow you to work on small areas of a board with ease. Instead of running the whole board through an electric planer to remove a small area of ugliness, you can usually remove it with a couple well-placed swipes of a handplane.

But exactly where you put those swipes is the topic of this short tip.

Here I'm working on a contemporary Arts & Crafts cabinet in maple for the master bath (OK, you caught me, it's a flipping potty cabinet). One of the structural details of the cabinet is that it has a thick base piece and top cap that are attached to the carcase.

The top cap and base are face-glued to the carcase. Getting the pieces to mate can be tricky. There are a lot of surfaces to get flat, and the fit between the carcase and the top cap and base will be highly visible (to me and my spouse, at least).

To encourage mating, I recommend friction (I think our company's human resources department is going to come down on me for this tip).

First secure the carcase against your bench. Then take the mating piece and rub it vigorously against the carcase. About 10 swipes will be enough. Remove the mating piece and then get yourself down low so you can see light reflecting off the carcase. The high spots on the carcase and its mating piece will be burnished and will be shinier than the low spots.

Mark the high spots with a pencil. Then remove the shiny spots using a plane with a short sole, such as a low-angle block plane. Remove the high spots from both the carcase and the mate. Then repeat the process until you get the fit you want.

RUB THE TWO SURFACES TOGETHER *(as shown above), then mark the shiny high spots with a pencil.*

REMOVE THE HIGH SPOTS USING *a plane that has a short sole. Then go back to rubbing.*

Handplanes & Dovetails

How a moving fillister plane can make dovetailing easier.

When most people think about cutting dovetails, they think: handsaws. However, there's more to dovetailing than sawing. You also need to be mindful of your handplanes when you're dovetailing. They can create gaps or help prevent them.

When I'm dovetailing a carcase, a bunch of drawers or even smallish boxes, my planes are heavy on my mind.

HOW PLANES ARE TROUBLEMAKERS

First, let's talk about how handplanes can cause gaps. If you cut your pins and tails for your box then plane all the inside surfaces, you are asking for trouble with the final fit of your joint. Planing the inside surfaces of your pin boards will make you look like a crap-tacular sawyer.

Don't get it? Think about it for a minute: The interior surface of your pin board contains the wide triangles that fit into your tail board. Every stroke of your handplane on the interior of your pin board makes the joint looser and looser by removing the widest part of the joint (this same advice holds true for the belt-sander crowd).

You can, however, plane the interior surfaces of your tail boards with little consequence. The more planing you do, the more trimming you will have to do after assembly, but this is really no big deal.

So how do you avoid this problem? Plane the interiors of all your surfaces before you cut your joinery. This is a good idea for many reasons. First, planing helps remove any twist or bow in your stock, which makes joinery easier. And second, it prevents your joints from getting looser as you refine their surfaces.

For casework, here's how I do it: First, I dress all my long-grain surfaces with a jointer plane. Then I cut the joinery. I assemble the carcase. Trim

IF I REMOVE ANY MATERIAL *from the inside of this pin board, the joint will become gap-tacular.*

WHEN CUTTING A CROSS-GRAIN RABBET, *first draw the tool backward so the nicker can define the shoulder. This results in cleaner cuts (and is historically accurate, thank you Peter Nicholson).*

the proud nubs. Smooth plane the exterior. Then I am done with it.

Now that we know that handplanes have an evil side, how can we use them to tighten our dovetails? Use a moving fillister plane to cut a shallow rabbet on the inside of each tail board.

THREE ADVANTAGES

This shallow rabbet is the width of your stock's thickness (use a $\frac{3}{4}$"-wide rabbet for $\frac{3}{4}$"-thick stock). And the rabbet is less than $\frac{1}{32}$" deep. What does this rabbet do? It makes transferring your marks from your tail board to your pin board (or vice-versa) much easier. The mating board nests right into the rabbet so you don't have to fuss around with lining things up on the baseline.

It also offers a second advantage: forgiveness. One of the most common problems with dovetailing is that your miscuts show up on the inside of your case or drawer. The small rabbet on the tail board does a nice job of hiding and gaps or small overcuts on your pin board. The result is that the inside of your assembly looks tidier.

And finally, the miniature rabbet also helps you chisel out the waste between the tails. The shoulder of the rabbet prevents you from overcutting past your baseline on the inside of your tail board – this allows you to work more quickly on this part of the joint because you don't have to worry about your chisel drifting past your baseline while chopping things out.

Senior Editor Glen D. Huey showed me this trick with the rabbet in 2002. He was using it to line up pieces of differing thicknesses, but the rabbet also made transferring the marks from one board to another almost foolproof.

I use a moving fillister plane to cut the shallow rabbets. A true moving fillister has a depth stop and fence to regulate the depth and width of the cut – plus it has a nicker that scores the cross grain ahead of the cut. This reduces tearing.

This shallow rabbet, which is used by other dovetailers such as Rob Cosman, is completely worth the effort to make it. It takes just a few strokes with your plane and prevents an endless cycle of fussing and adjusting.

The Veritas Skew Rabbet Plane meets all the criteria to make this cut, as does the Philly Planes moving fillister plane and vintage moving fillisters. The Lie-Nielsen Skew Block Plane (with nicker) is lacking only a depth stop (you have to count the shavings and be careful if you use it for this purpose).

HERE'S THE COMPLETED RABBET. IT'S *less than* $\frac{1}{32}$" *and a bit more than* $\frac{1}{64}$". *It's all you need.*

HERE I'M PUSHING THE RABBET *against my pin board. This makes transferring the shape of the tails a can't miss affair.*

THE RABBET ON THE INSIDE *of the tail board also helps me when chiseling out the waste between the tails. It prevents me from over-cutting past the baseline.*

How I Use a Plow Plane

These traditional planes excel at making grooves and wasting away material for the other planes. Here's how to master it.

Plow planes are some of the easiest joinery planes to use – once you know a few tricks to getting good results. I struggled with the tools until Don McConnell (now a planemaker at Clark & Williams) set me straight years ago with one simple piece of advice:

"Each hand should have a separate job," he said. "One hand holds the fence. The other pushes the tool forward."

Before that point, both of my hands were engaged in job sharing. My hand on the fence was also pushing forward. My hand on the tote was twisting the tool to keep the fence tight on the work.

Here are the other things I've learned about gripping a plow plane over the years:

1. It's a bit like sawing. The hand that holds the tote (or the stock) should be directly lined up with the cut and should swing free. Sometimes this means getting your body over the work (a low bench is helpful here). If your forearm is not in line with the skate of the tool, it's gonna be a roughie.

2. It's a bit like jointing an edge. For my fence hand, I wrap the web between my thumb and index finger around the stems (sometimes called posts) of the tool. I reach my fingers around the fence and touch the work and the front edge of the bench if possible. My thumb is pressing down. If you joint edges of boards by hand, you'll recognize this hand position immediately.

WORKHOLDING: KEEP IT SIMPLE

There are lots of ways to hold your work for plowing. If your end vise and dogs are positioned near the front edge of the bench, you can usually pinch things directly between dogs. You also can use a sticking board, which is a little shelf that holds your work.

Or you can do what I do: Clamp a batten to the benchtop to brace the edge of your workpiece. And plow into the tip of a holdfast. This is very quick for plowing drawer parts – there's no clamping and unclamping and you can work with a bunch of different lengths easily.

SET THE FENCE

Set your plow's fence so it is parallel to the skate and the desired distance from your cutter. The most common cut I make is a $1/4$"-wide groove that's $1/4$" from the fence. Conveniently, the brass section on my folding rule is exactly $1/4$" long, so it's easy to set things at a glance.

BEGIN AT THE END

You can use a plow plane like a bench plane and make full strokes that run from the near end to the far end. But I have found this to be sometimes troublesome. Sometimes the cutter will follow the grain in the board and the tool's fence will drift away from the work. The results are ugly.

WHEN GROOVING A DRAWER SIDE, *this is the setup I prefer. The hold-down acts as a stop. The thick board keeps the board from sliding to the side.*

I THINK THE FENCE SHOULD *be parallel to the skate of the tool. I'll check it at the toe, the iron and the heel.*

Instead, I start at the far end of the board and make short cuts. Each succeeding cut gets a little longer until I am making full-length cuts. The advantage to this is that if your plane wanders, it will only be for a short distance and the next cut will correct the error.

After you are making full-length cuts there's little danger of the tool wandering.

RESULTS AND THEN …

When the tool stops cutting, that means the depth stop is touching your work. So stop stroking. The edges of the groove might be a little furry – that's typical even for the best work. That's why I wait to smooth plane my pieces after I have grooved them. That removes the fur. See the photo below for what the groove looks like when I'm done.

THE FIRST CUT WITH THE *plow begins at the end of the board nearest the camera. This helps prevent accidents you cannot recover from.*

EACH STROKE IS A LITTLE *longer until you are plowing the entire board. Keep the skate in the groove – it's faster.*

THE SHAVINGS SHOULD BE FAIRLY *thick – you don't want to do this all day. These shavings are .015" thick. I could probably go a little thicker in pine.*

WHEN CUTTING IN SOFTWOODS OR *with the grain of a board the groove should be neat like this. When you work against the grain, it can be a little ugly. You can score the extents of the groove with a cutting gauge before plowing when working against the grain. That will keep the top edge clean.*

Planing a Dovetailed Box

By understanding how wood and your planes work, you can plane a dovetailed box all around without breaking out the fragile corners.

There are lots of people who will show you how to handplane the edge of a board. A few less who will show you how to really flatten the wide face of a board. A smaller number will show you how to flatten a glued-up panel and even fewer who will demonstrate how to plane an assembled carcase.

While working on this dovetailed 19th-century schoolbox, I took some photos as I dressed the exterior of the assembled carcase. Have a minute? Get the alcohol!

Really, get the alcohol. A dovetailed carcase has a lot of end grain, so moistening the end grain with denatured alcohol will make the work easier.

Set up a planing platform for your carcase. Big carcases can be sleeved over the end of your bench.

Small carcases and drawers can be worked on a platform that's clamped to your bench.

As with all aspects of hand work, everything begins with stock selection. I try to pick boards with the straightest grain so I can plane them in both directions – from the ends and into the middle of the carcase. This avoids blowing out the end grain of the pins and tails.

If the board has a pronounced grain direction (which stops me from planing both directions) I'll use a plane with a high pitch to do all the smoothing work – this also allows me to work from the ends and into the middle. High-angle planes can ignore grain direction. And, despite what you've read, you can plane end grain with them. Sharpness fixes almost anything.

MOISTEN THE END GRAIN TO *make it easier to plane. I like alcohol because it's not terribly toxic (to your skin).*

SHARP FIXES EVERYTHING. TRIM THE *end grain of the pins. Try not to plane the face grain just yet.*

If THE SURFACE HAS TO *be flat to receive moulding, use your jointer plane to true up the surface. Note: I'm lifting up in the middle of my pass, then working from the other direction. Check your work to ensure things are getting flat.*

WHEN SMOOTH PLANING, WORK FROM *the ends and into the center. Avoid running off the far end, which can result in the ends breaking off.*

TRIM THE PINS

I trim the pins with a sharp block plane. The reason I prefer a block plane is that it's quite narrow, so I can work in small areas without planing away stuff I want to keep. You can skew the blade to make the cut easier. And don't forget the alcohol. Work from the end toward the middle – but just trim the end grain, not the face grain.

With the pins trimmed on both ends of one face of my carcase, I need to make a decision. If I'm going to attach moulding to the carcase, I want to ensure those areas are dead flat. (Bending moulding = no fun.) I'm attaching base moulding around this box so I trued its lower section with a jointer plane. Note that I start the plane at the end, work into the middle and lift off in the middle.

Check your work with a straightedge to make sure you're not creating a hill in the middle of your panel. If you are, work the center only until you get it flat.

SMOOTH THE FACE

Then use a smoothing plane to dress the face. Start from the ends and work to the middle, lifting at the end of the stroke. At the moment your joints' baselines disappear, you're done.

One difficulty people have here is with boards that have a pronounced grain direction. Here's how I deal with it: Plane "with the grain" on the carcase face for the majority of the panel. Lift off only at the very end.

Then come back and dress the other direction with a high-angle plane, working only a short distance. That way if you have to scrape, it will only be a small area. Now plane the other side of the carcase using these same techniques.

TRIM THE TAILS

Now trim the end grain of the tail boards. Moisten the end grain with alcohol and work from top to bottom (or bottom to top). This prevents you from having any blowout on your tailboards. When the tails have been trimmed, grab the jointer plane and smoothing plane and work from the ends and into the middle again, just like you did on the other two faces.

Note: There are other ways to tackle this job. You can plane a small chamfer on all four corners and plane straight through on all four faces of your carcase. This is faster but risky. If your chamfer isn't big enough, you're toast. You also can fetch the belt sander or random-orbit sander. But you wouldn't be reading this book if you like to sleep with your sander.

TRIM THE TAILS FROM THE *top to the bottom. This will not blow out the end grain. However, be careful not to spelch the bottom edge of the box too much (unless it's going to be covered by moulding.*

Raising a Panel by Hand

A couple cutting gauges and a rabbeting plane
are all you need for a simple beveled panel.

When I was about 12, I raised my first panel with a block plane, and I did it by hand. Since that time my voice has gotten deeper, I've gotten furrier and my methods have changed a bit.

Now when I raise a panel, I'll usually rough out the shape on a table saw then I'll clean up the nasty sawblade marks with a skew block plane.

However, raising a panel entirely by hand is actually quite easy to do and doesn't require a lot of tools. All you need are a couple cutting gauges and a rabbet plane. Though I show using both metal and wooden rabbeting planes in this article, I prefer using a metal rabbeting plane because its fence has a longer reach, so I can make a wider bevel.

The first step is to back off the nicker in your rabbeting plane. Though you have some cross-grain cuts to do, the nicker isn't going to help you. Next, set a cutting gauge and your rabbet plane so they are making the same width of cut.

USE YOUR CUTTING GAUGE TO *define the field all around all four edges of your panel. Begin with light strokes then increase your downward pressure to make a fairly deep cut. This bevel is 1⅛" wide.*

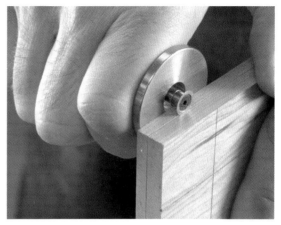

USE A SECOND CUTTING GAUGE *to define the thickness of the finished tongue. Run the fence of the gauge along what will be the backside of the panel. Make this cut on all four edges.*

BLOCK PREVENTS SPELCHING

NOW SINK A RABBET THAT *is the width of your bevel and about ⅛" deep. Work both cross-grain bevels first. Note the block of wood at the end of my stroke that prevents me from spelching the edge.*

THEN SINK THE SAME RABBET *on the long-grain sections of the panel. Don't press too hard on the fence. The skewed blade will pull the fence against the panel.*

NOW SHIFT THE FENCE SO *the tool will take a slightly wider cut – usually ⅛" wider will do it. Why? The bevel is longer than the rabbet. Tip the plane and work the rabbet into a bevel. Work down to the line on the edge of the panel.*

USE A MULLET THAT IS *the depth and width of your finished groove to check the edge. When the tongue fits and the corners look good, stop planing.*

USE YOUR EYES. CLEAN UP *the cross-grain bevels first. Then the long-grain bevels. With each pass of the plane, you'll see the bevels come into the same plane. Sometimes I'll use a rabbeting block plane or skew-block plane to dress the surfaces and clean up any wonky areas. A plane with a skewed blade makes cleaner cuts on the cross grain.*

I Need Something Like a Ruler

Here's a quick tip for planing thin stock when your regular planing stop is just too beefy.

Several years back I was fitting some ¼"-thick mullions and muntins into a door and needed to plane the little suckers to remove marks left by a saw.

Planing thin stock can be a real pain. I've seen how other craftsmen do it. Lonnie Bird drives escutcheon pins into his benchtop (or a planing board) and works against those. It's a neat trick. David Charlesworth attaches the stock to a planing board temporarily with cyanoacrylate. This is fantastic for long stock especially.

Here's how I came up with my method. I like to use planing stops because they are fast. And as I was considering how to plane these little nubbins of wood I was staring off into space outside my shop window and the tool rack hanging before it.

I remember thinking to myself: "For this planing stop, I need a really thin and rigid piece of material. Something with really square edges so they'll grab the work. I need something like a steel ruler."

So I searched over the junk pile in the window well behind my bench. (Note: This is my secret shame area. Though I don't have a tool well in my bench I have a junky window well instead.)

None of the little bits of wood in the window well fit the bill. They were too thick or their edges weren't crisp. Then it occurred to me: Hey moron, why not use a steel ruler?

And so I did, and I continue to use my slender 12" Shinwa to this day. It works great. I clamp it to the bench and go to town. (And now to go get some ginseng to improve my acuity.)

HERE YOU CAN SEE HOW *I use my regular planing stop, a clamp and a ruler to create a nice stop for thin boards.*

In the End, End Grain Bites

Try to work the face grain whenever possible. End grain is a bear.

Whenever I get into some serious hand-work, I always try to boil down the processes so that I can 1) remember it myself and 2) occasionally explain it to others (including my children, who are slack-jawed with boredom).

As I was cleaning up the half-lap joints for a Stickley 603 tabouret on my workbench, I was reminded of one of the guiding principles: Don't work the end grain unless you have to. End grain is unruly. It is usually confined to small surfaces that are hard to work accurately. And working it carries the risk that you will rip out chunks of precious face grain as well.

This is why I don't own any side-rabbet planes. In all my years of working wood, I have honestly never encountered a situation where I had to have those tools and no other tool would do. (Boy they look cool, though.)

Here are some other examples of this principle at work:

■ If a dado is too skimpy, I'll thin the mating shelf's face grain instead. The face grain is so much easier to plane, my tools don't have to be as sharp, my work is less at risk and it is another chance to remove tear-out in the shelf. If I have a lot of material to remove, I'll slightly bevel the underside of the shelf. No one will ever see it, and it's fast.

■ Same goes for rabbets. Avoid planing the end grain of the mating board. Plane the long-grain edges instead.

■ When fitting a face frame to a carcase, I'll tend to make the stiles 1" too long. This creates "horns" on the frame assembly. After attaching the face frame I saw the horns flush (the horns are end grain) and plane the long grain of the rails. I do the same thing when building doors. Crosscutting is easier than planing end grain.

So when I was fitting the first half-lap shown in the photo above, I cut my shoulders just a hair tight. So I took two swipes on the face grain on the edge of the mating piece. Perfect fit.

By PLANING THE LONG-GRAIN EDGES *(instead of the end grain in the half-lap), fitting this joint was far easier.*

Fancy French Footwork

An interesting feature of old workbenches makes planing across the grain just a little easier.

One of the best things about building old-style workbenches (like Andre Roubo's bench shown in the photo above) is that there are little lessons you learn by using them. At times, you learn the lesson unconsciously and it takes a couple years for you to even learn that you learned it.

One morning I was flattening the panels for the blanket chest I'm building for the Summer 2008 issue of *Woodworking Magazine* by planing them directly across the grain – what Joseph Moxon calls "traversing" in his 1678 book the "Mechanick Exercises."

So I'm minding my own beeswax while traversing, and I notice something I've been doing for a while without really thinking. While traversing, I wedge my left foot under the workbench's stretcher, and I use that foot to help pull my body forward on the push stroke.

So I paused and I pulled my left foot out from under the stretcher and tried planing with both feet planted on the floor instead. That felt a lot like working. So I wedged my foot back under the stretcher and returned to work.

Did Roubo design this workbench with this little detail in mind? It's hard to say. My limited understanding of Roubo's 18th-century French hasn't uncovered any reference to this detail of his workbenches. But the stretcher's location has always been curious to me – it's only 5" off the floor. Other benches I've worked on (and constructed) put the stretcher considerably higher off the floor.

Why would you put the stretcher higher? A stretcher that is higher (and wider) is more likely to resist racking forces when you are planing on the workbench. So how does my workbench resist rack-

ing? By putting most of its strength in the top of the bench. The legs are tenoned into the top so the lower stretcher doesn't have as much work to do.

If you have a low stretcher, give this footwork a try and let me know what you think.

RESPONSES FROM READERS

When I constructed my Roubo bench a few years ago, I followed the guidance in the magazine article pretty close. Being a new woodworker then, I didn't question the stretcher height from the floor. After using the bench for a few years, I always find my foot underneath the stretcher. Fast forward to a little more experience: I am now in the middle of constructing a Roubo/Holtzapffel bench – a big bench with a twin-screw vice. During the design, I particularly paid attention to the stretcher height off the floor as that has become something I've grown accustomed to using. *Roderick Drumgoole*

Question: What does your foot do with a stretcher that is higher off the floor? Is your balance off? Does your foot slip forward on a return stroke? *The Village Carpenter*

Answer: I can't do this on my European bench where the stretcher is 13" off the floor. It does work with the other benches, such as the Holtzapffel from *Woodworking Magazine*, which is 6" off the floor.

With my foot wedged below the stretcher, I'm actually quite balanced. My foot stays wedged there on both the thrust and return – though on the thrust my toe isn't pushing very hard against the stretcher. It feels a bit like using a rowing machine.

Working Round Tabletops

The offcuts from sawing a round tabletop can assist in holding it for planing.

Preparing small tabletops or irregular-shaped tops for finishing can be difficult with hand-planes. If the top has a lot of mass, you can usually count on friction to help hold the top in place. Or you can screw it down from the underside – assuming the underside is not a show surface.

But sometimes the best solution is to make some cauls to grip your work, which is what I did this morning in the shop to plane the top of some 18"-diameter tabletops for the Spring 2008 issue of *Woodworking Magazine*. The cauls are made from the scrap parts that fell off when I cut the tops to rough shape on the band saw.

Then I skipped the scrap pieces through my planer to reduce their thickness (I also could have used a jack plane). Then I bored ³/₄"-diameter holes in the cauls so they would press-fit over my ³/₄"-diameter round dogs in my benchtop. Finally, I pinched the top between the two cauls using my wagon vise (though any end vise can do the trick).

HERE YOU CAN SEE HOW *the bench dog is buried in the caul and that the caul is thinner than the top.*

When I've done this on workbenches with square dogs, the solution is to cut the pointy end of the caul so it is flat. Then you brace the flat against your square dog.

No matter how you rig your cauls, pinching the work between two cauls has some advantages, as long as you don't use too much pressure. With two cauls you can rotate the top to work cross-grain if necessary or move the top so it's more convenient to plane.

This arrangement works great with belt sanders. It's not necessary if you use a random-orbit sander to prepare your work. Then you can just place the work on a blanket and get to work.

RESPONSES FROM READERS

Vises with large jaws (such as twin-screws) often have multiple dog holes in the top of the outer jaw. If there are corresponding holes in the bench-top, three or four dogs will hold a round board very securely. Also, Festool's MFT tables have dogs which make this sort of thing very easy.

Narayan

Question: Thanks for the tip. Always looking for ways to get more out of my bench. Now, what's your tool of choice for cleaning up the edges – router? files? spokeshave? *The Village Carpenter*

Answer: It depends. Typically for round tops I'll use a router compass followed by a spokeshave or scraper. If the top is irregularly shaped (an ellipse perhaps) I'll use a pattern bit in a router and a pattern. Then spokeshaves and scrapers.

If it's a funky top (think: amoeba), then I'll use rasps, shaves and scrapers. Sometimes files.

Crazy for Chamfers

This detail lightens the look of a piece and is easy to create with a special plane — or freehand.

Anyone who has worked with me for about five minutes knows that I really like chamfers on my work. Stop chamfers, such as those found on early English and American work, are particularly attractive to my eye.

I also like through-chamfers, and my favorite tool for making those is the Veritas Chamfer Guide. This $22 accessory for the Veritas Block Planes is beyond clever. It beats up and steals the lunch money of traditional chamfer planes. I have a nice English version of one of these old planes that I bought years ago from Patrick Leach, and it just does not compare.

The genius of the Veritas guide – patented in 2003 – is that you can set it to make chamfers up to ½" wide with unerring precision. Set the guide to create the chamfer you want. Keep stroking until the plane stops cutting. Victory!

There is one downside to the guide: Veritas doesn't make it for other brands of block planes. I'm sure it would be a nightmare for the company to offer it for other brands because there are as many kinds of block planes as there are flavors of gum.

I tried fitting the Veritas guide to some of the Stanley block planes in my shop and could find only one (the venerable Stanley No. 65) where this worked well. The only problem with the retrofit on the Stanley No. 65 was that I had to scavenge a knob off my Veritas plane to prevent the host from rejecting the transplant. So that's not much of a solution.

So if you do have a Veritas block plane, I highly recommend this attachment. If you don't own the plane, I highly recommend you try freehanding things. When I'm working in my shop at home and am sans Veritas, I use my old Sandusky jack plane instead.

Those chamfers aren't as tidy, but they look good enough. And the nice thing is I can make freehand chamfers at any angle, not just 45°. To make freehand chamfers, lay out the two lines – one on the face of the board and one on the edge – with a marking gauge. Then go to town with the jack. When you get close to the scribe lines, switch to a plane that takes a fine cut to finish the chamfer.

Both techniques work better (for me) than a router with a chamfer bit, which can leave nasty chatter marks that have to be sanded or planed out anyway.

FREEHAND CHAMFERS HAVE A SLIGHT *irregularity that pleases the eye. If you are going to chamfer a moulding on a case piece, chamfer a long stick, then cut the miters from that so the corners will match.*

Sticking Boards & Bodger's Mitts

A sticking board helps you make mouldings. A bodger's mitt helps prevent blisters.

Moulding planes are some of the coolest planes in a toolkit. Each one is like a modern router, but without the dust, the roaring universal motor and a bit spinning at 20,000 rpm.

Like all hand tools, moulding planes require more skill and initial set-up than a power tool. Plus, you need the right accessories – some people call them appliances – to make them shine. And because many moulding planes have irons that have complex shapes, they can be intimidating, even to a veteran sharpener. But once mastered, moulding planes are addictive. Now, I probably wouldn't want to trim out a house with moulding planes, but when making short runs of mouldings for a cabinet, they're efficient tools because they are always set up to make their profile. You just grab them and go.

The most useful accessory for moulding planes (and planes that form rabbets) is a sticking board. There are lots of forms of sticking boards. Mine is a long section of stout wood with a low fence along one long edge. It also has some kind of way of stopping the work at the end of it. Examples I've seen have a wooden block with a nail jutting out. Mine has four screws that I can adjust up and down (or remove) to match the profile of the moulding and keep out of the way of the tool.

First secure your sticking board to the bench (there are many ways to go about this). The example in Robert Wearing's classic "Making Woodwork Aids & Devices" has a spine that runs on the underside of the sticking board. The spine hooks over the front edge of the benchtop and is secured in the face vise. My sticking board is pinched between dogs.

With a moulding plane you plane a little differently than with a bench plane. Begin with short strokes up by the stop. Gradually increase the length of your strokes. This process creates a track for your plane to ride in and makes cleaner profiles. Note that my left hand is pushing the tool against the fence. My right is pushing forward. Each hand has but one job.

Speaking of hands, the leather thing on my right hand was given to me to try by Charles Murray, the hand-tool guru for the Woodworkers of Central Ohio (WOCO). One of the other members had found a reference to it in an old book where it was called a bodger's mitt. So, of course, they made some of them to try out using scraps of leather from Tandy Leather and some snap closures.

The bodger's mitt is supposed to protect the right hand when using planes, particularly moulding planes. So last week I gave it a try. I did half a run of moulding without the mitt. Then the rest of the run with the mitt. I like the mitt!

HERE'S A LEATHER BODGER'S MITT *on my right hand. After using it for several months I think it's comfortable (it is a bit sweaty in the summer).*

Build George Ellis's Planing Board

If your benchtop is iffy in the flatness department,
this accessory can help.

I've looked at a lot of old workbenches, and I've only seen a few that exhibit signs of being flattened. I always look at toolmarks on the benches and what I typically find are toolmarks that are recent and some that are quite old – based on the patina of the gouged wood and the amount of grime that has accumulated.

So benchtop flatness is a red herring, right? Maybe. If you work a lot on a bench that isn't flat, you'll see it affect your work. A low spot in the top will prevent you from planing the middle of a board. You'll only be able to plane the ends of the board.

One possible solution is that woodworkers who toiled on less-than-ideal benches would use a planing board. Planing boards are thick assemblies that you lay over your benchtop and are set up to restrain the work. I first stumbled on them in the book "Modern Practical Joinery" by George Ellis. Despite its "modern" title, it's an old book.

I made a planing board using Ellis's description and text, and it works quite well. It's an unusual piece of work: It's a frame assembly and inside the frame are seven slats that float in grooves and can be slid a bit back and forth. Here's where it gets a bit odd: The frame's rails and stiles are 1⅜" thick; the slats are 1½" thick. The slats are proud on the bottom of the planing board. The top of the planing board is cleaned up flat and flush all around.

The differing thicknesses, I believe, might keep the whole thing flatter in the end. The center of the planing board will always be planted on the benchtop. You can easily true the underside because it is proud and then flip the thing over and true the whole thing. That's a working theory. I have a few others as well.

There are two planing stops at the end that adjust up and down. You can also restrain work for cross-grain planing by inserting wedges between the slat and pushing the work up against the wedges. This works great.

And how do you keep the planing board on your bench? The book is quiet on this. I have mine

HERE YOU CAN SEE THE *joinery of the planing board before it is assembled. It's like a door with loose slats instead of a fixed panel.*

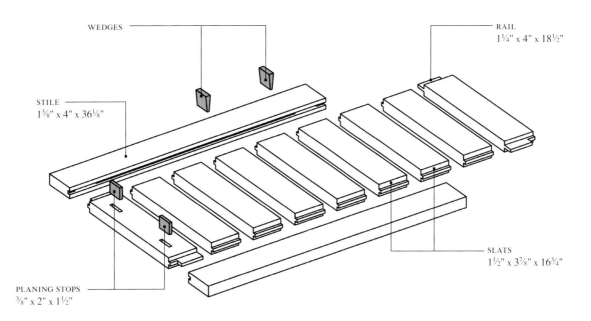

WEDGES

RAIL
$1\frac{1}{4}$" x 4" x $18\frac{1}{2}$"

STILE
$1\frac{3}{8}$" x 4" x $36\frac{1}{8}$"

SLATS
$1\frac{1}{2}$" x $3\frac{7}{8}$" x $16\frac{3}{4}$"

PLANING STOPS
$\frac{3}{8}$" x 2" x $1\frac{1}{2}$"

PLANING BOARD

pinched between dogs and against a dog at the back of the bench. I'm going to change this arrangement eventually. I plan to put a hook on its front edge (just like on a bench hook for sawing). Then I'll push the thing against a planing stop in use. There's no need to have a tail vise.

CONSTRUCTION DETAILS

Here's the cutting list for a planing board that will handle stock that is sized for typical furniture work. If you build bigger pieces of furniture (armoires) then you'll need a bigger planing board.

- 2 Stiles: $1\frac{3}{8}$" x 4" x $36\frac{1}{8}$"
- 2 Rails: $1\frac{3}{8}$" x 4" x $18\frac{1}{2}$" ($1\frac{1}{4}$"-long tenon on both ends)
- 7 Slats: $1\frac{1}{2}$" x $3\frac{7}{8}$" x $16\frac{3}{4}$" ($\frac{3}{8}$" x $\frac{3}{8}$" stub tenon on both ends)

After dressing your stock, plow a $\frac{3}{8}$" x $\frac{3}{8}$" groove down one long edge of each stile. Cut $\frac{3}{8}$"-thick x $1\frac{1}{4}$"-long haunched tenons on the ends of the rails. Cut matching mortises in the stiles. Cut the $\frac{3}{8}$" x $\frac{3}{8}$" stub tenons on the ends of the slats.

Bore the two $\frac{3}{8}$" x 2" through-tenons in one rail for the planing stops.

Dry-assemble the frame, clamp it up and make sure the slats will move when the assembly is put together. If everything works, glue up the frame and clamp it. When the glue is dry, dress the underside of the planing tray flat. Then flip it over and dress the entire top surface flat. Fit your planing stops and get a few wedges you can insert between the slats.

PLACE WEDGES BETWEEN THE SLATS *to create stops for your work.*

THE STOPS CAN BE USED *when planing stock with the grain or across the grain.*

HISTORY & PHILOSOPHY

The 12-step Program for Smoothing Planes

While making gossamer shavings is fun, getting the work done is also important.

The first handplane I ever bought was a *Popular Mechanics* block plane I purchased one night at Wal-Mart. There was no blade-adjustment mechanism. No adjustable mouth. And the iron was so soft that it might actually have been made of iron (instead of steel). The tool was a bonafide piece of junk.

As I set out to use the plane on a project I expected to be frustrated. (That's the way the story usually goes, don't you know.) But surprisingly, the plane actually worked, and I can remember clearly using it to trim some apron pieces flush on a low sitting bench I was making. One of the shavings was like gossamer; at that moment, I was hooked on planes.

Like many woodworkers, I became as obsessed with those shavings as I did with the tools that made them. No matter what plane I bought, I fussed and fussed with it until it made those magical .001"-thick shavings. My Stanley No. 5 Type 11 jack plane (a $12 flea market special) got souped up with a new iron, and I worked the sole until the plane was per-

---

"Have no fear of perfection — you'll never reach it."

— Salvador Dali (1904 – 1989)
Surrealist painter

---

fect. Same with my jointer plane. And even my rabbet planes. And on and on.

It took me a few years to realize what a huge waste of time a lot of that tuning was. With all my planes set to take fine shavings, it took forever to get anything done – further cementing the myth that hand tools are slow. Then one day I had my second epiphany with handplanes, and I remember it as clearly as my first.

I was smoothing up the side of an entertainment center and there were some serious low spots. I worked the piece for almost an hour before I started thinking about buying a belt sander. Something clicked in my head. I put down my super-tuned smoother and picked up my jointer plane. I set it to take a thick .006" shaving. In two passes, the whole side was true. Then I picked up my smoother again – still set to take a fine shaving. In two passes, the whole side was shimmering and gleaming and perfect. Right then my world turned upside down. Instead of focusing on tuning a tool to take a fine shaving, I focused on tuning my coarse tools to take a thick shaving without chattering. I started using my coarse tools more and my fine-set tools less. And I became a much faster builder.

So many woodworkers I know are obsessed with fine shavings. It seems proof perhaps that we are masters of our tools because we can make them perform this parlor trick. If this sounds like you I encourage you to try something. Take a board fresh from your powered planer. Flatten it with a finely set smoothing plane and count the passes you make to get it ready to finish. Now flip the board over and set your jointer plane to take a thick shaving. How thick? As thick as you can take while still easily maintaining control of the tool. Flatten that board. Then come back with a smoothing plane. Count your strokes.

Fascination with Fore Planes

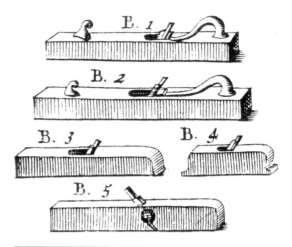

One of the most powerful handplanes is also the most ignored by the modern woodworker.

In 2008 I got deep into reading Joseph Moxon's "Mechanick Exercises" – the first English-language treatise on the craft of joinery. Published in 1678, the "Exercises" cataloged the tools and practices of the blacksmith, joiner, house carpenter, turner, bricklayer and those who make sundials.

For the modern reader, the book is a slog. The printed English word of the 17th century seems convoluted. Sentences run on longer than we are accustomed to, and the sentences are interrupted by asides that wander a bit.

Truth be told, you get used to it after a few pages. Then the hardest thing becomes the occasional unfamiliar word – for example, "dawks" means "hollows" – and the odd tool. My favorite example: the pricker. The pricker is a marking tool that perhaps resembles a square-shanked awl. But in Moxon's glossary he says the vulgar term is "awl" and instead the proper word is "pricker." So as of today, the filthy word "awl" has been banished from our shop in favor of the much more polite "pricker."

Every time I read Moxon I learn something interesting and useful. But what is most fascinating is how little has changed in 330 years. The tools and the methods are familiar – once you strip away the "shall yets." Except for one important difference.

What strikes me during this reading of Moxon is his affection for the fore plane – a tool that is typically 16" long, which is shorter than a jointer plane and longer than a jack plane. The fore plane has a blade with an obvious curve and is used to quickly remove material.

Moxon spills more ink on the fore plane and its use than he does on any other single plane. He discusses how it is used with its iron set both rank and fine. How it is moved across the board. How it trues faces and edges. The jointer plane gets some discussion, but not nearly as much as the fore.

Then there's the discussion of the smoothing plane. Here is the entire entry on the smoothing plane (cleaned up a tad):

"The smoothing plane marked B.4 must have its iron set very fine, because its office is to smooth the work from those irregularities the fore plane made."

That's really about it. There's no protracted discussion of wispy shavings or strategies to reduce tear-out (though Moxon suggests that high planing angles are important in one part of the book).

Our obsession with smoothing planes might be thoroughly modern. Or perhaps there's another way to look at this (bear with me, I know this is getting long).

Recently we had Matt Grisley from Leigh Industries in our shop to demonstrate his company's new dovetail jigs. During our day together, he made an astute observation about hand work. I wrote it down after he said it. And it went something like this:

"What's interesting to me is how woodworkers who love hand tools also love the heavy machinery – the big planers, jointers and table saws. And they don't seem to have much affection for the power hand tools, like the router and biscuit joiner."

And he's right. I am deeply indebted to my planer and jointer. I would get rid of five of my smoothing planes before I got rid of my jointer and planer. (Don't worry; I'd still have at least five smoothers left.)

I am obsessed with my heavy machinery like Moxon's workmen were attached to their fore planes. For these are the tools that get the brute work done, that make woodworking possible. The finesse work stands on the shoulders of the fore plane and machinery. Now if you'll excuse me I'm off to the shop to fiddle with my square, saw and pricker.

New Year, New Tools, New Tolerances

Trying new tools (and techniques) has its risks and rewards.

Every Tuesday night we ritually torture our children with a meal that we call "New Food Night." The kids have to eat something they've never eaten before – it can be as simple as coq au vin, but we've also ranged as far as ostrich and bison. In exchange for eating the new dish, the kids get one U.S. dollar and a small prize, usually a small plastic animal.

After a couple years of this schedule my girls have become accustomed to it (or they are suffering from Stockholm Syndrome). But some nights are rough. The most difficult dinner of all was when I made homemade chicken noodle soup. Tears – enormous ones. Shaky bottom lips. Slumping in the seats to a horizontal position.

All for chicken, wide egg noodles, carrots, celery and broth.

A FORM OF SELF-TORTURE

Every year I torture myself on Jan. 1 by forcing myself to put away some beloved tools and start using tools that I haven't embraced. For 2006, I put away my traditional bench planes and used Veritas bevel-up planes: a jack, jointer and smoother. After 12 months of hard use, I'm glad I did it. I now know the limitations and advantages of these tools. First the bad: I still don't dig the location of the adjuster (it's too low) or the shape of the handles (which I can fix with a rasp). But then the good: I really like the low center of gravity. I also like how you can tighten up the mouth to admit one-half of a gnat's

hinder with little effort. And I really like how you can hone an ultra-high angle on the blade to make a plane that mocks interlocked, reversing exotic woods.

So on Jan. 1 of 2007, I set the bevel-up tools aside and took out my Sauer & Steiner unhandled York-pitch smoothing plane. I have made peace with this tool and it is a great user, but I don't grab it automatically whenever I need to do some general smoothing. Maybe I'm not familiar enough with the grip – there's no tote on this plane. Plus, there's no mechanical blade adjuster or lateral adjustment lever.

But whether the thing turns out to be chicken soup or coq au vin, this is its year.

Its first major task was finishing up the top of an English workbench for a photo shoot on Thursday. After completing the bench, I started building the accessories you need: bench hooks, a sticking board and some stuff that grabs round and octagonal work. The sticking board, which is designed for holding long, narrow work for shaping, is about 6' long. When I placed it on the bench I noticed it wasn't sitting flat on the top. At first I thought it was the sticking board that was bowed. But after jointing the sticking board again and checking everything with straightedges, I determined there was a hollow in the middle of the benchtop, right up at the front of the bench.

This is the worst place for a hollow in your benchtop. Period.

So I went to work with a jointer plane, working diagonally across the top both ways. Then I worked with the grain of the top with the jointer plane, and then with the Sauer & Steiner smooth plane. Sweet. I checked my work with feeler gauges. I did this out of curiosity – not habit. I get asked all the time how flat a benchtop needs to be for handwork. Until today my answer has been: Flat enough so your work doesn't bow under planing pressure.

That's not a good answer when dealing with readers who need an answer that has a number attached to it. So with the feeler gauges and the straightedges I determined that I shoot for a top that is flat in the critical working area (the front half of the bench) to about .004" along 6'. Is that extreme? I don't know. But that's when my work started to behave predictably under the planes.

So is this a good start to the year? I don't know. I'll have to noodle it.

A HOLLOW RIGHT BELOW WHERE *the jointer plane is sitting was causing me endless trouble. A flat workbench makes a difference.*

THIS ENGLISH-STYLE WORKBENCH IS EXCELLENT *for planing faces and edges – once you get the top flat enough.*

Without Power – But Not Powerless

The only things stopping you from handwork are you and darkness.

We had two crippling power outages in our office during 2007. When the electricity goes out here, the computer screen flickers. Then your left hand twitches to hit the keys to save your work. Then the building goes dark. Except for a few groans, the building gets as quiet as a cathedral as work halts.

Except for me, of course.

At the time, I was between big projects in the shop, so I was working on a few small-scale pieces to clear my head. I built a small dovetailed silverware tray using some scrap cherry and I've built a couple picture frames for some paintings that have been sitting around the house.

My taste in art has always been a bit on the odd side. Lucy, my wife, and I prefer to buy what most people call "outsider art," a term I've never liked. (Kinda like the way I hate the word "blog.") These artists are street preachers, visionaries, homeless or mentally ill. We started buying this stuff when we lived in South Carolina and were exposed to artists Howard Finster, R.A. Miller and a few others. We've amassed a small collection during the last 17 years and have recently plugged into the same sort of network here in Cincinnati.

A GOOD EXCUSE

One of the projects was an Arts & Crafts-style frame for a painting by Barb Moran that we purchased at a street fair in August. It's always a challenge to get into the shop when you're also trying to get a magazine to the printer. But there is nothing like a power outage to change your priorities.

While the table saws, routers and miter saw were quieted, I spent the afternoon fitting the mortise-and-tenon joints to this frame and preparing the surfaces for finishing. Thanks to the afternoon light from our shop windows, the tear-out in the white oak was easy to see and remove. It was, all in all, a nice break from gerunds and dangling participles.

The funny thing about the power outages is that they take down all of our systems except for the emergency lights and the electric auto-flush toilets in our building. I suspect that senior editors Glen D. Huey and Robert W. Lang are making plans to hotwire the building's commodes to our shop's sub-panel in case of a third power outage.

Not me. I'm kind of looking forward to it. I just first need to get my left hand in shape to be able to hit the "save" key a little faster.

EVEN WITHOUT ELECTRICITY, WORK CONTINUES *in our shop. Here I'm prototyping a picture frame for a piece of folk art for our family room.*

The Sindelar Tool Collection

*After collecting tens of thousands of the world's most
beautiful tools, cabinetmaker John Sindelar is ready
to show them off in a new tool museum.*

John Sindelar stands in front of a door at the back of his thriving cabinet and millwork shop in Edwardsburg, Mich. The door opens into blackness and Sindelar turns around for a moment before entering.

"This room," he says with a sly grin, "is like church to me."

He flips on the light and walks into the small paneled room. The room is filled with antique tools. No, strike that last sentence. The room is filled with tools that you never thought existed or that you would see in person. Tools that you have only heard about, seen in auction catalogs or drooled over in Sandor Nagyszalanczy's books "The Art of Fine Tools" or "Tools Rare and Ingenious" (Taunton).

And not just a few tools. Hundreds and hundreds of vintage tools lined up on tables, shelves and a display case made from a harness for an elephant. Few of the tools are under glass. In addition to the tools, there are two comfortable chairs against one wall and under a panel of stained glass. And that is a good thing because I have to sit down.

This is just one of the five rooms filled with tools. Sindelar has so many tools ("Probably, tens of thousands," he guesses) that he keeps a significant number in storage. In one adjoining room there is a wheelbarrow filled with a stack of plow planes.

In another room there's a wall of rare infill miter planes. In the front room – the biggest room – the walls are lined with vintage workbenches. Tools cover the benches, axes cover the walls, the floor is covered in boxes (that are filled with tools).

That this collection exists is remarkable. Getting to see it is something else. And what Sindelar has planned for it just might change your vacation plans someday. Sindelar is actively making plans to build a 30,000-square-foot public museum and woodworking school that will show off his collection and teach woodworking skills.

He has three locations in mind – near Williamsburg, Va., Harrisburg, Pa., or perhaps in North Carolina. He sketched up plans for the building, which would look like a French castle, and turned them over to an architect to develop. He wants the museum open for business by 2010.

Opening a tool museum on this scale sounds like an unlikely feat for anyone. But once you meet Sindelar and hear his story, you are unlikely to doubt that it could happen.

A Trained Farmer and A Block Plane Into the Drink

Sindelar, who is from that corner of Michigan near Chicago and Indiana, had a father who was a

The rear-most room of Sindelar's collection contains an impressive array of plow planes and a wooden lathe that Sindelar brought back from a trip to Italy.

An ivory plow plane made *by Jim Leamy (jimleamy planes.com) to commemorate Sindelar's 25th year in business.*

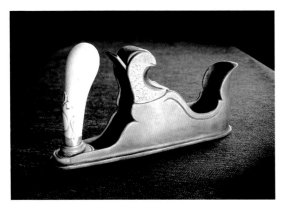

An unusual European ivory-handled plane. *The plane shows signs of use (lots of hammer taps on the wedge), and its construction suggests it is a scraping plane.*

carpenter and contractor. Sindelar himself was help-ing him set nails by age 5 and built his first apart-ment building as a teenager.

But it was farming that spoke to him. As a young man Sindelar leased a 350-acre produce farm then went to college to study agricultural manage-ment. He graduated and immediately got approved for a loan for $400,000 to launch his own farm.

That night, he thought, "That was too easy." He says he started running the numbers and con-cluded that if he had one bad year on the farm, he could lose everything. He eventually decided to fol-low in his dad's footsteps as a builder, though he still yearns to farm and will occasionally volunteer to plow the fields owned by local farmers just to get his hands dirty.

So Sindelar entered the building trade, and as a young man of about 21, he found himself in Florida building high-end residential homes and working under a French-Canadian carpenter who had a taste for good working tools.

One day the French-Canadian carpenter told Sindelar that it was time for him to start buying his own tools. So Sindelar purchased a new standard-angle Stanley block plane, the kind you'll find in tool buckets all over the country. He presented the plane to his boss for inspection one day on a job site.

"He studied it for five minutes," Sindelar says. "He never used it. He threw it into the Intercoastal Waterway and said, 'You have to start buying good tools and learn to take care of them.'"

Sindelar obeyed. From that point on, he tried to buy a good tool every week, a practice that con-tinues to this day, though now his tastes run more to mint Holtzapffel miter planes than hardware-store tools. And he also takes great pride in tending to

his collection. Every evening after finishing work at his business, Sindelar Fine Woodworking Co., he'll gently clean a tool or two in his collection.

His day job involves woodworking, though not the kind practiced by the tools he collects. Sindelar Fine Woodworking is a modern commercial cabinet-shop filled with power equipment and a half-dozen employees. The company tackles jobs that range from outfitting high-end horse trailers, to remod-eling the interiors of two state capitol buildings in Michigan and Ohio, to supplying wooden fittings to Georgie Boy RVs in neighboring Elkhart, Ind.

When you walk in the front door of the shop you're between the company's spray booth and the sanding area. The machining area spreads out before

One of the most sought-after *saws is the Woodrow & McPar-lin panther saw. Most collectors are lucky to have one example. On the day we visited Sindelar, he had three.*

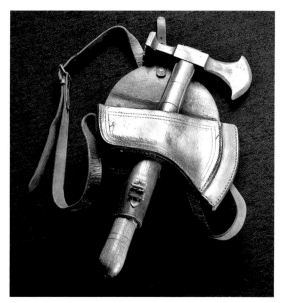

A FRENCH MARKING HATCHET WITH *a well-patinated leather sheath. Sindelar says this example is unusual in that the owners initials were still on the poll – those were usually ground off when the owner died.*

AN EARLY ADZE WITH AN *unusual hand-carved handle showing a horse and rider.*

AN ENGLISH STAIRSAW, USED FOR *cutting dados in stringers. Note the ingenious depth stop by the blade.*

you; a warehouse beyond that is stacked to the ceiling with bunks of lumber. Sindelar's office doesn't even offer many clues as to his tool-collecting passion – there are piles of paperwork, shelves of trade catalogs and modern office furniture. But once you pass through the back door of the office, everything changes. The hum of the machinery disappears and it's just rooms and rooms of tools.

This tool cache hidden in the back rooms of an industrial park is an apt metaphor for Sindelar's life as a collector. Though he has been a collector of tools for many years, few people knew of him until about eight years ago. Sindelar tried to keep a low profile in the collector world as he quietly fed the back rooms of his business with vintage tools.

That introverted approach – common among collectors – all changed when Sindelar met Roger Phillips, a long-time collector in La Jolla, Calif. Phillips also came up in the trades – his woodworking enterprise had a reputation for outfitting the interiors of banks, corporate offices and casinos. Phillips had been collecting since 1945, and when Sindelar saw his collection, he says he could think only one thing: "Wow. I want this."

With Phillips's guidance, Sindelar kicked his collection into high gear. He went from buying $100 tools to $10,000 tools. He sold his collection of Stanley tools and began buying one-of-a-kind tools in Europe.

"It's an obsession," he says. "I need to get into an AA program."

When other tool collectors go to Europe, they have secret spots to hunt for old tools that they share with no one. But when Sindelar told Phillips he was going to Europe, Phillips handed him a list of all his favorite haunts.

"Roger is just so open about everything," Sindelar says. "It really changed my life."

He also took a cue from Phillips when he decided to get involved with other tool collectors and open his collection for inspection. In the process, Sindelar has also developed a reputation as a collector who likes unusual tools with an artistic flair. Fellow collectors pull him aside during auctions and say, "Hey, I've got something you have to see."

And as a result, Sindelar's collection has evolved into something that is filled with some of the most recognizable vintage tools that have appeared in recent books on tool collecting, plus newly made tools, such as a fleet of plow planes made by Jim Leamy, and infill planes made by Bill Carter and Wayne Anderson.

A lot of vintage tools have tall tales behind them – antique collecting is like that – but Sindelar says that he stays focused more on the form of the tool than its particular provenance or the myth behind it.

He shows off a tool chest that is covered in handplanes that look like nothing else that has ever been manufactured. The planes are ornate: brass sides, steel soles, shapely totes and knobs. The level of detail on some of them is outrageous for a working tool.

So where did they come from? The story, Sindelar says, is that they are from Germany. He buys them from a guy who gets them from another guy. And that guy says they came out of a school for blacksmiths and silversmiths. When the students left the school, they would leave one of these example tools behind, where it would be displayed on the wall.

Does Sindelar believe the story? He shrugs. "Tool collectors have a lot of stories," he says. "I like the planes." They are attractive tools and have odd labels: A. Stohr & Son, Schuhstopsel, Hildesheim, Durchmesser.

A STAINED GLASS WINDOW IN *one of the rooms housing Sindelar's collection. When all the lights are off this is the only source of illumination.*

Not all the tools are so mysterious. There's a shapely French marking hatchet in a leather sheath. The sawyer's initials are cast into the poll of the hatchet so he could mark the felled tree as his own. There's a Phillips Plow Plane, patented in 1867, with an ornate cast iron frame. There's an English stairsaw with a depth stop that works like a depth stop on a fillister or dado plane. There's even a Stanley jointer plane that's painted gold. "That's a private joke I have with another collector," Sindelar says.

TOOL CHESTS LINE THE WALLS *of the rooms housing Sindelar's collection, and all of them brim with tools.*

A Place for the Past and Future

And now Sindelar wants to show it all to the public. He envisions a museum that will also have a woodworking school. His initial plan was to build it near Williamsburg, Va., to take advantage of the history-seeking tourists there. Since then, he also started considering the Harrisburg, Pa., area. And since his plans for his museum have gotten out, he's been contacted by officials in North Carolina who think the museum, the school and the state's furniture-making history would be a good combination.

Sindelar says he thinks the museum would be a winner because it would appeal to people beyond tool collectors. Many tool museums and collections tend to focus on manufactured tools. Tools that have been patented are hot items these days. Old Stanley tools have always been a popular item for collectors.

But Sindelar's collection is all about the artistic form of the tool. He's more interested in buying something that will take your breath away rather than a collection of all the patented tools from 19th-century Connecticut. And that's why he thinks the museum would succeed.

Sindelar regularly escorts people through his collection, he hosts meetings of tool collectors and even opens his doors to the public on occasion to benefit a charity.

When he shows people around, they are overwhelmed by the tools, no matter if they are woodworkers, collectors, young or old.

"I've especially been amazed at how women, in particular, like the tools," he says. "And it's because they're all one-of-a-kind.

"They're ..." and Sindelar pauses as he looks for the right word, "just pretty."

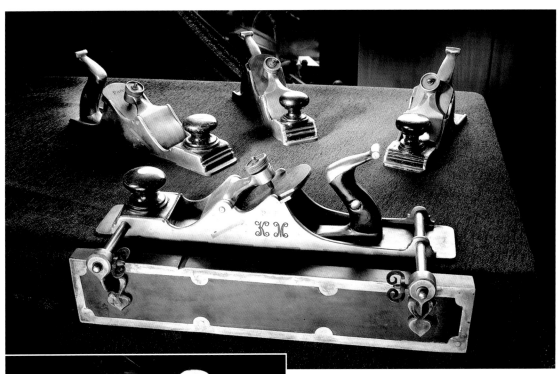

SOME OF THE UNUSUAL PLANES *that Sindelar acquired through a middleman. Little is known for sure about the planes, except that they look like nothing else. The bench planes (above) include a plane with a hefty fence integrated into its design. The other grouping (left) shows a fixed-sole compass plane and an unusual plane that was designed to plane boards to one specific thickness.*

The Mystery of Miter Planes

*An evolutionary dead end or
a misunderstood and useful tool?*

The so-called miter plane has always been something of an enigma lurking in the tool chest for the modern user. After setting up and using a fair number of these blocky planes it seems unlikely to me that these tools were designed solely for planing smooth a hand-sawn miter.

Except for a couple of trades – picture framers come to mind – mitering on the large scale that demands a dedicated miter plane is an infrequent chore for a cabinetmaker or joiner. Much cabinet- and sash-work mitering can be handled by a chisel and a guide.

Perhaps, some have proposed, the name "miter plane" is the incorrect term for the tool. The Stanley catalog lists this tool as a cabinetmaker's block plane, and the tool was particularly favored among piano-makers.

Both facts suggest that the tool had perhaps more than one function in the traditional shop. So last year I decided to investigate the history of the tool and also to try using this style of plane in a variety of unusual ways in my own shop. I got out the books and put away my set of bench planes for the time being. It was time to start looking back.

FROM AN UNEXPECTED FRENCH TRADE

Metal-bodied planes have been traced back to Roman civilization and the 4th century. And other examples surface from Europe as early as the 16th century, including some that look like the miter plane we're familiar with. But from a user's perspective, the most obvious fact about these tools is that they were unlikely to have been used on a shooting board. The iron sole is sometimes proud of the sidewalls. Or the sidewalls aren't even flat. These planes look to me like they served a purpose other than shooting miters.

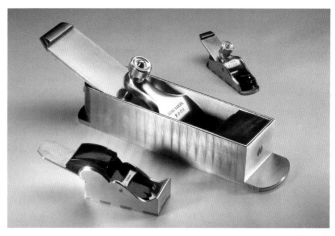

A DOVETAILED MITER PLANE MADE *by Robert Baker (center). This boxy tool is typically what we call a "miter plane" but it's unlikely it was used exclusively for mitering.*

Some solutions to the mystery came from the Manhattan apartment of Joel Moskowitz, a tool collector and founder of the Tools for Working Wood catalog and web site. As interesting as Moskowitz's tool collection is, what is equally impressive is the quantity of printed material on tools and the trades he has gathered over the years that line the walls of his apartment.

Moskowitz himself has often wondered about miter planes, especially the curious way they appear in England in the late 18th and early 19th centuries without any evolutionary precedent, including their inclusion in the inventories of Christopher Gabriel & Sons (a planemaker and tool dealer on Banner Street in London).

Moskowitz points to the French as the source of this form of metal-clad tool. Three early sources clearly show metal-clad planes. André Félibien's "Principes de L'architecture" (1676); Denis Diderot's "L'Encyclopedie," a collection of 71,181 articles on the state on the arts, sciences and trades in France between 1751 and 1772; and André Jacob Roubo's "L'Art du Menuisier," a multi-volume treatise on the manual arts published between 1769 and 1775.

What is curious is that the plates that show a metal-clad plane are not where you might expect them, which would be with the traditional cabinet-making and joiner's tools. Instead, it is in the marquetry section. Moskowitz speculates that the highly skilled French marqueters would use the metal-soled planes to smooth the exotic woods they used in their work. Before the French Revolution, France was a rich country, and the court could afford to support such high-end work and the craftsmen and tools that produced it. After the Revolution (1789), there was no such well-heeled royalty.

However, soon after the Revolution, these metal planes show up suddenly in England, Moskowitz

EARLY METAL PLANES LOOK LIKE *what we could call a "miter plane." However, they likely weren't for shooting miters. Many examples had the sole proud of the sidewalls, such as in this modern interpretation of an early plane by Wayne Anderson.*

notes. The Industrial Revolution made metal planes easier to build, England was become richer and perhaps French craftsmen fled to England. Of course the demand for marquetry tools would be small, so it's logical that planemakers tried to sell the metal plane to the cabinetry trades, Moskowitz says. In any case, the miter soon became a mainstay of early planemakers and likely evolved into the classic bevel-down infill plane that remains desirable today to collectors and users.

Using Early Style Planes

Miter planes are characterized by an iron pitched at 20° to 30° or so with the cutter secured with the bevel up. This "bevel up" configuration allows the user to maintain the tight mouth of the tool as the iron is sharpened back, even if the iron decreased in thickness (which was common among early cutters). It also allowed the user to change the cutting characteristics of the tool by whetting (sharpening) a higher pitch on the iron. While I don't know of any reference to early craftsmen changing the pitches on the irons of their miter planes, they certainly were aware that different pitches produced different results, as evidenced by the early wooden tools that have surfaced with different pitches.

For my own experiments, I examined a number of historical examples of miter planes (both cast and dovetailed examples) and worked extensively with three planes: The cast Lie-Nielsen reproduction of the Stanley No. 9 and two custom-built miters from Wayne Anderson: an "improved" dovetailed miter plane, and a metal tool that was based on very early examples of European tools that resemble miter planes.

That plane, shown at left is a small tool, 7" long with an 1½"-wide cutter. The sole is proud of the brass cladding on all four sides and the brass is peened through holes in the sole to secure it. What is interesting about this tool (and other European examples like this) is that the mouth of the tool is located farther back from the toe than most users are familiar with. The mouth on this one is located almost centrally between the toe and heel of the tool.

This changes the cutting characteristics of the tool significantly. It is far easier to begin a cut with this tool than it is with similarly sized modern bench planes, such as the Stanley No. 2. It also excels at trimming joints flush. The oversized toe is easy to balance on the proud section of the joint before the trimming cut. It also is easier to plane edges with this tool than with a block or chariot plane because the longer toe directs the plane into the cut. I've long thought that one of the functions of the adjustable

mouth on a block plane was to prevent the corner of your work from catching in the mouth. With this old-style miter plane, this was never a problem.

I even used it as a small-scale smoother and found it a great tool for planing out the occasional hollows missed by a jointer plane. Ironically, the one task I couldn't use this miter plane for was shooting miters on a shooting board.

As far as ergonomics go, the plane was comfortable to use. The extension and "handle" of the toe offered two different hand positions. The rear of the plane is gripped with fingers curled under the iron or with the hand resting over the wedge with the fingers grasping the sidewalls.

The Improved Miter Plane

The so-called improved miter planes were an advancement among English planemakers. The front infill was replaced by a more shapely bun. And various makers, such as Spiers of Ayr, experimented with different ways of making the rear infill more comfortable to grasp. Ultimately, however, these advances would be eclipsed by the popularity of planes with rear totes. This plane could be used for actually shooting miters, which it does quite well, once you figure out a grip on the sidewall and lever cap.

Like historical examples, the mouth of this Wayne Anderson improved miter is closer to the toe than in the old-style plane. So it doesn't have any of the working advantages of that unusual (and almost forgotten) older configuration. However, this plane is obviously easier to set up than the old-style plane. The snecked iron allows you to retract the iron with small hammer taps instead of rapping the brass stock of the tool. And the lever cap allows you to hold the iron with far more pressure at the cutting edge, and even to tweak the depth of cut by snugging up the lever-cap screw.

Once again, I tried using this plane for a wide variety of tasks, and I found it well-suited for more than I expected. At 9" long it is much more like a traditional-sized smoothing plane, and it could be wielded that way with ease. The ergonomics are less challenging than you might expect. With a slightly lower workbench the plane was comfortable to use for several hours at a time (I built a large tool cabinet and a couple tables with this plane). In fact, I had no complaints until I switched back to my bench planes and the rear tote immediately seemed more comfortable. However, I kept coming back to this tool because of its sweet feedback and the fact that I could quickly configure it to plane tough tropicals, at which it excelled.

THE NO. 9 CABINETMAKER'S BLOCK PLANE

The Stanley No. 9 looks a like a traditional miter plane, but it has always offered some improvements that set it apart from the older tools. Like a block plane (a later invention), the No. 9 has an ingenious adjustable mouth. Paired with the bevel-up design of the iron, you can quickly and easily configure this plane to handle just about any wood, no matter how difficult or easy it is to work.

The extraordinary mass of the tool and its large sidewalls make it the best shooting plane I have ever used, hands down. Accurate shooting on larger pieces demands some mass and a sole of some length. At nearly 11" long (some originals come in at 10") this is the ideal length for shooting both end grain and miters.

The Lie-Nielsen version comes with a cherry side handle that screws into the sidewall. This handle assists your grip during shooting. Original No. 9s can be found with a so-called "hot dog"-shaped casting that screws to the sidewall for this task. I obtained a reproduction "hot dog" handle that fit the Lie-Nielsen and found it much to my liking. In fact, I prefer it to the cherry side handle.

LIE-NIELSEN IRON MITER PLANE. A *remake of the Stanley No. 9 cabinetmaker's block plane of the last century.*

I DO A LOT OF *hand sawing in my shop, so a shooting board is an oft-used appliance. After working with a variety of tools, I've found that the more mass you have in the plane, the easier it is to shoot the edge accurately. Here, I've installed a reproduction "hot dog" side handle on the tool.*

After my positive experiences with the older miters, I decided to use the No. 9 for other tasks. Surprisingly, it is comfortable to use flat on the bench. I spent two days planing stiles and rails with it and was impressed with the knob at the rear of the tool. It is much more comfortable than expected. At the toe of the plane, you have two options. The extensions on the sole allow you to accurately register the tool on narrow edges, as with the other miter planes. When used flat on the bench, you grip the toe like you would a wooden-stock plane. Both grips are quite comfortable. Do not believe the naysayers when it comes to this tool until you've tried one yourself.

After six months of using these planes and shunning my bench planes I am not ready to give up either. There is something remarkably different about using a miter plane. Part of it is the grip, of course. And part of it is the different feedback you receive from a bevel-up plane. But there is something more.

The miter plane is not just an evolutionary deadend. In fact, as I work with them more and more I think that I am just beginning to unlock a few more of their secrets that are – for now – out of my reach. Perhaps if a few more people will take their miter planes off the shelf and into the shop then some of the tool's other mysteries might be revealed.

FOR MORE INFORMATION

Lie-Nielsen Toolworks
lie-nielsen.com, 800-327-2520

Anderson Planes
110 Monroe St., Big Lake, MN 55309
andersonplanes.com, 763-486-0834

The Ghost in the Machine

*Old technology can
teach us new things.*

When you're a professional writer, people tend to give you cranky manual typewriters as gifts. They don't expect you to use them, per se. But they do expect you to display them in your home.

Good thing I'm not an undertaker.

For years I despised manual typewriters and rolled my eyes any time one of them showed up at my door with a bow on it.

My hate affair with these clackety, dinging beasts began in journalism school. Though our school had modern computers, the school decided that the Basic Writing students should use manual typewriters only.

This seemed more like a punishment than a valid method of teaching me how to write about fires at double-wide trailers (my specialty). But the school prided itself on weeding out the less committed students. After four years, my class was one-third its original size.

So every evening my head ached from the pounding of letters against platens from the fingers of 20 would-be scribes in my Basic Writing lab. My pinkies ached from pressing the shift key. The smell of correction fluid made me wince.

I bought my first Macintosh computer that year and never looked back. Until one weekend in 2009.

SIMPLE LESSONS

My youngest daughter became curious about one of the typewriters in the basement, so I pulled it down and got it working for her. Like most children, she's pretty fast on a keyboard, but watching her struggle on a typewriter was a revelation.

The manual typewriter had taught me some critical lessons.

1. Use the fewest words possible to say something.

2. Make as few mistakes as possible.

3. Always think two sentences ahead of the one you are typing.

Without those three lessons, I doubt I'd have this job.

When you are a woodworker, people tend to give you beat-up wooden-stock handplanes as gifts. They don't expect you to use them, per se. But they do expect you to display them. Good thing I'm not a proctologist.

My mom gave me one this summer for my birthday that made me shake my head. It's an old jointer plane, probably craftsman-made from ash or something ring-porous and oaky. The maker included the pith of the tree in the body – generally a no-no in planemaking. And the body has cast itself into a wacky rhombus shape.

I took one look at the tool when it came out of the box and set it in the corner of our sunroom. This week, something compelled me to take a closer look. I knocked its wedge loose and removed the chipbreaker and Ward iron. The iron has been ground away to almost nothing, but it is interesting. It is perfectly crowned – just like I crown a jointer plane blade. And the face of the iron has clearly been polished during honing.

This was a working tool. I took a close look at the sole. Ignoring the holes from some insects, it was obvious that the sole was burnished from hard use – it was the best-looking surface on the entire tool.

So I resolved to get this thing working. Perhaps it has a few more lessons to share with me.

A Brush with Greatness (and Smallness)

One of the largest legends in the tool collecting world stands under 4'.

In May 2007 I got a chance to show off my new Holtzapffel workbench at the Sindelar Tool Meet, talk to a bunch of tool collectors and buy some tools I've been coveting for too long.

But the absolute highlight of the entire event was a brush with greatness.

You see, I got to meet "the boy."

OK, some background for the uninitiated: Tool dealer Patrick Leach (supertool.com) has been selling tools on the Internet for as long as I've been buying them. Every month, Leach sends out an e-mail newsletter that is (hands-down) the best-written tool newsletter in the business. His tools for sale are always the cream of the crop and his descriptions are often hilarious.

(By the way, Leach is also the founder of the Blood & Gore web site, the best online reference on Stanley planes, and started Independence Tool with Pete Taran, which made the dovetail saw that Lie-Nielsen now sells. That saw launched the premium handsaw market.)

Anyway, one of my favorite parts of Leach's newsletter is that he has a "Tool of the Month," which is usually the most unusual, minty or rarest tool on offer. And every month, one of the photos features Leach's son holding the tool.

As I've been getting this newsletter for years, I've watched the child grow up, and Leach always peppers the tool's description with some comment about "the boy" or the "tool youth." For example: "Fresh from stuffing his mouth with Oreos while playing with his toy motorcycle, the tool youth wasn't too happy to pose with this one, the much coveted #164 low-angle smooth plane …."

So one afternoon at the tool meet I took a moment away from my demonstrating to browse some of the tool dealer's tables. I was looking at a small router plane when I glanced up. Now it's rare for me to be speechless (just ask the magazine's staff), but I saw The Boy and all I could do was stutter: "Uhhhh, it's … uhhhh … The Boy!"

He and his father were set up right by the entrance to the building that houses the collection. Leach was working the crowd, cracking jokes and making deals. The Boy was helping out, arranging the tools and tending to the tool bargains that were arrayed on the blue plastic tarp off to the side.

"The best tools are back over here," The Boy called out to the crowd.

I obeyed him and went to have a look. I snatched up a brass router plane made by a patternmaker and an accessory for my brace that would allow it to accept small round-shank bits. The Boy was right.

I wanted to say something like, "I've known you since you were just a wee lad holding an ebony plow plane in a bouncy seat." But that sounded stupid. And I'm sure that it would seem creepy if I started talking to The Boy, so I just admired him from afar. If you've ever wondered about it, The Boy is a good kid. He helped Leach the entire weekend and was one of the most well-behaved elementary-school kids I've met.

Other highlights: Getting to meet toolmakers Paul Hamler and Jim Leamy (I ordered one of Hamler's smallish router planes, shown above). Konrad Sauer from Sauer & Steiner was there as well. I know Konrad quite well and we spent our evenings trying to find a decent beer (we looked a lot, but that's another story for another kind of book). I did learn that Konrad has a weakness for powdered sugar doughnuts. John Sindelar, the host of this incredible event, bought about 3,000 doughnuts for the event. No lie. Konrad ate his fair share.

A Softwood Scraper Mystery

This homemade scraper plane seemed like it was a dog until one day.

Sometimes a craftsman-made tool surfaces that is just plain mysterious and wondrous. One day in 2006 I spent a morning with Carl Bilderback, a semi-retired Chicago-area carpenter who has an astonishing collection of handsaws and dang-good collection of other tools. We were working on a story together about resawing with band saws, but he also really wanted to show me an oddball scraping plane he'd bought years ago.

The thing looks a bit like a Stanley No. 112 scraper plane with some major differences. First, this plane holds the scraper at one angle only – 90°. The Stanley No. 112 adjusts to an infinite number of angles. And the craftsman-made tool has an odd knob in front of the tote that adjusts the scraper iron up and down in the mouth.

Carl bought the plane years ago (and said he paid too much for it, by the way). And when he started using the thing on hardwoods he found "it

didn't work worth a damn" no matter what he did. So the thing sat on his shelf.

Years passed. Then one day Carl had some tear-out problems on a piece of pine around a knot. Scraping pine is generally a difficult proposition, but for some reason Carl's hands reached for this tool and he took a couple swipes. Like magic, it scraped the tear-out smooth and also scraped the knot to perfection. Since then, this tool has become Carl's go-to plane for softwoods.

So today we did a little experiment: We set up his Stanley No. 112 with a bit of a forward pitch and scraped some white pine. We could pull a decent shaving, but it left an unacceptable and wooly surface. Then we planed the pine with the oddball plane. It left a perfect surface, ready to finish.

Carl said that he can set up his Stanley No. 212 scraper plane with a perfectly vertical frog to somewhat imitate the oddball scraper plane, but he said it takes a lot of fussing to get everything working right – both the pitch and the projection. The oddball plane is super simple: Just drop the scraper in, turn the knob and go.

The plane was surprisingly well made in many respects. The sidewalls were welded to the sole and it had evidence that it was once zinc-plated. The one apology for the tool was that the front knob was too close to the mouth of the tool, and shavings would bunch up behind the knob. But beyond that, I was very impressed.

"Someone," Carl said, "might want to think about making one of these tools for sale."

Routers Without Cords & Without Brand Names

Oddball craftsman-made router planes are a common find at tool meets.

One of my favorite old tools to fix up and use are small patternmaker's router planes. Each one of these little tools is unique, usually inexpensive and easy to get functioning.

They also can be gorgeous examples of craftsmanship, or as ugly as an Allen wrench jammed into a plate of rusted steel.

The tools are fairly common because they were made by pattermakers for their own use, according to tool collectors I've talked to. Sometimes the patternmaker would use a common Stanley tool as the pattern for the craftsman-made tool. And that's why you sometimes see router planes that look like slightly shrunken Stanley router planes in bronze.

The coolest craftsman-made router plane I've ever seen is owned by Carl Bilderback, a semi-retired carpenter and tool collector who lives outside Chicago. He writes for *Popular Woodworking* on occasion and whenever I'm up there to take photos of his work I always catch myself looking at his router plane with lustful thoughts.

It's fancy. It has a bronze base, a beautifully knurled adjustment mechanism and tiny little turned handles. You can see a photo of it in the February 2008 issue of *Popular Woodworking*. Carl is using it during an article on repairing mistakes.

The router shown in the photo above is a more typical example. I bought it for $15 at a tool swap. It was sitting on a blanket with a bunch of other little bits of rusted metal.

Fixing one up is easy. I started working on this one at 4:10 p.m. and was trimming tenons before 4:30 p.m. rolled around. The irons on these are almost always soft steel, which means they are easy to hone, but that you'll be sharpening them often. The only other downside to these tools is the cutter is on a round shank, which can rotate during heavy use (so rough it up with #220-grit sandpaper).

I polished the flat face of the cutter on my waterstones during two songs on the radio. Then I trued up the bevel on a diamond stone and honed a micro-bevel on the waterstones. You can't use honing guides to sharpen the L-shaped iron, but it's easy to work the iron by hand.

The only other thing to do was to clean up the sole a bit. Oxidation on a bronze-base tool will leave nasty marks on your work at first. I cleaned up the base on some sandpaper stuck to a piece of granite.

If you'd like one of these tools for yourself, the best way is to join the Mid-West Tool Collector's Association (mwtca.org) and attend one of the local or national meets. You will have 20 or 30 to choose from. I've found a few on eBay, but I like buying them in person because you can make sure that the iron can be tightened up well. There's nothing worse than an iron that shifts around in use.

Editing the History of Handplane Adjusters

Most people think that Norris adjusters were invented by Thomas Norris. The Stanley catalog begs to differ.

To most handplane users there are three principal ways to adjust the cutter in the tool: You can use a Bailey-style adjuster made popular by the U.S.-made Stanley planes, you can use a Norris-style adjuster made popular by T. Norris & Sons in its English infill planes, or you can use a mallet and tap the thing into position.

For years the debate had raged about which sort of adjustment mechanism is best (the American, the English or the Neanderthal). Me, I prefer the Bailey-style adjuster in metal-bodied planes, but that's not the reason I'm writing this. Instead, it's to explore a little wrinkle about the history of the Norris-style adjuster. As tool collector and carpenter Carl Bilderback told me: "Norris might have made that adjuster popular, but they didn't invent it."

Exhibit A is the Stanley No. 12 Victor "Pocket Plane," made by Stanley between 1879 and 1884. Bilderback showed me this plane from his collection in May 2007, and I was intrigued. After taking the sucker apart, it's clear to me that the adjuster is indeed almost identical to a so-called Norris-style adjuster, which wasn't patented in England until 1913 (patent No. 11526-13). Leonard Bailey patented his adjuster in 1878 (you can read the original patent on Google patents if you like).

The adjuster on the No. 12 works exactly like the adjuster on my Norris A5 smoothing plane. There are two threaded sleeves that (with the help of a couple studs) control both the projection of the cutter and its position in the mouth of the tool.

The No. 12's adjuster works quite well. Bilderback had even sharpened up the blade on it and let me use the little guy for a bit. It was pretty sweet. In fact, it was so sweet that toolmaker Paul Hamler has developed a keen interest in the plane and asked to borrow the tool so he could make a copy of it.

So perhaps we need to start calling both types of mechanical adjusters "Bailey-style" adjusters. (I really doubt that will happen.) But this little bit of research actually opens the door to some more research (if you've ever known an academic, you know that this is always the case, even when the additional research would be really uninteresting). Dig into the description of Bailey's patent for the No. 12, and he admits that he wasn't the first to come up with this idea for an adjuster, though he doesn't name the person who beat him to the idea. Curious.

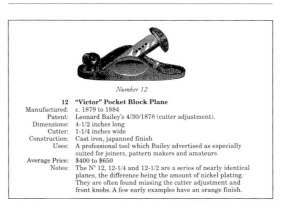

Number 12

12	**"Victor" Pocket Block Plane**
Manufactured:	c. 1879 to 1884
Patent:	Leonard Bailey's 4/30/1878 (cutter adjustment).
Dimensions:	4-1/2 inches long
Cutter:	1-1/4 inches wide
Construction:	Cast iron, japanned finish
Uses:	A professional tool which Bailey advertised as especially suited for joiners, pattern makers and amateurs.
Average Price:	$400 to $650
Notes:	The Nº 12, 12-1/4 and 12-1/2 are a series of nearly identical planes, the difference being the amount of nickel plating. They are often found missing the cutter adjustment and front knobs. A few early examples have an orange finish.

HERE'S JOHN WALTER'S WRITE-UP OF *the tool in his wonderful (but out of print) "Stanley Tools: Guide to Identity and Value."*

That's Not a Collection; It's a Large Working Set

A brush with a bit of handplane arcanum results in a minor obsession.

A lot of people ask to see my tool collection. I tell them I don't have one – I'm a user, not a collector. If I utter that line again, however, I'll be a liar.

Somehow during 2008 I started acquiring edge-trimming planes. I've owned a Lie-Nielsen version – a right-handed copy of the Stanley No. 95 – for many years, and that one version of that plane was all this woodworker really needed.

But in 2008 I heard Thomas Lie-Nielsen tell the story of how he got started in the planemaking business in the 1980s to a group of students at the Marc Adams School of Woodworking. I'd heard the story before: Lie-Nielsen began making the edge-trimming plane after picking up the business from machinist Ken Wisner.

This time, the story was different because one of the students at the school (Jeff Skiver) brought one of the Wisner planes to the class to show. As I held the little sucker, I thought it would be cool to own one of these Wisner planes as a piece of modern planemaking history.

So I started trolling eBay with little luck. The Wisner planes are hard to come by because there weren't many of them made. Meanwhile, we got the new Veritas versions of the edge-trimming plane in iron, and (mystery of mysteries) those ended up in my tool chest. Then I stumbled upon an AMT ver-

sion of the tool for sale that I couldn't pass up. The AMT version is, by the way, a complete piece of dung. Its red velvet bag is nice, however.

I knew I had crossed over the line into being a "collector" when I started regretting not buying the stainless steel version of the plane that Veritas offered but is now sold out.

And in 2008, I finally got my Wisner.

Thanks to some help from Skiver, I found a Wisner plane and snagged it. When it arrived, I was thrilled. Not only is it well made, but it is the first used tool I've ever bought that came perfectly sharp and ready to go. That's the good news.

Here's the bad news: My Wisner plane has an iron body with a brass lever cap. So now I'm going to have to look for a Wisner with a bronze body. And the Veritas version in bronze.

And that stainless Veritas plane. Curses.

JEFF SKIVER'S BRONZE WISNER PLANE *ignited my collecting lust.*

New Toothing Plane; Familiar Maker

Toothing planes were used for planing gnarly surfaces or for preparing a surface for veneer. What is special about this one is its previous owner.

In 2008 I bought a toothing plane from a Midwestern tool collector. I've always wanted one of these tools, and this one is particularly nice.

Toothing planes are lot like scraping planes: The iron is vertical. What's different is that toothing plane has a serrated cutting edge – instead of a smooth edge with a tiny hook, like you would find on a scraper plane.

You sharpen toothing irons like a standard plane iron: Sharpen the bevel and the face to as high a grit as you like then go to work.

Toothing planes can be used in a couple different ways. Some people use them to flatten a board's surface. The vertical pitch of the iron (and its toothed shape) prevents tearing in gnarly woods, and the serrated teeth allow you to take a fairly good bite.

You can use them in virtually any direction on a board: with the grain, across the grain, diagonally or against the grain. The thing won't tear out your grain.

And the iron doesn't have to be at this high pitch for it to work well. Modern toolmakers offer toothed blades that you can use in other tools. Most people use them in bevel-up jack planes and smoothing planes.

Other craftsmen use a toothing plane for traditional veneering jobs with hide glue. According to old texts, the toothing plane would prepare the substrate – flattening it and giving it some "tooth" –

before you apply the adhesive and the veneer.

No matter what you use it for, a toothing plane is an interesting experience. When used diagonally, it makes a weird granular dust. When used with the grain it makes tiny curls that tend to break apart quite easily.

I'll probably use this tool for both of these sorts of jobs – they're handy and simple tools. This one was probably made by the craftsman, and the maker was likely German. The "horn" at the toe is a feature of many European planes.

Oh, there's one other feature of the plane I like. The name stamped on the toe (see below).

I WISH I HAD A *good story about the origin of this tool, but I don't. The tool collector who bought it acquired it during a tool swap meet. So there's no cool history to share – just the mystery of me wondering what sort of work the other "C SCHWARZ" did.*

Almost a Plane Wreck

The perilous flight of the world's most valuable tool.

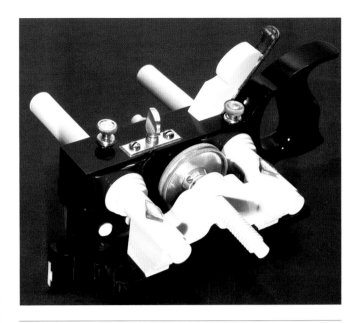

Half of the airplane's hydraulic system had failed at take-off; the other half failed as the plane was 10 minutes from the Atlanta airport. So the flight crew prepared the passengers for an emergency landing because they were going to hit the ground at about 200 miles an hour.

"Arms crossed; heads down," came the instructions from the crew. Clarence Blanchard was about to do as he was told, but there was something nagging at him so much that he just had to stand up and rummage through the overhead compartment.

Blanchard, you see, just happened to have the world's most expensive tool in a 1971 hard-case Samsonite above his head. He retrieved the ebony and ivory handplane and cradled it between his legs. Then he waited for the plane to hit the ground.

The story of Blanchard and the now-famous Sandusky centerwheel plow plane began on the last day of June 2004 with a phone call to Blanchard's office at Brown Auction Services in Pownal, Maine.

The woman on the phone had a relative who wanted to sell an antique handplane, and asked if Blanchard's auction house would sell it for them. Blanchard said he would be willing to take a look, and so they e-mailed him some photos.

When he saw the tool on the computer screen, he knew it was special – despite its crust of 100 years of coal dust. This was a "presentation" tool made by the Sandusky Tool Co. in Sandusky, Ohio, likely to display at the 1876 Centennial Exposition.

After the Sandusky Tool Co. fell on hard times and was sold in the early 20th century, some of its assets went on the block about 1934. A local construction magnate, John Charles Feick, wanted that plane badly. After the sale he walked out of the building and handed the tool to his son, Thomas, who was then 4 or 5 years old. John told his son he bought the contents of the entire building just to own that tool.

The plane remained in the family then passed to Thomas, who retired to Florida and kept the plane there until a phone call summoned Blanchard to fly south to retrieve it during the 4th of July weekend.

While in Florida, Blanchard disassembled the tool to get it through airport security. The metal parts went in his checked luggage; the ebony and ivory parts into his carry-on. And as the airplane lost altitude on its final descent into Atlanta, Blanchard says he wasn't afraid for his life.

Instead, he feared what would happen to the tool after the plane went down and Blanchard tried to leave the airplane with lots of officials around. "What would I do," Blanchard says, "if one of these great big guys tries to take it away from me?"

The airplane landed smoothly. And the Sandusky plane – which Blanchard affectionately calls "Sandy" – was unscratched.

Three months later in Harrisburg, Pa., lot #308 opened up at $64,000. Until that moment, the record for any single tool sold at auction was about $32,000. There were three bidders left when the plane hit $100,000, and the gavel fell at $104,000. With the buyer's premium, the total price was $114,400 plus sales tax (the buyer was a Pennsylvania tool collector in the audience).

Avrum Silverman, a Massachusetts tool collector, says the room erupted in cheers when bidding hit $100,000 then in applause for the buyer when the hammer dropped. "I don't think there's anything out there that can top this plane," he says. "It came out of nowhere. It has never been written about and it was only rumored to have existed. What else can top this plane?"

Choose a Vintage Handplane

Old handplanes can be a good bargain, if you know how to purchase them.

Whenever I teach a class on handplanes, I'm amazed at what the students bring to set up and use. I've seen Holtey planes and Harbor Freight planes in the same class.

And there's always at least one student who brings an entire box of vintage planes that he or she bought at a garage sale (price $5). And this is where I usually find the biggest pieces of garbage and the brightest jewels.

Because many beginning woodworkers have trouble telling the difference between a good user and slag, I'd like to discuss two of the hallmarks of good planes and bad ones: the sole and the frog.

But before we dive in, let me offer one caveat on my advice. Almost any plane can be made to work in some fashion. With enough time, effort and luck you can make almost anything passable. The problem is that in the vintage market, the poor planes and the good planes might cost exactly the same. So why buy a problem child?

Funky Frogs to Avoid

Call me old fashioned, but for metal planes, I think the frog should be a piece of cast metal – not some thin piece of stamped and bent steel. I've worked with students who have planes with stamped-steel frogs and have yet been able to get one working to my satisfaction.

I don't have a photo of a stamped frog to show you. But you'll know it when you see it. The frog will be hollow and have thin walls.

BAD FROG – MORE LIKE *a toad. Here's a painted frog from a Stanley Handyman smoothing plane. This is a rough casting that has been painted red. It's unlikely to be satisfactory for high-tolerance smoothing operations.*

BETTER FROG. THIS IS A *frog on a no-name No. 3-sized smoothing plane. Note that the bed for the blade has been linished or machined, but there's not a whole lot of surface contact between the frog and the blade. This can be made to work well (flatten the face of the frog on a diamond stone). But it's easy to do better.*

Another thing I look for: painted frogs. If the entire frog was painted at the factory, that usually means that the thing is just a rough casting that hasn't been machined. Quality frogs are machined in several places so the frog mates securely with the body of the plane and the iron.

In my experience, the more area that is machined, the more solid the tool is in use. Check out the photos on these pages as a guide.

THE SOLE OF AN OLD MACHINE

When purchasing a vintage plane, the flatness of the sole can be critical when making a purchasing decision. So I'm going to man-up here and talk about how I approach this potential problem.

The soles of vintage handplanes can be warped for a variety of reasons. Perhaps they were poorly manufactured. Perhaps they weren't properly stress relieved and the casting moved over time. Perhaps they were abused.

Whatever the cause, an out-of-true sole affects the way a plane cuts when trying to take thin shavings. When I purchase a vintage handplane that I am going to use for smoothing or jointing, I'll check its sole with a straightedge and feeler gauges.

Some people will instead skip the feeler gauges and just look for light between the straightedge and the sole. I think this can be misleading (the gaps look alarmingly large) and it doesn't tell you how much of a convexity or concavity you have. That's where the feeler gauge comes in.

I assemble the plane completely, apply a working tension to the lever cap and retract the iron into the tool. Then I set the plane upside down in a vise. I don't clamp the jaws down – I merely position the jaws to support the tool's sidewalls.

Then I place the straightedge on the sole of the tool and start with the feeler gauge that is .0015" thick and see if I can slip it under the straightedge at any point. Then I move the straightedge and try again. If I can slip the gauge under the straightedge

A FINE FROG – A *prince, really. This is a frog on an early Stanley No. 6. Look at the acres of contact area between the blade and the frog. These planes are easy to tune to a high level. As a bonus, I find these early planes to be less expensive than other vintage planes because they usually are crustier on the outside. But like a lobster, it's what on the inside that really counts. Even better than this frog is the Bed Rock-style frog, which is completely machined on the underside. Bed Rocks are generally bulletproof.*

I'll switch to a thicker leaf, such as .002" and try that. I keep moving up in thickness until I cannot slip the gauge under the straightedge.

Do enough testing and you'll get a good topographical map of your sole. But how do you read the map? Your sole doesn't have to be dead flat to work great. The plane's sole has several critical areas that need to be coplanar. Check out the photo below. All the Xs are the critical areas. However, you don't really want the sole to be convex in the areas behind or in front of the mouth. Big hills are bad news.

Then it's time to make a call. For a plane for rough work, almost anything is acceptable because its shaving is so thick. For a jointer plane or a smoothing plane, I get concerned when the sole is out in a critical area by more than .002".

So what do you if the sole is out of whack? If it's a jointer plane, I'll keep looking. I have had difficulty in the past flattening jointer plane soles. Plus there is no vintage plane shortage. If it's a smoothing plane I might still buy it. I can true those easily.

"X" MARKS THE SPOTS WHERE *the sole needs to be coplanar for high-tolerance work.*

USE A FEELER GAUGE TO *look for low spots in the sole. Begin with the thinnest gauge.*

Out of the Dark Ages

*A before-sunrise visit
to Lie-Nielsen Toolworks.*

It's about 7:30 a.m. on a Wednesday, and I am severely deprived of caffeine as I follow Thomas Lie-Nielsen through the narrow passages of his tool factory in Warren, Maine. He moves so quickly up and down the steps that I'm always five paces behind, despite my longer legs. Tom flings open a door on the second floor and unwraps his scarf and coat in one fluid motion.

Tom has invited me to attend one of his company's weekly staff meetings, where he hands out paychecks and talks shop with the employees of Lie-Nielsen Toolworks. I catch up with him a few beats later and he's already sorting through papers on a desk.

But even before this early morning meeting with all the employees, Tom holds another meeting with a few key employees in this bullpen that serves as the office for him and several other employees. They briefly look over some production numbers, discuss the health of a few machines then head to the shop floor. The all-employee meeting is held in an area directly behind the Lie-Nielsen showroom where employees heat-treat the blades and assemble the planes before shipping them out.

At this early hour the sky above Warren is dark and so are the halls of the toolworks. But as I step onto the shop floor I squint. My eyes adjust to the bright lights above – then I see it. Something that is completely startling.

No, it's not the company's No. 4½ anniversary plane in bronze. It's the people in the room. There are dozens of them standing around the boxes filled with castings and lever caps and chipbreakers. Tom is moving around the room handing out a stack of paychecks, calling out each person by name and chatting with them briefly.

Within a few moments all of the employees are performing stretching exercises and Tom is sketch-ing out the news of the day. One of the new machines has some bearings that need replacing. The sales numbers from the West Coast woodworking shows are in. The block plane group has been making its production numbers regularly this week.

The employees clap at the news, except for a group standing near me. It's the block plane group, and then it dawns on me. I'm just a bit amazed that there could be a group of people who make block planes. In fact, it's amazing that there are so many people in this world who all build hand tools in this post-handwork, post-industrial country.

I've had this feeling before, mind you. A few years ago I toured the Veritas manufacturing facility in Ottawa, Ontario, and was struck dumb at how many people were engaged in building hand tools. I followed Rob Lee around the Veritas plant and warehouse for more than two hours – and we still didn't see it all.

It's experiences like this that give me real hope for the future of craftsmanship on this continent. In order for woodworking in North America to survive, there needs to be a steady supply of good quality new tools (both with a power cord and without) available to the public. Without those new tools, the craft is destined to become just a quaint sideshow at living-history museums and on television.

It's actually somewhat of a miracle that we still work wood at all. It is, after all, more expensive to build a piece of furniture from scratch (in hours, tools and time) than it is to buy a piece of furniture from a discount furniture outlet. But still we persevere. All of us.

Mark Swanson, Lie-Nielsen's patternmaker, chatted with me for a moment as the early morning meeting geared up. Then he said: "You better do your stretches, too."

So I did. And I'm glad to be a part of this.

Lie-Nielsen Planes for $38

Buying premium tools isn't like buying a car. They don't plummet in value.

These days investing in a few premium hand-tools might have less financial risk than the stock market.

Just about every week I get an e-mail or phone call from a reader asking me if they think that premium handplanes from Veritas, Lie-Nielsen and Clifton are worth the extra expense. I think they are worth the money, and I always tell the person the following:

"If you don't like them, you can always sell them on eBay and get most of your money back."

This morning I decided to run some numbers to determine if I'm full of poo. So I checked the price of 36 recent eBay transactions in 2009 for Lie-Nielsen tools. It was mostly planes, but the list included a couple sets of chisels, a saw and a screwdriver.

Here are some typical prices:

■ The Lie-Nielsen No. 164 low-angle smoothing plane. Retail: $265. eBay: $235.

■ Large shoulder plane. Retail: $250. eBay: $220.02.

■ Lie-Nielsen No. $4^{1}/_{2}$ bench plane. Retail: $325. eBay: $250.

There were a few surprises on my list.

A couple sellers actually made money. A rabbeting block plane and a chisel set sold for more than the retail price. That can be caused by bidders fueled by testosterone or by other factors (including the fact that the buyer could be in another country).

On the whole, the Lie-Nielsen tools sold for an average of 16 percent less than the full retail price. If you averaged out all the transactions, the average Lie-Nielsen tool sold for $38 less than the retail price.

So there you have it. My collection of Lie-Nielsens is doing better than my 401(k).

COMMENTS FROM READERS

I did a similar study, off and on, for an extended period of time and came to a similar conclusion. Virtually everything sold for at least 80 percent of the original purchase price, and I didn't include shipping costs. Most sold for 90 percent or more. The ones that didn't tended to be the less-popular tools. For example, the No. $5^{1}/_{4}$ jack and No. $10^{1}/_{4}$ bench rabbet sold at 79 percent of their values; a No. 2 sold at 69 percent. So those were relative losers.

With the recent price increases at Lie-Nielsen, I think that tools purchased under the old prices will do much better, even make money. That's assuming that you can stand to part with those treasures.

Richard Dawson

Chris is right on. I do a lot of tool buying and selling on eBay, and fine tools that are well taken care of retain most, if not all, of their value. Some increase in value with limited production, e.g. Bridge City Tools' commemorative stuff. I've bought all my Lie-Nielsens off eBay (most of them during a Microsoft Live promo period with 20 percent to 30 percent off … watch for that again!). I'm confident that I'll be able to sell at the same price if and when I were to sell them. So buy your Lie-Nielsens off eBay and they're essentially free! The equation is further tipped in your favor as some toolmakers have a propensity to increase pricing of products with regularity.

Even if you lose the $38 with buying a new tool … say you hold it for four years – isn't it worth it to rent a premium tool for $10 per year? If you buy a new tool, just don't get it engraved or personalized as that will reduce its selling value.

Charles Davis

Planing in Circles

In its heyday, Stanley Works made some of the best tools around. These days, they are competing with their past greatness.

I almost never get a phone call from the public relations people at the Stanley Works. Perhaps they are too busy selling garage door openers or thinking up double-entendre and obesity jokes to accompany the company's line of Fat Max tools.

But in 2002, the phone rang, and it was Stanley.

The friendly public relations person had heard that I'd just reviewed jack planes in *Popular Woodworking* magazine and that Stanley had won the "Best Value" award. Could he get a copy of the review right away? And could they use it in their marketing materials?

At that moment I knew this was going to have a storyline that ended with me telling him that the tooth fairy didn't exist.

Yes, I replied, Stanley won the award. Yes, I'd be happy to send him a copy of the review. Yes, they could use the test in their marketing materials.

"However," I said, pausing for a moment, "I don't think you're going to want to use the review."

And so I explained: When I set up our review of metal-bodied jack planes, I included all the major brands on the market at the time: Lie-Nielsen, Clifton, Record, Shop Fox, Anant and Stanley. And then, as a lark, I put a few vintage Stanley planes into the test.

The vintage Stanleys in the test were about 100 years old and were bought at flea markets and on eBay for anywhere between $12 and $35. As you can probably guess, the vintage Stanley planes blew the doors off most of the new planes (except the Lie-Nielsen and, to some degree, the Clifton).

It was a fair fight. These vintage planes needed work. The soles were a bit wonky. The irons and chipbreakers needed work. The frogs weren't perfectly tuned. But even though these vintage Stanleys should be retired to the old-folks home for cast iron, they were easier to set up than the new planes. The controls were finer. Heck the 100-year-old fit and finish was better than those on the Record, Shop Fox and Anant.

The guy from Stanley Works was perplexed by my explanation. But he still wanted the review for his files, so I sent it to him that very afternoon.

And now bear with me for a second story that begins with my phone ringing.

It is from a reader who wants help choosing a tool – the kind of call I get about five times a week.

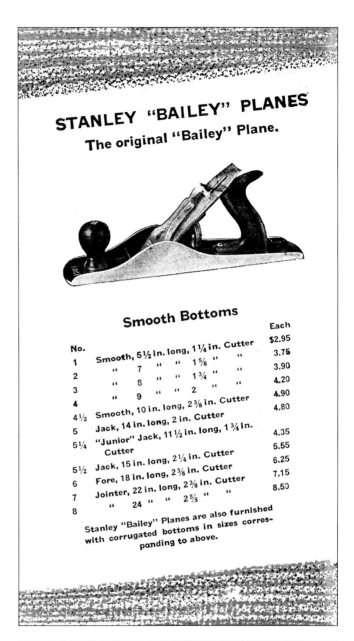

This guy wants some help buying a bit brace. No problem. I rattle off my standard favorites: The North Bros. 2101A brace and a couple from Peck, Stow & Wilcox. And I throw in a plug for Sanford Moss's web site (sydnassloot.com) as a great place to research and buy the brace of his dreams.

"Um, thanks," the guy says, "but I wanted to buy a new brace."

Huh? Why would anyone want to buy a new brace? The best braces ever made are still littering the planet and can be had for less than the price of a tablet of Oxycontin (not that I know anything about the price of illegal prescriptives).

"I don't like used equipment," he explains. "I want to be the first person who uses it. When I take it out of the box, I want it to be perfect."

The reader then asked me about three brands of new braces he'd seen in catalogs. We went over the details of each one: junk, tremendous junk and crap-tacular junk. He settled on purchasing the brace about which I had the fewest bad things to say. We both hung up the phone bewildered.

Sometimes I forget that there is a certain consumer who won't buy anything that has been used. With all of the sturdy old houses on the market, they would prefer to buy something new in the suburbs that doesn't have the same level of craftsmanship or detailing.

I used to get fairly worked up about this fact, but in the last few years, I've come to embrace it as a good thing. Here's why: These people are helping expand the marketplace for high-quality new tools. They are the consumers who help ensure that Veritas, Clifton, Lie-Nielsen and other manufacturers will have a customer base.

Their buying habits have encouraged competition among makers and have exposed more of their fellow woodworkers to the wonders of high-quality modern tool manufacturing. I myself started into the craft with vintage planes and balked at the price of Lie-Nielsen (and later Clifton and Veritas) planes when I first encountered them about 12 years ago. But after using the tools, I think they're a tremendously good value.

The whole thing is a bit of a chicken-and-egg situation. Does the availability of quality new tools increase the interest in traditional tools? Or does an interest in traditional tools fuel the availability of new quality tools?

I'm not smart enough to answer a chicken-and-egg paradox. But I am smart enough to recognize that the world works in cycles. You see, last week I got an e-mail from a public relations person at Stanley Works ….

THIS BRACE BY NORTH BROS. *of Philadelphia is better than any new brace I've encountered. Why would you buy a shoddy new one when the old ones are so superior?*

THE FRONT KNOB ON THIS *vintage Stanley No. 6 is perfectly turned rosewood – a far cry from the plastic handles of modern inexpensive planes.*

DESPITE THE BROKEN TOTE, THIS *vintage Stanley plane steals the lunch money of the company's modern output. All of the controls still work as well as the day the plane was made.*

A Piece of History from The Early Bronze Age

Ken Wisner's little plane led to a larger handplane renaissance.

When a young Thomas Lie-Nielsen set out to start making premium handplanes in the early 1980s, he launched his business with an adaptation of the Stanley No. 95 edge-trimming plane.

But Lie-Nielsen wasn't the first person to make this tool in bronze. That footnote goes to machinist Ken Wisner, who made the planes in small batches and sold them through the Garrett Wade catalog. When Wisner decided to get out of that business, he turned over his patterns to Lie-Nielsen, who took them to Maine and set up shop in a shack on his farm.

I've always wanted to own one of these Wisner planes – partly out of curiosity and partly out of my desire to own a piece of history. But they're hard to come by, and they're expensive.

So in 2007, I got a little schoolgirl thrill when Jeff Skiver pulled a Wisner out of his bags of tools during a class on handplanes at the Marc Adams School of Woodworking. He wasn't looking to sell it, and I won't tell you what he paid for it. Suffice it to say that Skiver practically stole it from a starving widow who had substantial medical bills.

The Wisner is an interesting piece of work. On the one hand, the main casting was nicely polished and the machined areas were crisp and clean. But the thumbscrew on the lever cap was black plastic (the screw itself was metal, however). And the main screw that joined the lever cap, iron and body casting was an off-the-shelf hex-head screw.

Wisner signed his name on the plane with some sort of rotary tool (perhaps a Dremel). And the blade was thinner than the Lie-Nielsen version.

Of course, when you are blazing a trail like Wisner, you have to overlook details like this and appreciate the fact that this plane exists. Plus, look at what this little plane led to in Warren, Maine.

And if anyone has a bronze Wisner plane they'd like to part with (for the sake of history, natch) please drop me a line.

READER COMMENTS

The Wisner plane is certainly an elegant and well-executed design. However, as Chris points out, it seems surprising and maybe even a little disappointing that the work includes, and is therefore somehow marred, by the inclusion of off-the-shelf parts.

Isn't it interesting that we as a society eschew standardized parts? Even if only when looking at collectable items. Perhaps it is our association of standardization with "mass produced."

When this plane was produced I am guessing Mr. Wisner considered alternatives, but custom manufacturing is expensive and he probably had to balance aesthetics with cost. I do agree that a slotted fillister, pan or binding head screw would have been a nice alternative. But when you are just starting out there are compromises to be made.

Imagine if Stanley had decided to use a single type of screw for the frog or chipbreaker. Though it would give the collectors fits, it would certainly ease the proper restoration of a neglected plane.

Are "custom-made" and "large-scale manufactured" truly mutually exclusive terms? Can a unique design that is also mass produced hold its value? I think the premium hand-tool makers have been relatively successful at threading the needle.

Murphy

Friends, Krenovians & Countrymen

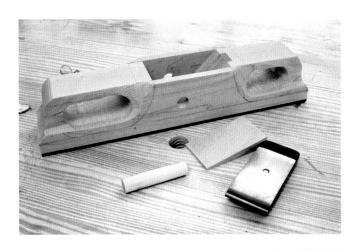

Early Roman planes were considerably different than modern ones. I built a Roman-style plane from a modern kit.

In 2006 I built two wooden planes from a kit sold by Ron Hock of Hock Tools. The kit is designed to be used to make a wooden handplane much like the ones popularized by James Krenov while he was at the College of the Redwoods.

When I took the parts out I got to looking at them and realized: "Hey, these could be used to build a Roman-style handplane." So I decided to build one plane like a Roman plane and the other like a Krenov-style plane.

Why build a Roman plane? (I mean, besides the fact that my mother must have dropped me on my head.) Well, I've always been interested in the odd grips offered by these tools. They seem designed to allow you to really press the plane down effectively, and one of the reasons I struggle with wooden planes is that I find them difficult to keep pressed to the work.

This plane is based on the Saalburg Roman plane shown in W.L. Goodman's "The History of Woodworking Tools." This plane survived because it was thrown down a well when the village was sacked by barbarians, according to Goodman. The dimensions for the plane kit are pretty close to the Saalburg plane, though not exact – mine will be a little short.

The iron on both the Saalburg plane and on the Hock plane is 1½" wide. Unlike a typical Roman iron, the Hock Tool iron and breaker are short. In the Roman examples, the iron will jut out several inches from the top of the stock. The extra iron will add weight and make the iron a little easier to tap left and right to adjust its projection. The iron in the Hock kit is bedded at 45° – Roman planes are typically pitched much higher – between 50° and 66°.

The kit from Ron Hock (hocktools.com) includes everything you need to build the plane: wooden components already cut to shape, the wooden cross-pin, a wedge and an iron and cap assembly. I was a little skeptical when I saw that the directions were a single page, but boy was the kit easy to put together. The plane shown above is the result of two hours of work. The Krenov-style plane was an even faster build because it didn't require shaping the elaborate grips.

First I glued the sidewalls and sole of the plane together. The wood for the body and sole was in good shape, though I tweaked one sidewall with a couple swipes of a block plane to get it to fit perfectly. Then I bored out the two grips using a 1"-diameter Forstner bit. Then I started shaping the grips with a handsaw and rasps.

When I first put my hands into the grips and got into planing position I was surprised by how good the body felt with those grips.

I'm interested in how the wooden body will react to humidity changes. Coffin-bodied smoothing planes are shaped to expose the maximum end grain, which allows them to react to humidity changes quickly. This plane has even more end grain exposed – right up against the area where the wedge and blade are, and at the front and toe. It could be good; it could be bad.

"Everything's a kit."

— Michael Burns, instructor
College of the Redwoods' Fine Woodworking Program

REVIEWS

BENCH PLANES

EXOTIC PLANES

JOINERY PLANES

MOULDING PLANES

SPECIALTY PLANES

Two Planemakers

Lie-Nielsen Toolworks and Lee Valley Tools have changed woodworking with their premium handplanes. Meet the men behind the brands and learn the real differences between the tools.

Thomas Lie-Nielsen reaches into a cardboard box to fetch a tool his company plans to manufacture in the coming year. He pulls out a wooden pattern of a router plane, a well-shaped and handmade version of the tool as it will look when it's later cast in ductile iron.

Like many of the tools from Lie-Nielsen Toolworks in Warren, Maine, the plane is recognizable as an adaptation of a classic tool – in this case the Stanley No. 71. Though as you examine the wooden pattern, you do notice subtle refinements, including an improved adjuster.

"A tool that looks like it was drawn in CAD is a failure to me," Lie-Nielsen says about the tool's almost-Victorian curves. "It might be fine, but it doesn't satisfy me."

More than 400 miles away in Ottawa, Ontario, Robin Lee offers a similar preview of tools that will be produced under the Veritas name by Lee Valley Tools. During this tour, Veritas is gearing up to build a bullnose plane. There's a beautifully made wooden pattern to show, and a plastic one, too. And the plane exists in a virtual environment on the company's servers as well.

Lee and a tool designer show off the plane's features and demonstrate how they tweak a tool's design in the computer to improve its balance and look. The Veritas bullnose plane looks like what you'd expect when you hold a bullnose plane, to be sure. But its DNA is impossible to trace to one historical example. The tool looks modern, and it has features never before seen on a bullnose – such as set screws that tweak the blade left and right. And it feels different in the hand thanks to holes and finger depressions in the body.

"Function is first," Lee says. "We're trying not to design from plane numbers, No. 1 and No. 2 and so on. Plus, people have changed. We're a lot bigger. There have been changes in nutrition and lifestyle. Muscle development has changed. We do less physical work. Our grips have changed. We have fewer callouses."

During the last two decades, these two toolmakers – Lie-Nielsen and Lee Valley – have transformed the way that thousands of woodworkers flatten and shape wood. Both companies have devoted enormous energy to do something almost unheard of: Produce high-quality hand tools in North America. While the planes cost more than many hand-held

ROBIN LEE IN THE COMPANY'S *flagship retail store in Ottawa, Ontario. "When we develop a tool we look at what will make it more usable for the average person. An inexperienced user should be able to get as much out of a tool as an experienced user."*

THOMAS LIE-NIELSEN IN HIS FACTORY *in Warren, Maine. "How a tool looks is important, but I don't do things for strictly decorative purposes."*

power tools, both brands have thousands of users who enthusiastically spread the word that well-made hand tools are worth the expense.

Both companies have succeeded while corporations, such as Stanley and Record, have abandoned efforts to make quality hand tools in the United States and England. In fact, demand is so strong that both Lee Valley Tools and Lie-Nielsen Toolworks struggle at times to keep up with their customer's orders.

And while these two tool-making companies share many similar goals, the way they design their tools is different. For those woodworkers looking to purchase a premium plane, many agonize about which brand to get. They debate the differences in nauseating detail on the Internet. They call woodworking magazine editors for opinions. And ultimately, some end up buying handplanes from both companies.

The brands are indeed different – not only to look at but in use as well. And the differences can be traced to the passionate personalities behind each company.

THE SELF-TAUGHT PLANEMAKER

Thomas Lie-Nielsen doesn't have a traditional office. In a back room of his factory there's a large open space with worktables, a workbench that the company is developing for sale and sweeping views of the Maine landscape. The shelves on the back wall are filled with tools his company made, plus antiques that are being studied.

Lie-Nielsen shares this room with other long-time employees, and he sets up his laptop computer on a worktable to answer e-mail, phone calls and questions from employees. Today Lie-Nielsen examines a bit for a metal milling machine that's bored with tiny holes to carry lubricant to the cutting edge. Lie-Nielsen and Joe Butler, then the vice

president of the company, debate the merits of the tooling and Lie-Nielsen asks how much the bits cost. Butler tells him.

"And you think my tools are expensive?" Lie-Nielsen says with a laugh.

Surprisingly, Lie-Nielsen isn't a formally trained machinist or engineer, but he probably would be welcomed into any factory. Since establishing Lie-Nielsen Toolworks in 1987 in a decrepit woodshed, Lie-Nielsen has become personally accomplished at casting bronze, heat-treating steel and machining tools.

He was born in 1954 as the son of a Maine boat builder and grew up surrounded by craftsmen who built wooden boats with hand tools. His father's

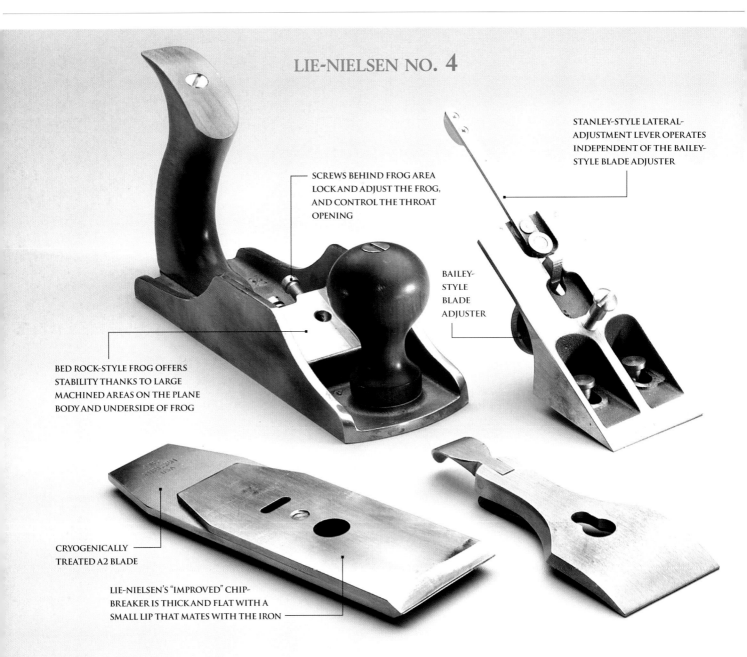

LIE-NIELSEN NO. 4

STANLEY-STYLE LATERAL-ADJUSTMENT LEVER OPERATES INDEPENDENT OF THE BAILEY-STYLE BLADE ADJUSTER

SCREWS BEHIND FROG AREA LOCK AND ADJUST THE FROG, AND CONTROL THE THROAT OPENING

BAILEY-STYLE BLADE ADJUSTER

BED ROCK-STYLE FROG OFFERS STABILITY THANKS TO LARGE MACHINED AREAS ON THE PLANE BODY AND UNDERSIDE OF FROG

CRYOGENICALLY TREATED A2 BLADE

LIE-NIELSEN'S "IMPROVED" CHIP-BREAKER IS THICK AND FLAT WITH A SMALL LIP THAT MATES WITH THE IRON

business, Lee's Boatshop, also had a machine shop and would cast the lead keels for its boats on the beach.

Lie-Nielsen enjoyed making things and considered becoming a boat builder; he recalls a visit to a yacht designer during high school as a pivotal career moment. When Lie-Nielsen asked the designer for advice about boat building, the designer handed over a set of old plans for a boat.

"He said: 'Here, take these. Everything you need to learn is right there. You don't need to go to school,'" Lie-Nielsen says.

Lie-Nielsen went to Hamilton College and studied English and history. After school he ended up in New York City while his wife attended gradu-

ate school there. An ad for the Garrett Wade woodworking catalog in *Wooden Boat* magazine caught his eye, and he landed a job with the Manhattan mail-order company run by Garry Chinn. There he had a front-row seat as Stanley and Record discontinued their specialty planes and allowed the quality to slip on their bench and block planes. He heard customers complain.

There were some cottage toolmakers making a few of these desirable tools, but they were a drop in the bucket. One of these toolmakers, Ken Wisner, made a version of the Stanley No. 95 edge-trimming plane and sold them through Garrett Wade. Lie-Nielsen heard that Wisner was looking to get out of the business. At the same time, Lie-Nielsen

VERITAS NO. 4

NORRIS-STYLE ADJUSTER CONTROLS BOTH DEPTH OF CUT AND CENTERING OF BLADE IN THE THROAT

FROG ASSEMBLY EXTENDS ALL THE WAY TO THE SOLE OF THE PLANE AND INCORPORATES THE REAR HANDLE (CALLED THE "TOTE") INTO THE DESIGN

SET-SCREWS TWEAK BLADE'S POSITION IN THE THROAT

STANLEY-STYLE CHIPBREAKER

A2 BLADE

was looking to return to Maine. He worked out a deal with Wisner, bought a run-down farm in Maine and began making tools in the woodshed when he wasn't growing food, or tending the sheep and milk cows.

He developed the patterns for the skew block plane he now sells, and built a new shed on his property. A friend who ran an art foundry would cast the bronze, and Lie-Nielsen started investing in machines and tooling.

Customers and the woodworking press began to take notice. When David Sloan from *Fine Woodworking* magazine called Lie-Nielsen for the first time, he was picking blueberries on his land. Since then, it has been a story of almost-constant expansion.

Lie-Nielsen got divorced, sold the farm and moved the business into the building he now occupies – which was once an icehouse and later a factory that built one-man submarines. He struggled to find foundries that would handle his small volume and demands for quality. Until he found the right foundry, he cast the bronze tools himself. It was the same story with the blades for his tools.

As his volume increased, he found the right foundry and the right people in the steel and heat-treating industry to provide him with cast bronze and ductile-iron tool bodies and quality irons.

The company has outgrown its building several times and construction seems constant. During this visit in early 2004, Lie-Nielsen is juggling his warehouse and new chisel-making operation and he's about to break ground on a 7,500-square-foot

HERE YOU CAN SEE SAW *handles being prepared for finishing at Lie-Nielsen's satellite factory. Though produced by modern methods, the handles are decidedly inspired by 19th-century designs.*

VERITAS NO. 6 FORE PLANES *after the frogs have been machined. Unlike a traditional No. 6, the Veritas has its mouth located further back than the Stanley versions.*

expansion. He's even had to acquire a factory in a nearby town for his saw-making, handle-making and his patternmaker. He now employs almost 70 people.

Lunch today is at his laptop with some fellow employees – the debate is pizza or hamburgers. The work is constant and every year seems to be a pivotal one. After building up his line of hard-to-find specialty planes, Lie-Nielsen then took a gamble by building bench and block planes, which competed directly with mass-produced Stanley and Record planes. Lie-Nielsen planes can cost five times as much as a new Stanley plane, but people continue to buy them.

"There was some price-resistance at first," he says. "But we proved that quality sells. I price the tools so I can make money but people can afford them."

And some of his tools have changed the way people work wood. His low-angle jack plane launched a revolution in the hand-tool world and people began embracing larger tools that cut with the iron's bevel facing up. He now offers chisels that have raised the bar among Western tools, and he struggles to keep up with demand, despite dozens of competitors that make chisels. Next up is workbenches. And then?

"We want to offer as complete a kit as possible for the hand-tool woodworker," he says. "Future planes will obviously be more specialized now that we have the full range of bench planes: compass planes, spokeshaves, panel saws, veneer saws. My list is longer than it has ever been."

LISTENING TO CUSTOMERS IS A FAMILY TRADITION

Somehow, Robin Lee violates the laws of time and space. Visit almost any woodworking discussion forum on the Internet, and you're sure to run into him there. He monitors and chimes in almost

BOTH LIE-NIELSEN AND LEE VALLEY *use ductile iron for their plane bodies. This material is nearly unbreakable and stable. Here Lie-Nielsen shows off one of the castings that has been brutalized to show how it won't crack.*

daily on these forums – though he's never trying to directly sell product. Mostly he's reading about woodworkers' experiences, answering questions asked directly to him and occasionally tantalizing others on the forum with images of the tools that are coming from Veritas, the manufacturing arm of Lee Valley Tools.

Competing tool manufacturers are often bewildered by the energy Lee pours into this endeavor, but Lee sees it as the same thing he has done his entire life while growing up under the wing of Lee Valley Tools: He's listening and responding to the needs of customers.

Lee was 15 when his father, Leonard Lee, started Lee Valley Tools from his house in 1978. The company's first catalog was laid out on the family's kitchen table with the assistance of Garry Chinn, the founder of the Garrett Wade catalog (and the person who also gave Lie-Nielsen his first job in the tool industry).

"We do share roots," Lee says of Lie-Nielsen, Chinn and Lee Valley. Lee Valley's first taste of manufacturing tools was actually the result of a partnership with Garrett Wade to produce a line of tools under the name "Paragon." That short-lived venture led Lee Valley to become a tool manufacturer, though planes were not at the top of the company's list then. "Stanley and Record were still pretty good at the time," Lee says.

From those humble beginnings at the Lee home, the company has grown to more than 900 employees who run the catalog operation and 11 retail stores in Canada. With more than 5,200 woodworking products in the catalog – 550 of which they make – Lee Valley is likely the largest hand-tool catalog in the world.

Part of that success is the result of offering good tools at a fair price. And part of that success

is the result of the company's legendary customer service. Lee learned that lesson well as he worked full-time hours after school and during summers for Lee Valley.

"I enjoyed every minute of what was virtually slave labor," Lee says with a laugh. "That's typical for a family business. But I really found that I enjoyed not only the tools, but the industry and the people we serve."

When he was home between sessions at the University of Waterloo (where he studied engineering, specializing in management sciences and ergonomics) he sifted through the comment cards and letters from customers. He estimates he has personally read tens of thousands of these.

"My real education came from customers," he says. "The formal schooling will teach you how to think. In dealing with the customers, I learn something every day."

In fact, Lee points to customer comments as the starting point for designing a tool. About a third of the company's tools sprout from customers. "We

A VERITAS EMPLOYEE CHECKS THE *machining on a plane's frog. Most home woodworkers don't have the correct instruments to measure tolerances or the skills to correct them. If you think your premium plane isn't right, contact the manufacturer before fixing it yourself. You could make it worse.*

read every comment card," he says. "We file them and keep them as a reference so we can go back and see trends."

Lee Valley employs 12 people in research and development (R&D), including five product designers. Tucked under the eaves of the company's headquarters in Ottawa, the designers work in sleek office cubicles with high-powered computers. But their shelves are packed with prototype, vintage and new tools.

Though Veritas planes have modern lines, it would be a mistake to say they are a rejection of past forms. Many of the details and features on Veritas planes have appeared on tools, if however briefly, some time in the last 200 years. Yet some of the features on the tools are truly original – the company holds a number of patents on its line of hand tools.

Through a doorway from R&D is a large storage room with a woodworking bench where these ideas are put to the test.

Though Lee isn't part of the R&D department, he spends a fair amount of time guiding their efforts. Today the product designers and Lee are working with three tools: a concave-sole spokeshave, a low-angle jack plane and the company's spokeshave kit.

Lee takes a couple swipes on a board with the jack plane and offers some comments about the tool's balance. Then he shows off one of the features of the plane he's proud of. It's a small, adjustable stop in front of the blade that prevents the adjustable mouth from striking the iron and damaging it. It also allows you to rapidly clear the mouth

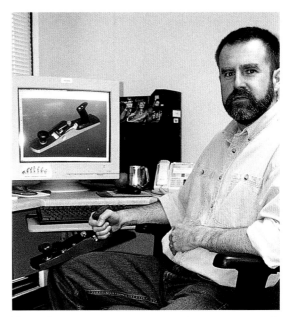

TERRY SAUNDERS, THE CHIEF PLANE *designer at Lee Valley Tools, shows off the CAD drawings that led to the prototype low-angle jack plane he's holding.*

of shavings should it clog. He demonstrates this feature by quickly clicking the mouth open and shut. If you want you can even slam the mouth open and shut without striking the iron.

The knob is simple and ingenious. Innovations like this get Lee very excited.

It's fair to say Lee's passion for product development comes naturally. His father recently turned over the reins of Lee Valley to Robin. Now Leonard Lee focuses his efforts on designing and producing new surgical instruments and procedures for Canica Design, including a scalpel that sprung from the Veritas Carver's Knife.

And the Lee family tradition is likely to continue. Both Robin's son and daughter – now college age – have grown up working in every department. "They started with the manual labor – the landscaping," he says.

And they are both refining one of the most important traits of the Lee family. His daughter is now doing product-management work for the company.

"She really enjoys the research," Lee says, with obvious pride, "and listens well."

COMPARING THE BRANDS

The tools that spring from the labor of these two companies are indeed different, from their price tag to how they feel in use.

But you should know that any comparison of two planes is troublesome – planes are personal tools. So the following opinions should be taken as only one person's experiences. But for what it's

ONE OF THE BIG CHALLENGES *for Lie-Nielsen and Lee Valley is to produce handles that are comfortable but that can be made with a minimum of hand work. Here, a Lie-Nielsen saw handle is machined to shape.*

THE VERITAS BULLNOSE PLANE SHOWN *with a vintage Preston version of the same tool. The Veritas plane has features and a shape that favors ergonomics and function over the classical form.*

worth, I have worked with both brands for years. And I have a long history with many of the tools.

On the topic of price, the Veritas planes are almost universally less expensive than the Lie-Nielsens. In 2004 there were 12 styles of planes made by both companies. If you bought all 12 from Lie-Nielsen, you'd spend $2,580. From Veritas, that same linep would cost $1,799 – 30 percent less.

Price is only one factor. Unlike a router or drill, planes are lifetime tools. So I personally don't focus as much on price as I do on the tools' working characteristics, how it behaves during use. Does it fight me or work for me?

VERITAS BENCH PLANES

The overall design of Veritas's four bench planes is quite different than a Stanley plane. Many of the Veritas's features have appeared on other tools, but the Veritas combines them in a new way.

The frog – the metal casting that supports the iron – is the most unusual part of the design. The rear handle is actually screwed to the frog. And the bottom of the frog is incorporated into the sole of the plane. This unusual frog allows you to close up the plane's throat without changing the depth of cut.

I've never had problems with the stability of this frog – functionally, it's a success. It does have two aspects that annoy me slightly. Having the frog visible on the sole makes it trickier to sight down the sole when setting the blade – the back of the frog creates a black line that looks like the black line created by your blade. Also, you have to navigate a screwdriver through holes in the lever cap, chipbreaker and iron to reach the screw that allows you to open or close the throat. That takes fiddling.

To adjust the depth of cut, Veritas planes use a Norris-style adjuster. This adjuster, made popular on English smoothing planes, allows you to change both the depth of cut and to center the blade in the mouth with one mechanism. (Stanley planes use two separate mechanisms.)

Veritas's Norris-style adjuster is precise and robust, with a respectable half-turn of slop in its mechanism. Even better, the Veritas designers have avoided a common problem with Norris adjusters: When used in an infill plane, it's easy to cinch down the lever cap so tight that when you turn the Norris adjuster it commits suicide by stripping out. With the Veritas plane you can tighten the lever cap as much as you please and the worst that can happen is that you'll push the chipbreaker out of position. I cannot destroy this adjuster – and I've tried.

I don't like the position of the adjuster above the tote, however. This is personal preference, but I like the adjustment mechanism directly in front of the tote.

The sidewalls of the Veritas hold two small set screws. These finely center the cutter in the mouth and prevent the cutter from slipping out of position. I'm of the opinion that lateral adjustment levers on all planes are too coarse for high-tolerance smoothing. I usually end up tapping the iron with a small hammer for my final adjustments. The set screws are slower than tapping the cutter with a hammer, but beginners will likely find them an asset. I don't use them much on the bench planes.

The cutter is made from A2 steel and the chipbreaker resembles the Stanley version. Though I'm not wild about this classic chipbreaker design in principle, I must admit that Veritas does a fine job of making them – I haven't had one give me trouble since my first encounter with them on Veritas's first-generation No. $4\frac{1}{2}$ plane.

LIE-NIELSEN LOW-ANGLE JACK PLANES BEING *readied for shipment from the factory in Maine. Both companies hand-assemble each tool.*

The handles are now made from bubinga (my No. 4 has the original stained maple knob and tote). The rear handle is larger than I prefer, though other craftsmen I respect disagree with my assessment. I don't consider it uncomfortable. Veritas has been tweaking its totes and knobs, and a redesigned tote is being worked on, Lee says, so stay tuned.

LIE-NIELSEN BENCH PLANES

The Lie-Nielsen bench planes, from the diminutive No. 2 up to the No. 8, are modeled after the Stanley Bed Rock line of planes, but with better materials and machining tolerances.

The Lie-Nielsen frog is mated to the plane's body via a large machined area. This stable design was abandoned by Stanley years ago in favor of cheaper methods – and is one of the things that make new Stanley planes squirrelly today. The Lie-Nielsen frog is bulletproof and rock solid.

You open and close the mouth of the plane by first loosening two screws behind the frog then turning a screw centered between them. Finally, you retighten the screws and adjust the cutter before going to work. I've never been a fan of the trial-and-error method of adjusting the frog. I admit that opening and closing the mouth of a bench plane is an infrequent activity; when I do change it, it takes some fiddling. Here's why:

A SURPRISING AMOUNT OF HAND *work is involved in building handplanes. Here a Lie-Nielsen employee flattens the unbeveled side of a plane iron using sandpaper.*

Because the frog rests on a machined ramp, moving the frog also changes the depth of cut of the blade. So to find out how tight your mouth is, you tweak the frog, reset the blade and make a sample cut. I usually go through three rounds of this before I find the opening that reduces my tear-out and allows the shaving to pass.

The plane uses a "Bailey-style" system of regulating the depth of cut: You turn a large wheel in front of the tote to change the cut. A lever above the tote tweaks the cutter's position left and right.

The blade adjuster of the Lie-Nielsen is precise and responsive, though I wish it had a little less slop – it's almost a full turn of the wheel. This is a function of the Bailey-style mechanism; on vintage planes there can be as much as two turns of slop. The adjuster is positioned perfectly in front of the tote so you can make adjustments by simply moving your fingertips. As I mentioned with the Veritas, the lateral adjustment of all planes is coarse – hammer taps get you where you need to be.

While all those elements resemble those found on a vintage Stanley, others do not. The iron is cryogenically treated A2 steel, and the chipbreaker is different than the one found on vintage Stanleys. The Lie-Nielsen resembles chipbreakers found on some vintage infill planes: It's flat, thick and has a small lip on the end where it mates with the iron. The chipbreaker is the cat's pajamas – I wish all planes were equipped with it.

MODERN PLANES HAVE FAR MORE *machining than vintage tools. On this Veritas spokeshave, the mouth and sole are milled out on precision equipment. This extra work means less blade chatter for woodworkers.*

AT VERITAS, EVERY TOOL HAS *a checklist that must be followed at assembly-time. These checklists are continually fine-tuned for better results and faster work.*

The handles are available in cherry or rosewood. The knob and tote are attractive and comfortable in my hands. My only complaint is that the screw for the rear tote works loose after heavy use – an annoyance on many other planes as well.

COMPARING BEVEL-UP PLANES

In addition to bench planes, both companies sell "low-angle" jack, jointer and smoothing planes. These tools are essentially oversized block planes. Unlike bench planes, these have a cutter with the bevel facing up (it faces down on bench planes).

These tools are simpler than a bench plane – there's no chipbreaker, the blade-adjustment mechanisms have fewer parts, and you open and close the throat of the tool by sliding an adjustable shoe forward. As with the bench planes, there are differences between the brands.

The Lie-Nielsen low-angle jack plane is simple and robust. The depth of cut is regulated by a knob in front of the tote. However, there's no lateral-adjustment mechanism. Sharpen your iron as square as possible and center it in the mouth of the tool with hammer taps. The Lee Valley version of this tool is equally robust and offers a Norris-style adjuster with lateral adjustment. Plus, the plane has set screws in its sidewalls to tweak the iron's position. I find both planes easy to set, though first-time plane users might like the extra blade-adjustment features on the Veritas.

You adjust the throat of both tools by loosening the front knob and sliding an adjustable shoe forward and back. The Lie-Nielsen has a lever to assist this process, though I occasionally bang the shoe

into the iron using this system. The Veritas is a bit different. There's no lever to help dial in the setting. But there is a small knob in front of the throat that acts as a stop (preventing you from hitting the cutter's edge) and it helps you dial in the throat opening precisely. I quite like the system.

The Veritas is wider – it has a $2\frac{1}{4}$"-wide cutter compared to the Lie-Nielsen's 2" cutter. Wider isn't always better; it depends on the scale of your work. The cutter on the Veritas is $\frac{1}{16}$" thicker than the Lie-Nielsen's, and the Veritas is heavier – 5.7 pounds compared to 4.6. One significant design feature worth noting is the position of the mouth on each plane. The Veritas's mouth begins $4\frac{3}{4}$" from the toe of the tool. The Lie-Nielsen's begins $3\frac{15}{16}$" from the toe. Having the mouth set back a little makes the tool easier to start because you don't have as much of the tool hanging off the board. Also, positioning the mouth back a bit offers some advantages to planing the edges of long boards.

The other differences are subjective. I prefer the handles on the Lie-Nielsen, though Veritas has made some changes to its handles that make them more comfortable for me.

Both companies also make a smoothing plane using the bevel-up configuration. For the most part, the differences between the brands mirror those for the jack planes. The one notable exception is that the adjuster on the Lie-Nielsen version, the No. 164, is quite different. It's actually a Bailey-style adjuster that has been reconfigured to work on top of the lever cap. It's a smooth-acting adjuster, but there are some extra parts involved, including a small plate that has to be affixed to the cutter to engage the adjuster. This plate has to be removed when sharpening with a jig and has to be precisely placed for the adjuster to work. This is the way the original Stanley worked, and I've always thought it was a little fussy.

CONCLUSIONS

Every week, someone asks my opinion on which brand is better. Let me tell you what I tell them: Both brands are machined to tolerances that exceed those of vintage tools (and, in some cases, exceed what's necessary for woodworking). Both brands are made using materials that are superior to what's needed for home woodworking, such as the A2 irons. Both brands of tools can be tuned to do the finest work. I can consistently make equally thin shavings (.001" thick or less) with either brand with equal ease.

So the differences come down to looks, price and features. And that's where my biases come into play. For bench planes, I favor the Lie-Nielsens. I prefer the Bailey-style adjuster, especially its location by the tote. I also like the wide range of plane sizes available. Though the Veritas line of planes makes sense as a system, I've found that after using all of the sizes available, I like having a small smoother, such as a No. 3, in my arsenal. And I also gravitate to the long bench planes, including the No. 8. My preferences could be debated, but they are real.

For the bevel-up planes, I prefer the Veritas low-angle smooth plane to the Lie-Nielsen version. The adjuster is simpler and my fingers feel less crowded on the tool. For the low-angle jack plane, it's a toss-up. I cannot argue with the features or engineering of the Veritas. It's likely the best plane the company has ever built. But the Lie-Nielsen was one of my first premium planes, and I have a lot of miles on it. It's always appealed to my eye and my hands, and was the tool where I first discovered the benefits of a bevel-up tool.

So for this tool, I choose both. I keep the Veritas low-angle jack at work and the Lie-Nielsen version at home. Like many woodworkers, I end up using both brands of tools. And Lee says this is something he's seen time and again.

"The difference is like jazz or classical, which do you prefer?" he says. "We co-exist in the market. And the existence of the other is better for both businesses. And for woodworkers."

FOR MORE INFORMATION:
Lee Valley Tools/Veritas
800-871-8158, leevalley.com
Lie-Nielsen Toolworks
800-327-2520, lie-nielsen.com

Building Planes One at a Time

Most woodworkers appreciate things that are well-made, fashioned by hand and extraordinarily useful. So it's little wonder that Wayne Anderson stays quite busy.

From a small basement workshop in Minnesota, Anderson makes custom infill planes one at a time to sell to woodworkers and collectors. Unlike many manufactured tools, Anderson's planes marry solid plane mechanics with fluid curves that would be difficult – if not impossible – to create using machines. One recent chariot plane from his workshop resembles a scarab beetle. The front grip of the small plane at right is filed into the shape of a curved acanthus leaf.

And though some of these tools look delicate, they have the souls of small tanks. The sides and soles of the planes are joined with hand-filed double-dovetails. The wooden infills are secured with brass or steel pins that are peened in place. The soles are hand-lapped dead flat. The mouths of the tools are extremely fine.

The result of this alchemy are tools that are beautiful to the eye and spookily responsive in your hands.

During the last five years I've examined more than a dozen of Anderson's planes and used four of them in my shop for a variety of tasks. They all work as well as any handplane – vintage or new – I've ever owned.

Despite the fact that many of his tools lack a mechan-

WAYNE ANDERSON FILES THE BED *of a chariot plane in his basement workshop. Tools on the back wall serve as inspiration and they lend a hand with the woodworking on occasion.*

ical adjuster, I find it unnecessary. Because every part fits so perfectly, the tools respond predictably and precisely every time I pick them up.

Setting the irons is an easy task with a hammer. Anderson's planes generally have a generous surface for bedding the A2 irons. When you drop a freshly sharpened iron on the bed it practically sticks there because the parts fit so well. A couple hammer taps and a turn of the lever cap screw are all it takes to get the plane working.

I'm not alone in my assessment. Ralph Brendler, one of the ringleaders of the Internet-based e-mail list called "oldtools," owns a few of Anderson's planes that he uses regularly.

"If I had my druthers, every plane in my cabinet would be from Wayne," Brendler says. "The miter plane he built me so far exceeded my expectations. I was just stunned when I opened the box. … My jaw hit the floor."

ENGINEERING & ARTISTRY

For Anderson, his planemaking business is the logical culmination of his artistic tendencies as a boy and his career path as an adult. He worked as a machinist, then in a metal fabrication shop and as a mechanical designer.

Add to that a passion for collecting vintage tools and it's little wonder that Anderson stays busy building tools. Or that he has recently shifted into high gear by going part-time at his day job so he can focus even more on building planes for clients, almost all of whom are repeat customers. One enthusiast owns 14 of Anderson's planes.

Anderson's path to becoming a professional planemaker began several years ago when he and a friend would haunt the local woodworking supply stores. One day Anderson was in a used tool store where they had a copy of the now-famous poster of the H.O. Studley tool chest – a small wall-hung tool chest that holds more than 300 artfully fit hand tools.

"I found myself riveted to that image," he says. "Something clicked. And I decided to amass a small collection of vintage tools."

So Anderson began buying old tools. As he plunged deeper into collecting, Anderson stumbled on a story about British infill maker Bill Carter and was so intrigued that he decided to make an improved miter plane for himself. He still owns that tool.

"I call it 'plane-a-saurus,'" Anderson says with a laugh. "It had $^3/16$"-thick sides and a $^1/4$" bottom. It's butt-ugly, but it functions well. It's like your kid's artwork. It's not worth a nickel, but you wouldn't sell it for a million bucks."

Encouraged that he could make a functioning tool, Anderson built more planes (lots more) and started posting pictures of them on the Internet. Woodworkers began to take notice and ask Anderson to make planes for them. Now he spends his time filing and fitting and fussing with all the details that go into one of his planes.

He has a few machines that assist his work: a small drill press and band saw lend a hand. And he recently purchased a small benchtop milling machine to cut the mouth of the planes. But much of the work is by hand and by eye.

TWO PLANES FROM WAYNE ANDERSON: *A full-size smoothing plane with ebony infill (top) and a small plane inspired by some of the earliest metal-bodied planes from Europe.*

What's most striking about his finished tools is how they don't look much like anyone else's tools. Unlike some contemporary planemakers, Anderson doesn't revel in making reproductions of classic infill tools from Norris, Spiers, Mathison or Slater. Instead, Anderson's keen eye and impressive collection of files create planes with fluid sidewalls, sculpted and scalloped wedges and details that are found on fine furniture more than on tools.

"I was never one to copy a Norris or a Spiers," Anderson says. "Those were the production planes of the era. I was never impressed with the style."

As you can imagine, one-of-a-kind hand-built planes are more expensive than manufactured ones. Anderson's planes can start at $1,000.

But Anderson's tools have an undefinable appeal that cannot be boiled down to price alone. A lot of hand work goes into the furniture I build, and there is something fitting about using a hand-made tool in my work.

From a pragmatic point of view, Anderson's planes are quite reasonably priced compared to the cost of the vintage infill planes that are prized by tool collectors. Vintage tools of this caliber are far more expensive and may or may not even be usable. In fact, other toolmakers and collectors consider Anderson's planes an astonishing bargain for what you get.

Anderson says he isn't driven by money. He merely prices his tools so he can stay busy making them, that he can do the kind of work he wants and make a tool that's within reach of the serious plane user.

"These are user planes," he says, tapping the table for emphasis. "It's a tool. Take it into the shop and use it."

FOR MORE INFORMATION
andersonplanes.com, 763-486-0834
110 Monroe St., Big Lake, Minn. 55309

Veritas
Low-angle
Smoother

*A well-made, versatile plane
that's a great value.*

When Stanley manufactured the No. 164 low-angle smoothing plane from 1926 to 1943, it was intended mostly for working on end grain, butcher blocks and the like.

These planes didn't sell too well, so you might wonder why modern planemaker Veritas decided to introduce its own version in 2002. The truth of the matter is that the Veritas Low-Angle Smooth Plane is much better-made than the vintage Stanley. The body castings are thicker, the blade is beefier and the blade-adjustment mechanism is simpler to operate and more versatile. On top of that, modern woodworkers have learned how to customize these tools easily to make them ideal for any smoothing task.

Unlike in a bench plane, the iron in a low-angle smoothing plane sits in the body with the cutting bevel facing up, similar to a block plane. With the iron factory-ground at 25°, the tool is ideal for planing end grain, trimming miters and smoothing face grain that's straight. Boards with tricky grain are a problem in this stock configuration, but if you simply grind the bevel of the iron to 38° or steeper, you can create a higher cutting angle that makes this tool ideal for smoothing the trickiest face grain out there.

In fact, you can make this tool do the work of several planes by purchasing a few replacement irons (available from the manufacturer), grinding different cutting angles on them and swapping them out when your work demands it. (Lee Valley Tools now offers replacement irons for this tool ground at 38° so you don't have to do it yourself.)

Once I started experimenting with different grinding angles, the Veritas Low-angle Smooth Plane became one of my favorite tools.

The plane's body is made using indestructible ductile iron, so the plane will survive a fall to a concrete floor. The sidewalls are ground square to the sole of the tool, which makes the plane ideal to use with a shooting board to trim the end grain of parts.

The handles are comfortable to hold for long periods of time. Some woodworkers will like the fact that their fingers aren't jammed behind a frog assembly, as they are with a standard bench plane.

Another big plus with this tool is that the mouth of the plane can easily be closed up tight thanks to an adjustable toe piece similar to what you find on a block plane. You simply turn the front knob to loosen the toe piece, move it where you want it and turn the knob back to lock your setting. My only quibble with this system is that it's almost too easy to move the toe. In the last couple years I've had it slide back unexpectedly and strike my freshly sharpened iron. Current versions of this tool have a small stop that allows you to set the mouth to the same position every time.

My only other gripe with the plane is that the sides of the A2 iron aren't parallel – they taper so the iron is narrower at the back. This makes it difficult (and sometimes impossible) to secure it in common side-clamp honing guides. The sides have to be tapered to allow you to laterally adjust the iron to get a perfectly square cut.

Those minor quibbles aside, the Veritas Low-angle Smooth Plane is an impressive tool, and one I frequently recommend to woodworkers who are getting started in exploring handplanes. You'll be hard-pressed to find a better all-around premium handplane for the price.

FOR MORE INFORMATION
leevalley.com, 800-871-8158

Lie-Nielsen Low-angle Jack Plane

Quite possibly the perfect plane.

I've used many different planes, but none is as versatile, easy-to-use and robust as the Lie-Nielsen low-angle jack plane.

This 14"-long plane is based on the collectible Stanley #62 plane, which has not been manufactured since the 1940s. Unless you're a collector, there is little reason to seek out the old Stanley version because it's more expensive and less durable than the Lie-Nielsen.

Essentially, the low-angle jack plane is what would happen if you wedded a block plane with a bench plane. You have the mass and length of a jack plane, but you also have the simpler mechanism, adjustable throat and bevel-up blade design of a block plane. For beginners especially, the combination is hard to beat. Here's why:

The standard Bailey-style bench plane has more adjustments than the low-angle jack, which make the Bailey tools more difficult for beginners.

For example, if you're working with figured wood and want to close up the mouth of a bench plane to reduce tear-out, you have to adjust the plane's frog forward. This operation involves a screwdriver and sometimes requires disassembling the tool. With the low-angle jack plane, there is no frog to adjust. All you do is unscrew the front knob a bit and adjust a lever to open or close the mouth.

Another advantage of the low-angle jack's design is that the cutting bevel of the blade faces up, unlike a bench plane where the bevel faces down.

If you purchase a couple replacement blades for this plane, you can hone different cutting angles on the blades. The stock blade has a 25° bevel and sits in the plane at 12°. Add those two numbers together and you have a 37° cutting angle. This pitch is great for end grain.

Grind a 33° bevel on the blade and the plane will have a standard 45° pitch (33° plus 12° equals 45°). Grind a 38° bevel and you have a high-angle pitch of 50°, which is great for difficult woods.

So what can you use this plane for? In the modern power-tool workshop, this plane can handle a lot of chores. It's great for planing down doors and drawers to fit. You can remove saw marks from the edges of boards.

You can even use it as a smoothing plane to remove the machining marks from the faces of your boards. Hand-tool purists might turn up their noses at this notion and say you need a shorter smoothing plane for this operation because it gets into the hollows of the board. But I've found that if you surface your lumber with machines, it's flat enough for this plane to work rather well as a smoother.

No matter how you use this plane, you'll find that it exceeds your expectations. The machining is impeccable. The cherry knob and tote are perfectly formed and comfortable to use. And the blade has been well heat-treated, which allows it to take and keep a superior edge. The body is made of unbreakable ductile iron (standard gray iron planes can shatter if you drop them) and the blade cap is bronze.

With almost every tool I own there is always something small I wish was improved or a bit different. But that's not so with the low-angle jack, which I've been using for years now. As the handles of this tool patinate with age and the blade gets progressively shorter, I find it more and more useful. And I occasionally wonder how I ever did without it.

FOR MORE INFORMATION
lie-nielsen.com, 800-327-2520

Clifton Bench Planes

Excellent intentions; inconsistent execution.

When woodworkers talk about modern handplanes, you often hear them rave about Lie-Nielsen and Veritas and complain bitterly about their newly made Stanleys. But when it comes to Clifton's line of Bed Rock-style bench planes, what you mostly get is silence.

American woodworkers I've talked to during the last eight years actually have more questions than they do opinions about this British-made line of premium planes. They wonder about the quality of manufacturing and machining, and how the tools compare at the bench to more the Lie-Nielsen planes and the Canadian line of Veritas planes.

After almost three years of working with the Clifton planes, I've found that they can be tuned to a very high level of performance – what you would expect from a Lie-Nielsen, Veritas or highly tuned Stanley Bed Rock. But what I've also found is that the manufacturing is a bit inconsistent. Some of the Clifton planes have been nearly perfect out of the box, while others have had problems that required considerable effort on my part or – in two cases – for the tools to go back to the seller.

On paper, the Clifton bench planes can be a bargain or more expensive – depending on the exchange rate with the English pound (when they were introduced they were a bargain). Like the Lie-Nielsens, the Cliftons are based on the venerable Bed Rock pattern but have some enhancements: thicker castings, fancy brass fittings, bubinga handles and an improved iron and chipbreaker assembly.

But it wouldn't be fair to say the Cliftons are a British clone of the U.S.-made Lie-Nielsen plane. The Lie-Nielsens are cast from ductile iron, which renders them nearly invulnerable to breakage.

The Cliftons are made using the same grey iron used in Bailey-style planes, and the tools can crack from a nasty fall from bench height. The Lie-Nielsens have an exotic cryogenically treated A2 alloy cutter, while the Cliftons stick with tried-and-true high-carbon steel.

There's a bitter disagreement among handplane users about how sharp you can make A2 and if it's a fitting tool steel for handplanes, particularly for the demands of smoothing. That discussion could fill an entire magazine issue, but my shorthand opinion is that A2 takes a little longer to sharpen, but it is perfectly suitable for handplanes and appears to keep a working edge longer than high-carbon steel.

SOME ARE PERFECT; SOME HAVE SOME PROBLEMS

The first Clifton plane I purchased was the smallish No. 3, and it was one of the first tools off the boat in 2001. It was practically perfect. Like all the Clifton planes I tested, the mating between the frog, sole and iron was excellent. The iron itself required little work – the back was remarkably flat and the chipbreaker fit perfectly with no tweaking. The sole of the plane needed no flattening. It was, all in all, as much as I could ask of any premium handplane. A second No. 3 purchased later proved similarly perfect. Then I purchased the No. 5 and I began scratching my head.

I'm not a nut about flattening the soles of planes, but if they don't behave as expected, the sole is one place I'll look for trouble. Sure enough, this No. 5's sole was too high at opposing corners. In other words, it was warped and rocked slightly on the work. According to a straightedge and feeler gauges, it was out of true by .005" (Clifton's literature states its maximum deviation should be .003"). That was the same amount of warpage I found on the Indian-made Anant jack plane and the British-made Stanley jack. Otherwise, the plane was in good shape; after a grueling sole-flattening session, the tool was a winner.

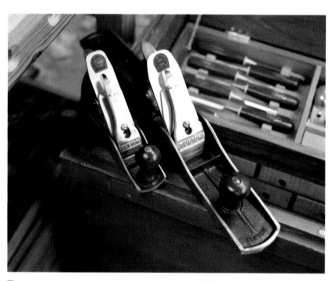

FROM AN AESTHETIC POINT OF *view, the Cliftons have a decidedly English look to them and appear at home on my toolbox, an adaptation of Benjamin Seaton's famous tool chest.*

The No. 4 I tested had a different problem. The hole stamped in the chipbreaker was located in the wrong place and it looked like the dog that regulated the iron's position was ground a little differently than the other Cliftons in our shop. As a result, the iron had to be almost fully retracted into the plane's body to take a fine, .001"-thick smoothing cut. That's not right. So the plane went back to the seller; they gladly replaced the chipbreaker and the plane worked well after that.

Finally, the No. 7 showed up. The sole was decent, the iron didn't need a lot of work and I was happy with the tool for the first year. Then, while flattening my benchtop, I turned the plane over to wax the sole and noticed a chip behind the mouth. A few months later I was shooting the edges of a couple boards to glue up a panel and I tweaked the lateral-adjustment lever. It moved a little too easily. The dog that engages the iron had broken loose – a weak weld apparently. This plane also went back to the seller and it was replaced promptly.

Another small gripe came when dealing with the tote on two of the tools. They could not be tightened sufficiently – I suspect the bubinga had contracted a bit as it dried. So I had to hacksaw off about ⅛" from the threaded rod that holds the tote in place. It was a minor inconvenience, but it was another thing that had to be tweaked before I could go to work.

GOOD-LOOKING OR FLASHY? YOUR CALL

And then there's aesthetics. To my eye, the Veritas planes are designed to look like modern tools, with angles and lines that belong to this cen-

HERE YOU CAN SEE THE *dog that popped off the lateral-adjustment lever on the No. 7. This shouldn't happen after only a year of use.*

tury – not the 20th and definitely not the 19th. The Lie-Nielsens have one foot planted firmly in the past, subtle refinements and a workmanlike appearance. The Clifton bench planes, on the other hand, have somewhat of a Victorian look to my eye. The top edges of the plane's wings are rolled and highly polished. The lever cap is emblazoned with the Clifton logo and has brass fittings. Add to that the bubinga handles and the British racing green paint and you have a tool that makes a statement.

Are the Cliftons worth purchasing? If you expect perfection out of the box, you might be disappointed, depending on the particular tool you receive. But if you know you might have a little tuning ahead, the Cliftons are superb and will last you your entire life.

In the end, it's my opinion that Cliftons are far better planes than the modern-day Stanleys or Records (now defunct). But they don't quite meet my admittedly high expectations when I spend more than $200 on a tool.

FOR MORE INFORMATION
Tools for Working Wood
toolsforworkingwood.com, 800-426-4613

LIKE THEIR BED ROCK ANCESTORS, *the Cliftons have a fully machined mating surface between the plane's body and its frog. This makes for a stable and confident tool.*

Technical Specifications

Nos. 3, 4, 4½, 5, 5½, 6, and 7 available

Iron: 0.12"-thick high-carbon steel, hardened to Rc 60 to 62 (specification according to the manufacturer)

Chipbreaker: Clifton's "Stay-Set" model, which allows you to remove a front shoe piece (instead of the entire chipbreaker) for simpler resharpenings

Buying A Jack Plane

We review 7 brands of jack planes.

Though all the jack planes in this review look basically the same – they're all based on Leonard Bailey's 19th-century designs – there are fundamental differences that separate a cheap plane from a more expensive one.

Like all tools, it comes down to three things:

- The design of the tool
- The materials used
- The quality of the manufacturing process

DESIGN: THANKS LEONARD

Two of Bailey's patented ideas show up on most of these planes. The way you adjust the depth of the cut on all these planes has remained basically unchanged since Bailey patented his idea in 1867. All the planes but the Record also use Bailey's idea for securing the lever cap.

However, there are significant differences in design among these tools. Two of these planes – the Clifton and the Lie-Nielsen – have a superior way of securing the frog to the base. Commonly called Bed Rock-style frogs, these were patented in 1895 and were used on Stanley's premium bench planes. Unlike other Bailey-style planes, Bed Rock planes have a large machined area where the frog mates with the base. Depending on the brand, Bed Rock frogs have three to five times as much contact between the frog and base compared to standard Bailey planes. Without a doubt, this reduces chatter. The Bed Rock frogs also allow you to move the frog easily without disassembling the plane.

MATERIALS: NOT JUST A PRETTY KNOB

More expensive planes are generally made using better materials. The cutting iron will be thicker and properly heat-treated. Parts that are plastic on one plane will be brass or bronze on another.

Except for the Lie-Nielsen, all of the plane bodies in this review are cast using grey iron. There's nothing wrong with grey iron, but it is brittle and will crack or break when dropped from, oh, about bench height. Ductile iron, which is used by Lie-Nielsen, is about as strong as cast steel. A Lie-Nielsen plane should be safe from even sledgehammers. That strength comes at a cost, however; Lie-Nielsen's jack plane is the most expensive in our test.

Another important difference between Lie-Nielsen's planes and the others is the cutter. Lie-Nielsen's A2 steel iron has been cryogenically treated, which means you will have to sharpen it less.

Anant

This India-manufactured tool has its followers, and it's no wonder. You can purchase a complete set of seven Anant planes for the price of a single Lie-Nielsen jack plane. Of course, the real question is: Should you? The sole was remarkably flat on the Anant, second only to the Lie-Nielsen. But the iron needed a lot of work to be serviceable. Fine-tuning the plane to take a nice smoothing cut proved tricky. The adjustment knob had to be spun more than three times before the iron would advance or retract – more than any other plane in our test. Also, the adjustment knob had sharp edges that needed to be sanded down before it would be comfortable. We give the Anant points for wooden handles, but they were lumpy and poorly finished. You can easily refinish the handles for a custom fit. In all, the Anant did better than expected, though we found the vintage and premium-priced planes outmatched it.

FOR MORE INFORMATION
Highland Hardware, 800-241-6748 or highlandwoodworking.com

Clifton

The toughest skirmish in our test was when we pitted the Clifton against the Lie-Nielsen. Both are based on Stanley's long-discontinued Bed Rock model, and both excel on nearly every front. The biggest disappointment with the Clifton came with the sole. It needed a lot more work than the Lie-Nielsen's – in fact, the largest gap we could find between the sole and a straightedge was more than three times bigger than the gap we found on the Lie-Nielsen. That said, we've set up three other Clifton bench planes that had soles that were much flatter than this one. Once fettled, the Clifton is a real champ at the bench. It has excellent heft and feel, and the adjustment knob is responsive to your slightest whim. The Bubinga handles are comfortable in use and attractive when at rest.

FOR MORE INFORMATION
Tools for Working Wood, 800-426-4613
or toolsforworkingwood.com

MANUFACTURING

What really separates the inexpensive tools from the expensive ones is the care taken to fit the parts into a tool that is easily set up and adjusted. This truly is the "fit" in fit and finish.

If a frog doesn't mate well with the body casting, you're in for a world of hurt. The only thing you're going to make is chatter marks. If the sides of the plane aren't ground at 90° to the sole, you'll never be able to shoot an edge that's 90°. And if the sole isn't ground reasonably flat, or if it warps because it wasn't properly stress-relieved, you don't have an inexpensive plane in your hands, you have an expensive anchor for a bass boat.

As a result, one of our primary concerns was how all the parts worked together. We checked each sole for flatness by placing a straightedge across the sole and measuring the low spots using a feeler gauge. We checked the flatness of each frog face by flattening them on a diamond-impregnated sharpening stone and checking our progress. We also checked the cutting irons in a similar way by flattening the irons' cutting faces on the diamond stone.

At last it was time to cut some wood. After lapping the soles, frogs and irons flat, we set up these planes for use. All of the editors tried the planes on hardwoods, softwoods and exotics. To test the durability of the iron's edge, we used each plane on a nasty piece of purpleheart and then observed the cutting edge to see how dull it had become.

It's fair to say you get what you pay for when it comes to jack planes. But it's not fair to say that the inexpensive planes were universally bad. It's more accurate to say that the manufacturing was inconsistent among the lower-priced tools. For example, the sole of the Anant was outstanding, but the iron required an unacceptable amount of work. On the Shop Fox plane, the situation was reversed. The sole was quite warped, but the iron was in nice shape. Of all the planes, the one that required the least setup was the Lie-Nielsen. From the sole to the frog to the iron, everything was perfect.

The Clifton was in the next best shape. Its only flaw lay in the sole, which required more work than I expected. This could be an anomaly with the tool in our test, however. Other Clifton planes I've set up had soles that were in better shape.

The rest of the planes required several long hours of work before they'd ever touch a board.

On the inexpensive planes, the area that requires

Lie-Nielsen

Record

At $325, you're probably wondering if this tool is intended for collectors or users. While I know of a few people who collect these tools, the Lie-Nielsen was designed for hard use and will earn its keep in your shop. Of all the planes in our test, the Lie-Nielsen required the least fettling. The sole was in exceptional shape out of the box (it took a lot of searching to find any gap between the sole and straightedge). The blade was in perfect shape and ready for a light honing. And all of the parts mated perfectly. In use, the Lie-Nielsen is at the top of the heap. Everything moved smoothly and the plane was taking long, wide and wispy shavings from a board with only slight adjustments. The cherry handles are beautiful and comfortable. The Lie-Nielsen is a combination of excellent manufacturing and premium materials (including indestructible ductile iron and rustproof bronze). For these reasons, it is a lifetime tool.

We were dismayed by the poor fit and finish on the test model we purchased. One side wing was poorly ground and the back of the iron was completely and weirdly discolored. The sole was in average shape. However, this plane has got it where it counts. I like the cap that uses a screw instead of a lever to secure the iron assembly, which is the mechanism on all the other planes in our test. The shape of the handles is nice, though the plastic gets slippery after a few minutes of hard use. All the adjustments were smooth, and the Record was easy to get set up and cutting. The fact that there is no frog-adjustment screw at the rear makes adjusting the frog a tricky matter, but this function isn't as important as it is on a smoothing plane. If this plane is on your shopping list, we recommend you examine it before you buy, or be ready to send it back to the seller if the plane doesn't meet your personal expectations.

FOR MORE INFORMATION
Lie-Nielsen, 800-327-2520 or lie-nielsen.com

FOR MORE INFORMATION
Discontinued, but widely available used

most of your attention is, of course, the frog – particularly where all those parts sandwich together. This is the area where most of the inexpensive planes ran into trouble. The cap-iron screw is what holds everything down. If it's too loose, your plane will chatter like a pair of wind-up teeth. If it's too tight, the iron will refuse to budge when you turn the adjustment knob.

If nothing works, look to the chipbreaker as the culprit. If it's too springy, it will bend the iron, which forces you to really torque down that cap-iron screw. Don't be afraid to bend the chipbreaker until you get a tight fit between the chipbreaker and iron. However, after you bend the chipbreaker, make sure the iron isn't bending under the pressure. That also causes a plane to chatter.

In the end, we came to the conclusion that there are two paths to follow. For those on a budget, we recommend you buy a vintage Stanley plane (about 100 years old if you can), purchase an aftermarket Hock iron (and an aftermarket chipbreaker if you can spare a few extra dollars) and spend a day in the shop tuning it. You'll spend about $50 all told and end up with an outstanding tool.

The second path is with the premium planes. If you've never used a Lie-Nielsen or a Clifton, you're in for a real shock. There is an astonishing difference between these planes and the less-expensive tools. Once you've used one of these planes, you'll never want to go back.

It's our opinion that the Lie-Nielsen edges out the Clifton thanks to its superior materials (ductile iron, bronze and the cryogenically treated A2 iron) and the unerring consistency of its manufacture. However, if you prefer your tools with an English accent, you'll be well served by the Clifton.

Shop Fox

This entry to the world of jack planes comes from China with an attractive price tag. While this tool has some things going for it (such as an oversized adjustment knob and half-decent blade) it struggled on some other fronts. Most notably, the chipbreaker was entirely too springy and bent the iron when engaged. Once we hammered out a good deal of the spring in the chipbreaker, things started to work better. Like the Stanley 12-205L, the Shop Fox was difficult to tune initially. If the cap-iron screw was even slightly overtightened, the blade would refuse to advance or retract. If you loosened the screw, you would quickly run into chatter problems. The handles are painted wood, which is better than plastic, but the front knob was a bit too small for average-sized hands. All in all, we think you might want to wait a bit for the manufacturers to work the bugs out of this one before you buy it.

Stanley Type 11

This flea-market special really held its own against its shiny new cousins. We restored four of these vintage planes and found that they all needed as much work as a mid-priced new tool. They also needed a new iron. Spend the extra $38 to buy an aftermarket Hock iron (888-282-5233) or one from another manufacturer. You will be amazed at the difference it makes. Once your plane is set up (expect a long afternoon of work), we think you'll be pleased. The rosewood handles are a pleasure to hold. Iron adjustment is smooth (though we've all found the blade-adjustment knob to be a little on the small side). Our only caution in buying one is you have to keep a sharp eye for cracked or rewelded castings, and soles that are warped or bent because they were dropped while in service. If you're a scrounger and are willing to do a little work on your plane, we recommend the Stanley Type 11 as a best buy.

Stanley 12-205L

Stanley makes a "contractor grade" version of this tool with a few more niceties (a frog-adjustment screw, brass fittings and more machined areas between the frog and body casting). We've tested that version, too, and if you buy a new Stanley jack plane, it's the one to buy. The 12-205L has a plastic knob that's difficult to use for adjusting the iron; and getting the chipbreaker, lever cap and cap-iron screw all working together takes some intense fiddling. If the screw is too loose, the plane will chatter on your work. If the screw is too tight, the iron won't move when you turn the blade-adjustment knob. Speaking of that knob, you need to turn it two revolutions before it will advance or retract the blade. The contractor version is more on par with the Record in performance and ease of use. If you buy a new English-made Stanley for fine woodworking, spend a few extra dollars to get the upgraded version.

FOR MORE INFORMATION
Grizzly, 800-523-4777 or grizzly.com

FOR MORE INFORMATION
Available at flea markets and eBay.com

FOR MORE INFORMATION
Amazon, amazon.com

Test-driving Exotic Infill Handplanes

We spend three days with the world's most expensive planes.
Are they just jewelry? Or do they work better than your plane?

There are times when I wish I could find my first handplane. It was, by most standards, an utter piece of junk. I had bought it after college during a late-night run to Wal-Mart, and my purchase was guided by the fact that it was blue, cheap and the only block plane I could find on the shelves that evening.

So it was surprising (then and now) that the tool actually worked quite well. It didn't have a blade adjuster, the sole was rough and the steel in the cutter was as gummy as Juicy Fruit. But when I put the tool to wood it made that sweet "sneeeeck" sound of a perfect curl of wood being sliced from its mother board.

It was the first step in my journey. Since that day in 1993 I've slowly upgraded my handplanes. After buying a Stanley jack plane, the blue plane went into my carpentry toolkit. Then it went into a box in the basement. And now I can't find it. Occasionally I do get a pang of longing for it. But never have I wanted that block plane more than the day I pushed a $6,600 Karl Holtey A13 infill plane over a piece of curly maple.

A custom-built Holtey A13 is for many handplane enthusiasts the pinnacle of the planemaker's art – perfect in form, function, fit and finish. And when I first used the A13 I got the same sort of heady feeling you get when you master a handplane for the first time. However, like any buzz, after about 20 minutes of work with the A13, the buzz wore off and I began to think (somewhat) rationally about this beautiful piece of steel and brass under my command.

I set the A13 aside and picked up a plane made by James Krenov, the author of "The Impractical Cabinetmaker" (Linden) and planed the same piece of irascible maple. Then I tried a $2,800 Sauer & Steiner panel plane, a Bill Carter jointer plane, a $1,300 A13 from Darryl Hutchinson, a small $775 smoothing plane from Wayne Anderson and more infill planes from custom builders Robert Baker and Brian Buckner.

That was a very good day.

Before you wonder if I've won the lottery, let me explain. Many of these planes (and a dozen more) were loaned to us by a generous and trusting man named John Edwards. Edwards, a retired automotive engineer from Detroit, amassed his collection of modern handplanes after years of saving and careful purchasing. He and I are both handplane geeks, so we got together in February 2006 in the magazine's shop, tuned up these planes and put them to work, deliriously making shavings on boards both mild and wild.

We also invited many of the makers of these tools to have a look at the planes on a following day. See the story "Mavericks for a New Era" on page 254.

After three days of using these tools, I recorded my impressions in a legal pad, took some photos and now am ready to share what we found. There were a few surprises, some disappointments and a small revelation at the end. If you've ever gazed longingly at some of these beauties on the Internet or at woodworking shows and wondered, "But do they work well?" you're about to find out.

HOLTEY A13: PERFECT TO THE NTH DEGREE

I actually never thought I'd get to use one of these planes. In fact, this plane almost didn't make it here in time after getting tangled up in U.S. Customs for a breathtaking bit after its trip from Holtey's shop in Sutherland, England.

Holtey was one of the early pioneers of the modern infill makers. And his reputation, quality of work and prices all reflect the fact that most people see him as the top of the heap.

KARL HOLTEY'S A13 (BACK) AND *his new 11-S (front) both proved to be formidable planes when put to work.*

Karl Holtey A13

SOLE LENGTH: 9"
WEIGHT: 6 lbs. 2 oz.
PITCH OF IRON: 50°
MOUTH OPENING: About $1/64$"
IRON: S53 steel, .183" thick, $2^1/4$" w.
CONTACT: holteyplanes.com or (UK) 01549 402500

Karl Holtey 11-S High-angle Smoother

SOLE LENGTH: $6^1/2$"
WEIGHT: 2 lbs. 5 oz.
PITCH OF IRON: 60°
MOUTH OPENING: About $1/32$"
IRON: S53 steel, .168" thick, $1^1/2$" w.

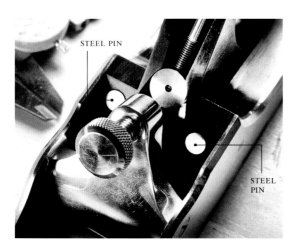

SEE THE TWO STEEL PINS *in Holtey's A13? The iron is bedded against these and a steel plate at the throat – not the wood. Most unusual and interesting.*

The Holtey A13 is based on a classic pattern of English plane made by the venerable Norris company. And it's one of Holtey's signature planes (his other, the No. 98, will be discussed shortly). Once you hold one of the tools you understand a bit of the Holtey mystique. The man is a perfectionist. No matter how closely you examine his tools, you cannot find cosmetic flaws. They are finished both inside and out to the highest degree. Here is just one example: Where some makers (both historic and new) will leave the bed of the plane with a few file marks (which you'll almost never see because the bed is covered by the iron), Holtey does not.

In fact, the bed of the tool is where we got our first surprise. Holtey secures his irons to the body in a way that's unlike any other infill toolmaker I know. In other infills the iron rests directly on the wooden infill below it. Sometimes there is a steel plate down by the mouth that offers support as well, but mostly it's the wood that's in charge. Some enthusiasts say it's this wooden bed that makes the tools special.

But Holtey's A13 mocks that assertion. His irons don't even touch the wooden infill. Instead, the iron rests on a steel plate by the mouth and two raised steel pins embedded in the tool's bed. What's the advantage? In my experience it made the cut much easier to adjust. Even with the tool's lever cap cinched down super-tight, the iron could still be adjusted with little effort – or risk. Many old Norris infill planes have adjusters that were stripped out by people who tightened down the lever cap too much and then adjusted the iron.

The Holtey A13 is surprisingly comfortable to use and has a wicked-heavy presence on the wood. What I didn't like about it was it was uncomfortable to hold the tool upside down when sighting down the sole – a common operation when trying to center the blade in the mouth of the tool. The tool's front bun is hard to grasp in this position.

That's a quibble, really. I think I was looking for something – anything – to disappoint me on this tool. Not much cropped up. It's as close to perfection as you can get. If I had an extra $7,000 I'd love to own one.

HOLTEY 11-S: A HIGH-ANGLE SOLUTION

This new model from Holtey isn't based on an old plane – it's one of his original designs. When I first saw it I thought it looked as comfortable to use as a brick. And on that point, I was mostly wrong. The 11-S is easy to cradle with your hands and to control, thanks to its diminutive size. After a lengthy planing session my right hand began to rub on the back edge of the blade, which was annoying, but not awful.

The high cutting angle (called the "pitch") of the tool made it a remarkable smoothing plane. There was nothing in our shop that it couldn't handle with ease – and I rooted deep into our scrap pile. Unlike Holtey's A13, the iron is bedded directly on the wooden infill and the lever cap is removable; it hooks around a pin that passes through the sidewalls of the plane. This feature makes it easy to remove and install the iron.

The only disappointment with this tool is one shared by many of Holtey's tools, and that's the particular alloy of steel used in the plane's cutter. The alloy, called S53, wears astonishingly well. But I found it difficult to sharpen. Some of my stones wouldn't touch it, and I had to resort to diamond stones to get a keen edge. Even then, I wasn't confident I had gotten the best edge. This is a personal opinion, but I prefer steel that is easy to sharpen, especially with smoothing planes.

Compared to other Holteys, the 11-S is a bargain: about $1,500 with the way the dollar was trading at the time. This is a sweet tool that cries out to be used. I hope it doesn't sit on a collector's shelf.

"It is far better to work with one plane, one saw, one chisel and a few accessories, all of them good, honest steel, properly sharpened, than it is to have a cellar full of inadequate devices."

— "How to Work With Tools and Wood" (1942) from Stanley Tools

My frustration with the No. 98 was in getting the iron to drop onto the pin shown here on the adjuster. It took much fiddling. Once in, however, the tool is a sweet user.

Karl Holtey No. 98

SOLE LENGTH: 9½"
WEIGHT: 4 lbs. 3.7 oz.
PITCH OF IRON: 22°
MOUTH OPENING: About ⅟₆₄"
IRON: S53 steel, .176" thick, 2⅛" w.

HOLTEY NO. 98:
A DESIGN THAT CHANGED THE RULES

The No. 98 (about $2,900 in 2006) is another of Holtey's original designs and it is a groundbreaking tool. It was one of the first modern "bevel-up" smoothers, and Holtey's trailblazing has led to a surge in the popularity of this style of tool.

That said, for a variety of reasons, the No. 98 was my least favorite of the Holtey planes I tested. The adjuster, while ingenious, is fiddly when it comes to installing the iron in the tool. The iron is bored with a series of holes. You drop the iron onto a pin that projects from the plane's adjuster. Because the hole and the pin have a tight fit, it took me a good deal of messing about to get the iron in place on the pin.

In use, the tool is remarkably balanced and has a sleek modern look that appealed even to my traditional tastes. And it performed admirably. With a steep 38° microbevel on the cutting edge, the resulting 60° pitch made it a formidable smoothing tool.

CLASSIC PLANES A13:
A MORE AFFORDABLE WORKHORSE

Like Holtey, Darryl Hutchinson of Devon, England, also makes a version of the Norris A13. Hutchinson's plane is similar in form to the Holtey plane, but it's different in the details. Overall, the level of fit and finish and perfection is lower. But considering that Hutchinson's A13 cost about $1,300 in 2006 – about one-fifth the price of the Holtey A13 – it's a value among premium tools.

The plane works remarkably well – as anything costing more than a grand should. It has a fine mouth and high pitch to the iron, which make it ideal for fine finishing cuts. Because of the vast price difference, it's not really fair to compare it directly to the Holtey, so here are my general impressions.

The tote is pretty comfortable, though it had more flat areas than I like – I wished it were more sinuous. The front bun is sizable and I didn't find it as comfortable as an old-fashioned Stanley-style front knob during long planing sessions.

The adjuster works quite well and had little slop in its mechanism. I found it remarkably easy

DARRYL HUTCHINSON'S A13 (RIGHT) WITH *a Ray Iles A5. Both are English makers who produce tools that very much evoke the classic infill planes of the 19th and early 20th centuries.*

Classic Planes A13 by Darryl Hutchinson

SOLE LENGTH: 9"
WEIGHT: 5 lbs. 15.5 oz.
PITCH OF IRON: 50°
MOUTH OPENING: Less than ⅟₆₄"
IRON: A2 steel, .192" thick, 2¼" w.
CONTACT: classic planes.com or (UK) +44 01647 432841

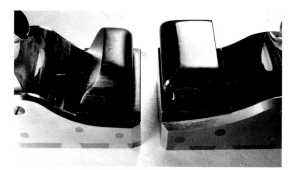

HERE YOU CAN SEE THE *differences between the front buns of the two A13s – Holtey's is on the left; Hutchinson's is on the right.*

to get the plane running smoothly and making very sweet cuts. It's not a fussy tool.

There were some minor cosmetic things: The bed of the tool is essentially unfinished and is covered in file marks. Among its premium-priced peers this is unusual. And there were a few drips of finish in the channel for the adjuster. All in all however, the tool is quite solid, unpretentious and ready to go to work. I quite liked it.

BILL CARTER A1: BEYOND MASSIVE

Bill Carter is another English tool maker, and he was probably the earliest of the modern infill makers. His hand-built infill planes have inspired toolmakers all over the world since he started building in the 1980s.

The jointer plane I used for this article is, like most Carter planes, a work of art. Carter has an excellent and eccentric eye: The dovetails in the sole are filed in the shape of a cupid's bow and he has a reputation for adding images of elephants to the sidewalls of his tools. Plus, though all his tools are obviously new, Carter ages the metal and builds them with a decidedly old-world charm.

This jointer plane is as interesting as the man who built it. The story goes that Carter built it first as a 36"-long tool, but when he took it to auctions and tool sales to show, it was simply too long to fit into the allotted space in his car. So Carter chopped a bit off each end. He sent the "offcuts" to Edwards when he bought it and suggested Edwards use them as (wait for it …) sanding blocks.

This jointer plane has the presence of a museum piece. The metal is beautifully chamfered and the wooden infill is gracefully shaped. It is absolutely exquisite to behold. But pushing it is another matter. It is my opinion that infill jointers don't fit the American style of work. They are too heavy to wield for any length of time by mortals. After 10 minutes of pushing this tool up and down my bench, I was ready for a nap. Also, the front infill is difficult to grip – or perhaps I never found the right grip.

I own a small Carter miter plane, and I have used several of his other planes so I know they are eminently usable tools. This jointer deserves a place above the mantle, or as part of an upper-body workout program.

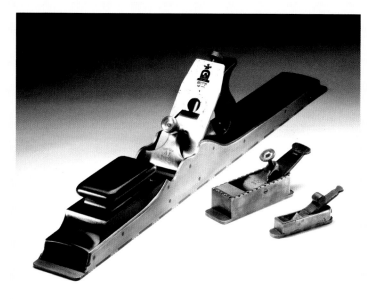

THE BILL CARTER JOINTER PLANE *dwarfs two smaller Carter miter planes. Carter sometimes uses recycled materials – the little plane is made from a backsaw.*

Bill Carter A1 Jointer Plane

SOLE LENGTH: 28"
WEIGHT: 12 lbs. 5.5 oz.
PITCH OF IRON: 47°
MOUTH OPENING: Less than $^1/_{32}$"
IRON: High-carbon steel, .169" thick, $2^1/_2$" w.
CONTACT: billcarterwoodworking-planemaker.co.uk

SAUER & STEINER:
NEW KID ON THE BLOCK

Konrad Sauer is a graphic designer turned furniture maker turned toolmaker. And all three of those traits are evident in his world-class workhorses. Sauer, who lives and works outside Toronto, incorporates classic touches from historic infill planes such as the venerable Spiers and Norris brands. But he blends them in a way that makes his tools both classic and distinctive. All of his tools look unmistakably like they are in the same vein, even his custom work.

As far as workmanship, Sauer's planes are at the top of the heap. I could find no flaws in the four bench planes that I inspected closely (two panel planes, one unhandled smoothing plane and a jointer plane). The metalwork was excellent. And the wood showed off Sauer's strengths as a furniture maker. The infill material he selected was itself astonishing, and the small details – fillets, curves and chamfers – were gorgeous.

But how do his planes function? Remarkably well. Everything clicks and fits together in a workmanlike manner. There's no fussing with this or

that. The adjuster is precise yet not precious. The iron is well bedded on a massive steel throat plate and wooden bed. And the tools (all of them) are a joy to push. Naturally, the high pitch and impossibly tight mouth relegate the panel plane I tested (about $3,000 in 2006) for smoothing large surfaces, which it does with great aplomb.

Sauer's business, which has kicked into high gear in the last couple years, will surely flourish because of his energy and the exquisite finished product.

SAUER & STEINER NO. 4:
FINISHING MAGIC

I'd really like to hold up this tool for special mention. It lacks a rear tote, which will turn off some users, but I found the plane a delight to wield. The coffin shape of the body and gracefully shaped infills conspire to make this a tool that you unconsciously reach for while working. Like the other unhandled tools I tried, there is a tendency for your hand to rub on the back edge of the iron a bit during long planing sessions, but that's a small price to pay. Because of the No. 4's tight mouth (I tried to

A SAUER & STEINER JOINTER *plane (left) with two panel planes by the same maker. The Sauer & Steiner planes all have consistent lines.*

THE SAUER & STEINER NO. *4 smoothing plane is unexpectedly comfortable. Note how the knuckle of my index finger rubs the back of the iron; this can be uncomfortable after hours of planing.*

Sauer & Steiner Panel Plane

SOLE LENGTH: 14³/₄"
WEIGHT: 7 lbs. 15 oz.
PITCH OF IRON: 50°
MOUTH OPENING: Immeasurably tight
IRON: High-carbon steel, .186" thick, 2¹/₂" w.
CONTACT: sauerandsteiner.com or 519-568-8159

Sauer & Steiner No. 4 Smoothing Plane

SOLE LENGTH: 7¹/₂"
WEIGHT: 4 lbs. 4.7 oz.
PITCH OF IRON: 50°
MOUTH OPENING: Immeasurably tight
IRON: High-carbon steel, .186" thick, 2¹/₂" w.
CONTACT: sauerandsteiner.com or 519-568-8159

KONRAD SAUER MADE FURNITURE BEFORE *he made tools. And it shows here in the sculptural front bun on one of his panel planes.*

HERE YOU CAN SEE IN *detail how carefully fit and detailed Robert Baker's work is.*

photograph it but failed because it was too small) and 55° pitch, it's for finishing cuts alone. This was, to me, one of the most appealing tools of the whole bunch.

ROBERT BAKER BOX MITER: STEEPED IN HISTORY

Baker has been making infill planes for a long time for builders of furniture and musical instruments. But his main line of business is in restoring old tools (and sometimes furniture). He's quite famous for his restoration work – many gorgeous and important tools have passed through his shop. I think it's clear that his link to tools of the past has heavily influenced the tools he builds today. They have an unmistakable old-school feel.

The enormous miter plane of his that I got to use was simply an awesome piece of engineering and design. The decorative pattern worked into the sidewalls of the plane was something I'd never seen anything like before (and in fact a couple other toolmakers have wondered how he does it). The wood is finished to a high-grade furniture look. And the details are right-on. This tool was designed to be used on a shooting board and both of the sides were almost exactly perfectly 90° to the sole (the right sidewall of the tool was an airtight 90°; the left just a smidge off). As someone who has tried to "fix" a misaligned sidewall on a few tools I can tell you that this is no small achievement for a handmade tool.

The weight of the plane made it a formidable shooting board plane; your fingers fill right in next to the lever cap like they should live there. The tool was not comfortable when used upright like a bench plane – but few box-shaped miter planes are.

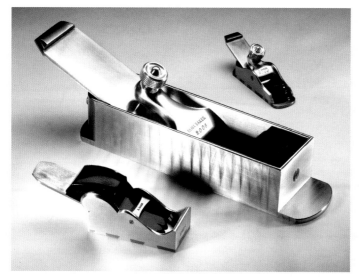

BAKER'S AMAZING AND HUGE MITER *plane, with two smaller examples of his work.*

Robert Baker Box Miter Plane

SOLE LENGTH: 10½"
WEIGHT: 6 lbs. 1.5 oz.
PITCH OF IRON: 20°
MOUTH OPENING: Immeasurably tight
IRON: High-carbon steel, .180" thick, 2³⁄₁₆" w.
CONTACT: 1 Fieldstone Road
York, ME 03909
or HoltzGear@aol.com
Note: Baker does not have a catalog or web site.

BRIAN BUCKNER MITER: AN AMAZING AMATEUR

Buckner isn't a professional toolmaker – he does sell some of the planes he makes, but he also holds a high-tech day job in state government. What is particularly interesting about his tools is the level of detail he achieves because he doesn't have to put food on the table by selling his planes. As a result, everything is over the top. The chamfers he files into the steel sides are (and there's no other word for it) downright sexy. He used Damascus steel for the sidewalls of this plane, which gives the tool an unmistakable graphic look. The ebony front bun has the presence and precision of a well-made chess piece.

This tool is what's called an "improved miter" pattern of plane. It's a form that is related to the box-shaped miter shown at right and below. What's improved about it? Well you can use it like a smoothing plane, which is something I've become comfortable doing. Buckner's tool fit in my hands and was effortless to get it set and taking beautiful shavings.

A DETAIL OF THE OUTSTANDING *woodwork on Buckner's miter plane. Ebony is absolutely no fun to shape in this manner.*

BRIAN BUCKNER'S IMPROVED MITER (REAR) *and one of his unusual rabbeting infill planes – both with Damascus steel sides.*

Brian Buckner Damascus Miter Plane

SOLE LENGTH: 8⅛"
WEIGHT: 2 lbs. 10.1 oz.
PITCH OF IRON: 20°
MOUTH OPENING: Tiny
IRON: High-carbon steel, .182" thick, 1⅝" w.
CONTACT: sydnassloot.com/bbuckner/tools.htm

WAYNE ANDERSON SMOOTHER: NO TWO ALIKE

First, some full disclosure: I own this particular plane and have been using it regularly for several months now. Anderson's planes are all built with Swiss-watch mechanicals and European old-world flair. Every one of his tools is a little bit different than the ones he made before, even if it's the same basic form. They all have an organic and human-made quality to them that sets them apart from manufactured tools.

This tool, which was made in late 2005, has some unusual characteristics. First, there's no chipbreaker. This makes the tool simpler to set up – an errant chipbreaker can cause serious clogs. But it also makes the shavings bunch up in the mouth. Chipbreakers have one excellent benefit in bevel-down planes: they push the shavings up and out of the tool. With this smoothing plane (and others I've used without a chipbreaker) the shavings will never eject entirely out of the mouth. That said, this tool has yet to clog on me. The shavings simply pile up and come out of the tool in a less dramatic fashion – it's more like they foam up from the mouth rather than spit out.

The diminutive size of this tool would suggest it's only for makers of tiny boxes. Don't believe it. I've used this tool for smoothing large surfaces, even tabletops. And it's excellent for sneaking into small hollows to remove tear-out. As with the other unhandled smoothing planes, you will rub your hand against the iron during extended use. I've taken to putting a preventive bandage there before long planing sessions.

AND IN THE END

The final revelation came when I put Krenov's handplane through the same paces as I did the other tools. By comparison, Krenov's small polishing plane (7½" long) is crudely made – the wooden

A PLANE BUILT BY JAMES *Krenov (foreground) next to a plane made by Ron Hock from one of his plane-building kits (it also works very well).*

stock looks like it was roughed out with a band saw and knife. The chipbreaker on the iron was roughly ground with many little facets. The mouth was tight ($\frac{1}{32}$") but not extraordinarily so. When I disassembled the plane I found that the bed down by the mouth had a layer or two of blue painter's tape affixed there, perhaps to close up the throat.

But the plane held its own with every other plane on my bench in terms of performance. As did my "work-a-day" tools from Veritas and Lie-Nielsen. The same goes for other high-end tools I've already written about: the Ray Iles A5, the Clark & Williams smoothing plane and the new Bridge City variable-pitch plane, which I had only limited time with. Even my vintage Stanleys had nothing to be ashamed of.

I discussed this finding with several toolmakers, none of whom were surprised by it. Robin Lee, the president of Lee Valley Tools, summed it up this way: "The wood doesn't care." And he's right. Thomas Lie-Nielsen, founder and owner of Lie-

Nielsen Toolworks, put it this way: "A plane is just a jig for a chisel." And he's right, too.

If your planes meet the minimum basic requirements of a plane: a sharp cutter that's firmly secured at an appropriate angle for the wood you're working, the tool will do an excellent job. So if you think that buying a very expensive plane will make all lumber bow down before you and your tool, think again.

But there are good reasons to buy custom planes – and they're the same reasons people buy custom furniture when they could go to a discount store and buy an entire bedroom suite for $500. Some people like handmade and exquisite things. And thank goodness, because our mass-manufactured world can use a few handmade touches.

These were the thoughts that were flying around my head as I packed up all the tools used for this article to ship them back to their owner. As I taped the last box and swept up the mounds of shavings we made, I resolved to tear apart our basement looking for my little blue $15 block plane. It just might have some high-end work ahead of it – until I win the lottery, that is.

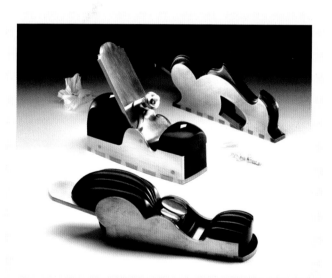

THREE WAYNE ANDERSON PLANES: A *rhino-horn shoulder plane (rear), a coffin smoothing plane and chariot plane.*

Wayne Anderson Coffin Smoothing Plane

SOLE LENGTH: 5$\frac{1}{2}$"
WEIGHT: 2 lbs. 1.7 oz.
PITCH OF IRON: 57°
MOUTH OPENING: A sliver
IRON: A2 cryo-treated steel, .189" thick, 1$\frac{1}{2}$" w.
CONTACT: andersonplanes.com or 763-486-0834

WITH NO CHIPBREAKER, SHAVINGS TEND *to collect in the mouth. However, the tool doesn't clog, it just doesn't eject shavings as quickly.*

Mavericks for a New Era

When word leaked out that John Edwards and I were going to be setting up and using all of the planes featured in this article, toolmaker Wayne Anderson remarked: "Boy I would like to be a fly on that wall." After some thought, we decided to open up the door for a day and invite as many modern toolmakers as we could on short notice.

Surprisingly, many of them came. And even more surprisingly, many of them were meeting one another for the first time in our shop. The toolmaking attendees included:

- Wayne Anderson (Anderson Planes)
- Robert Baker (a custom maker)
- Brian Buckner (a custom maker)
- John Economaki (Bridge City Tools)
- Ron Hock (Hock Tools)
- Joel Moskowitz (Tools for Working Wood)
- Thomas Lie-Nielsen, Kirsten Lie-Nielsen, Mark Swanson (Lie-Nielsen Toolworks)
- Robin Lee, Terry Saunders (Veritas/Lee Valley Tools)
- Konrad Sauer (Sauer & Steiner)
- Larry Williams, Don McConnell (Clark & Williams)

We spent the entire day in our shop swapping personal stories, using all of the tools and generally having a good time. In hindsight, I think we were lucky that a meteor didn't hit the building that day or modern toolmaking would have been set back about 20 years.

KONRAD SAUER AND TERRY SAUNDERS *look for tear-out on a particularly nasty piece of wood.*

DON MCCONNELL TWEAKS THE SETTING *on a Clark & Williams smoothing plane.*

BACK ROW (LEFT TO RIGHT): *Christopher Schwarz, Thomas Lie-Nielsen, Kirsten Lie-Nielsen, Mark Swanson, Joel Moskowitz, Clarence Blanchard (from the Fine Tool Journal), Mike Jenkins (also from the journal), John Economaki, Robin Lee. Middle row: Konrad Sauer, Ron Hock, Wayne Anderson, Don McConnell, Larry Williams, Terry Saunders, Robert Baker, Brian Buckner. Kneeling, front left: John Edwards.*

Wayne Anderson:
Infills of a Different Breed

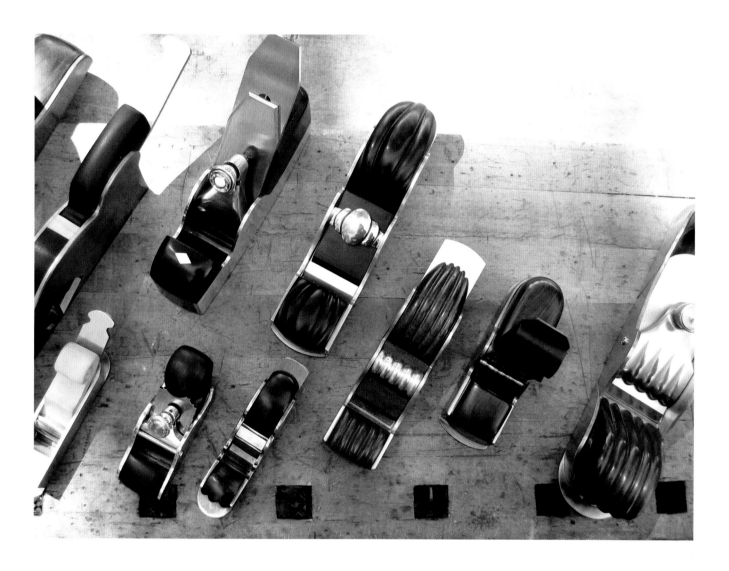

A toolmaker who takes cues from the past but doesn't copy.

It's a bit of a weird scene – part Paris fashion show and part down-home barbecue. A couple dozen tool collectors (and users) from the Midwest have gathered around a cabinetmaker's bench that's set up in an Illinois field and are chattering like old friends do. This gathering is the ninth meeting of what is affectionately called "Galootapalooza," a summer event where old-tool enthusiasts get together to swap tall tales, tools, tricks of the trade and eat pork shoulder.

This year several of the guys have brought along infill planes made for them by Wayne Anderson, a mechanical designer from Elk River, Minn., who builds custom tools in his off hours. As the infills start to come out of boxes and bags and land on the bench, the talk subsides. And by the time there are more than a dozen of the planes on the bench, all you can hear is the birds and the wind blowing through the trees.

Someone steps forward and lines the planes up. Someone else lets out a low, wet and appreciative whistle. And then the cameras come out and people start to take pictures of the family reunion assembled on the benchtop.

One of those photographers is Anderson himself, who has flown in to Chicago for the event. Seeing all his tools together is a bit of a shock for him, too. The tools were assembled one-by-one in his basement and then sent out into the world. And now he can see all the double-dovetails, naval brass, ebony and lever caps he's slaved over during the last three years.

ANDERSON'S UNUSUAL INFILL TOOTHING PLANE *is made with a vintage iron. The owner, Ralph Brendler, uses it to prepare thin wooden bands to make Shaker oval boxes.*

What's most striking about his tools is how they don't look much like anyone else's tools. Unlike many contemporary planemakers, Anderson doesn't like to make copies of classic infill tools from Norris, Spiers, Mathison or Slater. Instead, Anderson's keen eye and impressive collection of files create planes with fluid sidewalls, sculpted and scalloped wedges and details that are more often found on fine furniture than on tools.

"I was never one to copy a Norris or a Spiers," Anderson says later that evening over a beer. "Those were the production planes of the era. I was never impressed with the style."

So when Anderson set out to build handplanes he drew more on his artistic drive (which first blossomed in childhood) than he did on the traditional forms. But there is one strong similarity Anderson's planes share with the old-school English tools. His planes work as well as any infill plane – vintage or modern – that I have ever used.

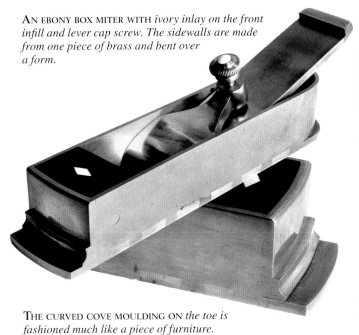

AN EBONY BOX MITER WITH *ivory inlay on the front infill and lever cap screw. The sidewalls are made from one piece of brass and bent over a form.*

THE CURVED COVE MOULDING ON *the toe is fashioned much like a piece of furniture.*

THE FLUID LINES OF THIS *chariot plane made of cocobolo have an almost Victorian flair. Note the patina on the sidewall – this plane is a user.*

THIS DIMINUTIVE THUMB PLANE CAN *be held in your palm, but it is just as detailed as its larger cousins.*

ADAPTED FROM A PLANE SOLD *on eBay, this stunning shoulder plane has two sets of sidewalls – the steel wraps around a second layer of brass.*

I'm not alone in my assessment. Ralph Brendler, one of the ringleaders of the Internet-based e-mail list called "oldtools," owns a few of Anderson's planes that he uses regularly.

"If I had my druthers, every plane in my cabinet would be from Wayne," Brendler says. "The miter plane he built me so far exceeded my expectations. I was just stunned when I opened the box…. My jaw hit the floor."

ANDERSON PLANES ON THE JOB

For the last four months I've been using one of Wayne Anderson's improved miter planes as a daily worker in my shop – primarily as a smoothing plane, but also as a block plane and even to shoot the occasional miter. I'm of the mind that these so-called "miter planes" weren't actually used much for mitering by 17th- and 18th-century craftsmen, but that's a topic I explore in the section called "Mystery of the Miter Plane" in this book.

My Anderson plane is an excellent worker. When the tool first showed up in my office I was a bit intimidated about using it, covering it with fingerprints and dinging the gorgeously shaped ebony infills. But the plane simply begs to be used, and after 30 minutes of admiring Anderson's workmanship I took the plane to the shop to sharpen the A2 iron and put the tool to work.

From a working perspective, Anderson clearly understands plane mechanics. The bed is perfectly true and in the same plane as the section of the steel sole leading up to the mouth. The bed is, in fact, as finely finished as the rest of the wood in the plane. With some infill planes, the wood can shrink enough over time to disrupt the perfect bedding provided by the wood and sole. Anderson uses exceptionally stable wood (ebony in many cases) that has been kiln-dried and then allowed to stabilize in his shop. (Of course, you can always file an infill bed flat if the wood moves – I've done it myself to a couple

vintage planes.) As delivered, the sole is dead flat within .0015" across its width and length.

The A2 iron in my plane is from the shop of toolmaker Vlad Spehar, though Anderson also uses irons from other makers, including Thomas Lie-Nielsen. (For smoothing planes with adjusters, Anderson generally uses Norris-style adjusters from Bob Howard at St. James Bay Tool Co.)

The iron drops smartly into place in the bed, like it was made to sit there. I cinch up the lever cap and then tap the snecked iron a bit with a hammer to center the iron in the mouth and get it projecting just right. The iron responds exactly as it's supposed to, a testament to the care taken with construction.

I pull a board of curly maple out of the rack – a scrap from a contemporary dresser I built long ago. I keep this board around because it's a good test bed for new planes that come into the shop. The grain of this board changes direction a couple times and

THIS IMPROVED MITER PLANE MADE *by Wayne Anderson has been set up like a smoothing plane and performs astonishingly well.*

the curl is prominent. It's a tough board for many planes to surface without tear-out.

But not the Anderson plane. I start with a light cut and take some sub-.001" shavings and the plane performs flawlessly. But perhaps even more telling is how well the plane handles the board as I increase the projection of the cutter to take a .007"-thick shaving. The plane remains in control, the iron refuses to chatter and the board is clear of tear-out. I put down the tool and wonder what sort of person can make a tool that looks this good and performs so well.

From Weaponry to Woodworking

Anderson's father and grandfather were Chevy dealers in his hometown, but Anderson, 52, was destined to work with a different kind of iron. As a child he was a sketcher and a sculptor. He considered majoring in art in college, but changed his mind.

"I quickly realized that there's a reason for the term 'starving artist,'" he says.

So he turned his attention to mechanical design. He never made it past the first year of college and then spent three years in a machine shop and then three more years in a metal fabrication shop for an electric utility. Anderson now works as a mechanical designer. For 11 years he worked for Caterpillar, and then United Defense, a defense contractor.

Then he became a full-time toolmaker.

"I did a lot of virtual design on computer – not with my hands," Anderson says. "I suppose it (planemaking) is the antithesis of what I did. I have to be making something with my hands."

That affection for handwork first lead Anderson into a woodworking hobby. He and an engineer friend would haunt the local woodworking supply stores. One day Anderson was in a used tool store where they had a few copies of the now-famous poster of the H.O. Studley tool chest.

"I found myself riveted to that image," he says. "Something clicked. And I decided to amass a small collection of vintage tools." So he began buying old tools (he's now holds the title of director of area A for the Mid-West Tool Collectors Assn.). One day Anderson read a story about British infill maker Bill Carter. Intrigued, so he decided to make an improved miter plane for himself.

"I call it 'plane-a-saurus,'" Anderson says with a laugh. "It had 3/16"-thick sides and a 1/4" bottom. It's butt-ugly, but it functions well. It's like your kid's artwork. It's not worth a nickel, but you wouldn't sell it for a million bucks."

Anderson made more planes (lots more) and started posting pictures of them on the Internet. People began to take notice and ask Anderson to make planes for them. Today he spends about three hours each weekday in the shop and as many as 14 to 16 hours a day on weekends – yard work permitting. He has aspirations to turn planemaking into his full-time job.

He's willing to try new forms, take risks and even throw the occasional experiment into the garbage. He's built an infill toothing plane (the first one I've ever seen). He's also built an astonishing low-angle jack plane that has an ingenious way of removing the iron. And then there's a shoulder plane he built that has brass sidewalls wrapped by steel ones on the outside – a real looker.

A Hand-made Tool

A typical Anderson infill plane is created mostly by hand. He begins by roughing out the dovetails and the shapes of the sidewalls on a metal-cutting band saw, but the final shapes are achieved by hand-filing. The same goes with the wooden infills. Though he may size the wood to rough shape on his band saw, all of the finished work is accomplished by hand.

At any given time, Anderson will have 75 different full-size files and another 75 needle files of all shapes and sizes, which handle all the intri-

Without a doubt, this is *the most comfortable unhandled plane I've ever used. Its wicked-tight mouth and low cutting angle make it an ideal plane on end grain.*

Here's something you don't see *every day: a low-angle infill jack plane. The handle is thick, substantial and surprisingly comfortable to hold.*

cate shapes of the wood and brass in Anderson's designs.

One of the most astonishing details is the brass cove moulding on the toe of the miter plane he built for Brendler. The cove marks the transition between the curved front of the plane's brass body and the steel sole. Anderson makes it sound like simple work. After roughing out the shape on a piece of flat brass, he refined the cove with files and then relieved the backside of the brass to prepare it for bending. This process, which is much like kerf-bending in furniture-work, ensures the front will bend over a form without creating ugly folds in the toe-piece.

Anderson is equally skilled with shaping wood. One of his recent low-angle chariot planes has a wedge that resembles a traditional shell carving. At

THIS 9"-LONG SMOOTHER IS BEDDED *at 50°, making it ideal for working difficult woods.*

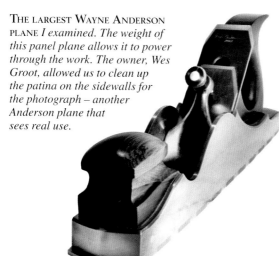

THE LARGEST WAYNE ANDERSON PLANE *I examined. The weight of this panel plane allows it to power through the work. The owner, Wes Groot, allowed us to clean up the patina on the sidewalls for the photograph – another Anderson plane that sees real use.*

first it seems a showy detail that would make the plane difficult to grasp, but that assumption turns out to be dead wrong. Because of the shell carving the plane fits just right in the hand. The recesses of the shell help you control the tool without using an iron grip. And the plane takes full-width end-grain shavings with ease from hard woods such as birch.

One of the pleasures of handling an Anderson plane is being able take in the small touches throughout the tool. Anderson works to a very high level of fit and finish, but there are still subtle marks of the maker. Deep in a recess you can see the subtle scratch of a file. Look closely at the sole plate of one of his miter planes and you can see how they are built from two pieces of steel and joined at the mouth.

The work is even more impressive when you take into consideration how reasonable Anderson's rates are compared to buying high-end vintage tools. In 2004 an Anderson plane cost between $80 and $100 per inch of length – my 9" miter cost $900. *(Ed note: His prices have gone up since then, but they are still reasonable compared to other custom makers.)*

Some people have wondered how Anderson can charge so little for this level of work, while others contend – of course – that his tools cost too much. Anderson himself isn't worked up about the economics of the business. He sets his prices so he can build what he wants and stay busy – without pushing the price outside of the realm of a serious user.

"These are user planes," he says, tapping the table for emphasis. "It's a tool. Take it into the shop and use it."

I'm a believer. My Anderson plane has become one of my favorite tools. I've made a place for it in my tool cabinet right below my Lie-Nielsen No. 62 low-angle jack and next to my Preston bullnose plane.

The miter plane's brass sidewalls are now developing a nice patina, and the front bun has a small ding from my wedding ring. I think it looks better (and works better) after every project I use it on. And after another 12 months of hard use it's going to be ready for a trot down the cabinetmaker's bench at a future Galootapalooza.

FOR MORE INFORMATION

Anderson Planes
110 Monroe St., Big Lake, Minn. 55309
andersonplanes.com, 763-486-0834

Galootapalooza
(past and future events), galootapalooza.org

Wayne Anderson Smoother

A high-angle tool of last resort, this small plane can go anywhere and plane almost anything.

Despite the amount of bronze and iron in my tool cabinet, most woodworkers need only three bench planes: A fore plane to reduce the thickness of boards, a jointer to flatten them and a smoother to prepare them for finishing.

That's in a perfect world. In reality, we work with a material that is unpredictable, cantankerous and vexing – like my first redheaded girlfriend.

During the last few years, I've gradually folded a fourth plane into my arsenal, and now I cannot imagine working without it.

It's a small smoothing plane with a steeply pitched iron (a 57° angle of attack), no chipbreaker and a mouth that a gnat would have a hard time squeezing through without damaging his hinder.

This is my plane of last resort. When my 50°-pitch smoothing plane leaves torn grain in its wake, I pull out this plane. It doesn't care if there's a grain reversal in the board. Or if I'm planing against the grain. Or if the grain is interlocked. When set for a fine cut, this plane almost never fails me.

This plane has become a staple of Wayne Anderson, a custom planemaker in Elk River, Minn. This form of plane started out several years ago with Anderson's interest in high-angle planes without a chipbreaker. He built this version for writer Kerry Pierce to test for a competing magazine. Then I bought the plane from Anderson.

Since that time, I've fallen head-over-heels for the plane, and Anderson has pushed the tool's design in new directions for other customers. If you're not familiar with Anderson's work, he's a bit different than other custom makers. He seldom makes the same tool twice. The profile on the rear of the iron might change. Or the shape of the sidewall or lever cap will morph. But the tool still looks like itself – like a fraternal twin.

As to the function of the tool, you could set up a 6"-long block plane to do the exact same job, but there's no way the tool will look as good or fit your hand so well.

With this small smoothing plane, the coffin shape of the body lets you squeeze the tool right in the middle by its mouth. And having mastered the tool, I find I can change the depth of cut merely by squeezing and pressing at the center of the tool, or by releasing that pressure. The weight of the plane (2 lbs. 2 oz.) keeps the tool in the cut without chattering (try that with your block plane) even when I use little-girl pressure to control it. The result: Thin shavings; no tearing.

The rear bun is rounded nicely so it feels good against my right palm, and the tall iron keeps my hand right where it should be.

The short sole (about 5½") allows you to plane in areas that longer smoothing planes can't get to. When I say this I don't mean tight little spaces inside a cabinet, I mean the small and large hollows that occur on any flat board. A small tool rides the gentle waves of a board where a longer plane skims off the peaks instead. And when you're trying to get a tabletop looking right (perfect flatness be darned) a short plane is invaluable.

If you're thinking of investing in one custom plane, this plane would be an excellent addition to any standard lineup. These tools start at $950.

FOR MORE INFORMATION
andersonplanes.com, 763-486-0834

Sauer & Steiner Toolworks

Near perfection from one pair of young hands.

The minting of a new toolmaker can have as much to do with skill as it does with serendipity. For Konrad Sauer, his journey from art director to furniture designer to custom toolmaker began about 12 years ago when someone positioned a cherry cupboard next to the booth of an antique tool dealer.

Sauer and his soon-to-become wife, Jill, were looking for furniture for their place and happened upon the cherry cupboard. Sauer wanted it – badly. But he couldn't in any way afford it on his salary as a young art director in Toronto.

While staring at the cupboard that he couldn't buy, his eyes alighted on the antique tools in the next booth. His gaze drifted back to the cupboard. And then back to the tools. A light bulb went off in his head.

"These," he said about the tools, "made this cupboard."

Sauer decided to learn to build furniture and to do it mostly with hand tools, which he thought would be much less expensive than power tools. He quickly mastered the Bailey-style bench planes and started wondering where he could get a bit more performance in the plane department. He asked around until he had a fateful conversation with Doug Evans, an Ontario tool dealer (and a founder of the now-defunct Shepherd Tool Co.).

Sauer: "Where do I go from here?"

Evans: "Do you have an infill?"

Sauer: "What's an infill?"

Evans sold an unhandled Spiers coffin smoothing plane to Sauer, and then it was only a matter of time before Sauer & Steiner Toolworks would be born and Sauer would say farewell to his job as an art director and become a full-time – and quite successful – custom toolmaker. And all before he turned 35.

CLASSIC DESIGNS WITH REFINEMENTS

Sauer & Steiner tools are cast solidly in the great infill-making traditions set by Stewart Spiers and Thomas Norris. And while Sauer's tools are unapologetic tributes to these great planes, they have a distinct personality that clearly is the product of Sauer's upbringing, training and artistic talents. You can see this in the details of the entire Sauer & Steiner line.

The Sauer & Steiner No. 1 panel plane is a good example. At first glance it looks like a pretty faithful Norris No. 1. But then you get a good look at the front bun. The bun on a Norris is nice enough: sculptural, sinuous and nice to hold. The front bun on the Sauer & Steiner is something else entirely: There is a small and perfect fillet that traces a square

KONRAD SAUER SPENT NEARLY 10 *years as an art director who built furniture on the side before taking the plunge into full-time toolmaking.*

on the top of the bun. The curve on the bun's sides is more symmetrical in size and shape. And the corners are astoundingly crisp. Despite all the extra shapes on the modern bun, it is just as comfortable to hold as the classic Norris.

Side by side, the Sauer & Steiner front bun makes the Norris's look like the knob on a barn door in comparison. This isn't supposed to be a criticism of Norris planes – they were mass-produced (and very expensive) English planes. But it shows that Sauer's woodworking skills flow through his work in an unusually high fashion. In fact, it is his affection for, sourcing of, and skills with wood that distinguish his tools from other makers past and present.

The metalwork I've examined on Sauer & Steiner tools is universally flawless, despite the fact that he doesn't have any metalworking tools in his Kitchener, Ontario, shop. But what is most surprising is the consistency in all the tools that come out of his shop, in design and workmanship. They all look like the same "brand" of tool with little details that are shared among the jointer, smoother and panel planes.

This "branding" of the Sauer & Steiner line is no accident. And to understand how Sauer's line of planes evolved, it helps to go back – way back – to follow the development of this toolmaker.

A Fearless Geek

As a student, Sauer describes himself as "the geeky kid who was always drawing things." And by the time he had gotten to high school, the art program and industrial arts program of his schools had become his two homes. In art class, he would come up with harebrained ideas of things to try. And his industrial arts teacher would help him give it a go, whether it was welding or metal sculpture.

The most important lesson Sauer learned there, he says, was that there is no harm in trying anything new. That lesson would become a key the first time Sauer picked up a hammer to peen together the metal shell of an infill plane.

After graduating, Sauer didn't want to go to a university to get a traditional liberal-arts education. He ended up studying graphic design; when he completed the program he became an editorial illustrator at a newspaper, then worked in packaging and finally landed as an art director at an advertising and communications company, where he worked for almost 10 years.

The years he spent as an art director proved surprisingly valuable to Sauer in his latest profession. As an art director at a small company, Sauer learned a great deal about the business world and he worked with more than 100 other businesses and watched them thrive, survive and sometimes fail. He learned how to treat suppliers.

"Even now, whenever I go to pick up materials, I bring my checkbook and pay them right then," he says. "That is good business."

Dealing with clients honed his interviewing skills – he spends as long as two hours with a potential tool-buying customer to find out exactly what he or she needs for their work. Designing web sites, television commercials and entire media campaigns honed his marketing skills – the Sauer & Steiner web site and brochure would make some Fortune 500 companies jealous.

Once Sauer started building furniture, he caught the attention of *Canadian Home Workshop* magazine, and he started writing for them on the side. Then Evans – the man who sold Sauer his first infill – made a fateful request in 2001. He asked Sauer to do some demonstrations at a woodworking show at Durham. Evans also asked a man named Joe Steiner to demonstrate at the show.

Sauer and Steiner were across the hall from one another during the show and they hit it off quite well. During that same show, the show's attendees showed an enormous interest in the infill planes on display. After the show, Sauer, Steiner, Evans, Ben Knebel and Dave Shepherd got together and started

A Sauer & Steiner No. *4 plane with bronze sides and a 50° pitch. The mouth aperture of this tool is almost unmeasureably small.*

One hallmark of Sauer & *Steiner planes is that they are remarkably consistent, to the point that you wonder if they're manufactured and there's a quality-control department.*

KONRAD SAUER'S PLANES ARE DISTINGUISHED *by his attention to both the wood and the metal. Here the bun of a panel plane is shaped like an exquisite chess piece.*

wondering if there was a market for a modern 21st-century infill. Evans, Knebel and Shepherd thought that a kit would be a good idea – they went on to found the Shepherd Tool Co., which made infill plane kits, finished infills and other tools. Sauer and Steiner were more interested in building finished planes for themselves.

"Joe and I went our own way," Sauer says. "We threw money in our own pot, sat back and had to figure out how in the hell these things were made."

Mystery No 1: dovetailing the steel sidewalls to the sole.

"Dovetailing metal seemed insane," Sauer says. "But it turned out to be the easy part. You have to remember: Joe made teeth for a living; I was an art director."

They made their first set of planes. Though each tool was based on a Spiers smoothing plane, each plane looked different. "We put them together," Sauer says. "His felt like crap to me. Mine felt like crap to him. But then it became obvious to me: We were building tools suited for one user."

Someone liked what she saw and asked the guys to build one for her. They gave her a price ($1,000) and braced themselves for rejection. But it didn't come; instead she said: "Great, when can you start?" Sauer & Steiner were in the planemaking business.

ROCKY ROAD, SEPARATION AND STABILITY

Sauer lived in Toronto; Steiner in Woodstock. This turned out to be a struggle. They each had separate shops. To produce consistent work, they had to shuttle parts and partly assembled tools back and forth. There was a lot of driving, late nights and insane hours. Eventually, Steiner decided to leave the business; Sauer decided to soldier on, keep Steiner's name on the business and become a full-time planemaker.

At the outset and even today, one of Sauer's biggest competitive advantages has been his access to excellent wood through a distributor who took a liking to Sauer and Steiner. Actually "excellent" doesn't even begin to describe the wood he uses. Much of it is quite old; some of it dates from the 1920s. It is beautiful and stable stuff.

"The wood part is the most challenging part of it," Sauer says, "especially finding it."

Aside from the high-quality wood, Sauer also spends a pretty penny for his metal. Instead of mild steel, Sauer insists on using O1 steel for his plane soles. O1 can be five times as expensive as the mild steel; but it's more stable and easier to lap flat in the end.

Until recently Sauer cut the dovetails for the plane bodies by hand with a hacksaw, but he has since switched to a vendor that uses water jets to cut the rough shapes, which Sauer then refines with a file before peening the shell together by hand.

About half of his business is in making smoothing planes, though he's had a spate of orders for jointer planes since he made a trip to a woodworking show in England. "There's something different about their working methodology there," he says, "they're very comfortable with infill jointers."

Most customers order one of the standard planes from his line-up on his web site, though each is customized to the user (Sauer will typically ask for a photocopy or scan of the customer's hand). And each tool can be further customized in even smaller ways, such as the width of the iron.

DESPITE THE FACT THAT JOE *Steiner is no longer part of the business, Konrad keeps his name on the planes and the business.*

AND PERFORMANCE?

I had the opportunity recently to test-drive several Sauer & Steiner planes that belonged to John Edwards, a Detroit-area woodworker and tool collector. Among the planes I used were a No. 4 smoothing plane ($2,200 Canadian) with bronze sides and a coffin-shaped body, a couple panel planes ($3,500 Canadian with an adjuster) and a jointer plane ($4,850 Canadian with an adjuster).

All four planes were finished to a high degree compared to many antiques I've examined and many new custom-made tools that have passed through my hands. In my estimation, Sauer's planes are fit to a degree that rivals those of planemaking legend Karl Holtey. However, Holtey's planes definitely have the edge when it comes to the final finish. Inside and out, Holtey's are perfection, and they are still unrivaled on that measure.

Still, the shiny knobs and polished sidewalls are not what cuts the wood. And so I put a Holtey A13, 11-S and No. 98 up against the Sauer & Steiners to see if they performed any differently on mild walnut, curly maple or some unpleasantly unruly Lyptus. The short answer is: I couldn't find much difference among any of the tools, even on the belligerent Lyptus, an engineered mahogany-like exotic. That result should come as no surprise – money can buy beauty but not skill.

Still, while all the planes made nice shavings and left shimmering, perfect surfaces, how I got to that pleasant point was a bit different with each tool. The Sauer & Steiner planes are well-balanced, comfortable to wield and easy to adjust. They are not in any way fussy – unlike many (but certainly not all) infill planes. While many tools and I have a rocky period where we resist each other at first, the Sauer & Steiner planes were well-behaved at the outset. I don't have any long-term experience with them

(yet), but I assume they'll become even more comfortable friends at the bench.

Considering Sauer's relatively young age, it's a bit exciting to consider that he has many years of toolmaking ahead of him, with time to mature and develop even beyond the high level he works at now.

And indeed, Sauer says that the work is still a challenge and is still not monotonous – a fear he considered as he entered the business full-time. In fact, he is still making plans for future innovations in his line: One tool he is now building is a Norris A5-style plane with ebony infill and all-steel metalwork, including the lever cap.

"It is all shades of gray," Sauer says.

He's also open to working with other sorts of materials (he's tried unsuccessfully to use plastic as an infill) and other configurations of planes – one of his most pospular planes today is a very small smoothing plane – just a little longer than a block plane – that can be wielded one-handed if you please. Spiers never made anything along those lines, as far as I can tell.

And while Sauer says he likely will always make handplanes, he keeps an open mind about the far future. He may, for example, concentrate more on his first love – making furniture. Now that Sauer knows what an infill plane is, and how to build a near-perfect version of one, making furniture should be a snap.

"This (toolmaking) has been opening a lot of doors for me," Sauer says. "It may not be the be-all and end-all, I will always be making planes. And I know that this field, woodworking, is the one I want to be in."

FOR MORE INFORMATION
Sauer & Steiner Toolworks
21 Maynard Ave., Kitchener, Ontario N2H 4Z6
sauerandsteiner.com, 519-568-8159

Fast (and Shapely) Friends

*A Sauer & Steiner smoothing plane moves into the pole
position with astonishing ease.*

All my relationships usually start out rocky. On my first date with my future wife, I almost blew it by presuming to order for her at the IHOP. (I thought it Southern courtesy; she thought it sexist piggery.) But after a few bumps I usually get along with almost anyone.

The same goes with tools and machines. When I switch to a new tool for testing, I usually have a few weeks where I don't trust it on real workpieces. So I futz with it on scrap until I'm confident the tool (and its user) are ready.

This week I'm building an Arts & Crafts-style frame for a painting and decided to disregard my cautious gut. After flushing the joints of the frame with my jointer, I picked up my Sauer & Steiner No. 4 smoothing plane and dove into the work.

At first, I thought it was a mistake. The tool's iron was sharp but it needed to be centered in its mouth. This plane has no mechanical adjuster, so you adjust the iron with hammer taps. With my other infill planes I use a small Warrington. I tap the sides of the iron to wiggle the iron left and right, and then I tap the back of the iron to increase the depth of cut. If I advance the iron too much I tap the steel or brass back of the tool to retract the iron.

So yesterday it was tap, tap, tap then (expletive deleted). I had advanced the iron too far and needed to rap the rear of the plane to retract it. (My other time-consuming option was to loosen the iron and start over.) The single curse word (sorry mom) was because the back of this beautiful plane shouldn't be struck with a steel hammer. It's gorgeous kingwood. I needed a wooden mallet to retract the iron so I didn't damage the infill. But here's the problem: I hate tapping plane irons with a wooden mallet. It feels mushy to me.

THE SAUER & STEINER NO. *4 smoothing plane is a working piece of art. And the wooden infill is exquisite.*

I wasn't pleased about using two hammers to adjust this plane, but then I remembered a tool I had purchased from Dave Anderson at Chester Toolworks. It's a plane-adjusting hammer with one brass face and one wooden face. (Lee Valley also sells a version, by the way.)

Three taps later and the shavings spilled from the center of the mouth of the plane as the tear-out left by the jointer plane receded like ugly floodwaters.

Some details: The Sauer & Steiner No. 4 smooth plane is 4 pounds, 5 ounces of perfectly fitted steel, bronze and kingwood. The overall length is $7\frac{1}{2}$". The coffin-shaped body is $2\frac{1}{2}$" wide at its most girthsome. The iron is 2" wide and is high-carbon steel – that's old school.

The Chester Toolworks plane hammer has a brass head with lignum vitae head at one end. The handle is ash and finished with linseed oil. It weighs 8 ounces and is 12" long. I paid about $50.

The money I spent on the Sauer & Steiner plane is, hands down, the most money I've ever paid for anything in my shop. The tool was an indulgence after a busy year with a couple extra teaching jobs on the side. When I ordered it, I also felt like I was reaching for something I wasn't meant to own – the same way I felt when I was dating Lucy, who was by far more talented and popular in college.

But I know that this plane will earn its keep. I have a lot of years ahead of me in the shop. And I'm loyal – I'm still married as well.

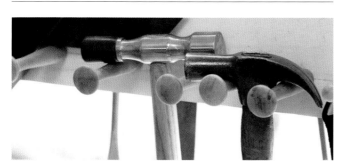

THE CHESTER TOOLWORKS HAMMER IS *ideal for precise work.*

FOR MORE INFORMATION

Sauer & Steiner Toolworks
sauerandsteiner.com, 519-568-8159

Chester Toolworks
chestertoolworks.com or sales@chestertoolworks.com

Brese Planes

From sheet metal to sweet metal.

When you use a custom tool that was designed and built by one person, you usually learn a lot about the maker without having to even have a conversation with them.

You can tell if they are more of an artist than an engineer. If they prefer utility to beauty. If they respect tradition or want to break new ground.

During the last few months I've been using a smoothing plane that was handmade by Ron Brese, and before I ever picked up the phone to chat with him, I knew he was a heck of an engineer and a die-hard traditional furniture maker.

How could I tell? Brese's planes are put together in an unusual and innovative way (more on that later) that belies a deep knowledge of metal, the tiniest details of his tool are well sorted, and the statistics and configuration of the tool suggests someone who has been using planes for a long time to build custom furniture.

But what you cannot tell about the tool from working with it is that it is quite a bargain for a piece of custom work: His 8"-long 800-255 smoothing plane is $1,542. It's a darn remarkable price for a tool of this quality.

The 800-255 plane is designed especially for taking fine cuts and for tricky woods. It's far more of a thoroughbred than a draft horse, as you can tell from its numbers. Weighing in at about 6 lbs., the tool has the mass necessary to keep it in the cut in tough timbers, yet the tote and distribution of the tool's weight allow you to use it for long periods without excessive fatigue.

The weight comes from the heavy $^3/_8$"-thick brass sole (though Brese says he is moving more to steel these days) plus the $^1/_4$"-thick brass sidewalls and $^1/_4$" thick iron. (The thick sole allows him to avoid using an accessory steel chatter block in the plane's bed, which saves labor and material.)

The iron is pitched at 55°, and the mouth aperture is tiny – less than .006" by my reading. And there is no chipbreaker. These details reserve the tool for fairly fine cuts, though you can easily pass a thickish .002" shaving through the mouth without difficulty. In other words, this could be your only smoothing plane if you wanted a Spartan tool kit.

The wood in the tester version was walnut, though Brese uses ebony, rosewood and other species upon request. And the wood is where you can see that Brese has a love for furniture. The wood

is finished to as high a degree as the metal, and it fits and flows like a cabinetmaker's finest work. It's really quite stunning and impressive.

And how does the tool work? I was completely impressed with the tool as a working example. It took fine shavings with no complaint and was predictable to set up and use. It outperformed all my vintage tools and stood shoulder to shoulder with my highly tuned premium tools that I've fussed over for years. My only quibble was I wish the iron were snecked so you could easily reduce the iron's projection without completely releasing the iron. But that's a small complaint for such a complex and well-thought out piece of engineering.

BUILDING TO RELIEVE STRESS

The story of how Brese became a toolmaker begins a couple careers ago when he was an engineer working for a sheet metal fabricator in the 1980s and early 1990s.

"Woodworking was a stress outlet from a day of work," he says. "Having an engineering background I migrated toward woodworking; I was raising a family and we had a need for furniture."

THE WALNUT INFILL ON THIS *smoother shows remarkable attention to all aspects of the craft, and it's remarkably comfortable to grasp.*

THE SMALL BRASS BUTTON PREVENTS *the iron from sliding to the floor when the lever cap is released. I also used it as a sneck to retract the iron a tad when setting it.*

THE CHAMFERED SIDEWALLS OF HIS *planes are just one more clue as to the care and attention that Brese lavishes on his smoothing planes.*

His wife, Julie, is an X-ray technician, so word got out around the medical community in their Georgia town that Brese built furniture. And though Brese preferred simple Shaker lines, his clientele migrated toward the 18th-century high style.

"I decided it (building furniture) was what I wanted to do," he says. "And I decided I should do it while I was young enough and had a backlog of commissions."

So he became a full-time furniture maker. And with the added work came the added dust, and the health concerns that go with it. He added air scrubbers and other measures, but adding more hand tools to go with his heavy woodworking machinery seemed a wise step.

He started using a lot of handplanes in his work, and found they were efficient, even in a modern professional shop. His work also evolved into a higher level as a result, particularly with his surfaces. There was a downside to the hand work: He was planing all day at times, and the tools tended to wear him out.

"I started looking at infill planes, but I saw the price as an obstacle," he said. "I had made a number of wooden planes, but they required an awful amount of effort to use them. So I started designing and using a few infill planes and putting them to use in my work."

"Do not hire a man who does your work for money, but him who does it for love of it."
— Henry David Thoreau (1817 - 1862)
American author and naturalist

After building 20 or 25 tools, his style of migrated to modern forms and then went back to a traditional look. He also found that the tools were less tiring to use in his day job.

"With an infill plane you seem to be able to do the same amount of work and not be tired at the end of the day," Brese says. "The plane gives you most of your leverage."

After experimenting with those planes, he thought that he could make them for sale and he started exploring other tool forms and processes to make them. And around the beginning of 2007, he was ready to go to market.

One of Brese's signatures with his work is how he joins the sidewalls to the sole of the tool. Historically, the shells of infill planes were either cast in one piece or were three pieces joined with dovetails. Brese says he was once browsing Karl Holtey's web site and was struck by how Holtey riveted his shells together using rivets that were integrated into the sole piece.

Brese then came up with a way to make the sole and sidewalls one piece using rivets that screwed into the sole plate and locked into the sidewalls thanks to a small chamfer on the rim of the rivet's hole.

UNLIKE THE TOTE ON A *Bailey-style plane, Brese's angles your hand higher, which helps press the tool into the work as you push it forward. It's also very comfortable to grasp.*

THE MOUTH ON BRESE'S PLANES *are incredibly tight, which makes them excellent weapons against tear-out.*

"I was intrigued with the dovetail but I also saw the drawbacks," Brese says. "Accuracy can be difficult. You almost have to estimate how much the body is going to draw when you peen it together."

Thanks to his engineering background, Brese was able to also streamline the operation so it was fast and inexpensive, with few tooling changes on his milling machine.

The results are remarkable. When the plane first showed up in our shop, it was impossible to see the joinery. Except for the fact that the shell was too perfect to be a casting, there were no clues about the joinery. After a few months of use, the patination of the shell revealed slight shadows of the rivets.

OTHER TOOLS IN THE LINE

But this tool isn't going to be his sole offering. In addition to this smoothing plane, Brese also makes a small unhandled smoothing plane, the 650-55 ($594), and he has a Norris A13-style plane (the 875). A panel plane in the works. He also has a kit he's developed, but he's not sure about the market for that.

And what's the next frontier in planemaking for Brese? Right now, it's securing one of the most essential raw ingredients: dense, dry and exotic wood for the infill material.

Recently he traded his way at an Athens, Ga., tool meet into a monster rosewood log that had its history intertwined with an international art student of Pablo Picasso's who fell behind in his rent, a mobile-home fire and an Atlanta exotic wood business.

And by the time the entire wild tale ran its course, Brese ended up with two rosewood logs in his shop that were so dense his hand-held power tools were almost worthless in the initial attack. His Sawzall almost came to a stop. His carbide-tipped sawblade on a circular saw didn't do much better.

But thanks to a handsaw and some gumption, Brese was able to break into the log so he could start processing it on his large power equipment.

"I'd cut some, take a rest, then cut some more. Then rest some more," Brese says. "After a long while, I had a nice prize."

The same could be said of Brese's new business. It's taken him two starts in other careers – and a lot of hard work and inspiration – to find just the right combination of skills to make something as beautiful as his extraordinary handplanes.

FOR MORE INFORMATION
Brese Plane
18 Eastside Drive, Thomaston, Ga. 30286
breseplane.com, 706-647-8082
ronbrese@breseplane.com

Philip Marcou

*A planemaker from the Southern Hemisphere builds
tools that excel when cutting exotic woods.*

When you purchase a new custom-made handplane with a price tag that has at least four numbers in it before the decimal, there is a small voice (the sane voice) that asks: "What, dear lord, are you purchasing?"

It's a good question. And now that I have handled and used handplanes from every major maker (including some tools with five-figure price tags), the answer is becoming clear to me.

You are not buying a tool designed to flatten and smooth domestic hardwoods – those can be had for $20. Instead, you are buying the same thing that customer buys when they plunk down $10,000 for a handmade custom chair or cabinet from an esteemed woodworker. More precisely, you are buying exactly what it is that you want, with no compromises or disappointments.

And so comparing a tool from one custom planemaker directly to another's is a bit ridiculous. After all, in the world of furniture, which is superior: A rocker from Sam Maloof or a chest-on-stand from James Krenov?

There's no correct answer. Here's why: Of all the dozens of custom tools I've handled during the last several years, I've been struck by how different one maker's work is from another's. Is a Wayne Anderson infill smoother better than a Sauer & Steiner smoother?

It's a bad question. One maker (Anderson) builds tools that are loosely interpreted from past work during the last five centuries. The other (Konrad Sauer) builds tools that have an undeniable pedigree that can be traced to specific shops at specific points in history. All the tools in this price category plane wood quite well. Heck, any tool with a well-bedded iron can do an astonishing amount of good work.

And so it was with great interest that I opened a box that arrived from New Zealand a few months ago with a plane that looked like it was a marriage between a Karl Holtey No. 98 and a Veritas Bevel-up Smoothing Plane. It turns out that the plane is neither, in fact.

It's actually a Philip Marcou original, and it is a format of handplane that is both familiar and foreign, both beautiful and a brilliant piece of engineering. Like all custom work, it's not for everyone. But it might just be exactly what you are looking for if you use exotic woods.

FROM SOUTHERN AFRICA TO PLANEMAKING

Marcou, 54, began woodworking at age 12 in his native Zimbabwe and became a full-time furniture maker in 1990 – a career that was launched by making 1,000 high-quality wooden coat hangers for a hotel.

He eventually settled on making military-style furniture – campaign chests, davenports and the like – as the centerpiece of his business. And his furniture work, which is on display on one of his web sites devoted to his woodworking (collectablefurniture.co.nz/), displays an obvious level of restraint, refinement and skill. Marcou says he never had to look for work while building in Zimbabwe; but as the political situation worsened (and continues to worsen now), Marcou made a change.

"I thought it better to leave while I still could, and New Zealand was the only chance I had," Marcou says in an e-mail. However, like in the United States (and other parts of the world), New Zealand has been flooded with low-cost furniture from Asia, a fact that has put many bespoke furniture shops on the auction block. Despite the dire

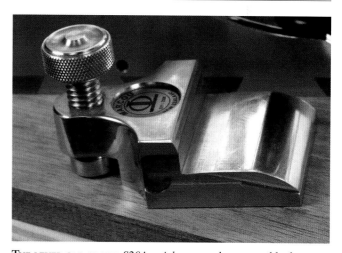

THE LEVER CAP OF THE *S20A weighs as much as many block planes. Note the machined slot on the sides of the cap. These slots mate with two shallow pins embedded in the sidewalls. As a result, the lever cap attaches to the plane body at multiple points: Against a traditional cross pin, against the shallow pins, at the front of the iron and at the back. Marcou says this "feature" actually was the result of an error on a batch of planes where he placed the cross pin incorrectly. He doesn't plan on making any more with this feature, but if you ask nicely ….*

business prospects, Marcou says he tried for two years to make his business in New Zealand work.

Then, for some reason, Marcou says he purchased a Veritas bevel-up smoothing plane. He was enamored with it, but he began mulling over some changes to the tool that he thought would make it more suited for his work. He put together his own handplane using a variety of metal- and woodworking machines, and since January 2006 has been making planes for a living and doing some furniture work whenever he can.

He has been developing a number of unusual planes during the last 12 months. None is a clear copy of any one historical form, yet all are interesting and are carefully conceived and engineered to solve certain pesky problems in woodworking.

This fall, I asked to borrow one of his tools for a shop test – an S20A bevel-up smoothing plane. Marcou readily agreed, and for the last few months I have been decoding this tool to find its true purpose in the woodshop.

THE MARCOU S20A PUSHES THE LIMITS

Fact No. 1: The Marcou S20A is the heaviest smoothing plane I have ever used. At 8 lbs. 13 ounces, the Marcou is more than twice as heavy as a Lie-Nielsen No. 4 bench plane in iron. Heck the Marcou's lever cap alone, at 1 lb. 8.5 ounces, weighs more than a Lie-Nielsen No. 60½ block plane.

The body is 11³/₁₆" long – somewhat north of a traditional smoothing plane and south of a jack plane. And its sole is 2³/₄" wide. The mass of the tool was an immediate concern of mine. You anticipate that the tool will simply wear you out after a few strokes. This is not quite the case. Because of

AT FIRST I THOUGHT THE *adjuster was too close to my knuckles. Not so. I wish it were placed a bit higher (somehow – I don't know how). But it is fairly easy to grasp in use.*

the tool's immense mass, you don't have to push the tool firmly down against the work to ensure a smooth cut (even in tough woods). Lightweight wooden planes are a joy to use in domestic hardwoods, but they can require a fair amount of downward effort on your part to maintain a controlled cut. With the Marcou, its mass does most of the pushing down. You just have to push it forward.

Getting the plane started in the cut requires the most effort; after that, inertia takes over and the tool isn't difficult to push. The return stroke seemed the most fatiguing to me, even though you're not cutting during this part of the stroke. Bottom line: The tool isn't tiring if you use it properly. If you prepare your stock with a jointer plane prior to a smoothing plane then the stock will require only minimal attention with a smoothing plane. Long planing sessions should be fairly rare.

The mass is an advantage when planing difficult woods, such as the timbers found in New Zealand and neighboring Australia. A plane's weight helps keep the cutter in the thick of things – not riding up and skittering over the wood.

Another important difference: The plane has its iron's bevel facing up and is bedded in the plane's body at 20°. This is much like a standard block plane – most larger bevel-up planes have the iron bedded at 12°. Why the higher angle? Again, it's for working difficult woods. The higher pitch allows you to easily get the plane up to high planing angles (up

THE BED OF THE PLANE *is serious business. Note how the adjuster is let into the bed and secured with a screw – repairs, if ever necessary, would be easy. Plus the entire bed is machined.*

THE MOUTH OF THE PLANE *is opened and closed with this plate. It's nice how you can grasp it from the sides to adjust it. It's much more precise than on a traditional block plane.*

near 60° counts as high in my book) without sharpening radically high angles on the iron. I have a 40° secondary bevel on the iron right now, which is easy to achieve with standard equipment. Add the 20° from the bed of the tool and I'm planing at 60° with little effort. And high angles are great for both difficult tropical woods and even irascible domestics.

The iron itself is worth remarking on. Most planemakers make a custom iron for each tool. Not Marcou. He uses a stock, off-the-rack 2¼"-wide A2 iron from Veritas. These irons, which are of high quality, are inexpensive and easy to obtain. So if you want several blades honed at several angles, it requires little investment. Also, Veritas has started making these irons in old-fashioned high-carbon steel – so you have even more options.

The mouth can be opened and closed by sliding a small shoe forward and back in front of the iron. The mouth is locked in place with two knurled thumbscrews on top of the plane near the mouth. I was surprised how much I liked this unusual configuration. Most of the bevel-up-style block planes have a shoe like this, but it is captured by the metal body of the tool and can be fussy to move with the supplied lever. The mouth on the Marcou S20A is adjusted faster and more precisely than other tools with this mouth. And, as a testament to Marcou's engineering skills, the mouth's tightest position is absolutely perfect for high-tolerance smoothing with a .001"-thick shaving or less. So closing up the mouth for a pain-in-the-burl cut is child's play – just shut your mouth all the way. In fact, the mouth aperture is so tight with this setting that the shaving is wedged between the mouth and iron until you take your next pass – that ejects the shaving.

Do you need a tight mouth? Holtey's No. 98 has a fairly open mouth and no way to close it up, for example. And there is an argument that sharpness

and the angle of the cutter is more important than a tight mouth. Perhaps, but I found that the mouth on the S20A really pointed out the advantages of a tight mouth in exotic woods. With the mouth open (and by open I mean about .010" or so), I would get tear-out when planing Jatoba against the grain. But when I closed up the mouth all the way – keeping the same settings on the iron – the tear-out disappeared. I don't need any more convincing. Tighten up those mouths on your smoothing planes when you are doing high-tolerance work in nasty woods.

A SURPRISING ADJUSTER

I've said it many times that I don't like Norris-style adjusters on handplanes. They can be fussy and fragile, and they are never positioned on the tool where I want them (which is directly in front of the tote and near my middle finger).

But the Marcou adjuster, like the one on the Veritas, is something special. I'm sure you could damage it if you really gave it a shot. And it's probably a bit more fussy to use compared to a good old Bailey-style adjuster. But the Marcou adjuster is a smooth piece of work with minimal backlash and none of the jerky movements with the old Norris adjusters. Though the bedding angle of the tool brings the adjuster up to ring-finger height on the rear tote, I still wish it were a bit higher so I could make depth adjustments on the fly. It's a minor quibble for an excellent piece of work, really.

The other blade-adjusting mechanism on the tool is a set of setscrews on either side of the iron, up by the cutting edge. These are standard on many Veritas planes, though I never seem to need them. They can help you laterally adjust the iron in a pre-

HERE YOU CAN SEE THE *thumbscrews that lock the mouth in position. Secure them firmly or they can come loose.*

THE FRONT KNOB IS OVERSIZED, *beautifully turned and very comfortable in the hand. Marcou makes a variety of custom knobs to suit your taste.*

THE TOTE OF THE **S20A** *is comfortable to hold as long as you don't grasp too tightly up by the horn. If this were my plane, I would relieve a couple small sections to make the tote fit my hand.*

dictable manner, though with a smooth adjuster like this I think the screws are moot. They're there if you need them; you'll probably outgrow them.

ERGONOMICS: GOOD AND OTHERWISE

Both the tote and the front knob are made using Rhodesian teak, which Marcou brought with him and has in limited supply. The front knob is larger than I expected ($1\frac{7}{8}$" in diameter), but I quite liked it and found it perfectly suited to my very slightly smaller-than-average hands.

The rear tote was another story. After about 20 minutes of heavy use, my right hand would tingle, especially my forefinger and thumb. I tried different grips (for example, switching to a three-fingered grip). Some things helped; some things didn't. When brought to Marcou's attention, he responded that the rear tote was a topic he was working on. He offered many useful solutions, some of which helped the tingling go away.

The best solution was to train my efforts on letting the left-hand knob do most of the pushing down. And then allowing the tote hand to focus on pushing foreword by holding the rear tote more near its base. This really helped.

A DOVETAIL JOINT NEAR THE *heel of the plane. All the joints are perfect. And the splay angle is quite attractive as well.*

FIT AND FINISH

The plane cost $1,995 at the time of this review in 2007. And so you have a right to demand a tool that makes no compromises with the fit and finish of its parts. It should be dang-near perfect. And the Marcou delivers on this point.

Marcou's cabinetmaking and machining sensibilities make this a tool of few compromises. The dovetails are seamless. The knurling on the knobs is crisp. The parts slide together in Swiss-watch fashion – the way the lever cap goes into the plane body is truly a marvel. All in all, no disappointments.

I finishing up testing this plane on a Wednesday afternoon in our shop in Cincinnati and boxed up to go to another woodworker. And I was sad to see it go, despite all the other high-quality tools that have passed through my hands. It's a different tool. It's not the same as a Wayne Anderson tool or a Konrad Sauer tool or a Bill Carter tool.

It's encouraging that none of the modern tool-makers are wading in different waters. There might be room for all of them – and perhaps a few more.

FOR MORE INFORMATION
Marcou Planes
Waihi
New Zealand
Telephone: +64 7 863 6016
marcouplanes.co.nz

Premium
Shoulder Planes

These useful tools were once simple and traditional.
Three modern makers have redesigned this tool
and added some features.

Shoulder planes are, in the opinion of some highly skilled craftsmen, the wood putty of the hand-tool world.

The first time I ever saw Frank Klausz, he was (as per usual) surrounded by rapt pupils as he dovetailed a box during a woodworking show in Ft. Washington, Penn. As Klausz sawed and chopped his pins and tails, his audience peppered him with questions.

One question really stood out that day.

"Mr Klausz," the guy said. "You and other woodworkers from Europe don't seem to use shoulder planes. Why is that?"

Without even a pause to ponder, Klausz responded. "I don't need them. I cut my tenons right the first time."

As a frequent user of shoulder planes, that truthful comment stung. Cutting your tenons dead-on is the way to go, but I don't do it enough by hand to master it, I'm afraid. And so the shoulder plane remains on my bench when I'm doing traditional work.

I had bought my first shoulder plane several years before hearing Klausz's assessment of the tool. My plane was an English-made Stanley No. 93, and I'd bought it after reading a glowing account of the wonders of shoulder planes in *Fine Woodworking* magazine.

I remember unwrapping the tool from its waxy paper, honing the iron keen and square, then cleaning up a rabbet at my workbench. The tool cut on one side of the blade, but not the other. So I Englished the blade left and right in the plane's body and tried again. No luck; the tool wouldn't cut on one side. So I put it away.

Every month or so I would fish it from my tool cabinet and give it another try on a piece of non-essential work. And every time the tool refused to take a full-width shaving. So I blamed myself as not being skilled enough to wield such a precision instrument.

Then one day the shoulder plane was perched on my workbench on its side with its sole touching a piece of work. I noticed that the sole didn't line up with the edge of my wood. So I grabbed the workpiece and put a square on it. The work was perfect. It was the shoulder plane that was messed up.

I put a try square on my shoulder plane for the first time ever and confirmed that the sole of the tool was not at all square to the plane's sidewalls. I was furious. I trotted back to our shop's edge sander and began power sanding the plane's sole with the side of the tool on the edge sander's table. After 10 minutes of work at the sander I walked back to my bench and my opinion of shoulder planes changed

THE LIE-NIELSEN MEDIUM SHOULDER PLANE *has classic good looks and simple controls.*

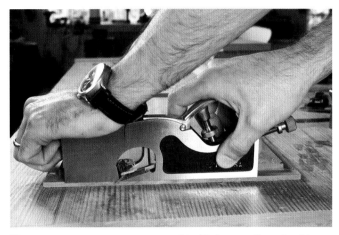

THIS TWO-HANDED GRIP KEEPS THE *Lie-Nielsen medium shoulder plane in the cut without too much effort. But the grip did require some getting used to.*

forever. The tool worked, and worker better than I thought possible.

SURGICAL INSTRUMENTS

Shoulder planes aren't just for truing the shoulders of tenons. If that were the only task they were designed for, I'd just fetch one of my chisels to undercut the shoulder of the joint and walk away. Shoulder planes adjust rabbets, dados, half-laps, bridle joints, tenon cheeks and any other work where one surface must be square to another.

Shoulder planes don't form these joints, but they do refine them so that everything fits the way the maker intended.

During the last 10 years I have become a shoulder-plane junkie and have tried every size and configuration available on the market. And I've concluded that most users are better served with buying a new tool instead of a used one. Trust me: You don't want to buy a used tool that you cannot send

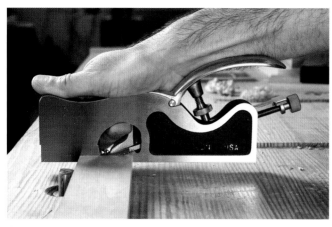

A ONE-HANDED GRIP MAKES MY *right hand look a bit claw-like. But this does focus the force of your hand right over the cutting edge, a major advantage when working the tool.*

WITHOUT A LATERAL ADJUST LEVER, *you must rely upon your ability to test the iron's position with your fingers or sliver of wood.*

back if the sole isn't square to the sides. Most flea markets and Internet auction sites are *caveat emptor*, and so shoulder planes with a warranty are the best choice in my opinion.

Three new commercial brands stand out as the best tools in my book: Bridge City Tools, Lie-Nielsen Toolworks and Veritas (sorry Clifton, I've just had a few too many defective Cliftons pass through my hands). I've worked with all three versions for some time now and have found they are quite different to hold and behold. Here's a close look at what I like (and dislike) about each version in the size that's close to ³/₄" wide.

LIE-NIELSEN
MEDIUM SHOULDER PLANE

The most traditional of the ³/₄" shoulder planes is the Lie-Nielsen model, which shares ancestry with the Record 042 and an earlier Preston version. These tools are distinguished by their attractive

and flowing lines. The lever cap of the Lie-Nielsen plane is a gently curved bronze wing that reflects the curve of the tool's body above its escapement.

I've always been attracted to the traditional look of this tool. But learning to hold it comfortably was a struggle at first. There isn't an obvious hold-me-this-way aspect to the tool. When I use it upright on my work to clean up long rabbets, I grasp the tool with my right hand enveloping the lever cap and my left hand pushing the tool behind the slight hump at the toe of the tool.

When I plane the cheeks of tenons, I used the plane one-handed: My right hand grasps the hump above the shaving escapement with my middle finger hooked into the escapement. The lever cap is locked against my forearm behind my wrist. It sounds (and looks) a tad awkward, but it is a good way to get an accurate cut. After a little practice, this grip feels natural.

When used on its side, I pinch the plane's sidewall above the escapement. There isn't a natural holding spot waiting at that location, though the plane responds admirably when used in that manner and is fairly comfortable when held this way.

The mechanism for adjusting the iron is simple and robust. The long iron drops into the plane body from behind, and a small groove in the iron nests onto the adjustment knob. The knob spins about half a turn before engaging the groove when you go from retracting the iron to advancing it. That's a tight tolerance. There is no mechanical method for adjusting the iron laterally left and right. You do that with finger pressure alone.

You adjust the mouth of the Lie-Nielsen using two screws. The screw on the top releases the mouth mechanism so you can change it. The screw at the toe of the tool allows you to dial in the mouth's aperture. This is the same method that most shoulder planes use to adjust the mouth, so I didn't have a problem with it until I tried the toolless method dreamed up at Bridge City.

The manufacturing quality of this tool (and all the others in this article) is quite good. The ductile iron is finished well (and is indestructible). The bronze is well-polished except on the underside of the lever. The A2 cryogenically treated iron holds an edge well, though edge-retention isn't as critical a component of a shoulder plane as having a straight edge is.

Conclusion: For the traditionalist, the Lie-Nielsen is the first choice. Its only downsides are the mouth requires a couple steps to adjust the aperture, and the ergonomics must be learned before you can really start to unlock its potential. The Lie-Nielsen Shoulder Plane is $195.

VERITAS MEDIUM SHOULDER PLANE

The ¾" version of the Veritas shoulder plane was hailed by its fans as the first ever comfortable shoulder plane to use. In many way, I must agree. The adjustable rear grip of the Veritas Medium Shoulder Plane allows you to comfortably wrap the web of skin between your thumb and index finger around the rear of the plane. Plus, because of the hole in the sidewalls, you can get a remarkably strong grip on the tool. Robin Lee, the president of Lee Valley Tools, often compares the grip on his tool to that of a handshake.

The small brass knob on the rear of the tool is adjustable and can be pivoted to your favorite spot (or even removed). I think of the rear grip of this tool to be similar to the pistol grip of a dovetail saw, whereas the grip of a traditional shoulder plane is more like that of a straight-handled saw or dozuki. It's just different.

I will say this: The Veritas required me to reprogram the way I approach my work. To get an accurate cut, I levered the tool into the work against my finger in the escapement and my hand's web on the tool's rear knob. Once I got familiar with this grip, the tool was a breeze to use accurately.

The Veritas shoulder plane has the most complex method of adjusting the iron. The advantage of the Veritas is that you can dial in a precise adjustment. The downside is that this process requires some time.

The Veritas's iron is shorter than the Lie-Nielsen's and mates with its adjuster in a slightly different way. The Veritas's iron is pierced with holes that drop on the adjuster's pin. The adjust-

THE VERITAS MEDIUM SHOULDER PLANE *shares a lot of the advanced features of the other Veritas planes. It has a modern rear end, but the toe resembles that of old infill shoulder planes.*

ment knob controls both the depth of cut and some lateral adjustment – it's a Norris-style adjuster.

But there is more. In addition to the lateral adjust function of the adjuster, you can control the position of the iron in the mouth of the tool using four setscrews embedded in the sides of the body. Some people love these screws. Some leave them alone.

If you are a lover of the screw, you can line them up to provide a precise channel for your iron so you can drop it back into place – perfectly – after sharpening. If you haven't yet tamed the screw, you'll sometimes unwittingly lock the iron in place so you can't get it out of the tool without backing out the screws a tad.

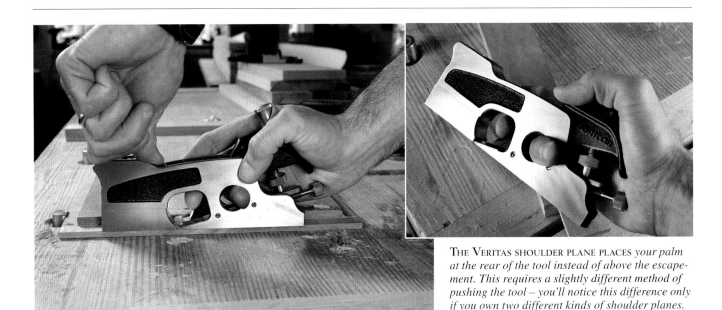

THE VERITAS SHOULDER PLANE PLACES *your palm at the rear of the tool instead of above the escapement. This requires a slightly different method of pushing the tool – you'll notice this difference only if you own two different kinds of shoulder planes.*

THE SCREWS IN THE SIDEWALLS *create a precise channel for the iron to rest in. The actual blade adjuster is a Norris-style adjuster.*

MOST TRADITIONAL SHOULDER PLANES WITH *an adjustable mouth work like the Veritas. Loosen the screw on top of the tool then adjust the mouth with the screw in the toe. Then tighten the screw on top again.*

In general, I keep the screws backed out and find the pressure of the lever cap keeps the iron in position just fine during a cut. The screws are optional.

Like with the Lie-Nielsen, the mouth of the tool is adjusted using a screwdriver. This isn't a frequent function with this form of tool anyway, so asking you to use a screwdriver isn't unreasonable.

The fit and finish of the tool is quite good, and you can purchase this tool with either an A2 or standard high-carbon iron. It weighs 2 lbs., which is a bit lighter than the Lie-Nielsen.

Conclusion: This tool looks unusual to a traditionalist (such as myself) at first – though it worked flawlessly from the start. The interesting thing is that you quickly become accustomed to the shape of the tool, particularly its unusual rear grip, and you forget that it's even unusual. The tool features some modern design touches and has features that appeal to the woodworker who likes being able to tune a plane in a most empirical fashion. The Veritas Medium Shoulder Plane is $179 for the tool with an A2 iron and $179 for the tool with a high-carbon iron.

BRIDGE CITY
HP-7 SHOULDER PLANE

The Veritas Medium Shoulder Plane appears to be a radical design until you lay your hands on the Bridge City HP-7 Shoulder Plane. This brass and stainless steel plane is different in every measurable way from its competitors except one: It cuts wood in the same accurate manner.

Where to begin? Let's begin at the end. The rear of the HP-7 is a stainless steel S-curve that fits nicely into the palm of your hand. As your fingers close on the body of the tool, they fall directly into the milled grooves on the side of the plane.

Recently I had 18 students take all of my shoulder planes for a test drive during a class on hand joinery. This tool was the only shoulder plane that didn't elicit the following question: "What's the best way to hold this tool?" With the HP-7, the grip is obvious.

What's not so obvious is how you remove and insert the iron. It doesn't come out the rear of the tool like the Lie-Nielsen and Veritas versions. Instead, you open up the mouth wide – it's easy because you don't need a screwdriver to do it – and lift the iron off the bed of the tool and out the mouth.

Removing the iron is easier than replacing it. Sometimes it can require a little fumbling to find the pin that mates with the hole in the iron – especially if there is any sawdust or sharpening grit present. You can't readily see the pin and hole without peering through the top of the tool.

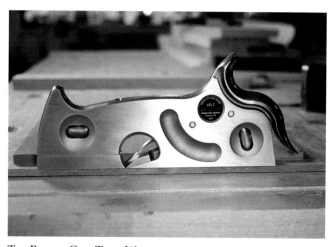

THE BRIDGE CITY TOOL WORKS *HP-7 plane combines contemporary styling with features you won't find on other tools. All of these features make the tool quite simple to set up and use.*

THE RHINO HORN AT THE *toe of the tool makes it comfortable to push. The rear grip is intuitive – more so than on most other shoulder planes.*

SPIN THE KNOB ABOVE THE *mouth plate and push the mouth forward (it's on a dovetailed way). Then you can lift the iron up and out of the body.*

When the iron is in place on the pin you then squeeze the stainless handle to lock it. This is probably the coolest feature of the plane. The lever cap and rear grip are linked with a pivoting mechanism. Lift up the grip and the iron is released. Squeeze the grip and the iron is locked.

You can adjust the tension applied by the lever cap on the iron with a hex wrench if need be, but I haven't found that to be necessary (instructions are included for doing this, however).

The iron adjustment is dead-nuts simple. A knurled knob by the grip controls the depth of cut. Lateral adjustments are handled with finger pressure.

The grip of the tool at the toe is also nice. The rhino-horn shape (a traditional touch) is good for pushing or pulling the tool.

The fit and finish is perfect – when the tool comes out of the box. The body is brass, and it quickly becomes patinated through use, though this can be polished away. The stainless grip has remained gleaming through months of hard service.

Conclusion: The design of the tool isn't (in my opinion) as radical as some of the other plane designs from Bridge City Tools, and perhaps that is why this plane tugs at my traditional heart stronger than I expected. Or perhaps I'm just a sucker for a brass shoulder plane. It strikes a balance between interesting features and traditional functionality. The HP-7 costs $589 (some are still available).

POSTSCRIPT

For many years, that quip from Frank Klausz made me feel a bit guilty about owning a shoulder plane, and I would keep the tool in a drawer instead of on my workbench. I would fetch it when the other people in my shop weren't looking or had gone home.

THE HP-7 IS SURPRISING AT *every turn. The lever cap engages and releases by lowering and raising the grip. It's intuitive and simple in use (though mechanically complex inside).*

But that became difficult because I ended up using the thing so dang much (after its trip to the edge sander). After several years of slaving in shame, I actually got to know Klausz and visited his shop in New Jersey.

I marveled at his plumb bob collection and the orderly way his shop was put together. And then I saw it. On the lower shelf of his tool cabinet was a 1/2" shoulder plane. I've never asked him about it, however, just like no one ever talks about wood filler.

FOR MORE INFORMATION

Veritas Medium Shoulder Plane
Lee Valley Tools
leevalley.com, 800-871-8158

Lie-Nielsen Medium Shoulder Plane
Lie-Nielsen Toolworks
800-327-2520, lie-nielsen.com

Bridge City Tools HP-7 Shoulder Plane
Bridge City Tool Works
bridgecitytools.com, 800-253-3332

D. L. Barrett & Sons

*Meet the young (he's just 18) and skilled hands
behind a near-perfect tool.*

While modern carpenters might show off at the jobsite by driving up in a fully loaded pickup truck, the 19th-century cabinetmaker did the same thing when he pulled out his plow plane from his tool box.

Plow planes were usually the most expensive tool in an early woodworker's tool kit. While all the other tools in the woodworker's chest might be iron or beech, the plow plane could be made from an exotic wood, be highly decorated and use complex adjustment mechanisms. In fact, sometimes a particularly fancy plow plane would be presented to an employee as a retirement gift.

To me, it's amazing that all this effort went into a tool that really did only one thing: Cut grooves.

Because plow planes were some of the fanciest tools made, they also are one of the most collectible today.

Unlike a number of tool collectors I know, I don't have a full-blown plow-plane obsession. Ebony screw-arm plows with ivory tips and silver fittings are beautiful and ingenious, but I've always thought that their flashy details somehow diminish them because they make them too nice to use – like a table saw with a solid-gold top.

In my work, I've always used metal-bodied plow planes, though they eject shavings into your hands, are cold and seem heavier than their wooden cousins. The overriding advantage of the metal plows, however, is that their fences are easier to keep parallel to the tool's skate than a typical wooden screw-arm plow plane.

As a result, what I've always wanted is a wooden-bodied plow that has a robust and easy-to-adjust fence. My search ended last year when I judged a toolmaking contest put on by the WoodCentral.com web site and sponsored by Lee Valley Tools.

For that contest, we judged more than 60 tools that had been brought into Lee Valley's board room in Ottawa, Ontario. The moment I walked into that room my eyes locked onto a beech-bodied plow plane with ebony arms and a simple metal fence-locking mechanism.

KYLE BARRETT HOLDING THE THIRD *plane he built.*

"In 1765 everything a man owned was made more valuable by the fact that he had made it himself or knew exactly from where it had come."

— Eric Sloane
"A Reverence for Wood"

When I finally got to pick the tool up, I was impressed by how lightweight it was and how the fence slid smoothly on its arms and locked with the quick twist of a thumbscrew. The real test, however, came when I started plowing grooves using a workbench that Lee Valley employees had moved to the boardroom.

The plow plane both glided over the work and removed a sizable shaving. It was the easiest groove I'd ever cut by hand in maple. This was a surprise. Usually with tools as complex as a plow or a moving fillister plane, there's a break-in period while the tool and its user circle each other and neither performs at the top of their game. This plow plane was different. It was like I'd been using it all my life. My first groove with the tool was a total success.

After a couple days of discussion, we awarded that plane first place for craftsmanship, and I resolved to track down its maker and ask that person to build one for me.

When I finally got in touch with him, I was shocked to find out that the maker was Kyle Barrett, an 18-year-old high-school student in Barrie, Ontario, who had built the plane in his father's workshop. I was even more shocked to learn that his prize-winning plane was only the second hand-plane he'd ever made.

'I Enjoy Seeing How Things Work'

Kyle's toolmaking adventure began years ago in his father's shop. Dan Barrett is a trained carpenter and cabinetmaker with more than 25 years of experience in building and teaching. When Dan built the family's living room chairs, Kyle was right there in the shop watching the process and helping where he could. When Dan built some shelves that looked like an airplane flying out of a wall, Kyle was there as well.

THE MOULDING ON THE FENCE *is remarkably crisp, even as it returns across the front. Here you also can see (if you look closely) the boxwood lining and the two sliding dovetails that attach it.*

THE SKATE IRON AND DEPTH *stop all come together seamlessly. The tapered A2 irons all seat firmly against the skate and are held securely by the wedge. The set of eight well-made irons is just one of the selling points of this tool.*

"I thought it was really cool getting to see how things were made," Kyle says.

Then Kyle took a shop class at high school and resolved to challenge himself by building a walnut grandfather clock. To make the beading on the clock's ogee bracket feet, Kyle had to make a simple handplane for the job.

"I really enjoyed that," Kyle says. So the pump was primed when he happened upon an ad for a toolmaking contest in one of his dad's Lee Valley flyers.

To enter the contest, he had to figure out what tool to build. As Kyle was flipping through "Wooden Plow Planes" by Donald Rosebrook and Dennis Fisher he spied a Hermon Chapin plow plane on page 98. That Connecticut-made plane was very similar to a Scottish-made Mathieson bridle plow, and Kyle locked onto that plane and resolved to build a version of it for the contest.

His plane combined elements of both the Chapin and Mathieson planes, and he added a couple significant details of his own. From Mathieson,

THE BRASS CAPS ON THE *ends of the ebony stems are wedged tight. The amount of detail on this plane is extraordinary.*

THE BEECH TOTE IS HAND-SHAPED *and has no hard lines to nip at your fingers.*

Tʜᴇ ʙʀɪᴅʟᴇ ᴍᴇᴄʜᴀɴɪꜱᴍ ɪꜱ ꜰʟᴀᴡʟᴇꜱꜱ *in workmanship and in function. The fence locks parallel to the skate every time, which saves an immense amount of fussing.*

Kyle took the basic overall shape and fence-locking mechanism. But he swiped an improvement from the Chapin: The plane's ebony arms sit in a brass liner on the tool's fence. Kyle also improved the tool by adding a boxwood facing to the plane's fence – it's attached with sliding dovetails.

Kyle and his dad both insist that Kyle did all the work himself, including the complex metalwork on the bridle mechanism. And after a few minutes of talking to Kyle, you have little doubt that he is capable of building a tool like this. He really knows his stuff.

"My dad was very adamant that I learned the proper techniques to use when doing anything," Kyle says. "He would always say that there was a right way and a wrong way to do something, and he would always go out of his way to make sure I was learning the right techniques. I could never have made the same quality tool without him passing on his knowledge and experience."

The plane took about 120 hours to build and almost didn't make it into the contest. At one point, Kyle said he mortised the plane's depth stop lock on the wrong side of the skate and he had to start building the body all over again.

"Do you remember what time the contest's deadline was for entries?" Kyle asks. "Well, we made it in with about three minutes to go."

The tool was fun to build, and Kyle was surprised by how well it worked, especially considering it was his second plane and how tricky it had been to line up the iron and skate of the tool.

A Nᴇᴡ Cᴏᴍᴘᴀɴʏ ᴀɴᴅ Cᴏʟʟᴇɢᴇ

Meanwhile, Kyle's father had also been making planes in his one-car garage, and with Kyle's interest in toolmaking ignited, Dan decided to start making planes for sale under the name D.L. Barrett & Sons.

Kyle, Dan and his younger brother, Jeremy, all work in the shop, which is filled with all the basic woodworking machines, plus a small milling machine, metal-cutting band saw and metal lathe.

As of now, the company offers three kinds of plow planes and three bench planes. In the works for the future are fillister, dado and moulding planes – most likely complex moulders. The plow planes come with a full set of eight tapered A2 irons, made by a Canadian company, which are also things of beauty. They taper gracefully from ⅜" thick to ⅛" thick at the ends. The unbeveled faces of the irons are remarkably flat and the V-groove that rides the plow's skate is crisp.

At the time of the interview, Dan and his sons were building nine tools: four Mathieson plows, three V-plows and two open-tote jack planes. But the plane-making work is sometimes interrupted by homework. That's because Kyle has just started in the tool and die-making program at nearby Georgian College.

"It's really neat, actually," he says. "Already I've learned so much about metalworking. There is so much more you can do to make it easier."

After a week of studying blueprint reading or machine processes, Kyle can be found in the shop

with his family working out some of the details of his planes. But after Kyle finishes the two-year program, he's not sure what he'll do.

"I don't know if I'll have enough skills to go out on my own as a toolmaker," he says. "I'm 18, and I'm not sure where I'm going yet."

A REMARKABLE WORKER

I hope Kyle continues as a toolmaker. After the contest ended, I asked him to build one of his plows for me that would be a worker in my home shop (instead of a trophy on the mantle). At the time I didn't even ask the price, though I consider the $2,250 (Canadian) price tag for the base model to be fair considering all the handwork and the full set of irons included with the tool.

The plane Kyle built for me is only slightly different than the prize-winning bridle plow. Instead of steel, mine has a bronze bridle mechanism. And it is signed "D.L. Barrett & Sons." Plus – I have to be fair here – I think my plane is even better than the plane that won the contest in February 2008. (Dan agrees with me, by the way.)

The plane feels like it is ready to go to work as soon as you pick it up. Unlike other plow planes, the controls of a bridle plow are remarkably intuitive – even power-tool woodworkers who pick it up understand the mechanism immediately.

All the brass fittings are perfectly mortised into the brass and ebony parts. The beech wedge is a seamless fit into the stock.

How does it work? I hate to think that anyone will buy one of these planes and put it in a glass dis-

play case. The D.L. Barrett & Sons plane is graceful and nimble in both hardwoods and soft. It is easily the nicest plow plane I have ever used.

Which begs the question: What did Kyle do with the tool that won the contest?

"It's in the shop," he says. "We have it in a place to keep it up out of harm's way. But I always like to take it down and use it."

FOR MORE INFORMATION:

D. L. Barrett & Sons Toolworks
112 Wessenger Drive, Barrie, Ontario, Canada L4N-8P5
dlbarrettandsons.com, 705-739-8905

THE PROOF OF THE PLANE *is in the thick, spiral shavings that peel off the board. You want to get the work done quickly, so a stable tool that can take a heavy shaving is a must.*

Veritas Small Plow Plane

Can this Canadian company improve one of the most highly evolved woodworking tools?

Unless you're involved in production woodworking (with plywood, MDF or worse), you probably would welcome a plow plane into your workshop.

I can remember the moment when I decided to buy one. I was making a pair of doors for a one-off bookcase, and I was routing the groove in the stiles using our shop's expensive router table. Despite my best efforts, the router bit grabbed my first stile and flung it across the shop about 15 feet.

The stile survived the javelin-style slinging, so I began grooving the next stile in the pile. Like the first stile, this one made an Olympic launch across the shop. But this time the stile's entire groove got chewed up by the router bit as the board made its hasty exit to kiss the floor.

There are some times when a machine is not the right choice for short-run work.

My first plow plane was a Record 043, an adorable English plane that came with three cutters that some Englishman had forgotten to heat-treat. Despite the fact that I had to sharpen the cutters every time I picked up the plane, I was hooked. I bought a Record 044 (the little guy's bigger brother), then a Stanley No. 45 and a No. 46.

Each of these tools had advantages. I liked the skew cutter on the Stanley No. 46 so I could make clean cuts across the grain. I liked the robust depth stop of the Stanley No. 45 and its weight, which kept the tool stable through the cut. And the Record 044 didn't get clogged as much as the baby 043.

I also purchased a couple nice wooden plow planes, but they had a variety of problems that kept them on the shelf and off the bench.

Sometimes, however, I feel I'm alone in my enthusiasm for plow planes. Plows seem complex and fussy to the uninitiated. In truth, plow planes are some of the easiest joinery planes to use. If you know the right tricks, they are simple to sharpen, simple to set up and simple to use.

So I was delighted when Robin Lee, president of Lee Valley Tools, pulled out the prototype for the Veritas small plow plane as we drank a couple beers after a trade show in Las Vegas in August 2007. Later that fall, Veritas loaned me a pre-production model to test for a few weeks. And once the company began manufacturing the tool in large quantities I snapped up one of the first ones and have been using it quite a bit in my work.

Allow me to spoil the ending: The Veritas plow plane is better than all of my other metal plow planes. Its Canadian designers fundamentally improved an already highly evolved tool. And the quality of manufacturing exceeds that of all my vintage metal plows. I do have a couple quibbles with the tool, which I discuss below, but overall, the Veritas Small Plow Plane is an impressive piece of work and an unqualified success.

ABOUT PLOWS

Any tool collector worth his (or her) salt knows that plow planes were the equivalent of jewelry for 19th-century cabinetmakers. The plow was the fanciest tool in the toolbox, and early woodworkers spent good money to get a tool that would impress their underlings and coworkers.

But that cachet was during the heyday of the wooden plow plane, and as metal planes pushed the wooden ones aside, the metal plows didn't keep the same luster as the wooden plows. Sure, there were some fancy metal plow and combination planes made, but since the invention of the powered router, the plow plane has been little more than a curiosity for modern woodworkers.

The new Veritas Small Plow Plane is probably a little ahead of its time. Though some hand-tool wood-

WHILE BENCH PLANES BEGIN AT *the right end of the board (for right-handers), plows and moulding planes begin at the left. You make a few short strokes at the end of the board to get the groove started. Then you lengthen each stroke until you are plowing the entire length of the board.*

A KEY POINT TO REMEMBER *with plow planes is that each of your hands has a different job. The hand on the fence pushes the fence against the work – nothing else. The hand on the tote pushes the tool forward – nothing more. Be sure to allow this arm to swing completely free – this will keep you straight.*

THE DEPTH STOP ON THE *Veritas isn't completely flat – the edges are relieved a bit. This gives you a softer landing when the depth stop contacts the work. You're less likely to mar your work with the leading or trailing edge of the depth stop.*

THE MOST WELCOME INNOVATION WITH *the Veritas is the collet-style locking system in the fence. It works like a router collet to hold the fence parallel and makes it impossible for you to lock the fence out of parallel to the tool's skate. I tried.*

workers are wildly enthusiastic about its release, the No. 1 question I hear is: What is it used for?

So here's a short explanation: Plow planes make grooves and (with some of the metal versions) some of them make small rabbets – the largest groove or rabbet that the Veritas Small Plow Plane can make with a single set-up is ³⁄₈".

Unlike bench planes, all plows work on different principles. You need to sharpen the cutting edge of your plow's iron square and keep it that way – otherwise your cutter could wander in the cut and it could become difficult to push the tool.

You start the cut at the left end of the board (this is the method for right-handers) with a few short strokes and then make each stroke longer and longer until you are plowing the entire length. Why? The tool will wander less this way because the already-cut groove will help guide the tool. If you try to plow the entire edge in one mighty stroke, changes are that the grain direction of the board will push your fence away from the work and then you will be weaving instead of grooving.

DETAILS ON THE VERITAS

As far as improvements go with the Veritas, the best place to begin is with the irons. The stock tool comes with a ¹⁄₄" iron, which is the most-used cutter for making grooves in rails and stiles to hold a door panel and for grooving the parts of the drawer to hold a bottom panel. You can buy four more cutters (¹⁄₈", ³⁄₁₆", ⁵⁄₁₆" and ³⁄₈") for an additional $65 or buy them individually.

All the irons are made from hard-wearing A2 steel, and the unbeveled face of the irons are flattened on Veritas's rotary lapping machines. This process makes polishing the unbeveled face a quick operation. I sharpened a complete set of cutters – from the wrapper to ready-to-plow – in about 30 minutes.

All of the irons come ground with a 35° primary bevel – the traditional angle for this style of bevel-down tool. This steep and blunt angle gives you a more durable edge and keeps the cutter from vibrating – plow planes don't have as much bedding as a bench plane. So when you sharpen the iron, don't add too much of a micro-bevel. Anything more than 40° threatens to violate the clearance angle of the cutter, which will prevent the tool from cutting.

There are lots of other small improvements to discuss. The depth stop is different than a traditional metal plow. The edges are relieved to prevent the stop from scratching the work. Plus, the knob for the depth stop has a wave washer beneath it, which prevents the depth stop from dropping out of the tool when you loosen the knob.

I did have one quibble with the depth stop. On the second plow plane I tried from Veritas, the stop would slip during use, no matter how tightly I cinched the knob. I've had this problem with other brands of plows, and Veritas officials said it can happen to their plow when the groove that the depth stop slides in is too finely milled.

The fix is to rough up the post of the depth stop and its groove with some sandpaper. About a dozen strokes with #100-grit paper did the trick. The depth stop has yet to slip again.

That minor fettling is completely forgiven when you consider the fence on the Veritas Small Plow Plane. Traditional metal plows use thumbscrews to secure the fence. And if you're not careful, it's fairly easy to lock the fence so it isn't parallel to the skate of the tool. A skewed fence causes all sorts of problems – the groove ends up wider than you intended, and it isn't the right size.

The Veritas uses technology from an electric router's collet to fix this problem. The metal shaft under the brass locking knob is segmented. When you tighten the fence knobs the fingers on the shaft squeeze the fence's rods so they are 90° to the skate. It really works.

The rest of the Veritas's controls will be familiar. The blade-holding and adjustment mechanism is much like those found on all plows. One knob holds the iron square in the tool. A second knob adjusts the depth. A third secures the iron's depth setting so it won't move.

A FINAL QUIBBLE AND
FINAL CONCLUSIONS

The only place where the Veritas didn't make a big step forward is providing a place to store the irons. I know this sounds minor. Perhaps it is, but every plow I've ever bought had a box for the cutters. Sometimes the box was wood but most times it was cardboard. Keeping track of the irons is an important long-term task, so a box would be a welcome addition. I consider the task to be important enough that I made my own box.

In use, the Veritas plow is a perfect worker. The wooden tote is kinder to the hand than any other

WHILE NOT AS COMPLEX AS *a Stanley 45's blade clamping mechanism, the Veritas Small Plow has all the features you need to ensure the iron stays put.*

THIS BOX TOOK FIVE MINUTES *to make on my table saw. The irons are ⅛" thick, so I plowed a single ⅛" kerf down a piece of scrap on my table saw. Then I crosscut the piece and taped up the sides. I'll make something fancier someday (yeah, right).*

metal plow I've used. The fence casting is easy to grasp using a variety of grips, and the tool has enough mass to stay in the cut and on line, even when removing thick ribbons of wood. The design of the fence is such that the tool is less likely to get clogged with shavings than my other metal plows.

My next task with my plow is to add a nice rosewood fence to the metal fence (clearance holes are provided) to make the tool even easier to use, and make it more familiar, like my No. 45 and my No. 46. And then I think I'll put the other vintage metal plows out to pasture by putting them up on my shelf in my office.

FOR MORE INFORMATION
Lee Valley Tools
leevalley.com, 800-871-8158

Raring to Rabbet

The Philly Planes Fillister is a hard-working tool with a fair price tag.

My first fillister plane was so pathetic it's a wonder I'm not the poster boy for DeWalt routers. But then, I don't look so good in yellow. Mom says I'm a winter.

About a decade ago I bought a Sargent copy of the execrable Stanley No. 78. I know I'm being hard on a plane that many people like and use. But every example I've used of this plane has a wobbly fence – no matter how tightly I cinched its thumbscrew.

So I was pleased to buy a C. Nurse moving fillister plane with a wooden body. It is a Cadillac; steel sole, brass wedge securing the nicker, smooth-acting and locking depth stop. But I've always been at a loss as to recommend a new maker for those woodworkers who don't want vintage. This week I received a moving fillister plane that I ordered from Philly Planes in England, and it is all I can do to stop typing and rush to the shop and cut some rabbets.

Philip Edwards, the man behind Philly Planes, has done a remarkable job of building a wooden-bodied moving fillister plane that works out of the box. (Another choice for those who like new planes

is the moving fillister version from ECE. I've also seen one from Clark & Williams.)

THE PERTINENT DETAILS

The Philly Planes moving fillister is $9^{3}/4$" long with a $1^{1}/4$"-wide skewed iron that's $1/8$" thick and made from O1 – oil-hardened high-carbon steel. The iron is pitched at 55° and the plane will cut rabbets up to $1^{1}/8$" wide and $1^{1}/8$" deep.

The fence is a $1/2$"-thick slab of beech secured to the body of the plane with two straight-head bolts and threaded inserts – which will ensure many years of long service. The depth stop adjusts smoothly with a knurled brass knob. Also a nice touch: The sole is lined with a sizable chunk of boxwood that covers rabbets up to almost a $1/2$" wide – again, it's another touch that says this plane is in it for the long haul.

Everything about the plane feels right, from the action of the wedges to the fit in the hands. And, as a bonus, it comes fully sharpened. And that's a good thing because I was ready to go as soon as it arrived. In use, the plane performs as a well-tuned vintage wooden-bodied moving fillister. Shavings curl up smartly out of the escapement and drop onto the bench. Rabbets form quickly, whether cross-grain or with the grain.

The price is £195. With our dollar that's about $306. Delivery time for me was about five weeks from the time I placed the order.

The moving fillister is as essential to a hand woodworking shop as a smoothing plane, and Philip Edwards makes a very nice version.

THE HAND-MADE WEDGE IS A *nice touch. After weeks of beating on it with a mallet it was remarkably unscathed.*

FOR MORE INFORMATION
Philly Planes
phillyplanes.co.uk

Veritas
Router Plane

Modern planemakers are turning their attention to the
joinery planes. But are woodworkers ready?

One of the delights of living in this age is getting to see the history of tool manufacturing almost repeat itself. In fact, if we thought of the recent renaissance of toolmaking as a movie, it's fair to say that this is a rare case where the sequel is better than the original.

For the last 10 years, modern hand-tool makers have focused their efforts on reviving two kinds of tools: the iconic bench planes that flatten and surface lumber, and what I call the "tweaking tools" – planes that refine a joint (shoulder planes and side-rabbet planes) or correct an assembly (block planes and chisel planes).

What has been missing from the catalogs from Lie-Nielsen Toolworks, Lee Valley Tools and Clifton have been the tools that cut wholesale joinery – fillister planes, dado planes, plow planes, router planes and (I shudder to suggest it) dovetail planes. But this situation is about to change. North American woodworkers are rapidly acquiring the skills to sharpen, set up and use the bench planes and tweaking tools; from there it's but a short and painless hop over to the joinery tools.

And that's why you should pay close attention to the new router plane from Veritas, the manufacturing arm of Lee Valley Tools. If this plane is successful – and it deserves to be – I think you'll see more joinery planes in the ever-fattening tool catalogs from these metal plane manufacturers and from the wood-lovers, Clark & Williams, which has been offering custom wooden joinery planes for some time. (And here's some inside scoop: The boys from Eureka Springs, Ark., have been showing a very sexy plow plane at shows recently. Perhaps Clark & Williams is a bit ahead of the curve here with that plow; but I can tell you it's a pretty fair curve.)

ROUTER PLANES: THE SEQUEL

The router plane is the descendant of the wooden "Old Woman's Tooth" plane, which was a wooden stock with a straight iron that extended below the sole and was secured by a wedge. I've used these planes a few times and don't much care for them. Yes, they will cut a flattened depression, but adjusting them is tedious because of that wedge; router planes require constant adjustment as you work. Plus, the wooden stock obscures where the work is going on and the tools can be difficult to push because they work mainly by scraping the wood. So it's little wonder that these tools evolved and that the next major jump would try to address these deficiencies.

The wooden D-handled routers (so called because of their shape) had the cutter secured in a hole in the stock so you could see the cutting action. And adjusting the iron became simpler (if not yet entirely predictable). The iron was secured by a metal collar that could be quickly loosened and tightened. I own a shop-made D-handle router and use it quite a bit. But though I can see a great deal more of the cut as I'm working, the big wooden stock gets in the way when I'm working in tight quarters and I tend to set the cutter to take too heavy or too light a cut when I adjust it. It takes a while for me to get into the rhythm of the tool.

THIS SHOP-MADE D-HANDLE ROUTER ISN'T *sophisticated, but it works quite well and can be built to suit any custom application. This model was built using an Allen wrench as a cutter – which is just the right hardness for the task.*

WHEN THE UPSIDE-DOWN SHOE CLICKS *against the base casting of the Stanley No. 71, your work is done. Sadly, this depth stop system seems like an afterthought. Whenever I've tried to use it, it's been less than ideal.*

The modern metal router – popularized by the Stanley No. 71 and its many variants – is what most of us think about when we talk about a router plane. It adjusts predictably with a wheel adjuster. You can always see where you are working and you can even mount the cutters to they can cut in tight spaces.

So what's left for modern planemakers to improve? Plenty, in my opinion.

Let's start with the depth stop on the No. 71. What, you didn't know the No. 71 sported a depth stop? Well it does, but it's a lame one in my book. The No. 71's depth stop is incorporated into the little metal shoe at the front of the tool. This shoe (and the metal rod attached to it) are supposed to close up the throat of the router for the instances when you need a bearing surface right in front of the tool – such as when making hinge mortises on the edge of a passageway door. If you take this shoe out and install it upside down so the shoe is above the tool (yes, it looks ridiculous) then you can use the shoe's metal rod like a depth stop.

The photo at below left shows this operation better than words can. The downside to this Rube Goldberg set-up is that the tool doesn't actually stop cutting when you reach your final depth – it's more of a depth "suggester." And then there's the small problem of the rod getting hung up on waste in your mortise. And sometimes the rod bangs into the good part of your work and makes a nice little rounded dent. Thanks Stanley.

The Veritas solution to this problem is elegant – and taken from the modern drill press. On the threaded post that controls the iron's projection there

are two threaded brass collars. Jam them against one another on any point on the threaded post and you can limit the depth of adjustment. There are even small holes provided in the collars so you can put a small metal bar or nail in there if you want to torque the two collars against one another. This is a good idea if you tend to over-torque things in general.

The adjustment mechanism on the new Veritas is a winner all-round. The adjusting wheel is big – its size makes it enormously easier to grasp than the skimpy Stanley wheel – which is ⅝" in diameter and an impossibly small ⅛" thick. Also worthy of note is that the thread pitch on the adjuster is finer on the Veritas than it is on the Stanley – one full turn of the Veritas knob lowered the iron by ³⁄₆₄". (The company reports it as ¹⁄₃₂"; it's probably my error or includes a bit of slop in the mechanism.) One full turn on the Stanley lowered it ¹⁄₁₆".

Other observations when comparing the adjusters side-by-side: The Veritas is far and away better-made. All the critical parts are machined and fitted precisely. The Stanley No. 71 uses two castings to lock the blade (a collar and a wing nut), both of them are crudely finished. It's not something that affects the tool's function, but it sure is amazing how far a little machining can go to make everything on the tool work so sweetly.

DO YOU NEED THE FENCE?

The fence on the Veritas is a $18.90 option to the base $149 tool (or you can buy both as a set for $159). The fence is a radical departure from the Stanley fence, which was a small casting bolted to the sole of the tool. The Veritas fence is more like the fence on the Stanley No. 78 fillister plane. The fence (almost ¾" wide and 3¾" long) slides on a rod that is then screwed to the base casting of the tool. The fence has two faces, one for referencing off straight edges and one for curves. Plus the fence has two holes so you can use a couple #8 screws to attach a longer straight wooden fence in place – or something custom.

The Veritas fence allows it to be used like a small plow plane, and it will get you as far as 2" in from the edge of your work. However, don't fool yourself, this isn't really a plow plane. It's not nearly

THE VERITAS DEPTH STOP IS *actually a jamb-nut system. For those who enjoy overkill in the torque department, Veritas has helpfully provided a ³⁄₃₂" diameter hole in each so you can put a lever in there and really jamb things up. Also note all the nice knurling and machining.*

The fence is pretty stable *for making shallow and narrow trenches in your work (think inlay). But try to use it as a plow and you'll run into complications – like adjusting the iron after completing only part of the groove.*

The Veritas comes with this *little sharpening jig. This can be secured in a honing guide (a jig in a jig!) or you can simply hold the jig and sharpen the bevel freehand.*

as stable. And the lack of a skate and proper depth stop make cutting a drawer-bottom groove with this tool something that you'd do only until you bought a proper plow.

However, the curved fence is useful for inlaying stringing on round tabletops. The fence is not a bad accessory, but if you have a good collection of hand tools already, I think you'll find it redundant.

Friendlier Cutters

One difference between the Veritas cutters and the Stanley cutters is that Stanley added a Vernier scale to the cutter so you could tell, approximately, how deep a cut you were about to make. The best things about these old scales is they get you in the ballpark faster than when you have no scale at all. This is particularly a factor when you are wasting away a lot of wood with other tools, such as a chisel, and are just batting cleanup with the router plane. I don't miss the scale, but it is worth noting.

One of the most frustrating things about any router plane is sharpening the cutters. The cutters are "L"-shaped and so even freehand sharpeners need to engage in some wrist gymnastics to get a keen edge. Luckily, the router plane is a joinery plane, and generally it does not produce a show surface. As a result, your cutting edges don't have to be as keen as what you'd put on a smoothing plane – anyone who cares if they have a little tear-out in the bottom of a dado joint can gather up their toys and go home now. (Low-relief carvers, who use the router planes for "grounding," or removing waste from the background, will disagree, I know.)

But you still need a pretty good edge. To make

things easier, the Veritas router plane allows you to disassemble the two larger cutters (the 1/2"-wide cutter and the 1/2"-wide V-shaped cutter) – separating the post from the business end of the steel. Then, Veritas includes a little sharpening jig you can secure to the detached cutting bits. This makes sharpening the cutters an act that's a lot like sharpening a narrow chisel or a marking knife. It's not as easy as a block plane, but it's a lot easier that sharpening something as small as your thumbnail.

The good news here is that the cutters are made well at the factory, so setting them up is pretty easy. The 1/4"-wide cutter was darn near perfect out of the box. The unbeveled side polished up in a few minutes and the beveled side was finely ground. The two wider cutters both needed a wee bit more work on the unbeveled sides, but nothing like the problems you'd find on plane irons 10 or 20 years ago.

All told, it took less than an hour from opening the box to get all three cutters sharpened and ready to go. And then it was time to put the tool to work.

Unusual Handles

When working with this tool, the knobs are the first things that strike you. They cant out at an angle that's about 35° off of 90° and are nice to look at. I don't find them a radical improvement compared to the straight-up Stanley knobs, though they aren't a deficit, either. All of the ways I grasp a router plane are comfortable for both knob configurations and the angled handles make the overall width of the Veritas plane only 1/2" wider than the No. 73.

However, sometimes that little extra can make all the difference. When you are plowing things out in tight quarters, it's always good to have the narrowest router plane possible (which is why they make small router planes as well).

The one interesting wrinkle with the Veritas knobs is that the company encourages you to customize the knobs to fit your hand or the work. Lee Valley sells a handle replacement kit for $7.90 that allows you to easily turn and mount custom knobs on this tool. Personally, I think these knobs are fine and I'm going to simply strip the lacquer off the rosewood knobs, sand them up to #400-grit and finish them with some oil and wax – I like that tactile feel on most of my hand tools.

The Veritas is what is known as a "closed throat" router, which actually makes it a lot more like the Stanley No. 71½ but I chose to compare it here to the Stanley No. 71 because that Stanley model has a depth stop – like the Veritas does – and it seems the more desirable tool to own – if only for its extra gizmos. The open-throat tools such as the No. 71 are supposed to offer better chip clearance and more visibility of the work. I didn't find either to be a problem with the closed-throat Veritas. And the fact that it's a closed-throat tool made it simpler to set up because there was no shoe to mess with, or to someday lose. Plus, closed-throat tools excel on edges, such as deepening grooves on door stiles.

After working with the tool for a couple months, I can report that the plane is an excellent user. It's nimble, adjusts predictably and is quite rugged (Veritas makes its iron planes from ductile iron, which is nearly unbreakable). The casting is a massive ¾" thick in places, making it quite rigid.

The irons are A2 steel and seem to keep their edge. I've actually been delighted by the smaller iron footprint of the tool – it's easier to balance on the edge of a door when cutting hinge gains. And perhaps the angled knobs assist in balancing the tool, too.

In addition to being an asset on narrow edges, the Veritas is also excellent for cleaning up angled dados and grooves – the cutters can really get into tight spaces. The other operation it was surprisingly good at was cleaning up or sizing tenon cheeks. I typically use a shoulder plane for this operation, but after seeing it being used on tenons in some of the Lee Valley marketing materials, I had to give it a try. With the V-shaped cutter, the Veritas produced an excellent and accurate surface. It's a bit slower than a dedicated shoulder plane, but it does function beautifully at this job.

But the biggest job ahead for this tool is that it make a lot of other woodworkers excited about the possibilities that joinery planes offer. Instead of setting up a router jig for three hours to make a 30-second cut to form an angled dado, you can simply saw to your lines and hog out the waste with a router plane. And soon, I hope, we'll all be ready to plunk down good money for a solid fillister plane with a rock-steady fence. And then a plow. And some dado planes.

I have a long list.

FOR MORE INFORMATION:
Lee Valley Tools
leevalley.com, 800-871-8158

TRY THIS WITH YOUR ELECTRIC *router with only five minutes to set things up. If your work involves angled or curved dados, you'll reach for this tool quite a bit.*

THE VERITAS ROUTER PLANE REALLY *excels at trimming tenon cheeks. Make sure the scrap is the same thickness as your work.*

After Hard Use

Lie-Nielsen vs. Veritas router planes.

Pint-sized router planes see a lot of use in my shop. Instead of using a trim router, I always prefer to cut mortises for hinges with a chisel and a router plane. So as soon as Veritas and Lie-Nielsen started making small router planes based loosely on the Stanley No. 271, I was first in line.

I now have many hours on both tools – I've sharpened each one about seven or eight times. And I have developed some firm likes and dislikes about each tool. The next paragraph is a spoiler, so if you like a little suspense when reading reviews, skip it.

Neither router plane is perfect. But nor is there one clear winner in the category. If I could combine the best of both tools (the Lie-Veritas?) I think it would be the router of my dreams. Here's the lowdown on each tool.

THE VERITAS SMALL ROUTER PLANE

First the good: This plane has a closed throat and is quite compact. The closed throat allows you to work on the edges of boards without any danger of the tool tipping. The downside to a closed throat is you sacrifice a little visibility.

The compact size is a big plus with the Veritas. The tool is 3¼" at its widest, and that is an asset when you are cutting hinge mortises inside assembled casework. Sometimes larger router planes are too big and ram into the top or bottom of your case. This little guy sneaks in everywhere I ask it to go. The fit and finish is excellent, as is the knurled brass locking knob. The iron is durable.

The downside: I don't care for the round shank that the iron is mounted to. No matter how tightly I secure the locking knob, the shank can shift if you take a big bite of wood with the plane. When the shank slips, usually the blade height doesn't change, but the iron rotates left or right. You can rotate it back, but there is the danger of changing your blade's prjection. So take light cuts.

LIE-NIELSEN SMALL ROUTER PLANE

The good: The blade-locking mechanism is incredibly solid and the iron never slips. The iron is mounted to a square shank, so there's no chance that the iron can rotate during heavy use. Plus, I quite like the fact the the blade-locking knob can be turned with a straight screwdriver. The knob is small, so this is a big plus.

I also like the curved fingerholds on the body. These are comfortable and feel right when you are skewing the tool into a hinge mortise. Plus, they give the tool a little sex appeal. The fit and finish on this tool is also excellent. The iron is quite durable.

The downside: The tool has an open throat. The almost ¾"-wide open section on the sole makes the tool unsuitable for work on narrow edges, such as cleaning up the ends of grooves in frame-and-panel work. If your work consists of a lot of work on edges, this isn't the tool for you.

Bottom line: I think the perfect plane for my work would be a router plane that had a closed throat, a compact size, curved fingerholds and an iron that had a square shank. Perhaps there's a vintage tool out there that meets these criteria, but I don't plan to start scouring eBay any time soon. Having both these tools covers all my needs.

HERE YOU CAN SEE THE *two throats of the router planes. The Lie-Nielsen (left) has an open throat. The Veritas has a closed throat.*

FOR MORE INFORMATION
lie-nielsen.com or leevalley.com

Sneak Peek

The new Veritas Side Rabbet Plane sneaks into corners.

Veritas has just released its much-awaited Side Rabbet Plane and Veritas was generous enough to permit me to test-drive it here in our workshop.

Though I still am getting comfortable with the tool, below are my initial impressions after trimming out about a dozen grooves and rabbets.

ABOUT SIDE RABBET PLANES

Side-rabbet planes are specialty tools that belong in the family of joinery planes. They are used to clean up and widen the difficult-to-trim walls of rabbets, grooves and dados. To be honest, some craftsmen don't use these planes. Instead of trimming a dado wider, they will trim the mating panel instead. Both perspectives work.

There are two kinds of metal-bodied side-rabbet planes (and there are wooden ones as well). The Stanley Nos. 98 and 99 have a right-hand version and a left-hand version so you can work with the grain in grooves in rabbets. The other format is to combine both cutters into one tool. Stanley did that in its No. 79 (with mixed results). And the English Preston version (and later Record version) got it right.

Lie-Nielsen makes versions similar to the Stanley in bronze. I've used them and they work well.

VERITAS'S SPECIFICATIONS

The Veritas Side Rabbet Plane is similar to the Preston plane: One cutter is on top. One is below. A handle is in the middle. Veritas, as always, has made improvements to the design that are beyond the "socks on a squirrel" variety.

The sleek handle – which reminds me of a beetle's back – pivots up and down depending on which cutter you are using. The handle is spring-loaded and doesn't slip during use – which is saying something because you have to apply significant hand pressure to these tools in use. The handle is comfortable. It burrows into your palm without poking you.

The other major advancement for the user is the

irons. Veritas has lapped the flat faces of these 01 (high-carbon) steel irons so sharpening them up takes only minutes. And when it comes to skew-cutting planes, this is critical. A small sharpening error with a skew plane and the tool won't function correctly.

The other thing to note about the tool is its depth stop, which locks quickly and squarely in either direction. You also can remove the toe piece of the tool with a screwdriver so you can work into the corners of stopped rabbets, grooves and dados.

In putting the tool to use, I was impressed (as always) with the irons and how easily they took an edge. Sharpening them without a jig is fairly simple work because the bevels are quite large and register firmly on a sharpening stone.

The only modification I'd recommend to the irons is to relieve the acute corner of each iron as it will dig in a little deeply in use (and will get worn away anyway). Veritas recommends this in the manual, and it is a two-minute job with a file. Be careful not to go too far – the point needs to extend beyond the sole a tad.

The real skill to learn with this plane is starting the tool. All the varieties of this tool have a small nose that you have to register against the sidewall of the joint you are going to trim. So it takes a steady hand to start a clean cut. Once you begin, the tool is easy to manage in the cut. The Veritas works in cuts up to $1/2$" deep.

Trimming the long grain of grooves and rabbets is easier than trimming the end grain in dados, so start with the easy stuff first. This style of tool isn't hard to use, but I wouldn't practice on a live project piece.

FOR MORE INFORMATION
Lee Valley Tools
leevalley.com, 800-871-8158

Clark & Williams: The Ultimate Wooden Planemakers

Test-driving Clark & Williams moulding planes.

THIS CLARK & WILLIAMS BEADING *plane is two pieces of beech and a single piece of steel. But it is one of the most perfect tools I have ever handled.*

W henever I'm in the presence of a piece of furniture that is designed and built to perfection – such as a chair by Brian Boggs – it is a humbling experience. Like I should just put my tools up for sale on eBay and take up a serious hobby of finally mastering tiddlywinks.

And after a few years of using planes from Clark & Williams, I should, by all rights, feel the same way. The planes that come from this planemaker's workshop in Eureka Springs, Ark., are as perfect a piece of woodworking as you will ever find. Every detail, inside and out, of the planes is crisp. The surfaces of the beech tools look as good as any piece of fine furniture at Winterthur. And the overall design aesthetic of the tools connects you directly to the best 18th-century British planemakers.

But here's the thing about these tools. When I use them I'm not humbled. I am, instead, inspired to push my furniture-making skills to their absolute limit. To make my furniture look as good as these planes look (and work).

I'm not alone. Whenever we have visitors in the shop (or whenever I teach), I put a Clark & Williams ³/₁₆" beading plane in their hands and show them how to use it. Within four or five strokes, they are hooked, usually forever.

I've owned a small coffin-shaped smoother from Clark & Williams for more than five years. But it wasn't until almost two years ago that I became totally ensnared. I got to borrow an entire set of hollow and round moulding planes, plus, I logged some time on the company's plow plane (for cutting grooves) and moving fillister plane.

The list of moulding planes I want has gotten to the point that I am considering teaching more woodworking classes somehow just to get the scratch up to buy them. Don't get me wrong. I don't think these tools are expensive at all. Considering the craftsmanship and handwork involved (not to mention the performance) I consider the Clark & Williams planes to be a bargain. A half-set of hollow and round planes (that's 18 planes) is $2,455. That's $137 per plane. Buying them one at a time is, obviously, more expensive.

Now, if you are interested in these planes but cannot afford the tools, your gut reaction might be to buy old moulding planes instead. This can be a perilous path. For every four moulding planes I buy off eBay, usually one is serviceable. The rest have warped wooden stocks, hopeless wedges or irons that verge on worthless.

So instead, I have a second option for you: Make your own. Larry Williams has a new three-hour DVD that is just out from Lie-Nielsen Toolworks that explains the process. Not just making the wooden stock, but about how to design the plane, how to sharpen and use the planemaker's tools and how to fabricate the irons. The DVD is a time capsule of traditional methods that have all but been lost and is enjoyable to watch even if you don't want to build a plane.

A few weeks ago a couple readers visited our shop, and one of them brought a couple of his Karl Holtey planes. Holtey makes the finest metal planes I've ever seen. Every construction detail is perfect, no matter how closely you look. We set up one of the Holtey planes and started making shavings on the nastiest Jatoba board we could find.

But the hero of the day was my little ³/₁₆" beading plane. After making their first bead, both readers were ready to order one for their shop. That beading plane is as perfect as anything I've seen from Holtey's shop. And I've seen quite a few.

If you ever have the opportunity to get your hands on a Clark & Williams plane, do not pass up the chance. The planes were my ticket to the next stage of craftsmanship. And they might well be yours.

FOR MORE INFORMATION
planemaker.com, 479-253-7416

Traditional Moulding Techniques: The Basics

A review of a Lie-Nielsen DVD hosted by
traditional woodworker Don McConnell.

Among all the many types of handplanes, it is the so-called moulding planes that generate the most confusion, consternation and frustration among beginning woodworkers.

Drawing a fair moulding profile, selecting the tools to cut it and actually proceeding with the work is enough to make many woodworkers cling to their collection of router bits forever.

If you're curious about cutting mouldings by hand, then I heartily recommend a new DVD from Don McConnell and Lie-Nielsen Toolworks that will lay the groundwork for you to understand the tools and how they are wielded.

And as valuable as these lessons are, I think the most eye-opening aspect of the DVD is that you get to watch McConnell make several profiles from start to finish. Seeing the profiles appear stroke by stroke, plane by plane, is a convincing argument that the work is fairly straightforward and do-able. Plus, the results are more beautiful than anyone can achieve with a routed and sanded moulding.

McConnell is, in my opinion, one of the most knowledgeable scholars on early woodworking tools who is working today. Plus, McConnell spent many years as an interpreter at The Ohio Village, as a professional hand-tool furniture-maker, and as a highly regarded ornamental carver in the Columbus, Ohio, area. I've always thought of him as the Indiana Jones of the hand-tool world – his encyclopedic knowledge of early woodworking is backed by years of putting his book-smarts to use at the bench.

As a result, this entire DVD is a jewel. McConnell, now a planemaker at Clark & Williams (planemaker.com or 479-253-7416), explains the basic anatomy of mouldings so you can understand the difference between Grecian and Roman shapes, and you can see how complex mouldings are in fact the assemblage of simple forms.

McConnell then demonstrates a couple basic complex moulding planes (the side bead and the ovolo) so you can see how a complete (usually simple) moulding can be created with one plane.

Then he moves into the hollows and rounds, which are the tools that you can use to create almost any shape or size of moulding. McConnell efficiently shows how to lay out a moulding on your work then prepare the profile with cuts from either a rabbet, plow or moving fillister plane. Finally, he demonstrates how the hollows and rounds bring the final moulding to shape with little fuss if you have followed the correct procedures. Proper rabbets help guide your hollow and round planes as they do their work.

In addition to creating several mouldings, McConnell also demonstrates how to sharpen moulding plane irons and how to maintain (and fix) their cutting profiles. He also shows how to properly saw (and shoot) your moulding so it can be applied to your project. That is followed by an eye-opening discussion of snipe bill planes, one of the least understood wooden moulding planes in the traditional toolkit.

When you're done watching the DVD, be sure to print out the accompanying glossary and bibliography on the disc. The glossary will help reinforce the names of all the shapes McConnell discusses in the DVD. And the bibliography suggests some books on furniture and tools that will help you build on the basic principles in the DVD so you can create well-proportioned, classic and crisp mouldings for your own work.

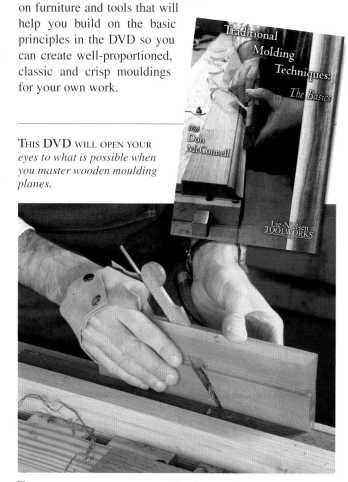

THIS DVD WILL OPEN YOUR *eyes to what is possible when you master wooden moulding planes.*

THIS BEADING PLANE IS AN *example of a complex moulder.*

A Close Look at the Veritas Premium Block Plane

*The Canadian tool-making company goes all out
to make a block plane for the ages.*

The unveiling of two new Veritas block planes in late 2008 thrilled some customers with their sleek design, and confused others. Is Veritas – a company historically focused on function more than form – changing its course with these new planes?

"It's not a direction change at all," says Robin Lee, the president of Lee Valley Tools and Veritas (the company's tool-making arm). "We have four planes coming out soon that are all under 100 bucks."

Instead, the new more-expensive planes are a way to provide a full range of choices for the customer, from Lee Valley's less-expensive Utilitas line of planes in a maroon finish, to the standard line of black planes that the company has been building since 1999, and to this new line of shinier planes that are designed for the customer who demands better materials, more features and a more refined design aesthetic.

"Some people want something that looks better," Lee says. "It's definitely a different aesthetic. But we have never meant for this to be a high-volume product. If it is a high-volume product, we'll go broke."

So why did Veritas produce it?

"What it is, is this is for (our) designers," he says. "You sit this plane besides other planes and they just look pedestrian."

During a 45-minute interview, Lee sketched out how these premium planes were designed and also discussed some of the new tools and redesigns that are on the drawing board for the Ottawa-based cataloger and manufacturer.

ONE FOR THE DESIGNERS

When Veritas designs any tool, Lee says, "price is always a concern. I want to put a tool in a customer's hands and have them wonder how we can build it for that price."

And during the last nine years, Veritas has done just that. The company's bench and block planes are almost always less expensive than those from Lie-Nielsen Toolworks and Clifton, its two major competitors. And while the Veritas planes stand toe-to-toe on performance with their rivals, the criticism has been that the Veritas tools aren't as nice looking.

Lee openly acknowledges this difference and says the company's first bench planes were designed

with interchangeable parts that made manufacturing efficient but didn't help the aesthetics. For example, the frogs and lever caps of the bench planes were all made to the same size then machined to fit whatever size bench plane they were building.

"We were a much smaller company then," Lee says. "We've grown and learned a lot." In fact, Lee notes that the company's bevel-down planes will be going through a redesign soon that will focus on the aesthetics of the tools.

When the idea came up for a line of premium handplanes, however, Lee said he threw a bone to his designers. "I told them to design the best possible tool regardless of cost," he says. The designers delivered plans for a whole line of planes. And then Lee went to work on the details.

"I'm a cheap guy," Lee says. "I want to get the most bang for the buck."

They decided to start with the smallest plane because it is the most difficult tool to design and will determine the look of the larger planes. The designers' plans called for a block plane that would end up costing $500. Then they sharpened their pencils to see if they could get the same design and the same

CHECK OUT THE ELLIPTICAL KNURLING. *This is neither simple nor cheap to produce.*

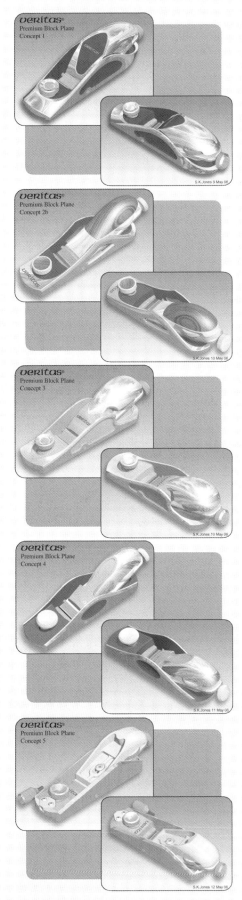

features for less. Here are some of the key features of the new block plane.

■ CORROSION RESISTANCE. Veritas started out experimenting with stainless steel and found it required a lot more manual work and cleaning during the manufacturing process. So the company settled on a ductile iron that is enriched with 22 percent nickel and about 6 percent chromium. This alloy is strong and definitely resistant to rust – a major complaint among hand-tool users. It's also more expensive (the nickel-based plane is $279; the regular ductile version is $179) and requires slower feed rates when it is machined.

■ A LONG AND ROUNDED NOSE. Many Veritas planes have more sole in front of the blade than traditional planes. This gives you more area that you can plant on your work before you begin a cut. Also, the Veritas designers did something tricky with these block planes: They encircled the movable sole plate entirely in the body casting. That's a lot more work, but it definitely dresses up the toe of the tool.

■ BETTER CONTROLS. The stainless steel knobs on the new block planes are something else. We see a lot of knurling here at the magazine, and the elliptical pattern on these tools is special. Another improvement: The plane's adjuster is locked in place in the tool's body and won't come loose when you remove the iron – a frequent complaint with this style of adjuster.

■ HAND CONTACT. It's hard to describe holding this tool. It feels heavier than the Lie-Nielsen low-angle block plane, but it's only about two ounces more on the scale. Because of the way the lever cap is integrated into the body, your hand touches

WITH MOST BLOCK PLANES THE *sole plate is visible from the front of the tool. The Veritas designers went all out and captured the plate in the plane's body.*

CONCEPT SKETCHES OF THE NEW *premium block plane that were provided by Veritas.*

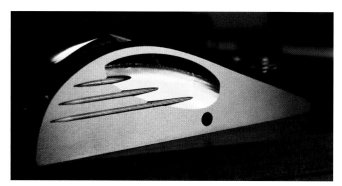

IS IT A PLANE OR *a car? The new Veritas block planes have sleek lines and flourishes that are also functional.*

WHAT'S NEXT FOR VERITAS

With the premium block plane out of the barn, the logical question is what is next for the designers who work in the loft space in Ottawa. Lee says the company plans to expand its premium line with a bevel-up jack plane and a smoothing plane. The bevel-up smoother likely will have its iron bedded at 12°. Both planes will have the same sculptural lines and have slightly different handles.

Also coming are some miniature shoulder planes in smaller widths, such as ¼", ⅜", ⅝" and a couple metric sizes. And what about saws? With the new Veritas dovetail saw now on the market will the company be producing a range of Western saws?

Lee says a carcase saw is in the works, and perhaps some other backsaws. But Lee says they don't intend to make full-size handsaws.

Anything else? While Lee described the frustrations of the Stanley's plane numbering system he mentioned that Veritas is working on a plane that ... well I'll just let him say it.

"We have a plane coming down the pike for which there is no precedent," he says. "There is no Stanley number that can be used to describe it."

It wouldn't be an interview with Robin Lee if it didn't have a little bit of mystery. So there you have it – something to look forward to.

FOR MORE INFORMATION
Veritas
leevalley.com or 800-871-8158

a lot of metal when you grab the Veritas. Also, the three milled grooves in each sidewall aren't just for show. They make the tool easier to grasp with less pressure. As someone who has flung a few planes across the room when planing, I'm happy to see this detail.

■ MOUTH STOP. In its recent bevel-up plane designs Veritas has added a mechanical stop to prevent the sole plate from slamming into the iron. In this plane, the stop has been shrunk down to a set screw. This is a good thing. Yes, you'll need a tool (it's included) to set the stop, but once you set it close, you'll never have to move it again.

■ THE IRON. It's A2 steel and is lapped on its unbeveled face so it takes a polish in seconds instead of hours. Though the A2 is fine, I hope Veritas can offer this iron in old-fashioned high-carbon steel. I like the ease of sharpening high-carbon steel and I find it works well at low sharpening angles typically used with block planes.

■ TOLERANCES. The plane is manufactured to tolerances that are twice as tight as the company's regular planes, and those regular tolerances already verge on the ridiculous.

With all these improvements, Lee says the plane is a good price at $279 for the nickel version.

"There's no margin in this for us," he says. "The cost is in the material and the machining – not the design."

Oh, and the thing cuts wood, too. This is a two-handed plane in my book. If you can wield it with one hand and take a heavy cut you probably can palm a watermelon. It took me about 30 minutes to get comfortable with the tool because I definitely think there is a right way and wrong way to hold it.

The wrong way is where you position your palm behind the tool and rest it on the adjuster. The knurling on the adjuster will chew up your palm after about 10 minutes of use. Switch to an over-handed grip and you'll find the sweet spot.

THE VERITAS BLOCK PLANE IS *as nice to hold as it is tool look at. Here you can see the sweet front knob.*

Wooden Miter Plane
from Philly Planes

*An English toolmaker reintroduces a plane
that hasn't been made for generations.*

Vintage wooden-bodied miter planes are fairly rare birds (at least in the Midwest), so I was quite eager to try a new one made by Philip Edwards in England (phillyplanes.co.uk).

While I'm well-versed in metal-bodied miter planes, I had to educate myself a bit on the history of the wooden ones before putting Edwards's plane to use in the *Popular Woodworking* shop.

John M. Whelan's seminal book "The Wooden Plane" (Astragal Press) says miter planes appeared in tool catalogs for about 100 years, starting in 1826. There are two major variations: an English tool with the iron bedded with the bevel facing up – like a metal-bodied miter plane. And an American version with the iron bedded with the bevel down.

Edwards's miter plane is mostly in the American style. The massive $\frac{1}{4}$"-thick cutter is bedded at 38° with the bevel facing down, like a traditional bench plane. The miter plane's iron is secured with a wedge and does not have a chipbreaker.

This turns out to be a good arrangement. Because the bevel is facing down in this tool, there isn't much of the wooden sole supporting the blade up by the tool's cutting edge. So the thick cutter is a must to prevent blade chatter.

However, the plane does have a bit of English in it. Edwards added a strip of dense end grain directly in front of the mouth of the tool – an English feature, according to Whelan. Because of the way miter planes are used, this is an excellent detail.

Miter planes can be used for a wide variety of chores – not just for trimming the short grain of a miter. The block-like shape of the tool allows it to be used on a shooting board for trimming end grain. Also, the plane serves as an excellent large-scale block plane – it's excellent for trimming the long-grain edges of boards. And the tool's 10"-long sole helps ensure your edges stay straight.

All in all, the plane is well-made. The wedge and the wooden body (called the "stock") are gon-calo alves, a dense tropical hardwood. The corners of the tool have handsome wide chamfers, like many early wooden-bodied planes. And the plane weighs in at 2 lbs. 12 oz., which gives it the kind of mass I like in a plane designed for a shooting board.

As far as fit and finish go, it is a quality tool, though not as refined as a plane from Clark & Williams in Eureka Springs, Ark. Nor does the Edwards's plane have the same price tag. Edwards

THE PHILLY PLANES MITER PLANE *excels on a shooting board, as shown here.*

charges £125 for the tool (with the state of the U.S. dollar these days, that's about $200).

My only difficulty with the plane came while I set it up. The wooden stock had moved during its trip across the Atlantic and the sole needed to be trued up. A few minutes on a sheet of sandpaper adhered to some granite and the tool was ready to go. Truing the sole of any of these tools will tend to open up the mouth of the tool, and the mouth on the tester went from infinitesimally small to about $\frac{1}{64}$", which is still a very tight mouth.

For now, Edwards is a part-time planemaker. His day job is carpentry – fitting kitchens, hanging doors and the like. Edwards also has been writing articles for British woodworking magazines (*Good Woodworking* and *The Woodworker*) and plans to become a full-time planemaker in 2008. His web site – PhillyPlanes.co.uk – already offers a variety of wooden planes and accessories, including a sweet mini panel-raising plane that I reviewed in the February 2008 issue of *Popular Woodworking*.

Both of these tools are excellent workers, and I recommend them without any reservations. If these tools are any indication, I think Edwards is going to succeed in his new venture.

FOR MORE INFORMATION
Philly Planes
phillyplanes.co.uk

Veritas
Small Scraping Plane

A first look at a new design for a small-sized scraping plane.

THE SMALL STRAIGHT SCREW CAMBERS *the blade. The hex-head screw locks the tilting palm rest.*

With the release of the new Veritas Small Scraping Plane in early 2009, lots of people are saying:
"Cool! I want one! Do I need one?"

Good question. Scraping planes are curious birds. The large scraping planes are typically used to dress tabletops and large panels that have unruly grain. Scraping planes can ignore grain direction, work large surfaces and leave a relatively flat surface – especially compared to a card scraper.

The small scraper planes work the same way, but I wouldn't want to use one for a banquet hall table. So they get used in other ways. You can use them like a block plane for dressing edges – this is how bodger Don Weber uses his Lie-Nielsen No. 212. If you have trouble bending a card scraper, the small planes are a good substitute as they are easy on your hands. And they can be used for evicting localized tear-out on a larger surface.

Veritas loaned us a Small Scraping Plane to test. I was involved in testing a pre-production model of the tool, so I was already familiar with the way it works. It is clever and easier to set up than the No. 212 model made by Stanley and Lie-Nielsen (I've owned the Lie-Nielsen No. 212 for many years). The Veritas also costs less money ($119; the Lie-Nielsen costs $160 to $175.) Both tools, I found, have plusses and minuses. Here's a look.

VERITAS: EASY TO SET BUT CAN CLOG

What makes the Veritas different is its blade system. Unlike the Lie-Nielsen, the Veritas uses a thin blade (.039" thick vs. .120"). The thin blade allows you to camber it by turning a small straight screw at the rear of the tool. This is much like the system on the venerable Stanley No. 80 cabinet scraper and the excellent Veritas Large Scraping Plane.

The net result of this system is that the Veritas scraping plane is easier to set up than the Lie-Nielsen. You insert the blade, tighten the clamp and give the cambering screw a turn. You're done.

The other new twist with the Veritas is the adjustable palm rest that gives the plane its Beetle-esque shape. It's clever – you move the rest until the plane fits your hand, then lock it in place with a hex-head wrench. Once locked, it's stable. You can force it out of position, but you have to work at it.

In addition to that ergonomic touch, the toe of the tool has a nice lip for your thumb.

My only complaint with the tool is the same one I had with the pre-production version. I think the tool clogs with shavings more easily than the Lie-Nielsen. I suspect – but could be wrong – that the cause of the clogging is that the blade-clamping mechanism is bigger and lower on the blade. And the tool's mouth is fairly wide open. What tends to happen is that you take a stroke with the tool, and on the return the last shaving drops below the sole. As you push forward for your next stroke, the stray shaving fouls the mouth.

If you pull the shavings out regularly, you won't have this problem.

LIE-NIELSEN: WON'T CLOG, BUT TRICKIER TO SET UP

The Lie-Nielsen uses a variable-pitch frog that allows you to set it for a wide range of pitches. This is handy for experienced users but sometimes frustrating for beginners. If you want a camber on your blade, you are going to have to add it while sharpening – there's no cambering screw on the tool.

This makes setting the tool a little trickier. You have to tap the iron left and right to get the camber in the center. Then you sometimes have to fine-tune the frog to get the shaving you want. After a while you get the hang of it, but I wouldn't want to learn to use the tool on live stock.

On the plus side, I can't recall this tool ever clogging. The mouth is tighter and the blade-clamping mechanism is fairly high. Shavings fall out and don't get pulled back into the mouth.

As to ergonomics, I think it's a draw. The Lie-Nielsen, while odd looking, is remarkably comfortable to my hand. And the Veritas is exactly whatever I want it to be.

FOR MORE INFORMATION
Veritas
leevalley.com, 800-871-8158

Afterword

On Saturdays I usually end up coming into the shop at the magazine to pick up tools that I need to do some woodworking at home. Sometimes, one of my kids will come along – usually hoping to score a candy bar from our company's vending machines.

One recent weekend I brought Katy along. As I packed up some mortising chisels, she picked up a No. 1-sized plane on my workbench and examined it. She's seen me do a lot of planing in her 8 years, but I've never really taught her much about it – we've focused on other skills.

Katy took a piece of pine on my bench, put it against the single-point stop and began to plane the board with the No. 1. Though my bench was too high for her, she moved confidently and naturally, peeling off shaving after shaving with that perfect "sneeck" sound.

I wanted to correct her grip and the way she overlapped her strokes, but instead I just watched her for about a minute. She stopped planing, reached into the mouth of the tool and pulled out the shavings.

"Look," she said, holding them up like a trophy. "I made these."

I smiled. And for the next 20 minutes we tinkered with the plane and her form and made a thick board into a much thinner one.

The point here is that planing is so simple that an 8-year-old can pick up the skills on a Saturday morning, and yet it is also so complex that this 300-page book only scratches the surface of all the things I'd like to tell you about this remarkable human invention. We're at the end here, but I'm afraid we're just at the beginning of your journey.

Handplanes are the most subtle and satisfying of the woodworking tools – there's a reason they are the symbol of the craft of furniture making. And they never stop giving up their secrets. After working with them for my entire life, I have yet to feel that I have fully mastered these tools.

It seems that no matter how good I become at planing, I will be better next year. I will produce flatter, better-looking boards with less effort and less thinking. I think that's why woodworkers have a different relationship with their planes than they do with their random-orbit sander.

Any woodworker can fully master the electric sander after about a day of working with it. But I have yet to meet anyone who has completely mastered the entire breadth of handplanes available, from the humble metal block plane to the exotic Japanese smoothing plane.

So like Katy, you better get started now. You have a long road before you, with lots of surprises and revelations ahead.